# TEXT ANALYSIS FOR
# THE SOCIAL SCIENCES

*Methods for Drawing Statistical
Inferences From Texts and Transcripts*

**LEA'S COMMUNICATION SERIES**
**Jennings Bryant/Dolf Zillmann, General Editors**

Select titles in General Theory and Methodology
(Jennings Bryant, Advisory Editor) include:

Norton/Brenders • Communication and Consequences: Law of Interaction

Perry • Theory and Research in Mass Communication: Contexts and
Consequences

Potter • An Analysis of Thinking and Research about Qualitative Methods

Perloff • Dynamics of Persuasion

Roberts • Text Analysis for the Social Sciences: Methods for Drawing
Statistical Inferences From Texts and Transcripts

Salwen/Stacks • An Integrated Approach to Communication Theory
and Research

For a complete list of other titles in LEA's Communication Series, please
contact Lawrence Erlbaum Associates, Publishers.

# TEXT ANALYSIS FOR THE SOCIAL SCIENCES

*Methods for Drawing Statistical Inferences From Texts and Transcripts*

Edited by

## CARL W. ROBERTS
*Iowa State University*

**LEA** LAWRENCE ERLBAUM ASSOCIATES, PUBLISHERS
1997 Mahwah, New Jersey

Lawrence Erlbaum Associates, Inc., Publishers
10 Industrial Avenue
Mahwah, New Jersey 07430

**Library of Congress Cataloging-in-Publication Data**

Text analysis for the social sciences : methods for drawing
   statistical inferences from texts and transcripts / edited by Carl
   W. Roberts.
        p.    cm.
   Includes bibliographical references and indexes.
   ISBN 0-8058-1734-4 (alk. paper). — ISBN 0-8058-1735-2 (pbk.
   alk. paper).
      1. Social sciences—Methodology.  2. Content analysis
   (Communication).  3. Social sciences–Research–Methodology.
   I. Roberts, Carl W.
   H61.T456  1997
   300′.1—dc21                                                    96-40299
                                                                       CIP

Books published by Lawrence Erlbaum Associates are printed on acid-free paper,
and their bindings are chosen for strength and durability.

Printed in the United States of America
10  9  8  7  6  5  4  3  2

*voor*
*Wies en Chantal*
*uit liefde*

# CONTENTS

Introduction                                                                    1
  *Carl W. Roberts*

1   A Matter of Definition                                                      9
    *Gilbert Shapiro and John Markoff*

**PART I:  METHODOLOGIES**

2   Thematic Text Analysis: New Agendas for
    Analyzing Text Content                                                     35
    *Philip J. Stone*

3   Semantic Text Analysis: On the Structure of Linguistic
    Ambiguity in Ordinary Discourse                                            55
    *Carl W. Roberts*

4   Network Text Analysis: The Network Position of Concepts                    79
    *Kathleen M. Carley*

**PART II:  APPLICATIONS**

5   Perceptions of Social Change: 100 Years of
    Front-Page Content in *The New York Times* and
    *The Los Angeles Times*                                                   103
    *Wayne A. Danielson and Dominic L. Lasorsa*

6  The Unobtrusive Measurement of Psychological
   States and Traits                                            117
   *Louis A. Gottschalk*

7  Labor Unrest in the Italian Service Sector:
   An Application of Semantic Grammars                          131
   *Roberto Franzosi*

8  Environmental Change and Conflict: Analyzing
   the Ethiopian Famine of 1984–1985                           147
   *Scott Savaiano and Philip A. Schrodt*

9  Assessing the Portrayal of Science as a Process
   of Inquiry in High School Biology Textbooks:
   An Application of Linguistic Content Analysis               159
   *Elizabeth M. Eltinge*

10 Applications of Computer-Aided Text Analysis:
   Analyzing Literary and Nonliterary Texts                    171
   *Michael E. Palmquist, Kathleen M. Carley, and
   Thomas A. Dale*

11 Reasoning in Economic Discourse: An Application
   of the Network Approach to the Dutch Press                  191
   *Jan Kleinnijenhuis, Jan A. de Ridder, and Ewald M. Rietberg*

12 Computer Programs for the Analysis of Texts
   and Transcripts                                              209
   *Roel Popping*

**PART III: PROSPECTS**

13 The Future of Coders: Human Judgments
   in a World of Sophisticated Software                         225
   *Gilbert Shapiro*

14 Developments in Computer Science With Application
   to Text Analysis                                             239
   *Robert Bechtel*

15 Text Analysis and Natural Language Database Systems          251
   *Albert L. Baker*

16   A Theoretical Map for Selecting Among Text
     Analysis Methods                                                 275
     *Carl W. Roberts*

References                                                            285

Author Index                                                          303

Subject Index                                                         309

# INTRODUCTION

Carl W. Roberts
Iowa State University

This book is for social science researchers with research questions applicable to relatively well-defined populations of texts. Although the book is accessible to readers having no experience with content analysis, the text analysis expert will find much new in its pages. In particular, this collection describes developments in semantic and network text analysis methodologies that heretofore have been accessible only among a smattering of methodology journals. In fact, it is originally with this volume that these two relational approaches to text analysis are defined and contrasted with more traditional, thematic text analysis methods. The emphasis here is on application. That is, this book's purpose is as an aid in answering the question, "Which text analysis method best affords answers to what research questions?"

Shapiro and Markoff's chapter introduces the reader to classical issues in content analysis methodology (e.g., the primacy of manifest vs. latent content, the requisites of scientific rigor, etc.). The authors develop a minimal definition of content analysis—a definition that encompasses methodologies far beyond the purview of this text. Whereas text analyses are only of texts or transcripts, content analyses can be performed on any symbolic material, be it visual, acoustic, tactile, or whatever. Beyond its limitation to texts, the domain of this book is also restricted to quantitative text analysis methods.

## QUANTITATIVE VERSUS QUALITATIVE TEXT ANALYSIS[1]

Generally speaking, there are two ways in which social scientists distinguish quantitative from qualitative analyses (cf. Vogt, 1993, pp. 183–184). On the one hand, qualitative analyses can be differentiated from quantitative analyses according to the level of measurement of the variables being analyzed. Shapiro and Markoff (this volume) argue, for example, that indiscriminate use of this quantitative–qualitative distinction has often resulted in the label, qualitative content analysis, being not only aptly applied to rigorous analyses of categorical data but also inappropriately applied to haphazard (and thus unscientific) analyses of such data. On the other hand, social scientists also distinguish their methods as quantitative or qualitative. Whereas quantitative methods are more deductive, statistical, and confirmatory, qualitative methods are more inductive, nonstatistical, and exploratory (cf. Berg, 1995, pp. 2–4).[2] It is only according to this latter distinction that quantitative text analysis is correctly understood as the subject matter of this book.

In a recent conversation Lyn Richards (of NUD*IST fame) made to me the intriguing assertion, "The distinction between quantitative and qualitative analysis reduces to one of 'timing'." The idea here is, on the one hand, that quantitative researchers specify their measures and tests in advance. In true confirmatory fashion they deduce hypothesis from theory and determine, prior to data collection, how to measure the hypothesis' central concepts. On the other hand, qualitative researchers typically explore their data, applying one classification scheme after another, before settling on that scheme (or schemes) that in their view resonates best with the data. Note that when applied to randomly sampled data, qualitative methods but not quantitative methods capitalize on chance. For example, it would be legitimate (based upon the application of prespecified measures and tests) for a quantitative text analyst to draw probabilistic inferences from a sample of paragraphs to the text population from which they were randomly drawn. However, because the qualitative text analyst's conclusions are based on repeated exploration of the sampled texts, these conclusions are more likely to reflect peculiarities of the sample, rather than characteristics representative of the larger text population. Thus, I suggest the following litmus test for distinguishing quantitative from qualitative analyses: If the method yields data matrices from which probabilistic inferences (i.e., $P$-values) can legitimately be drawn, the method is quantitative. Otherwise, it is qualitative.

---

[1]My thanks to Michael Bell for thoughtful comments on this section.

[2]The importance in this sentence of the two "more" qualifiers cannot be overemphasized. Quantitative and qualitative research are not mutually exclusive. Conclusions gleaned from field journals may be effectively supplemented with statistics, and probabilistic assertions about hypotheses may be convincingly buttressed by pithy quotations from a few of one's subjects.

It is critical that this litmus test not be misunderstood as embodying the defining distinction between quantitative and qualitative methods. Instead, the test is a mere artifact of the diversity between the methods' objectives. Qualitative analyses are usually performed not on randomly sampled data but on strategically selected case studies. Whereas the probabilistic inferences of quantitative analyses yield conclusions about the generalizability of one's findings, the logical inferences of qualitative analyses yield conclusions about the universality of one's theories. It is in this sense that Mitchell (1983, p. 203) said of qualitative analysis, "The single case becomes significant only when set against the accumulated experience and knowledge that the analyst brings to it." When a single case is anomalous, the quantitative analyst will likely dismiss it as entropic, whereas the qualitative analyst may see it as delimitative (i.e., as delineating a theory's proper or improper domain).

The pages of this book offer little guidance regarding the qualitative analysis of texts.[3] That is, it will be of little value to researchers who wish to examine theories' universality by drawing logical inferences from strategically selected case studies. However, this book will be useful to researchers who wish to test theory-driven hypotheses by drawing probabilistic inferences from samples to populations of texts.

## THEMATIC, SEMANTIC, AND NETWORK TEXT ANALYSIS

The sections on methodology and application are structured according to a three-fold distinction among thematic, semantic, and network methods of text analysis. These three quantitative text analysis methods differ according to the type of variable employed in each. Whereas in a thematic text analysis one examines occurrences of themes (or concepts), in a semantic text analysis the examination is of sentences (or clauses) in which themes are interrelated, and in a network text analysis it is of themes' and/or sentences' locations within networks of interrelated themes. The three are not mutually exclusive but may be combined in the same analysis.

### Thematic Text Analysis

Stone's chapter notes that computer-aided text analysis methods that originated in the early 1960s have become routine parts of business decision making in the last few decades. In sharp contrast to the top-down approach

---

[3]In contrast to the current paucity of books on quantitative text analysis, recent books on qualitative text analysis abound (e.g., Denzin & Lincoln, 1994; Feldman, 1994; Fielding & Lee, 1991; Kelle, 1995; Krueger, 1994; Marshall & Rossman, 1994; Miles & Huberman, 1994; Riessman, 1993; Silverman, 1993; Weitzman & Miles, 1995; Wolcott, 1994).

motivated in the 1960s by the grand theories of Lasswell, Parsons, and others, these business applications tend to use a grounded theoretical approach. Stone predicts a continued shift toward grounded, bottom-up thematic text analysis research with applied objectives.

Applications of thematic text analysis in this book are conspicuously nonapplied, however. For example, Danielson and Lasorsa trace changes in the occurrences of themes appearing on the front page of two prominent U.S. newspapers. These data are then depicted as indicating trends toward perceptions of a more dehumanized, quantitative, changing social reality. Other illustrations of thematic text analysis can be found in Palmquist, Carley, and Dale's Study 1 in which occurrences of robot depictions within science fiction are compared across three time periods, and in their Study 2 in which proportions of students who mention the same course-related themes and theme-pairs as their writing instructor (averaged across themes) or classmates (averaged across themes and classmates) are compared between semester beginning and end. Study 1 provides evidence for a trend from negative robot depictions prior to the 1960s to positive ones after the 1960s; Study 2 provides evidence for greater similarity of cognitive maps at semester end than at semester beginning both among students and between students and instructor.[4]

In fact, nearly all chapters discussing applications use theme occurrences among their variables. For example, theme occurrences appear to be a (minor) component in the calculation of Gottschalk's psychological scales and of Schrodt's WEIS scores. Franzosi's Tables 7.1, 7.2, and 7.4 are of theme occurrences, and Eltinge is explicit that theme occurrences play a central role in the development of her measure of scientific inquiry.

## Semantic Text Analysis

My chapter on semantic text analysis explains how texts can be encoded by fitting themes into a semantic grammar—a template that the researcher uses to capture essential elements of the phenomenon under investigation. For example, labor disputes can be encoded according to the three-place semantic grammar, Subject–Action–Object, and grievances can be encoded according to the two-place semantic grammar, DesiredAction–Object (cf. Franzosi, this volume; Shapiro, this volume). In applying a semantic grammar, however, parts of one's texts may be left uncoded (e.g., those parts that do not describe actors' actions or that are not grievances). In the chapter I develop a generic semantic grammar that allows one to encode themes and theme relations within every clause in one's texts.

---

[4]Cognitive mapping is referred to in Palmquist, Carley, and Dale (this volume) and elsewhere (cf. Carley, 1993) in ways that subsume thematic, semantic, and network text analysis methods.

Gottschalk's use of semantic text analysis dates back to the late 1950s—decades before any other researcher began nonthematic empirical work with texts. His pioneering efforts have until now had little visibility beyond the field of psychology. With a review of the last four decades of his highly productive career, Gottschalk's chapter is included as an acknowledgment of his groundbreaking contributions to text analysis methodology.

With both Gottschalk's and Schrodt's text analysis methods, texts are encoded by a computer program that generates scores on a variety of scales.[5] Whereas the Gottschalk–Gleser system produces measures of psychological states and traits, Schrodt's KEDS system yields event characteristics such as cooperation and conflict between pairs of actors. Thematic text analysis software such as the General Inquirer also yields scores (in this case, word counts within thematic categories). Unlike the General Inquirer, however, Gottschalk's and Schrodt's programs enlist parsers to identify theme relations required in calculating the scales. Because in scale calculation both of these programs use information on grammatical relations among themes, each comprises a tool for semantic, not thematic, text analysis.

Applications of semantic text analysis include Franzosi's chapter in which Italian government agencies were found more likely to intervene in domestic labor disputes that took place within the service sector than within the industrial sector. Here the analysis is of Subject–Action–Object relations among actors involved in Italian labor disputes as reported in an Italian newspaper during the first six months of 1986. Savaiano and Schrodt's chapter provides evidence that between 1982 and 1992 it was famine, not Ethiopian civil conflict, that drove refugees out of the country and into Sudan but that this conflict served to reduce Ethiopian conflict with neighboring Somalia and Sudan. In the chapter data from archival sources are analyzed in conjunction with conflict measures encoded from lead sentences in Reuters news articles on Ethiopia. Eltinge analyzes images of science as inquiry within a stratified sample of sentences drawn at random from introductory, genetics, and leaf-structure chapters within the 1956, 1965, 1977, and 1985 editions of Holt's high school biology textbook series. The analysis shows Holt to have been responsive to educator's early 1960s emphasis on scientific inquiry and to have depicted science as inquiry least often in chapters on leaf-structure (i.e., in chapters on an area of biology in which relatively little inquiry had occurred).

## Network Text Analysis

Carley's chapter on network text analysis develops a vocabulary for depicting the network as a set of interconnected statements, each of which is comprised

---

[5]In most cases, this software does not entirely automate the encoding process. The Gottschalk–Gleser system requires an initial division of text into clauses, and KEDS dictionaries are usually customized to fit the research at hand (cf. Savaiano & Schrodt, this volume).

of a pair of interrelated themes (or concepts). Carley describes and illustrates how concept positions can be depicted along three dimensions (viz., density, conductivity, and intensity), and how eight types of "concepts with particular communication properties" can be distinguished according to specific combinations of extreme values on the dimensions. Analyses that rank concepts along these dimensions may provide insights into which concepts are central in task accomplishment, consensus maintenance, and so on.

Both expert knowledge and the knowledge embodied in the statements of one's network can be used to generate new, logically implied statements that may not be explicitly stated in texts. For example, Palmquist, Carley, and Dale's chapter applies SKI, a program that is used to fill in networks with statements that an expert's knowledge of texts' social context generates out of the texts' explicit semantic and network information. Kleinnijenhuis, de Ridder, and Rietberg apply CETA to fill in networks with statements that are implied, not by expert knowledge but by the interconnected statements explicitly manifest within the texts themselves. This explicitly stated versus logically implied distinction is described in the chapter as giving new (and comparatively more rigorous) meaning to the classical distinction between the manifest versus latent content of texts.

The chapter by Kleinnijenhuis, de Ridder, and Rietberg provides this volume's only illustration of network text analysis. More accurately, in providing evidence of a 1968–1984 shift away from depictions of Keynesian thought in two Dutch newspapers' economic news coverage, the chapter contains a combination of both semantic and network text analyses. The semantic text analysis involves a set of $t$ tests that compare the frequencies at which specific nuclear sentences (i.e., statements or clauses) occurred in 1968–1976 versus 1978–1984. The analysis then proceeds to a second set of $t$ tests that compare the manifest versus latent influence reported from one meaning object (i.e., a theme or concept) to another. (Here, manifest influence is explicitly linked within a single nuclear sentence, whereas latent influence is implicitly derived from chain arguments among nuclear sentences.) The authors conclude that in the news the post-1977 shift away from Keynesian ideas may, in part, be due to journalists' attempts to rectify pre-1977 inconsistencies between influences explicitly reported and those implicitly suggested in their writings.

The applications section concludes with a chapter by Popping, in which brief descriptions and availability information are provided for software currently available for thematic, semantic, and network text analysis. Each program is classified according to one of these three types and then is subclassified within each type according to whether its primary use is as an instrument of diagnosis or as a medium for representing texts' intended meanings. This second dimension among text analysis methods is the topic of Shapiro's chapter with which the book's "Prospects" section begins.

## PROSPECTS

When computers were first enlisted as an aid for quantifying texts, it was commonly believed that they would, in time, entirely eliminate the need for coders to interpret the words being analyzed. Shapiro points out in his chapter that this belief has been realized, to a greater or lesser degree, in a class of instrumental text analysis programs. Of course, these programs do not eliminate the need for interpretation. Instead, they automatically "diagnose" texts' meanings by applying the researcher's rules of interpretation in a manner analogous to a medical doctor's application of interpretation rules in diagnosing a patient's symptoms. In contrast to this approach, Shapiro describes a representational orientation toward text analysis in which the source's intended meanings (not the researcher's interpretations) are encoded. Current developments in computer science are not sufficient to emulate, nor thus to automate, the coder's ability to infer beyond a text's words to the meaning(s) their source intended them to convey.

It is in Bechtel's chapter that a brief overview is given of the current state of these developments. After distinguishing the collection, preprocessing, extraction, and analysis stages of text analysis, Bechtel describes hardware and software developments that are likely to aid researchers in the first three of these stages.[6] It is here that the reader is introduced to technologies such as optical character recognition, machine translation, formal language theory, information retrieval, computational linguistics, pattern matching, production systems, and neural networks.

Also from a computer science perspective, Baker's chapter begins by noting that the structure of one's database delimits the types of queries that researchers can make of their data. He then develops three formal content models that specify the database structures required in respective software applications of thematic, semantic, and network text analysis. These database structures might be combined into a general purpose text analysis program that would afford queries appropriate to all three text analysis methods.

My concluding chapter picks up where Baker's leaves off. That is, if one can delimit the queries appropriate to each type of text analysis, it must be possible to delineate the universe of research questions afforded via quantitative text analyses. Because every quantitative analysis of texts involves the statistical analysis of a data matrix, the task of delineating this universe reduces to one of specifying the types of variables and units of analysis that can form the basis of the matrix. In this short chapter the reader will find this book's most concrete description of the thematic–semantic–network

---

[6]The fourth, "analysis" stage involves the statistical analysis and interpretation of a data matrix generated in the other three stages. Unlike the three prior stages, this stage is not unique to text analysis.

distinction—a prism through which to view the book's fundamental structure. Although the chapter should be read last, to pull together ideas from
throughout the book, it might also be read first, to gain initial insights into
the vision of quantitative text analysis depicted throughout.

## CONCLUSION

In this volume are descriptions and illustrations of cutting-edge text analysis
methods for communications research, cultural analysis, historical-comparative analysis, curriculum evaluation, event analysis, psychological diagnosis,
language development research—in fact, for any research in which statistical
inferences are drawn from samples of texts. The book's international and
cross-disciplinary content illustrates a breadth of quantitative text analysis
applications. These applications demonstrate the methods' utility for international research (e.g., Franzosi on Italy, Savaiano and Schrodt on Ethiopia,
Kleinnijenhuis, de Ridder, and Rietberg on the Netherlands, and Gottschalk
on analyses of German, Spanish, and Italian texts) as well as for practitioners
from the fields of sociology (Carley, Franzosi, Markoff, Popping, Roberts,
Shapiro), political science (Kleinnijenhuis, de Ridder, Rietberg, Savaiano,
Schrodt), journalism and communications (Danielson, Lasorsa), computer
science (Baker, Bechtel), psychology (Gottschalk), education (Eltinge), and
English (Palmquist).

This is an ecumenical collection that contains applications not only of
the most recent semantic and network text analysis methods but also of the
more traditional thematic method of text analysis. Its chapters provide
guidance regarding the sorts of inferences that each method affords and
up-to-date descriptions of the human and technological resources required
to apply the methods. Its purpose is as a resource for making quantitative
text analysis methods more accessible to social science researchers.

# 1

# A MATTER OF DEFINITION

Gilbert Shapiro
John Markoff
University of Pittsburgh

Researchers with the most diverse purposes have examined texts, recorded codes denoting some characteristic of those texts and then used a collection of such codes as data. Definitions of content analysis have tended to stress some of these purposes or some possible methods of accomplishing such purposes and have excluded others. Although there are significant differences among research projects, there are some significant common elements as well. In this chapter we offer a minimal definition of content analysis that covers a wide range of concrete research agendas. We also show how differences among standard definitions reflect central methodological issues that need to be addressed, rather than defined out of existence.

## THE NEED FOR DEFINITION

Normally, we hold that few strategies can so confuse a discussion as can an author's announcement of his sincere determination to use a common term in some clearly delimited manner. Nevertheless, a consideration of the boundaries of content analysis seems inescapable; at least, we find such discussions very frequently in the methodological literature. This need to define the term, we believe, stems from two opposite difficulties. At times, the explicit definition of the term, or the definition implicit in its use, can be so inclusive as to encompass any reading of text. At other times, explicit or implicit definitions restrict a term's application to a very small portion of the research activities that have been so labeled in the past. The boundaries of content analysis are problematic; hence we, like many other writers on the subject, find it necessary to attempt to delineate the range of research activities to which we believe it should apply.

Such broad categories of procedures are encompassed within some definitions and, more important, some patterns of usage of the term, that it is questionable that any common methodological principles can apply to them all. There are authors who seem to embrace literally any reading of text, albeit the most conventional of literary work. One example is Lerner's (1950, fn. 1, p. 212) description of his polemical answer to critics of the World War II research of the War Department embodied in *The American Soldier* as "a preliminary sketch for a more detailed thematic content analysis of responses to *The Soldier* and other significant books." Holsti (1969, p. 36) saw this article, which reads much like any other piece of controversial scholarly rhetoric, as an example of a content analysis. In such cases, we do not find any methodical marshaling of evidence, any explicit account of procedures for the selection of documents or sampling, or any indication of the invariable application of coding categories or tests of reliability. What we typically find is an extensive discussion of conclusions regarding the contents of some vaguely defined collection of documents, backed up by occasional citations; the systematic laying bare of methodology, warts and all, which we take to be characteristic of scientific work, is not seriously attempted.

Of course, there are the inevitable borderline cases. Davis (1938), at least, provided us with a list of the sources he studied to arrive at his description of the ideology of the mental hygiene movement. He also declares that these works were "gone through with the aid of a fixed questionnaire designed to discover certain things about each book" (p. 57), although we are not granted the privilege of reading the questionnaire, nor are we told the frequency with which he found each of its categories. Again, in his analysis of the American social pathologists' ideology, Mills (1942) generalized over the content of roughly 25 textbooks, of which he provided a list. He made no explicit claim, as did Davis, that he addressed identical queries to each text, but, in the time-honored fashion of literary or journalistic study, presented his general impressions of the contents speckled with occasional quotations.[1] We have no argument against the value of such studies but only

---

[1]As usual, Mills knew exactly what he was doing: "no one of the texts to be quoted exemplifies *all* the concepts analyzed; certain elements are not so visible in given texts as in others, and some elements are not evidenced in certain texts at all" (Mills, 1942, fn. 1, p. 165). "The quotations in the footnotes are merely indications of what is usual. The imputations presented must be held against the reader's total experience with the literature under review" (Mills, 1942, fn. 3, p. 166). Fair enough; we have no objections to the way Mills conceived of his work, nor, for that matter, to how he performed it. Note that Mills acknowledged that to properly assess his imputations, the reader must read all the texts that Mills read!

against the claim that they are somehow content analysis[2] and hence partake of the authority of science if performed by a professor in one department, whereas they are mere literary work if performed by a professor in another department or by a writer outside of the academy.

We believe that the designation of any work as content analysis as distinguished from the ordinary reading of text makes an implicit claim that the researcher is participating in a scientific enterprise. Such a claim must be based on something on the order of systematic or methodical procedures, and we would reserve the term content analysis for scientific work so conceived. At a minimum, there must be some rules (as opposed to feelings or intuitions) determining the text that is to be studied and some standard set of coding decisions that are to be applied to all of that text. The completion of this thought, specifying what, beyond the minimal requirement of systematic procedures, must be included among the defining criteria of content analysis, takes diverse forms for different authors, and much of this chapter is devoted to mapping the alternatives.

## REPRESENTATIVE DEFINITIONS

The following six quotations seem to us to provide a fair indication of the range of explicit definitions of content analysis in the methodological literature (cf. Berelson, 1971, pp. 14–18; and Holsti, 1969, pp. 2–3):

> *Bernard Berelson:* "Content analysis is a research technique for the objective, systematic, and quantitative description of the manifest content of communication" (Berelson, 1954, p. 489).[3]

> *Dorwin Cartwright:* "In the subsequent discussion, we propose to use the terms 'content analysis' and 'coding' interchangeably, to refer to the objective, systematic, and quantitative description of any symbolic behavior" (Cartwright, 1953, p. 424).[4]

> *Irving L. Janis:* " 'Content analysis' may be defined as referring to any technique a) for the *classification* of the *sign-vehicles*, b) which relies solely upon the *judgments* (which, theoretically, may range from perceptual discrimination to sheer guesses) of an analyst or group of analysts as to which sign-vehicles fall into which categories, c) on the basis of *explicitly formulated rules*, d) provided that the analyst's judgments are regarded as the reports of a scientific observer" (Janis, 1949, p. 55 [emphases in original]).

---

[2]Berelson (1971, p. 218) listed the Mills study as an instance of qualitative content analysis.

[3]This definition is identical with that in Berelson (1971, p. 18), but neither the restriction to the quantitative nor the restriction to the manifest is sustained for the rest of the book.

[4]Although this particular definition best fits our polemical needs, we find Cartwright's other formulation (1953, p. 421) more stimulating philosophically, in that he regards text or "qualitative material" as "phenomena" which, by "coding," are "converted into scientific data."

*Klaus Krippendorff*: "These observations suggest that content analysis be restricted to the use of replicable and valid methods for making specific inferences from text to other states or properties of its source" (Krippendorff, 1969, p. 70).[5]

*Charles E. Osgood*: "If we define content analysis as a procedure whereby one makes inferences about sources and receivers from evidence in the messages they exchange, then the problem falls precisely in the field of special interest of the psycholinguist" (Osgood, 1959, p. 35).

*Philip J. Stone*: "Content analysis is any research technique for making inferences by systematically and objectively identifying specified characteristics within text" (Stone, Dunphy, Smith, & Ogilvie, 1966, p. 5).[6]

The variety in these definitions is striking.[7] We find the following issues raised by their similarities as well as their differences:[8]

| What classes of symbolic objects are studied in content analysis? | |
| --- | --- |
| *Text Only* | *Text and Other Symbolic Material* |
| Krippendorff | Berelson ("communication") |
| Stone | Cartwright ("symbolic behavior") |
| | Janis ("sign-vehicles") |
| | Osgood ("messages") |

| What kind of intellectual product comes from a content analysis? | | |
| --- | --- | --- |
| *Description* | *Inference* | *Classification* |
| Berelson | Krippendorff | Janis |
| Cartwright | Osgood | |
| | Stone | |

[5]Krippendorff's later formulation is more ambiguous: "a research technique for making replicable and valid inferences from data to their context" (1980, p. 21). This formulation does not specify the kind of data, nor the meaning of the context, so we stay with the earlier statement in further discussion.

[6]This definition was repeated almost identically by Holsti (1969, p. 14). Holsti extended the possibility of content analysis beyond text to all kinds of messages, but, unlike Stone, he was not engaged in the development of a computer system for the content analysis of text alone.

[7]Recent literature on content analysis is scarce and adds no new elements to the range of definitions presented here. See, for example, Weber (1990).

[8]Some remarks on this (content?) analysis seem to be in order. We have relied exclusively on each author's explicit definition in arriving at our characterization of his positions. If we had paid attention also to his other text (viz., to the *context* of his definition), as well as, perhaps, to his other writings (especially to his actual content analyses) we would undoubtedly arrive at a superior result. Our limited rhetorical purposes do not warrant such extensive additional effort, however.

| *May (or must) a content analyst go beyond the manifest content to inferences about the "latent" content of the material?* | |
| --- | --- |
| *Manifest Only* | *Latent Permitted* |
| Berelson | Cartwright |
| | Janis |
| | Krippendorff |
| | Osgood |
| | Stone |

| *To what object of investigation is the description or inference to apply?* | | |
| --- | --- | --- |
| *The Text (or Other Symbolic Material)* | *Source* | *Its Receivers or Audience* |
| Berelson | Krippendorff | Osgood |
| Cartwright | Osgood | |
| Janis | | |
| Stone | | |

| *Must content analysis be "quantitative," or is the possibility of a "qualitative analysis" left open, at least by silence?* | |
| --- | --- |
| *Quantitative Only* | *Qualitative Possible or Silence* |
| Berelson | Janis |
| Cartwright | Krippendorff |
| | Osgood |
| | Stone |

| *What terms, redolent of the laboratory, serve to remind us of the identification of content analysis as a scientific pursuit?* | | | | |
| --- | --- | --- | --- | --- |
| *Scientific* | *Systematic* | *Objective* | *Replicable* | *Valid* |
| Janis | Berelson | Berelson | Krippendorff | Krippendorff |
| Stone | Stone | | | |
| Cartwright | Cartwright | | | |

## PROPOSAL FOR A MINIMAL DEFINITION

Our own views on the proper definition of content analysis are based upon what we regard as the requirements for progress in the development of the sciences of man. We seek a minimal definition, one that, although serving to exclude mere reading, still interferes as little as possible with the exercise of the methodological imagination by working researchers. We regard content analysis as best defined (today) as *any methodical measurement applied to text (or other symbolic material) for social science purposes.* Put otherwise (and we believe that we are saying the same thing again), the term refers to *any systematic reduction of a flow of text (or other symbols) to a standard set of statistically manipulable symbols representing the presence, the intensity, or the frequency of some characteristics relevant to social science.*

In discussions of content analysis, many authors assume that the term refers to the measurement of subjective phenomena, such as grievances, attitudes, values, ideologies, or political positions, but there is nothing in this definition (or most of those cited above) that excludes the measurement of objective facts described in the texts under study as well. In fact, as we try to show, the processing of text by researchers engaged in the measurement of incidents of collective behavior (e.g., riots, strikes, demonstrations, and so forth) based upon the coding of newspaper accounts has much in common with the measurement of such subjective variables as grievances. We try to justify our formulation, comparing it with the array of current alternatives quoted, using the questions listed here as our agenda.

## A COMPARISON OF ALTERNATIVE CONCEPTS OF CONTENT ANALYSIS

### What Classes of Symbolic Objects Are Studied in Content Analysis?

Stone, Krippendorff, and (by implication) Osgood restrict the term to studies of text—written language. Cartwright extends it to any symbolic behavior, which admits studies of music, visual art, body language, facial expressions, and other nonverbal symbolic or cultural materials. Our views on this question are tentative, even casual: If the methodology that develops in the study of nonverbal materials has enough in common with that of textual study to make it more convenient to include them under the same rubric, so be it. Krippendorff prejudged the issue, insisting that content analysis must not be restricted to the study of linguistic text on the grounds that "nonlinguistic forms of communication can be subjected to the same kind of analysis" (Gerbner, Holsti, Krippendorff, Paisley, & Stone, 1969, p. 5.). We would be delighted if this could some day be demonstrated; until then, we prefer to attempt to build the methodology of content analysis on the basis of more modest assumptions. We are skeptical about Krippendorff's apparent assumption that there is only one kind of analysis. What could the concept of discourse analysis, for which Krippendorff pleads in the study of text, mean in the case of visual art objects, for example?[9] Although we have an active interest in the use of nonlinguistic materials for social and cultural history, we would not want to be restricted in the development of content analysis methods to those techniques that could immediately be applied to nonverbal media; nor, we believe, would anyone else.

Clearly, the application of content analysis to cultural or symbolic products other than text depends heavily upon the methods chosen. Obviously, methods based upon concepts like words and sentences are married exclusively to linguistic material. If a human coder is used to categorize symbolic material in accordance with his understanding of its meaning, nothing in such a procedure requires that the symbols encoded be linguistic in character; they might as well be any other medium that is understood by the coder: visual art objects, facial gestures and body language, or even, we venture to suggest, culturally patterned episodes of social behavior.[10] This is only to recognize a fairly well-established practice. For example, in a study of magazine advertisements, coders were instructed, among other tasks, to code the presence of appeals based upon "positive interpersonal satisfaction." The words might be, "He'll like you better if you use Revlon," but, alternatively, his admiration might be portrayed pictorially; the coder instructions did not insist upon textual clues (Dornbusch & Hickman, 1959).

The most imaginative such work on culturally patterned episodes that we know of is the research of David Heise and his associates (Corsaro & Heise, 1990; Heise, 1988, 1991; Heise & Lewis, 1988) on how sequences of social events are patterned into culturally understood wholes. The raw materials are representations of sequences of actions: a videotape of children at play, an anthropologist's field notes, a historical document. Another very sophisticated analysis of nonverbal materials, a study of medieval religious art, combines the use of linguistic with visual material in an interesting way. Textual descriptions of the art objects are recorded, coded, and analyzed. " 'Data' in our case are descriptions of medieval pictorial sources that are formulated in a language that comes very close to the one used day by day by the researchers specializing in the field. Or, we should rather say, it comes close to it in its vocabulary, the syntax being transformed" (Thaller, unpublished paper).[11] If this technique, content analysis of the language used by experts to describe nonverbal materials, were to prove

---

[9]We understand discourse analysis to mean linguistic analysis of units larger than the sentence. There is no sentence, and no apparent analog to one, in visual communication.

[10]It seems reasonable to understand the structuralism of Levi-Strauss, Edmund Leach, and others as an encoding by the anthropological observer of social behavior that is taken as a symbolic language.

[11]In his study of national flags, Sasha Weitman (1973) similarly encoded verbal indications of the symbolic significance of colors.

powerful, debate over whether to classify such studies as content analysis might be gratefully bypassed; social scientists could study nonverbal material by means of an analysis of the text that experts use to describe it.[12]

The work of Karen Cerulo deals with musical and visual materials in a radically different fashion. Rather than carry out what she calls a semantic analysis of a symbol (e.g., what do a national flag's colors mean?), she studies its characteristics as a design (e.g., how many different colors does it contain?), which she calls a syntactic analysis. She measures aspects of such musical elements as melody, phrasing, harmony, form, dynamics, rhythm and instrumentation (Cerulo, 1992). For visual materials, she measures contrasts in hue, value, and chroma as well as geometric patternings. In both musical and graphical arts, she argued, symbols vary in their complexity along a "basic-embellished" continuum. Such variations in national flags and national anthems are supposedly meaningful reflections of the circumstances of their adoption: Politically turbulent regimes, for example, opt for unencumbered symbolic simplicity (like Libya's monotone green flag), whereas more stable polities generate much busier symbolic representations. Whatever the success of this particular connection, her work suggests a rich vein of possibility in the exploration of hitherto recalcitrant symbolic materials.

In a methodologically similar, if simpler, vein, Bergesen and Jones (1992) code shifts in dance choreography in New York. Dance, they find, exhibits a trend toward a minimal choreography from 1945 to the late 1960s. This trend then reverses, showing increasingly elaborate performances. The authors interpret this reversal as, among other things, a response to a decline of the position of the United States in the world economy, a circumstance threatening New York's position as the world center of dance, which generates more broadly appealing choreographic practice.

Because the strategic value of including such studies under the methodological rubric of content analysis is an open question, this book was organized under the more specialized category of quantitative text analysis—a phrase that implies no pre-judgment regarding the distinctiveness of verbal texts as objects of study.

## What Kind of Intellectual Product Emerges From a Content Analysis?

We see content analysis as a technique of measurement, rather than of description, as do Berelson and Cartwright, or inference, as do Stone and

---

[12]Interestingly, Paisley (1969), a content analyst of nonverbal materials, saw this kind of intervention by a human coder as inescapable for the study of visual materials but not of music. The latter has the note and phrase, which might be taken as analogous to the word and sentence, which can be identified without coder intervention. The more recent work of Cerulo (1992) suggests that Paisley's art–music distinction might be overdrawn.

others. This comes very close to the formulation of Janis, who sees it aimed at classification. These differences might appear more stark than they are. Measurement necessarily involves description, inference, and classification. There are, nevertheless, important divergences of viewpoint reflected in these formulations.

"Measurement" is used here in the broad sense that has become conventional in contemporary social science, *the assignment of symbols to objects or events according to rules.*[13] Hence, as is now customary, we admit as measurement operations that provide results in the form of nominal classifications and ordinal rankings as well as such higher levels of measurement as scales with equal intervals.[14] A division of the grievance lists drawn up by the French on the verge of revolution—the source of our own content analytic data (Shapiro & Markoff, in press)—according to their origins as above or below the St. Malo–Geneva line or the classification according to whether they were drawn up by assemblies of Nobles, peasants, or elected representatives of the local Third Estate, are examples of nominal measurements. The assignment of numbers representing, for each document, the number of grievances expressed against the system of indirect taxation illustrate a higher level of measurement.

In the light of our restriction of it to measurement, we find content analysis badly named. Social scientists sometimes wish to measure aspects of what is usually regarded as the form rather than the content of texts, as they have done in some of their most interesting studies in the past.[15] Even more important, we understand the sense of analysis to be much broader than that of measurement. The effort to analyze a society or a personality, or to learn something of importance about it exclusively by means of a content analysis of some of its literary products, is, in our view, based upon much more questionable methodological principles than the more modest (but sufficiently difficult) effort to measure one or more variables by means of some kind of processing of text.[16]

Stone, in emphasizing inference as the proper goal of content analysis, rejected the idea that content analysis should be devoted to "mere" meas-

---

[13]Our formulation revises that of S. S. Stevens to meet the demands of Clyde Coombs. Stevens (1951) defined measurement as "the assignment of *numerals* to properties, objects, or events according to rules" (p. 1, our emphasis). Coombs (1953, p. 472) objected that the restriction to numerical symbols misleads us as to the character of qualitative measures or nominal classifications.

[14]Galtung (1967) provided a detailed and systematic presentation of the logical foundations of measurement levels, their requirements, and the statistical methods warranted at each level.

[15]For example, Shneidman (1969) studied ways of drawing inferences that we, following common usage, would say were present regardless of the content of the argument.

[16]We much prefer to call our work, and other instances of measurement applied to text in the context of a research design, textual coding rather than content analysis, but we feel we must live with the familiar, if misleading, term, at least for the present.

urement on the grounds that its results would hardly be worth reading; only if inferences are made to some interesting characteristics of people or social behavior is the exercise worth the candle (Stone, Dunphy, Smith, & Ogilvie, 1966, p. 14). In the context of Stone's discussion, this principle makes sense. The Stone group assumes a research design in which the content analysis stands alone, as an independent means of research.[17] Under these circumstances, unless the content analysis results in something other than a set of measurements, it is a waste of time; nothing could be more dull than a list of measurements that take the form of symbols (such as numbers) attached to texts. However, if the measurements are there only in order to be related to other measures, the argument does not hold. The interest lies not in the numbers of the content analysis in themselves (which exist only as means to an end); nor in any inferences from those numbers, taken by themselves. It lies in the inferences made on the basis of the findings of the larger study in which those measures are embedded. Generally, this means that the interest lies in the relationships between the content analytic measurements and the other variables of the research design. If, as is common, those other variables do not exist, serious questions about the validity and the significance of the study are inescapable.[18]

As a matter of fact, we can go still further. The act of measurement in science, apart from a research design in which the measures are to be related to others, is an empty and meaningless ritual, and the conception of content analysis as a form of measurement therefore implies a design in which other variables are measured as well. The other variables might themselves be content analytic measurements, and this is surely very common. For example, in our own work, we are curious about the relationships among grievances: Do groups that express unusual numbers of grievances against the burdens imposed upon them by the state, such as taxation, also

---

[17]Stone had no objection to studies in which variables are measured by methods other than content analysis as part of the design. "Often an important part of the inference process . . . is information external to the texts themselves, with comparisons made to the text measures. Such external information is used to support inferences made from the content analyses of the texts" (Stone et al., 1966, p. 16). However, according to their own analysis, only 5 of the 23 studies reported in their book involve relating content characteristics to quantified variables outside of text analysis (Table 7.2, p. 245). Note that the inference process is made on the basis of text-derived scores alone. The correlations with external data are only of value for the purpose of verification.

[18]Our position on stand-alone designs versus content analysis as measurement has longstanding precedents. "Like other . . . exercises in content analysis the value of this study is limited by the fact that it tells us in a meticulous and laborious way what we know just as satisfactorily by an impressionistic inspection. The chief justification for such an expenditure of intellectual resources . . . would lie in the correlation of the variations in the one category with equally meticulously measured variations in some other category. Unfortunately, this latter step is omitted from practically all content analysis studies thus far" (Shils, 1948, fn. 73, p. 39).

express complaints against the ecclesiastical burden of the tithe? Or against seigneurial dues? Are we dealing with a means of expressing hostility to the state, to economic burdens, or to all outsiders interfering in the local economy? Such correlational hypotheses and their tests are legitimate, and, in fact, inevitable; nevertheless, there is something really unsatisfactory, even disturbing about any research study whose findings are based exclusively upon correlations among a number of scores derived from a content analysis. The enhanced validity of research designs that feature a multiplicity of indicators, many of which have different methodological rationales, is often discussed under the title of "multiple operationism" (cf. Webb, Campbell, Schwartz, & Sechrest, 1966; Webb & Roberts, 1969).

Fischer (1977) provided a fine example of an analysis that depends heavily upon this principle. In a veritable tour de force of imaginative historical measurement, Fischer included a study of the composition of family portraits as one indicator of fundamental change in attitudes toward the aged; he interprets his finding of a shift from the vertical format to the horizontal as an indicator of increased egalitarianism, that is, the decline of the status of the aged. (The difference is between a portrait with the father standing and the rest of the family seated and one with all standing or all seated.) Taken by itself, we find this analysis very interesting, which, of course, means that the fellow who thought it up is certainly very bright but is also likely to be very wrong. However, the atmosphere of Las Vegas tends to dissipate when we read that the following occurred at roughly the same time as portraits shifted from vertical to horizontal format (about 1800). New England towns gave up the practice of seating the town meeting according to age, in favor of the recognition of wealth; laws appeared for the first time providing for forced retirement of judges and civil servants; and "age heaping"—the discovery of large inequalities of age groups in census data that make no demographic sense—showed a switch from the common practice of exaggerating one's age to massive understatements of age. For example, since 1800, the U.S. Census generally shows far more 39-year-olds than 40-year-olds. Furthermore, the costume of men switched from a design clearly intended to make the young look older to one that was clearly intended to make the old look younger. For example, this era saw the decline of the wig and the rise of the toupee. Additionally, a study of the Oxford English Dictionary shows the concentration during this transition of the first known use of a differentiated pejorative vocabulary referring to the aged. Finally, inheritance laws shifted from those that gave important advantages to the firstborn male to equality of inheritance, reducing the power of the aged, and the proportion of children named after their grandparents steeply declined.

Perhaps the principle of multiple operationism can now be clarified in a phrase. If we were nervous and, at best, hopeful in assessing the chances for reliable knowledge to be based on Fischer's brilliant ploy with the portraits, now that we have received confirmation from so wide a variety of sources we are confident enough that the Age of the Democratic Revolution was something more than a political event and included a revolution in relations between age groups. In all likelihood, it was this fundamental change in social relations that, as Fischer contended, accounts for the shift in portrait formats.[19]

## May (or Must) a Content Analyst Go Beyond the Manifest Content to Inferences About the Latent Content of the Material?

As is evident in the definitions, the authors are at odds over whether content analysis studies the manifest content of communications, that is, the meaning as intended by the source, or its latent content, some meaning inferred by the analyst not acknowledged by or necessarily known to the author. Berelson restricted the term *content analysis* to descriptions of the manifest content, and, on the whole, Holsti did also,[20] whereas the other definitions include no such restriction; some even evince an infatuation with the latent.

Indeed, those, like Stone, who insist upon inference rather than description as the objective of a content analysis often imply that only the latent and not the manifest content of communication is of interest to the proper content analyst. Like Osgood's, our definition is noncommittal on the degree to which the producers or the audiences of texts must be conscious of the characteristics imputed to them by a content analysis. We take this position on pragmatic grounds: Any procedure that produces useful measurements is a valuable part of the social scientist's repertoire. Some social scientists (e.g., many historians and sociologists) are very much interested, for good reasons, in measuring aspects of the intended meaning of communications, whereas others offer exciting work based on measurement of states of which the subject of the research, be it the source or the audience, is generally unaware.

Before we can clarify our position, we must pause to inquire into what the distinction between manifest and latent content means. We find that meaning far from transparent. It seems to us that there is a sense in which any study of the meaning of text must be based, first, upon its manifest content. For example, before we can place a use of the term *fall* into a

---

[19]Webb et al. (1966, fn. 34, p. 9) suggest the happy term *triangulation*, to refer to this procedure: the use of multiple measures whose possible agreement inspires confidence because their defects differ radically from one another.

[20]An important qualification: "If we restrict our attention to coding operations, content analysis is limited to manifest attributes of text" (Holsti, 1969, p. 13). Similarly, he rejected interpretation at the coding stage (p. 12). Holsti wanted to delay any inferences to latent meanings until a second, or analysis, step. This is entirely consistent with our own conception of a two-step process of representational content analysis (Shapiro, this volume).

category of "fantasized flight," we must know that a particular use of *fall* means a descent due to loss of control. We would have to discover from its context that the term is not being used to refer to a season of the year, for example. If the text contained the sentence, *He saw the book fall off the table,* an analyst might see the use of *fall* as indicating the presence of a flight fantasy. If, however, the sentence read, *He went back to school in the fall,* the analyst is unlikely to do so. The reception of the manifest meaning of *fall* seems to be required before the latent meaning, the flight fantasy, can be inferred. Unless we are engaged in an analysis of the frequencies of character strings, typography, or the chemical composition of paper and ink, whenever we examine communications we first attend to the manifest meaning of the symbols, regardless of what inferences are later drawn from that meaning.[21] This observation suggests that we can regard references to the manifest content of a message as actually redundant; content cannot sensibly be called latent.

Although the terminology is confusing, those who speak of latent content often have some important and useful idea in mind. We believe that it is sometimes valid to infer from the manifest content of text characteristics of its producers or its consumers; these characteristics may be unknown to them or at least not admitted by them (e.g., their references to falling objects may reflect unconscious fantasy flights). The fact that the receipt of the message by the researcher or a coder as it was intended is an indispensable first step does not, by itself, establish that such inferences are inappropriate at later stages of analysis.[22] The restriction to the manifest by Berelson and Holsti is similar to an equally strange limitation formulated in the vocabulary of Charles W. Morris' "Theory of Signs" or "Semiotics." We are often told by authors influenced by this tradition that content analysis partakes of semantics and syntactics, but not of pragmatics; that is, it studies the relations of signs to meanings (or their objects) and the relations of signs to signs but not the relations of signs to people—those who use them, the sources or the targets of communications (cf. Janis, 1949, chap. IV; Kaplan, 1943; but also Stone et al. [1966, p. 18] for the contrary view that content analysis is a branch of pragmatics). We submit that almost all social science work generally classified as content analysis has been designed to tell us something about people, which, in social science, is the name of the game. Even when we engage in semantics, the effort to discern and classify the meanings in text, we are making inferences to some particular characteristics of the

---

[21]This is the reason for the great efforts invested by Stone and his associates in the disambiguation of words and phrases as part of their work on the General Inquirer.

[22]Berelson's dictum seems to us an arbitrary and unnecessary restraint on inquiry. Indeed, in listing and apparently approving such uses of content analysis as measures of the readability of text, Berelson seems to be forced by his pragmatic good sense to ignore his own rule: In no sense can readability be viewed as a part of the manifest content of a communication.

source, namely the intended meaning of the communication in the mind of the emitter. We cannot discover any utility for research work of a realm of meaning apart from symbol-using, interacting humans, regardless of its attraction for some schools of philosophical analysis.

In our search for a minimal formulation that will do the least harm to working researchers, we are happier with Osgood's (1959) definition: "a procedure whereby one makes inferences about sources and receivers from evidence in the messages they exchange" (p. 55). It permits the social scientist to use text to find out things about people, which is his vocation, and insists, as is only proper, that these inferences be based upon "evidence in the messages." It leaves open the question of whether the categories of inference refer to characteristics of sources or receivers that are known to or acknowledged by them.

Content analysis has lived in a kind of methodological ghetto. Its isolation from the methodological discourse of general social science has obscured the fact that the admissibility of latent inferences is only a special case of the classical problem of the validity of scientific measurements. Whether a scientist is justified in recording, based upon his reading of text, characteristics that are not known to or perhaps not acknowledged by its source or audience can only be properly evaluated on the basis of the usual criteria of the validity of measurements—procedures such as correlations with alternative measures that are commonly used to evaluate the validity of aptitude test scores, for example—not by arbitrary dicta in the form of "definitions of the field."

In contrast to those who insist upon the manifest, we find another group of authors who are infatuated with the latent. Particularly for those trained in dynamic psychology, only the latent seems to be important. They seek to avoid the superficial; whatever appears on the surface as the meaning of a communication must be of little interest. This is only a matter of professional blinders; many historians and sociologists are likely to find psychologically deep motives trivial in the perspective of their disciplinary orientations.[23]

Even though he admitted studies of the manifest in his ecumenical view of content analysis, Galtung (1967, p. 70), like Stone, saw them as generally trivial. He presented a table showing that when the manifest content is coded, theoretical relevance is likely to be low, whereas reliability is high. Conversely, if the latent intent is coded, theoretical relevance is likely to be

---

[23]The conception of content analysis as a stand-alone method of discovery of the latent is associated with a remarkable preference for factor analysis among its practitioners. We have been astonished to note that texts in content analysis will often have extensive discussions of factor analysis, with little or no mention of other multivariate techniques (e.g., North, Holsti, Zaninovich, & Zinnes, 1963, chapter VII). This privileged position of factor analytic models over, for example, multiple regression is understandable. Like content analysis, factor analysis is often used as a stand-alone method for the discovery of latent mysteries.

high while reliability is low. We do not grant the generality of this argument. Some studies based upon the coding of manifest content may have been trivial because the content analysis was allowed to stand alone. If the content analysis only yields measures that are used to explore relations with other variables, the significance of the inquiry depends entirely upon the larger research design.

In introducing the proceedings from the important Annenberg School Conference on Content Analysis in 1967, Gerbner also put forward a strong preference for the latent:

> But not all significance can be evoked by inspection nor is all significance accessible to casual observation. The purpose of any analysis is to illuminate or to make possible inferences about something that is not otherwise apparent. In the analysis of messages this particular "something" is a type of significance or "content" that becomes available to an analyst who uses particular methods for specific purposes. (Gerbner et al., 1969, p. x)

Clearly, any scientific study whose conclusions were obvious in advance is likely to be a disappointment (although such studies are occasionally necessary). This does not imply Gerbner's presumption that new and interesting findings must be in the form of content not accessible to casual observation. If the content analysis is pursued as an independent investigation, without reference to other data, then the only conclusions not accessible to casual observation would seem to be latent meanings.[24] If, however, the content analysis is a part of a larger research design, the covariations of variables characterizing that content with other features of social life are rarely obvious in advance of a systematic investigation.

## To What Object of Investigation Is the Description or Inference to Apply?

This is the issue on which the definitions most radically disagree. Is it the researcher's intention, as Krippendorff felt it must be, to discover properties of those who produced the text, that is, its source? Or may he also study properties of the audience for the text, as Osgood suggested? If so, what audience? Is the object of investigation the communication process?[25] Must he study only the text itself, as Berelson insisted?

---

[24]Even in this case, surprises are possible. In our study of the French Revolution grievance lists, we found categories of demands that are among the most frequent in the national sample, categories that have not been discussed in the work of scholars studying the documents by casual observation over a period of two centuries (Shapiro & Markoff, in press).

[25]In the explicit methodological formulations (but rarely in the research practice) of the school of Lasswell, Kaplan, Schramm, and Pool, much is made of the importance of studying communication as a process rather than studying the emitters or receivers of messages or the text itself (cf. Lasswell, 1946).

This last option (i.e., the text itself) has often resulted in content analyses that appear disembodied, disconnected from social life. As Galtung (1967) put it, "content analysis runs the risk of being suspended between senders and receivers, never really bearing on the social system" (p. 71). There are, of course, those whose interests properly lie in the text as such: those who study the vocabulary of Shakespeare's plays or who seek to establish the authorship of documents as revealed by unconscious linguistic habits (e.g., the classic work by Mosteller & Wallace, 1964). There are also many who claim to be studying "the text" only to avoid the difficulties of defending inferences to the source or the audience. Although Berelson's explicit principles approve only the study of text as such and never the study of its sources or its audiences, he admired many pieces of content analytic research that could not possibly be accepted by this criterion.

Just as some researchers claim to be studying only the text, some claim to be studying the whole society to avoid the specification of those sectors of the society whose views are supposedly reflected in the documents and the investigator's grounds for such contentions.[26] The dangers are well illustrated by the devastating critique by Mechling (1975) of research that attempts to measure child-rearing behavior of parents by a content analysis of manuals in which experts provide them with advice. The sloppy thinking that attributes a permissive or a highly structured set of values to the society is well served by the use of the contents of the manuals as an indication of parental behavior. Mechling (1975), however, demonstrated that "childrearing manuals are the consequents not of childrearing values but of childrearing manual-writing values" (p. 53). It is apparent that childrearing practice may differ substantially from group to group within the same society at the same time, and even those groups most likely to read the manuals can rarely be found practicing what the manuals currently preach. One can ask, "If that's what they're doing, why write a manual to convince them to do so?" We find it hard to believe that Mechling's findings would come as a surprise to Benjamin Spock.

When analyzing the source or the audience of written material, we are, of course, generally dealing with literate groups, and these are notably different from the illiterate in social and economic status. More broadly, most if not all symbolic products are patronized only by sectors of the society, and it is a primary obligation of the researcher to attempt to ascertain and communicate to the reader the groups that are represented, whether as source or as audience in his analysis. For example, it is a mistake to discuss the grievance

---

[26]The most sensational instance of such a use of content analysis has been in the work of McClelland (1961). Measures based upon the designs of Greek vase decorations and the contents of dramas and of children's readers are used to measure the level of achievement motivation attributed to the society as a whole and are correlated with a variety of indicators of economic growth.

lists of the French Revolution, the documents studied in our own research, as reflections of the views of an undifferentiated France in 1789, a democratic *vox populi*. They are the product of particular assemblies whose social composition was largely defined by law and, within limits, is generally understood. Nor should we rush to assume that, because we are studying written documents, the relevant audience is necessarily the literate. Not only are the latter a highly differentiated group, some parts of which produce or are exposed to different communications than others, but written or printed messages aimed at the illiterate—such media as the theater, sermons, and regular community readings—appear as surprisingly common and important in recent research in social history (cf. Bollème, 1965). Moreover, there are written messages of which the illiterate are at least coauthors. The grievance lists, for example, were discussed, modified, and endorsed in group meetings in which illiterates frequently participated, even though literate people placed the words on paper. Illiterate people have also produced documents, for example, in collaboration with scribes (e.g., wills) and magistrates (e.g., depositions).

We find among our definitions considerable controversy over the legitimacy of inferences to the characteristics of the audience rather than the characteristics of the source of the communication. Indeed, whereas Krippendorff defined content analysis exclusively as a means of inferring characteristics of the source, Osgood explicitly permitted studies of the audience. Our own definition is noncommittal: We insist only that the analysis be of use to social science, but of course we want any inferences to the audience as well as the source to be justified. We find at least two potentially reasonable defenses for an inference from the content of text to the characteristics of its audience. First, members of the audience are strongly enough affected by the communication for the latter to be taken as an indicator of their views (cf. Merritt, 1966). This requires very powerful communications indeed. A more commonly useful rationale refers to some feedback of the taste, the views, or the preferences of the audience on the communication content. The most familiar instance is when such a feedback is provided by a market mechanism by which the audience is free to choose whether or not to support the judgment of the editors by purchasing the product, depending upon its appeal.[27] We find it appropriate, for example, that Lowenthal (1956) chose the most popular magazines from which to draw the biographies to be studied for his classic analysis of shifts in the character

---

[27]There is often a temptation to make overly simple assumptions about the portion of the total communication that is being bought, supported, appreciated, or sought out, and that accounts for any persistence of the medium. For example, for many years the electorate of New York City usually voted against the editorial recommendations of the city's most widely read newspaper, the *Daily News*. Apart from differential rates of voting by educational level, this probably indicates that vast numbers of people read the newspaper for reasons other than agreement with the editorials—comics, lurid sex scandals, or excellent sports coverage for example.

of American heros, and that McGranahan and Wayne (1948) chose the longest running dramas in Germany and the United States for their study of national character differences. The feedback process would obviously have much less effect on the publication of books than periodicals and on a television special than on a series. Note that market mechanisms represent only the most familiar devices for such a feedback.

Sometimes the very distinction between source and audience might be obscure. McClelland's (1961) study of the use of the designs on ancient Greek and Peruvian vases as an indicator of the level of achievement motivation of the society provides an instructive instance. (The design characteristics associated with high and low levels of achievement motivation were projected from a study of the doodling of high and low achievement subjects—contemporary college students.) We speculate that, even in the absence of a market, a Greek artisan-slave who created vases that pleased his master was likely to create more vases over a lifetime than one whose work was objectionable and who may therefore have had his lifetime shortened. The more popular style of work was more plentiful and would be more likely to survive the centuries and thereby to enter into McClelland's statistics. By means of their selective support of particular producers or products, the populace may be said to join in the creation of culture (which might then be reasonably called popular culture), just as Vico (1961, p. 270) described the Greek people as the true authors of Homer's epics. There is a sense in which the audience then merges with the source, and the radical opposition between Krippendorff's definition of content analysis and Osgood's, in this respect, disappears.

Many studies that could be called content analytic by our definition address an important object of inference that is ignored in all the definitions that we have cited from the literature. Students of contentious events such as popular disorders or uprisings often use narrative sources such as newspapers, memoirs, and oral interviews to discover their data, and, if some quantitative manipulation of such event data is envisioned, utilize explicit schemes for systematic coding of the text.[28]

Tilly's (1981, 1986) extensive collection of data on collective conflict in 19th and 20th century France and England, Franzosi's (this volume) study of Italian industrial conflict, and Olzak's (1989b) work on nineteenth and twentieth century ethnic violence in the United States are examples of recent studies that involve extensive textual coding. In none of these instances is the object of inference the newspaper reader or the audience, nor is the research centrally directed to the attributes of the authors of these communications. Still less can it be said that the process of communication is itself of interest. The texts are taken as statements of facts to be suitably classified. The researcher is interested in the intended meaning of the communication,

---

[28]For recent trends in the study of events, see Olzak (1989a). For the methodological issues in one of the major sources for the study of events, see Franzosi (1987).

but the facts presented in the communication, and not its source or its audience, are the target of inquiry.

One might say that Tilly, Franzosi, and Olzak regard the authors of the communications they study as informants rather than as respondents. When, in a questionnaire study, we elicit responses from our subjects in order to infer some characteristics of those subjects from their responses, they are respondents; when, on the contrary, we enlist them as sources of information in order to learn something from their knowledge, they are informants. If, for example, we ask people their age, we are asking them to share with us information that they have available—a procedure much cheaper, if less valid, than chasing down their birth certificates. We are treating them as informants. In contrast, if we ask Americans their views on Bosnia, we are surely not trying to learn anything about Bosnia but rather about those whom we are interviewing. We are taking them as respondents. In the same way, when we use textual coding to identify and classify events, we take the reporters of these events as informants, for we wish to make inferences about the frequency and nature of the events they describe. Far from the center of our attention, the attributes of the author or the audiences of a communication are studied only as sources of possible error. For example, if we find that journals on the left attribute different political slogans to street demonstrators than those on the right, we would worry about whether the characteristics of author or audience are distorting the reality in which we are interested.

## Must Content Analysis Be Quantitative?

If Berelson and Cartwright required that the work be quantitative, Stone, Krippendorff, and Osgood insisted only on inferences, which could surely be qualitative. Note that Berelson and Cartwright alone insisted that the product must be a description, as well as requiring that all content analysis be quantitative. This clearly means that they wanted the description to be in the form of numerical measurements. We believe, in the light of their other writings, that they would admit a theoretical interpretation of the data that uses only words. It is important to note, therefore, that they differ from the others only in that they see the content analysis as complete after a numerical description has been produced, whereas the others would include within content analysis the subsequent activities of interpretation.

Our definition is permissive on this issue: Measurement includes operations that yield nominal or qualitative categories as well as ordinal or interval level scales. Note that this applies only to some of the studies that are often labeled as qualitative content analyses. Some would give the title to works based on literary or journalistic study of text lacking any systematic procedures. Berelson, for example, included Freud's analysis of Leonardo da Vinci's autobiography as a qualitative content analysis (Berelson, 1971, chap. III). He also classified what can only be called poor quantitative studies as qualitative;

these studies were based upon inadequate samples utilizing unspecified coding methods in a whimsical fashion. Nor was Berelson alone in muddying the waters this way. In introducing their computerized study of presidential nomination acceptance speeches, Smith, Stone, and Glenn (1966) referred to previous work on the subject: "Journalists have written many columns on the basis of qualitative content analyses" (p. 359).

As we have indicated, our emphasis upon the function of content analysis as measurement does not restrict us to quantitative results. A coder, having found a single instance of a class of events within a text, may be instructed to add one to a counter initialized at zero and to continue adding one (or some other figure) to the counter at every instance found. In this way, he will end up with a frequency, a quantitative or numerical value for each text. However, he may also be instructed to divide a set of texts into two classes according to the decision rule: "If at least one instance of an event of the defined class occurs, call the document an 'X'. Otherwise, do not." This would be a binary measurement, the simplest case of nominal measurement, which is, we believe, what is generally meant, or at least ought to be, by qualitative content analysis. In a study of diplomatic correspondence, for example, a researcher might be interested in classifying the documents into two piles: those that do and those that don't mention the possibility of war at least once. Whether this, or the number of paragraphs mentioning the possibility of war, is the better measure would have to be left open for resolution by experimentation in individual cases.[29] In our own work on the *cahiers de doléances*, we are interested in the number of grievances expressed in each document, for example, against privileges associated with the royal taxation system, but we are also very much interested in identifying those districts in which the Third Estate did not demand the procedure of "vote by head" in the Estates General. This was the pivotal constitutional issue of the spring of 1789, the issue over which the immediate break between the commoners and the privileged orders came, and an issue on which the Third Estate was almost (but not quite) unified. Any Third Estate assembly not associating itself with this position has special characteristics very important indeed to investigate.[30]

---

[29]George (1959) gave evidence, in one case, of the superiority of this kind of qualitative classification over quantitative counts as a means of propaganda analysis for espionage purposes in wartime.

[30]Some of the work called qualitative content analysis by Berelson and others might be best conceptualized as proto-content analysis in the sense that it constitutes a first step, a part of the job of measurement. Before there can be measurement there must be a set of categories with their symbols and meanings. The development of a codebook that indicates something of the range of the contents to be found, without indicating the frequency of each category, is often a very useful form of activity. It is not a measurement, however, but only the development of a part of the instrumentation required for the performance of that function.

The work of Heise (1988, 1991) is also qualitative content analysis in that Heise was not concerned with counts nor primarily with drawing statistical inferences through principles of sampling. In identifying narrative sequences, whether in children's games or stories, Heise's work meets strict canons of rigor (indeed, establishes new canons of rigor) and is a model of systematic procedure. Heise located structures but not structures simple enough to be expressed as quantities. They are described in a complex vocabulary of qualitative distinctions. The procedure is one of measurement in a nominal multidimensional space. Among many possible uses of Heise's techniques is exploring whether more than one episode of sequenced events can be fit by a particular abstract formulation (e.g., are two episodes of children's play, for example, instances of the same set of rules?) (Corsaro & Heise, 1990, p. 29). This is a measurement question.[31]

It seems to us, then, that the qualitative–quantitative distinction, as drawn by Berelson and others, unfortunately gathers together as nonquantitative both work that is devoid of any systematic character and the most scrupulously scientific work that identifies complex structures. If we instead distinguish work that does from work that does not have a systematic character (i.e., that is or is not engaged in measurement), Heise's work and other seriously scientific qualitative studies are included in content analysis whereas informal readings of text are not. In our view, there is a fundamental distinction to be drawn between research carried out with systematic procedures and a critical evaluation of data and methods in relation to theory and research that is haphazard or that involves no thought of the adequacy of the fit of the data and methods to theory. This distinction is a far more fundamental division in sociology than the more recent usage of the qualitative–quantitative distinction, a usage that distracts attention from the struggle for methodologies that advance knowledge.[32]

## What Terms, Redolent of the Laboratory, Serve to Remind Us of the Identification of Content Analysis as a Scientific Pursuit?

The greatest unanimity in our definitions appears in the requirement that content analysis must participate in the ambitions and the criteria of the

---

[31]One could imagine the development of similarity measures that would take this work in a quantitative direction and, if considered rigorously, would also raise issues of sampling. Is one's sample representative of the population of the children's games, stories, or conflicts that one wishes to analyze in terms of these measures?

[32]It is this more recent usage that is applied in the editor's introduction as depicting the quantitative domain of this book. In contrast with our usage, quantitative text analysis is described there as differentiable from qualitative text analysis in that only quantitative text analysis affords the researcher with probabilistic inferences from samples to populations of texts.

scientific tradition; all but one of the authors use one or more of the very similar adjectives "systematic," "objective," "replicable," or "valid" as symbols of this allegiance.[33] Indeed, the only criterion on which the definitions show a significant consensus is that whoever refers to his work as content analysis rather than as mere reading is making a claim to participation in a scientific enterprise as distinguished, for example, from a literary or a journalistic enterprise.

Our requirement that, to be regarded as content analysis, research must involve a methodical or systematic study of text is intended to exclude the use of the title to lend a scientific aura to ordinary reading. We can be somewhat more specific. We mean to convey, first, that all of the text or a portion of the text that is selected on the basis of explicit rules (such as a sample) must be subjected to analysis. The text that enters into analysis is not chosen by whim; it could not be, for example, the portion of the available material that appears interesting to a reader, even one of extraordinary sensibilities. The procedures whereby it is selected must be made public in sufficient detail to permit scientific criticism as thorough as is customary in public opinion polling, contemporary astronomy, census work, and industrial quality control. The terms *methodical* and *systematic* also refer to what is done with the portions of text that are selected for study. There must be some symbols—numbers, words, letters, computer codes—representing categories of analytic interest that are invariably considered, to be assigned or not after due deliberation, from all passages of text selected for study. In other words, it would not be a content analysis if a reader were to utilize one set of categories on one portion of text and another set on some other portion, in accordance with whim, a sense of discovery, or the onset of boredom.[34] Such a procedure is certainly not the only appropriate use of written material in social science or, for that matter, in ordinary life. We do not attempt to apply a consistent set of categories over a selection of text chosen by explicit rules when we read the morning newspaper over breakfast coffee, nor when we read a professional journal for the usual purposes. We also do not call such activities content analyses.

Although there is general agreement that content analysis must be somehow scientific, there is not, necessarily, agreement among these authors as to how they view the essential components of a scientific method. In fact, the literature reflects a profound methodological split (which is only dimly reflected in the definitions) over one fundamental issue: the application of a

[33]The exception is Charles Osgood, inventor of the Semantic Differential and Evaluative Assertion Analysis, whose exemplary writings should render any such confession of faith redundant.

[34]However, if one applies one set of categories to all text with a particular distinguishing characteristic and a second set to all of the rest, one is still using systematic procedures.

requirement for the operational definition of variables to content analytic categories and the associated question of the dispensability of human coders.

This issue is, of course, a proper one to debate: A very large number of important works of content analysis have been done with human coders, and the advantages of depending exclusively upon machines are considerable (Shapiro, this volume; Shapiro & Markoff, in press). The pros and cons are, however, not what interest us here, but rather the effort to preempt the issue by defining content analysis in a manner that would exclude the use of coders and, thereby, a vast literature. This is done more often by the implicit use of the term than by its explicit definition. For example, Stone and Weber (1992) launched their article on content analysis in the *Encyclopedia of Sociology* with a seemingly inclusive explicit definition: "Content analysis is a set of procedures for making reliable and valid inferences from images, speech, and text" (p. 290). But in the third paragraph, we are told, "In developing a content analysis procedure, investigators agree on what words in the text are to be used in drawing an inference" (p. 291). Implicitly, we are being told that the work of those investigators like Tilly (1981), Franzosi (1987), and Lowenthal (1956), who could not possibly catalog the variety of words that might signal the presence of the meanings they tabulate, is excluded from the field of content analysis. We contend that progress in content analysis requires that the issue be joined in debate, rather than dismissed by means of a restrictive definition of the field.

PART

# I

# METHODOLOGIES

# 2

# THEMATIC TEXT ANALYSIS: NEW AGENDAS FOR ANALYZING TEXT CONTENT

Philip J. Stone
Harvard University and the Gallup Organization

This chapter reviews how thematic text analysis applications in the social sciences have evolved over the last three decades. In contrast to an oft-noted decline in academic text-analysis applications, this chapter reports how business text-analysis applications have expanded, especially for analyzing open-ended interviews, making it perhaps one of the most extensively employed social science tools today. Noting that text analysis applications have shifted from testing broad theories to more grounded objectives, I anticipate how the capabilities of desktop computing compared to earlier mainframe computing will facilitate bottom-up approaches to thematic text analysis. With work competencies as an example, I illustrate how existing thematic text analysis resources can suggest ways for investigators to frame analyses from broadened perspectives, thereby further increasing the comprehensiveness of their analyses and the validity of their inferences.

## MEASURING THEMES IN TEXT

Clinicians, anthropologists, journalists, market researchers, and humanists are among the varied folk who have looked for themes in text. They have identified themes (or thematic imagery) in dream reports, folk tales, newspapers, focus-group transcripts, letters, and poetry, to cite just a few sources. Thus, it should not be surprising that many of those who systematically analyze text—from Lasswell's pioneering group of researchers to analysts today at organizations like Gallup—also describe their work as a search for themes. For them, measuring themes involves noting recurrent information embedded in text. What measurements they choose to make depends on what questions they want to address.

Random House's (Flexner & Hauck, 1987, p. 1966) unabridged dictionary defines a "theme" as the subject matter of a document, discussion, or meeting. An example given is that "the theme of the meeting was world peace." However, themes also are recurrent patterns that run through a text much as musical themes are melodic subjects embedded in musical compositions. Indeed, the analogy with musical themes probably has figured more in thinking about text analysis than has been acknowledged.[1]

Often a thematic analysis of text is quite informal and involves "more or less" judgments rather than precise numerical measurements. For example, people often make inferences about changes in what they hear and read. Someone who regularly reads about a political campaign in the press might note that Senator X has become more conservative in her speeches, drawing this inference from statements attributed to the senator over the course of a campaign. Indeed, more often than we probably realize, most of us informally analyze text to assess theme changes over time or to compare themes in different sources.[2]

It should be noted that, venturing beyond the dictionary definition, text analysts often measure such unintended text attributes as well as intended text subjects. Several examples from another chapter in this book illustrate this distinction. Themes as subjects are illustrated in this volume by Danielson and Lasorsa's descriptions of how much attention *The New York Times* and *Los Angeles Times* gave over a hundred-year period to communism and agriculture. Their charts show changes over time in the proportion of stories about these subjects—subjects that the journalists who wrote the articles intended to discuss. Themes as attributes are illustrated by their measure of quantification in these newspapers, again showing marked changes over time. Quantification usually was not the intended subject of the journalists who wrote the stories. Instead, quantification was an attribute of these stories that can be measured.

---

[1]My thanks to Signe Spencer for pointing this out.

[2]Not surprisingly, several attempts have been made to define, in a more delimited way, what is a theme. Berelson (1954) for example, defined theme as "an assertion about a subject matter" (p. 508), a definition that differs from the dictionary view of a theme as a subject matter itself. Following Berelson, several of us once suggested that such assertions naturally divide into two types: combinations of nouns and verbs (like *soldiers revolt* or *underpay workers*) that we proposed to call themes and assertions combining nouns and modifiers, like *nasty neighbor*, that we proposed to call images (Stone, Dunphy, Smith, & Ogilive, 1966, p. 36). We suggested that themes (defined in this way) often evolve into more static images, a process that might be interesting to examine. Neither we nor anyone else ever did much with this distinction.

"Theme" continues to be used in a loose, general way for analyzing patterns in text, but like an old shoe, the fit seems comfortable and does not cause much problem. More encompassing than the dictionary, in this chapter I treat themes as including attributes as well as subjects of texts.[3] Probably any further attempt to modify the term would be doomed to fail anyway, especially in face of humanists, clinicians, anthropologists, and others who will continue to use it as they always have.

## LIMITATIONS OF THEMATIC TEXT ANALYSIS

Any systematic thematic text analysis risks alarming those who worry whether it can do justice to a text's meaning. Some people will complain that a thematic analysis violates the text, especially if it does not fully consider the context from which the text was generated or if it is used to make inferences that the author did not particularly have in mind. Moreover, any translation of the text into numbers must further ignore the text as a whole.

These concerns have deep roots. Plato was suspect of written texts, for how, he argued, could readers surmise the intentions and context from which they were generated? Similarly, some qualitative researchers suspect text transcripts by themselves and instead use video cameras in an attempt to capture nonverbal communications, intonations, and surrounding context as well as what was said. In such cases as a dramatic courtroom scene, people rightly argue that a transcript is but a poor, inadequate trace of sights, sounds, smells, intonations, and emotional tensions of the original event. Certainly just a transcript of the song lyrics on MTV would not begin to convey what the performers intend or the audience experiences. Inasmuch as historians base their research on textual records apart from knowledge about context and intent that can only come from having been there, history itself becomes suspect.

### Content Lost

Science has been described, perhaps not totally with tongue in cheek, as "systematically throwing away information" in order to derive measures.[4] The first problem then comes from limiting the analysis to the textual record. This book's use of text analysis instead of the traditional content analysis—which also includes measuring themes in pictures and other modes of representation—makes this limitation explicit. Text can be daunting and

---

[3]The difficulty of distinguishing between attributes and subjects is not limited to text. A musical theme, for example, can be an attribute of a composition as well as its subject.

[4]I heard Kenneth Boulding use this definition years ago. I do not know where he got it or if he coined it.

complex enough without considering additional issues in evaluating themes conveyed by the setting or nonverbal communications.

Whether or not a reduction to the textual record is justified depends on whether what is learned is valuable and makes sense when put back in the context of the big picture. Angry parents, for example, have taken a close look at the themes in some MTV lyrics—even though many of us cannot begin to decipher what is being sung—because they are worried about the messages their children receive. For them, the text of the lyrics is important, even though the performers might dismiss it as but a minor part of the overall presentation.

As if the limitation to just text were not problem enough, a thematic analyst's second step in systematically throwing away information is to measure just themes in the text. Sometimes, themes are prespecified by the research question. Other times, investigators attempt to measure all the themes they can discern in the text. Some investigators will attempt to assess the presence or absence of a theme in a document, whereas others will attempt to measure the intensity, as reflected in the frequency with which the theme is present. In any case, here again is an occasion to miss the true intent of the message, no matter how many themes are part of the coding procedure. In the effort to make comparisons, more information is lost.

Finally, some thematic text analysts enlist computers in making their analyses. Unless there is adequate human backup to check on what the computer does, this technique risks making errors in identifying themes that not even a 7-year-old would miss. Arguing that computers provide even-handed coding, do not fatigue, and have complete rescoring reliability, some investigators nevertheless find this a risk they are willing to take, especially if their manual checks on text samples show that the computer is doing an adequate job.[5]

## Inferences Gained

Thematic text analysis, with or without computers, does not differ funda-mentally from analytic procedures used in many sciences. For example, a lab technician makes various measurements on an annual physical exam blood sample that range from traditional white cell counts to more recently developed high-tech measures, such as PSA indexes for men. Few would

---

[5]Contrary to popular impressions, most thematic analysts in the last quarter century have not enlisted computers to help with their task. For example, Smith's (1992) 702-page *Handbook of Thematic Content Analysis* describes only manual coding schemes and omits any discussion of computer-aided procedures. Most researchers find their task complicated enough without complicating it more with computers. Moreover, their research questions usually do not require analyzing an amount of text that would make manual analyses infeasible.

complain, however, that the measurements the lab technician makes violate the blood's unique essence or that the blood has been reduced to numbers. Nor would anyone be likely to confuse these measurements with the real thing when a transfusion is needed.

Both manual and computer-aided types of analyses share problems that stem from a lack of context. Much as patients sometimes complain that their doctors are more interested in their blood than they are in them, people may rightly complain that text analysts are more interested in the transcript than in understanding the situation. In their pursuit of testing hypotheses, some academic researchers allow themselves to ignore the original context in which a text was situated and instead focus on tables of statistics that their text analyses generate. Their research articles may seem remote from the object of study, much as blood-medicine journal articles may seem remote from their original clinical contexts.

However, if a whole-health physician makes good use of blood measurements as part of the evidence for making a diagnosis based on what is observed about the entire person—as well as the context within which that person lives—blood measurements may contribute to rather than detract from understanding, especially when they provide critical information that cannot be obtained in any other way. Similarly, a business consultant who uses thematic text analysis has to translate findings into actionable, valid, and responsible recommendations to the client, or the measurements are irrelevant. For both practitioners, numbers are only useful to the extent that they help make valid diagnoses and inferences.

The bottom line of whether any thematic analysis is worth doing is whether it delivers useful information. Making valid inferences from the information, however, may require clinical and other talents beyond measuring. It is not difficult, for example, to document the amount of violence on television (Gerbner, 1988) or the reduction in recent years of television news clips down to sound bytes (Adatto, 1990). The issue is what implications are to be drawn from these measurements, considering the functions of television in our society.

Thematic text analysis becomes especially worthwhile when used to predict outcomes and make nonobvious but valid inferences. The Gallup Organization, for example, has a proven ability, based on over a half-million job interviews, to use thematic indexes to identify those who will be outstanding performers in a particular job. Other examples include predicting whether mental patients will relapse on the basis of family members' "expressed emotion" (Vaughn & Leff, 1976), relating urban riots to "Black invisibility" in the press (Johnson, Sears, & McConahay, 1971), using a combination of action and thought themes to predict whether young field workers assigned overseas will do well (Ramallo, 1966), identifying from suicide notes who committed suicide (Ogilvie, Stone, & Schneidman, 1966), classifying people into standard diagnostic psychiatric categories such as depression (Gottschalk, this volume), and demonstrating convincingly to a court the existence of a social injustice in state history textbooks (Stone & Weber, 1992). It is easy to find themes, for we do it all the time. The question is what we make of them.[6]

## COMPUTER-AIDED TEXT ANALYSIS
## IN THE EARLY 1960s

The utilization of information-processing technology for thematic text analysis dates back to the 1950s when Pool, Lasswell and others first employed punched cards and tabulation machines to aid their manual efforts—Danielson and Lasorsa (this volume) quote Lasswell, Lerner, and Pool's (1952) admission that they could not have done their studies without machine tabulations. However, their research projects were still tedious to carry out and took a long time to complete, even with their tabulating machinery. Lasswell et al. (1952) opined that "perhaps the evolution of modern computing machinery may prove to be the key to the tremendously complex problems involved in the statistical analysis of language" (p. 63). However, for them the biggest advantage was not efficiency but an increased flexibility to go back to the data. As they noted several sentences later, "with the system actually used, tabulation was so laborious that, once the summary tables by periods were made up, it was almost never possible to go back for another look at them" (p. 63).

Many thematic text analysts would consider the most important advantage computer-aided text analysis offers to be the opportunity to utilize what was learned from one analysis in returning to the text for another look. Contrary to the notion that computers inherently distance researchers from the text, computers provide opportunities to get closer to it. For example, when a previously unnoticed theme is identified, computers aid the researcher to create a scoring procedure that captures this new theme and to go back and reanalyze the text.[7] To many of those who experienced the

---

[6]For further reading, Lindkvist (1981) provided additional perspectives on the limitations of thematic textual analysis by comparing content analysis with analytic semantics, structuralism, and hermeneutics, and Stone (1986) considered content analysis in relation to semiotics.

[7]To avoid shaping the analysis too closely to particular features of the text sample and thereby losing generality, researchers often split the text randomly in two parts and set the second part aside without looking at it. They then analyze the first half of the data as thoroughly as they can, creating whatever tailor-made categories this analysis would support. The validity of these measures is then checked by seeing how well they perform on the text that was set aside.

fatigue as well as the frustrations of manual content analysis, the computer would have offered considerable promise.[8]

Recognizing that mainframe batch-job computers put an undesirable distance between the investigator and the text being studied, considerable effort in the 1960s went into recoding text analysis programs into the machine language of the first smaller sized computers that investigators could operate themselves and also process considerable amounts of text (cf. Stone, Dunphy, Smith, & Ogilvie, 1966, p. 74). Users could instruct the computer to sort text, make retrievals, and make counts—most everything indeed except categorize words, which was still a mainframe task. Text was kept on magnetic tapes, and the researcher could pass over it as many times as needed to complete an analysis, with the results appearing on a high-speed printer. This capability made the investigator much more a part of a joint computer/human endeavor and provided a significant step toward realizing the interactivity that Pool and his colleagues had so wistfully envisioned.

Several different text analysis approaches emerged during the 1960s, some a direct result of computers becoming available. A 1967 content analysis conference that some 400 people attended at the Annenberg School of Communications in Philadelphia provided a forum for comparing these approaches. *The Analysis of Communication Content* (Gerbner, Holsti, Krippendorff, Paisley, & Stone, 1969) includes some of the discussions as well as the papers. Although some papers examined the content of visual records (Ekman, Friesen, & Taussig, 1969), music (Brook, 1969), and vocal information (Starkweather, 1969), most were concerned with text analysis.

One of the most salient contrasts at this conference was between analysts who used computers to factor analyze word counts and those who used computers to categorize text words and phrases according to a prespecified system. The advocates of the first approach claimed they were more likely to be true to a document's meaning because their approach was uncontaminated by theories (Iker & Harway, 1969). The advocates of the second approach looked to their categorization schemes as attempts to operationalize theory, including such grand theories of the time as the work of Lasswell and Kaplan (1950), Parsons and Shils (1951), and Osgood, Suci, and Tannenbaum (1957). Testing theories was their reason for doing content analysis in the first place. Some of the others at the conference, however, were neither interested in prespecified categories nor in handing their text analyses over to factor analysis programs. Advocates of a third approach looked to computers to help manage and organize textual information so they could work with it more effectively, much as earlier scholars had manually constructed Bible concordances to aid their work.

---

[8]See Barcus (1959) for a review of content analysis research between 1900 and 1958 based on about 1,700 studies, including some 500 Master's theses.

As illustrated by the other chapters in this book, the resources available to all three approaches have evolved considerably since the Annenberg conference. The first approach can benefit from new "unbiased by theory" techniques that uncover patterns in data. Factor analysis was never very satisfactory because raw text has too many different words, and word frequencies are not normally distributed—an assumption required in applications of factor analysis. Newer techniques, such as neural-net programs,[9] may prove more suitable. The second approach today can benefit from desktop computers that allow investigators to maintain larger, more comprehensive categorization schemes and to change them easily whenever the need arises. The third approach is now aided by an assortment of desktop computer tools developed for qualitative studies of text.

In retrospect, the projects reported at the Annenberg conference were but small demonstrations of what could be done in the future with the aid of computers. Compared to the convenience of today's desktop computers, researchers using computers at that time were hampered in almost every way. Research projects were made larger and demonstrations more difficult and expensive. Access to computers was relatively infrequent and although mainframe computers soon grew in capacity, users were then limited to memory partitions of a quarter or a half megabyte. The commercial charge for an hour of mainframe computer time, moreover, was about a month's wage for a secretary. Text itself had to be keypunched on cards for the computer and a megabyte of text was about six boxes (i.e., more than a person could carry).

Anticipating better, less costly computer access in years ahead, several projects were started in the 1960s with a view of creating social indicators on a larger scale. In 1964 a team at the University of Michigan worked with a content analysis group at Harvard to analyze open-ended answers to election-study survey questions about what people like and dislike about presidential candidates Goldwater and Johnson, as well as about the Democratic and Republican parties. Researchers at the National Opinion Research Center at the University of Chicago developed a text analysis procedure for survey questions about happiness and what people worry about. Political scientist Ithiel Pool, psychologist Robert Abelson, and sociologist James Coleman formed a company in New York called *Simulmatics* to apply computer-based procedures to the analysis of social problems, and *Inquirer* text analysis procedures became one of their tools (Stone & Bernstein, 1965; Stone, Dunphy, & Bernstein, 1966).

---

[9]SAS, for example, added a procedure for creating and testing neural nets in 1994. See Raud and Fallig (1993) for the application of neural nets to coding processes.

## THE ROUTINIZATION OF TEXT ANALYSIS: 1970–1995

Following Annenberg, many people felt that the use of computers for text analysis had been demonstrated and that further development could wait until computers were less expensive and less hassle to use. Moreover, the field of artificial intelligence was emerging, promising all kinds of text analysis capabilities if one would wait. Some moved on to other topics. Others continued with manual approaches, figuring that even with all the difficulties of training reliable coders, they still could be less fickle, costly, and difficult to manage than computers or computer programmers.

Nevertheless, some major computer-based text analysis projects continued during this period, usually at state universities that provided free mainframe computer time.[10] For example, Martindale (1990) reported on extensive research at the University of Maine studying cyclic patterns of regressive imagery as it occurs over centuries in poetry and prose. Namenwirth and Weber (1987) reported statistical studies at the University of Connecticut on value cycles in British speeches from the Throne and American political party platforms—what they called "wheels of time." Each of these books addressed new frontiers in identifying thematic patterns.

During this period, several businesses developed with specialization in text analyses. Only a few of them, however, enlisted computers for this. One of these, the Communication Development Company (CDC) in Des Moines, Iowa, is now over 15 years old, has a staff of over 100, and has accumulated a textual data base from hundreds of studies of over 6 billion words—at least 10 times more than all the academic computer-based text analyses combined. Indeed, a front-page article in the *Wall Street Journal* profiled CDC for its innovative approach (A maverick pollster promotes verbosity that others disdain, 1985).

The text analysis approach that has evolved at CDC is particularly interesting because it combines a priori categorization using text analysis dictionaries implemented in several languages with analyses targeted to a client's situation. Supporting text analysis critics who suspect that what people say on their own initiative is rarely the whole story, CDC has learned not to assume that people will say in focus groups, for example, what they really think about a topic. Instead, CDC developed depth-interviewing pro-

---

[10]As more institutions provided mainframe computing, granting agencies understandably became reluctant to fund others for the purchase of mainframe computing time. As Weber (1990) described, ZUMA, a German institute in Mannheim dedicated to supporting social science, has (partially in response to this trend) kindly taken over the maintenance and distribution of some content-analysis software. (See Popping, this volume, on the availability of *The General Inquirer III* and *TextPack V 3.0* from ZUMA.)

cedures in which they encourage respondents to talk at length about a topic. All generalizations, unfinished thoughts, incongruous thoughts, and vague demarcations are probed for further details as part of their active listening interviewing procedures.

CDC found that a respondent's identity in regards to a product or service has two parts:

$$Identity = Image + Relationship$$

In order to assess identity, it is necessary first to assess a respondent's image (including both the good and the bad news regarding that image) and then his or her relationship to that image. As a consequence, an interview transcript about what a person's national identity means to them would normally run for many pages.

CDC's categorization procedures assume that there are four major ways that people talk about a topic. For example, if the inquiry was what it means to have an identity as an American, some might emphasize its importance in realizing certain goals and gratifications, whereas others might emphasize the rules and responsibilities being an American carries. Still others would address the feelings and emotions they get from being an American, and some would emphasize the unique outlook and ways of understanding that being an American offers. CDC finds this categorization framework to be helpful in understanding how respondents relate to many products and services and uses these four measures to map clients' products and services against their competitors as well as against normative data on file.

CDC's work is guided by its theories, and it also uses detailed word-count comparisons and other text analysis tools to situate its analyses in the particular problems being studied. For example, a straight word-count profile showed car-rental agents who provide more customer satisfaction talk about renting "the" car than renting "a" car—which led to the finding that the more specific a rental agent is, the more satisfied the customer is. Actionable research findings in this way combine both generalities and particulars.

McBer is a company similar to CDC in that it has specialized for over two decades in analyzing texts of in-depth interviews. Both companies emphasize getting beyond initial responses to uncover underlying perceptions and motives. However, McBer is primarily concerned with helping companies select outstanding personnel. Moreover, its procedures for analyzing text have to date been manual. Founded upon the theories of psychologist David McClelland (the "Mc" in "McBer"), the company is now part of the Hay organization, a multinational consulting company.

Although McBer's tradition stems from analyzing stories told to picture stimuli for achievement, power, and affiliation imagery, it now analyzes transcripts for numerous competencies it has found to be important, depending on the particular job. Instead of limiting itself to picture stimuli—the Thematic Apperception Test developed by psychologist Henry Murray—McBer is most known for its Behavioral Event Interview in which people talk in depth (i.e., give blow-by-blow accounts) about two to three peak successes and two to three major failures at work. The interview often takes 90 minutes to 3 hours and results in a transcript approaching 100 pages.

McBer's approach to analyzing these interviews is described at length by Spencer and Spencer (1993). Normally, McBer constructs a specific competency model for each job by interviewing superior performers and less-than-superior performers who currently occupy the job. This interview is then used as the basis for selecting new superior performers. Over the years, McBer has created hundreds of job competency models involving over 10,000 job interviews. Such lengthy interviewing and intensive text analyses make for a research procedure that is used mostly for higher level jobs and jobs critical to the organization.

The Gallup Organization, known widely for its public opinion polls, has developed similarly well-grounded but less costly text analysis techniques that have been widely applied for personnel selection. Chairperson Donald Clifton, whose background is educational research, created interview instruments with open-ended questions not unlike those appearing in some IQ and educational tests. As at McBer, clients who enlist Gallup's services are asked to identify their outstanding and less than outstanding performers for a particular job. These people are interviewed in detail and the transcribed interviews are analyzed manually in detail to identify themes that distinguish superior performers in that job (Schlesinger, 1993). The result is a job-specific interview instrument that consists of multiple open-ended questions relevant to each theme, often including questions that ask people to tell about an instance in which they did a particular activity or avoided a particular behavior. Analysts are trained to listen for the presence or absence of particular themes in each answer, and these occurrences are then totalled into overall theme profiles. In some cases, personnel officers at client companies learn how to administer and evaluate these instruments themselves.

Curiously, focusing on textual themes to the exclusion of other contextual information works to Gallup's decided advantage. Most of Gallup's personnel selection interviews are by telephone, scheduled at a time convenient for the respondent. By excluding contextual information and focusing on the scoring of particular competency themes known to discriminate outstanding from ordinary performers, Gallup avoids some biases that might be contrary to American affirmative action laws. Instead of being front-stage in a strange interview setting, the respondent often is at home in casual clothes, enjoying a coffee—a more relaxed setting that Gallup finds conducive to an informative interview—and the interviewer focuses on administrating the interview in a friendly, efficient way. Sensitivity to context, when the issue is conforming to the law, can be a serious disadvantage, a lesson both Gallup and McBer know well.

Surprisingly, thematic text analysis appears to have been applied much less to studying media trends. As Neuman (1989) aptly argued, thematic analyses of media could be useful complements to public opinion polling by showing how the media set agendas or frame how people think about issues. Naisbitt (1982) described a systematic analysis of monthly data from some 6,000 local American newspapers. His company, the Naisbitt Group, found that newspapers from five states—California, Colorado, Connecticut, Florida, and Washington—served as bellwethers of major national trends, allowing him to identify what he called megatrends. Florida was included because of its elderly population in a country where the elderly are becoming increasingly important. Connecticut, Colorado, and Washington turn out to be bellwether states in many aspects of social innovation. California, of course, is a bellwether in many ways, although not everything Californian becomes popular elsewhere. Naisbitt's text analysis procedures were manual and resulted in a quarterly *Trend Report* for companies subscribing to his services. Moreover, his original medial text analysis has become a model for other trend analysts (Merriam & Makower, 1988).

All this media analysis has involved the manual coding of texts, with one exception, the pioneering work done by DeWeese (1976) at the Societal Analysis Unit of the General Motors Research Laboratories. DeWeese captured the news hole of a Detroit newspaper on-line as it went to press and used a version of Harvard text analysis software to monitor trends. Today, what DeWeese worked so hard to achieve is available to anyone who subscribes to major on-line media services such as Nexis.

Many companies today subscribe to electronic media services, often capturing texts by satellite as they become available, but they mainly use simple key-word matches (such as their organization's name and the names of their competitors) in order to select relevant articles and route them to those in the organization (such as a Lotus-Notes forum) who might be interested. Such selection and routing procedures help organizations be current and responsive to events, but they are unlikely to yield insights that a systematic media analysis can provide.

Why has CDC been so successful in enlisting computers for thematic text analyses while other companies have not? Basically, as long as the costs of manual analyses could be easily passed on to customers, businesses really had no pressing reasons to utilize computers. Being competitive simply did not demand it. Moreover, whereas CDC was fortunate in having a founding CEO who is well-versed in computing, other companies would have had to rest their future on computer talent that might leave. Such dependencies made poor sense, especially at a time when such talent was scarce.

However, for the past several years, McBer, Gallup, and other organizations have been transcribing their interviews on word processors, creating an electronic record of their primary data. Inasmuch as the interviews are now machine readable in any case, it is no longer an either–or decision regarding whether to use manual or computer-based procedures. Indeed, given the convenience of desktop computing, it makes little sense not to enlist the computer to do what it can do best and leave the rest to manual analyses.

Computer-based procedures may prove particularly helpful for thematic text analysis tasks that coders are poor at handling. Human coders are good at focusing on answers to specific questions and reliably coding the presence or absence of certain themes. Computers, however, may be better at scoring entire interview transcripts on a large number of themes. First, scoring many variables concurrently strains coders' bounded rationality. Second, the large span of attention this technique requires can lead to uneven evaluations, especially for coders who analyze transcripts day after day.

Each approach then has its own strengths and weaknesses. Some simple text analysis tasks that one might have expected to move to the domain of the computer will continue to be better handled manually, because somewhere embedded in the analysis is a very human judgment. Exploiting this complementarity also can help to keep research both systematic and well grounded, especially if human analysts can work interactively with computers to substantiate their findings.

Several new resources have also appeared during this period that should improve computer-based thematic text analysis. Most important is the development of procedures to identify different word senses, one of the most salient problems in computer-aided content analysis (Kelley & Stone, 1975; Stone, 1969). One approach to this has been to develop what Berleant (1995) called "word experts" that use nearby context to identify word senses. A second approach is to characterize the document as a whole, or at least 100 surrounding words, for identifying word senses. CDC compares counts on its four categories with norms for these categories associated with each sense of a word. It then chooses the word sense that has norms most closely matching the counts obtained on the surrounding text. Clearly there would be further gains by combining these narrow-band and wide-band approaches.[11]

During these 25 years, the social sciences have witnessed a shift away from grand theories to more practical, grounded research—a shift that is somewhat reflected in the choice of thematic text analysis procedures. Although much text analysis in the '60s was devoted to operationalizing the theories of Parsons, Osgood, Lasswell, and others, these theories receive less attention today. Fiske's (1991) four elementary forms of sociality, which

---

[11]Another major resource is Miller's (1990) WordNet, which groups thousands of English words into "synsets." WordNet should greatly facilitate creating comprehensive thematic text analysis categories as well as help with other content analysis problems.

he proposed as a framework for a unified theory of social relations, is a new grand theory with some elegant, admirable qualities but that has seemed to attract little interest compared to the attention that the overarching theories of the 1960s garnered. Instead, some of the more popular text analysis coding schemes correspond more to what have been called theories of the middle range, including the Peterson, Schulman, Castellon, and Seligman (1992) CAVE (Content Analysis of Verbal Explanations) procedures for measuring explanatory style and the Suedfeld, Tetlock, and Streufert (1992) measures of integrative complexity. Whereas the '60s emphasized being elegant and unified, the '90s appear to emphasize being grounded and practical as well as comprehensive enough to make valid inferences.

Perhaps one reason for the decline in the interest in overarching theories is that they in fact did not lead their advocates in unique directions that yielded unique, important insights. Weber (1990), for example, compared several major categorization schemes developed for content analysis and found that they tended to boil down to similar factor structures. Similarly, all the debate about different personality theories in the 1960s has boiled down in the intervening decades to the "big five" personality factors, with the dynamics of particular personality theories not adding all that much (Digman, 1994).

Neither grand theories nor reductionistic factor analyses offer the leverage that tailored, well-grounded instruments provide for such tasks as personnel selection. Yet let us take a closer look at how grounded and conceptual approaches in fact can complement each other, using job competency models as a case in point.

## COMPARING BOTTOM-UP (GROUNDED THEORY) WITH TOP-DOWN (CONCEPTUAL THEORY) APPROACHES

What kinds of insights do the more grounded approaches developed in the last 25 years add to the text analysis categorization schemes developed in the '60s and '70s? To gain some insight into this, we compared the domains of competencies that McBer and Gallup have repeatedly found to be useful with text analysis categories developed earlier. Do these grounded competency measures in fact map on to these earlier attempts to operationalize theories? Is the universe of these competency models, if generalized, roughly isomorphic with the categories embedded in these a priori text analysis categorization schemes? Have these competency models uncovered new domains that the earlier categorization schemes missed, even though they attempted to be comprehensive?

Our procedures involved two steps. Inasmuch as the Spencer and Spencer book provides generic competency models derived from the many job-specific competency models that McBer has created, Signe Spencer utilized these generic competency models as a guide to map Gallup themes in several hundred competency models for particular jobs.[12] This allowed us to identify themes common to both organizations and those used by one and not the other. It also allowed us to create a more comprehensive list of competency themes, partly because the two organizations approach competency analysis from different orientations.

The second step was to compare this combined list of competency themes with earlier text analysis categorization schemes. On the one hand, one might expect a better correspondence with earlier thematic categorizations than had been targeted to measuring a competency, such as one developed for measuring need achievement (Ogilvie, Stone, & Kelly, 1982; Stone et al., 1966). However, we were more interested in comparing the list with more general-purpose categorization schemes that employed many categories and represented several of the grand theories of the '60s.[13] Indeed, these general-purpose categorization schemes proved to offer more.

I find it useful to divide the combined Gallup–McBer competency themes into those working hard (i.e., striving), working with others (i.e., relating), and working smart (i.e., thinking). The earlier text-analysis categorizations turned out to include many categories concerned with each of these domains. In the realm of striving, there were categories of words for "try," "persist," "attain," and "goal reference" that are relevant to scoring competencies. In the realm of relating, there are many categories concerned with various levels of power (for example, "guide" and "control") as well as categories concerned with communicating and being accepted. In the realm of thinking, earlier dictionaries distinguished many thinking processes, including categories for relational, conditional, implicational, abstract, and primordial thinking, providing for a finer grained analysis of references to working smart than either McBer or Gallup developed.

There could be two reasons why the earlier categorizations provide more detailed attention to thinking. One is that more specific thinking styles do not distinguish superior from ordinary performers. The second is that thinking styles may prove particularly difficult for human analysts to score because an analyst's own thinking style may impact his or her ability to relate to other people's thinking styles. (This seems to be particularly true for scoring abstract, conceptual thinking.) In this domain, the computer-aided procedures may prove to be a particularly valuable complement to carry out what is more difficult for humans to code reliably.

---

[12]A team at Gallup then reviewed Spencer's organization of Gallup's themes and made some revisions.

[13]The main one selected is known as the Harvard IV-4 text analysis dictionary (Oglivie et al., 1982).

However, the earlier general-purpose categorization schemes also pointed to themes that may be important in obtaining a superior person for a particular job but that both companies are overlooking. One of the legacies of Parsonian theory is that our behavior is guided by the language and norms of different institutions. Example institutions are medicine, law, sports, arts, military, and business. Certainly, it stands to reason that if a person is going to do well at a job, then he or she should fit into the organizational culture and the language it uses. Gallup has a theme for business thinking, which refers to a bottom-line, profit-oriented business way of expressing ideas, but there are also similar themes for legal thinking, military thinking, expressive thinking, and the systems thinking that management expert Senge (1990) emphasized. Each of these languages has its vocabulary, which computers can identify with relative ease.

Inasmuch as both McBer and Gallup have their roots in psychology rather than sociology, it is perhaps not surprising that neither has given much attention to institutions. By comparison, CDC's categories are institution-oriented in identifying language use. Indeed, CDC's success in using their categories on a wide variety of problems supports the proposition that these may be important competency themes that have been largely overlooked. Scoring overall protocols for these types of language usage could be a worthwhile additional complement to the scoring methods now being used.

Computer-based categorization schemes for text analysis can have the desirable effect of stretching the conceptual envelope within which a problem is construed. To the extent that people easily draw on these tools to expand their thinking about what is relevant to a topic, these tools can help to make research even more grounded, helping them to notice features of the text they otherwise would miss. Would it not be interesting then, if these grand theory categorization schemes ultimately proved helpful as part of text analysis capabilities that expand researchers' awarenesses and provide a more comprehensive contextual grounding for making valid inferences?

## PREDICTING THE NEXT GENERATION OF TEXT ANALYSIS: A PLATFORM OF PLEASANT SURPRISES?

Technology no longer constrains researchers to one or another mode of analysis. Instead, it is feasible to consider a platform of desktop computer text analysis capabilities, illustrated in Table 2.1, that allows researchers to draw upon sequences of procedures that best suit their proclivities, to follow up on leads as they uncover textual patterns, and to check the validity of their discoveries. Moreover, given that only capabilities C and D in Table 2.1 must be language specific, this platform of capabilities allows researchers working on texts in different languages to share resources.

TABLE 2.1

A Platform of Thematic Text Analysis Capabilities

| Capability | Description |
|---|---|
| A. Searching text for occurrences of a specified text string | A self-explanatory capability that is now part of most word-processing programs |
| B. Counting word frequencies | Identifies words in text and counts each word frequency in each document; may also compare word frequencies across documents, usually with minimum word frequency cutoffs to limit display size |
| C. Standardizing word units | Redefines text units within text to facilitate making comparisons |
| 1. Decomposing complex words | Identifies embedded word roots, suffixes, prefixes, and infixes |
| 2. Linking words | Makes multiple word strings (e.g., in the form of idioms or names, such as United States, or split verbs) into one unit |
| 3. Disambiguating words | Uses word contexts to identify word senses in a manner that draws upon the local context (i.e., the immediate word window) and on overall document characteristics |
| D. Categorizing words and word units | Assigns category markers to words in raw text and to word units identified under capability C and counts the frequency of these assignments for each category within each document |
| E. Searching for combinations of word units, categorizations, and original text strings | Counts number of matches per document; may first cross-index all or a subset of text units and categorizations to produce immediate retrievals (possibly highlighted in colors that indicate type of match) for any search specification |
| F. Recognizing patterns | Aids pattern recognition either in the exercise of capabilities A, B, D, and E or in the application of procedures (e.g., factor analysis, cluster analysis, and neural net programs) that draw upon counts output from capabilities B, D, or E |
| G. Juxtaposing text segments | Displays similar or contradictory text segments, either by specifying retrievals or by dragging text segments with a mouse to a common window |
| H. Using nontextual information in conjunction with text analysis | Incorporates demographic, archival, and other data of nontextual origin into statistical analyses of counts output from capabilities B, D, E, and F |

Part of this platform for thematic text analysis can be borrowed from other text applications. For example, complex text-decomposing procedures (Table 2.1., capability C.1) have been developed to provide spell checkers for highly agglutinated languages like Hungarian that have too many word variants to be separately listed in spell-checker dictionaries.[14] Being able to work with word roots rather than each word inflection is helpful for languages like English but becomes essential for doing thematic analyses in these languages.

Other capabilities eventually may be obtained from automatic text abstracting, text question-and-answer systems, automatic text-routing procedures, and artificial intelligence research. One particularly valuable addition, for example, would be cross-sentence capabilities for automatically identifying the nouns referred to by pronouns. Additional capabilities are needed to help users make on-the-spot modifications and additions to the resources listed as capabilities C and D in Table 2.1. Useful tools may be drawn from database management packages, on-line bilingual dictionaries, and Miller's (1990) WordNet to facilitate developing new categories, make existing categories more comprehensive, and implement categories in different languages.

Finally, the capabilities in Table 2.1 that produce counts should be fully integrated with statistical packages that provide a wide variety of statistical and pattern-detection routines. This should be integrated with the analysis of numeric information from related data sets for performing both standard statistical analyses as well as less standard procedures such as neural net analysis.

By always keeping the original text easily accessible, researchers can more easily verify their inferences, especially those drawn from statistical analyses. Procedures for juxtaposing text were awkward at best in the days of mainframe computers, but now they can be as simple as dragging text segments to a common display. In these ways, a desktop software platform can indeed facilitate the closeness to the data that Pool and his associates sought.

As the platform of thematic text analysis capabilities becomes more fully developed, additional procedures may also be anticipated for linking visual information, such as film or video clips. Indeed, as the CD-ROM and 100-megabyte, floppy-size disks become a standard feature of desktop computing, these links may become commonplace.

Looking back to when text analysis was carried out on mainframe computers, it may well be that part of the appeal of general theories was that they provided a relatively broadside mapping of the text being studied. Inasmuch as researchers had infrequent access to the mainframe, they wanted to take away as much information as possible. Indeed, huge, unnec-

[14]For example, Morphologic provides a spell-checker of this type that comes with the Hungarian version of Microsoft Word.

essarily large printouts characterized computer use at that time. By comparison, desktop computing encourages a more grounded approach to research much like detective work, zeroing in on key evidence rather than making broadside passes over the data. This change in research style has already been noticed. For example, as CDC converts more of its computer procedures to desktop operations, it finds that its analysts give more attention to interactively exploring their data.

Even though thematic text analyses will become more grounded, easy access to various categorization schemes will help researchers find links to other studies, often uncovering similarities with their findings they did not anticipate. For example, three of CDC's categories map directly into three types of organizational cultures that Kabanoff, Waldersee, and Cohen (in press) derived by applying cluster analysis in a text analysis of documents from 88 Australian organizations. These in turn appear to map into three of Fiske's elementary forms of sociality.

As more desktop thematic analysis capabilities become readily available, the amount of text analysis will probably increase considerably. Weber's (1990) text on content analysis found a sizeable market of interested readers, for it went through more than one printing and was soon into a second edition, even though the book at the time could recommend very little software, some of it still running on mainframes. As documented by Popping (this volume), the variety of relevant software has greatly increased. At the same time, the amount of machine-readable text has become immense. Moreover, scanners and optical character recognition software have recently come of age, making it practical to scan printed texts and convert them to machine-readable form (cf. Bechtel, this volume).

Five predictions can thus be made with some confidence. First, the volume of text on the information superhighway, combined with the increased ease of using desktop computers, will generate an active arena of text processing activities. Second, the increase of these activities will be part of a significant social science contribution to help us better understand ourselves, our organizations, and our societies in an ever-changing world. Third, these activities will not be guided by overarching theories but mainly will be part of a grounded, bottom-up approach aimed toward making well-founded, valid inferences; however, computer-based categorization resources should help investigators broaden their perspectives and better situate their thematic analyses. Fourth, the division of labor between human coders and computer-based analyses will be guided by expediency and simple cost/benefit expectations, especially given that the text data are machine-readable in any case and that the two processes can easily be intermixed. Fifth, much of this thematic text analysis, including that sponsored by governments, will have applied objectives, as illustrated by content analysis applications in business over the past two decades. Whether these developments come about in an effective and efficient manner, and whether the applications will always be facilitative and helpful, as opposed to controlling and exploitive, remains to be seen.

## ACKNOWLEDGMENTS

I thank Donald Clifton, Charles Cleveland, Carl Roberts, Signe Spencer, Haihai Yuan, and members of my graduate practicum for their interest, questions, critiques, and contributions.

# 3

# SEMANTIC TEXT ANALYSIS: ON THE STRUCTURE OF LINGUISTIC AMBIGUITY IN ORDINARY DISCOURSE

Carl W. Roberts
Iowa State University

Semantic text analysis yields inferences about how themes are related in a population of texts. Initially, the researcher creates one of two types of semantic grammars, each of which provides one or more templates that specify the ways themes may be related. On the one hand, a phenomenal semantic grammar can be created to extract phenomenon-related information from a text population (e.g., "Among the population's grievances [the phenomenon of interest in this case], which were ones for the abolition of taxes?"). On the other hand, a generic semantic grammar may be developed to yield data about the text population itself (e.g., "Among all clauses in the text population, how many were grievances for the abolition of taxes?"). This chapter describes a generic semantic grammar that can be used to encode themes and theme relations in every clause within randomly sampled texts. Unlike the surface-grammatical relations mapped by syntax grammars, the theme relations allowed in this grammar only permit unambiguous encoding according to the meanings that clauses were intended to convey within their social context. An application of the grammar provides a concrete illustration of its role in the encoding process.

Semantic text analysis is a quantitative text analysis method in which not only themes but also grammatical relations among themes are encoded. The method involves a three-step encoding process. First, the researcher isolates a population of texts germane to the phenomenon under investigation.[1] Second, a semantic grammar must be acquired that specifies the relations that may be encoded among themes in the texts. Finally, the texts' themes are encoded according to the relations specified in the semantic grammar. Encoded interrelations may then be used as indicators of various characteristics of the phenomenon under study.

Consider, for example, the text population of *cahiers de doléances* of 1789 that Markoff, Shapiro, and their colleagues have been analyzing since the mid-1970s (cf. Markoff, 1988; Markoff, Shapiro, & Weitman, 1974; Shapiro & Markoff, in press). The *cahiers de doléances* are the documents produced by more than 40,000 corporate and territorial entities (e.g., craft guilds, parishes, towns, etc.) in the course of the king's convocation of an Estates-General—documents written as if in response to the open-ended query, "What are your grievances, and what do you propose should be done about them?" The documents were used to generate data on grievances, making grievances the researchers' phenomena of interest and, for the purposes of constructing a database for these grievances, effectively making "the grievance" the unit of analysis.

In essence, each grievance was encoded according to two syntactic components. (Or, if you prefer, a template with two interrelated fields was used in encoding each grievance.) First, there was the institution or problem area (i.e., the thing being grieved about). These grievances might be about the government, the economy, religion, the constitution, and so on. The second syntactic component of a grievance was the action demanded. These actions were encoded as demands to reestablish, to abolish, to simplify, to modify, to improve, and so on. In brief, the researchers designed a two-place Verb-Object (V-O) semantic grammar for the phenomenon, grievance.[2] The semantic grammar's application to a sample of texts from the *cahiers de doléances* yielded data that have been used to make inferences about public opinion on a variety of topics just prior to the French Revolution.

A second illustration can be found with Franzosi's (this volume) work on labor disputes. Applying a more complex semantic grammar to newspaper articles on Italian labor unrest, labor disputes (the phenomena of interest) are conceptualized as clusters of actors' actions toward each other (i.e., of Subject-Verb-Object [S-V-O] tuples). Like Markoff and Shapiro, Franzosi has

---

[1]Throughout this chapter I use "the phenomenon under investigation," "the phenomenon under study," "the phenomenon of interest," and "the unit of analysis" interchangeably. All refer to that phenomenon (as defined in the researcher's theory), sampled instances of which correspond to distinct rows in the researcher's data matrix, and measures on which are listed in the columns of this matrix.

[2]For each action (verb) toward a problem area (object), it was uniformly the king and his representatives (subject) who should act. Thus a more detailed Subject-Verb-Object syntax was unnecessary. This discussion presents only a simplified version of the researchers' semantic grammar. See Shapiro (this volume) for more detail.

used texts as a source of historical data. Yet whereas the former researchers commonly found more than one grievance per document (i.e., multiple units of analysis per text block), Franzosi had numerous S-V-O tuples per newspaper article and commonly multiple newspaper articles per labor dispute (i.e., multiple text blocks per unit of analysis). Thus, for Franzosi, the generation of dispute-specific indicators of whether one type of actor acted in a specific way toward another, requires a search for this information among all S-V-O tuples associated with each labor dispute.

## SEMANTIC GRAMMARS HIGHLIGHT STRUCTURES WITHIN TEXT POPULATIONS

The preceding illustrations demonstrate that in applying a semantic grammar to a sample of texts, the researcher assumes that the texts are structured according to the semantic grammar and that the phenomenon of interest is related to this structure in a specific way. In Franzosi's work, for example, newspaper articles are presumed to contain information on actors' actions toward each other, and labor disputes are portrayed as consisting of clusters of such actions. Thus, every semantic text analysis must begin by isolating a population of texts that exhibit the structure assumed in the research at hand.

On the basis of similar observations, Griemas (1984/1966) cautioned linguists to assemble a representative, exhaustive, and homogeneous corpus of texts prior to beginning analysis.[3] Even more strongly put, Halliday (1978, p. 32) argued that every utterance (or speech act) must be understood according to its "context of situation." Moreover, these situational contexts impose structural constraints on what statements are socially appropriate (cf. Lakoff & Johnson, 1980, p. 179, on the fit between statement and situation).

Linguists developed semantic grammars (or functional grammars; cf. Halliday, 1978, 1994; Propp, 1968/1928) as a strategy for describing text structure. Application of the strategy begins by identifying speech acts according to how they function within the genre of texts under analysis (e.g., as stating a situation, explaining a problem, responding to the problem, evaluating the response). The genre (e.g., of texts with problem–solution structure; cf. Hoey, 1994) is then characterized according to the sequence of functional forms common among its texts. The grammars underlying such sequences have been variously referred to as narrative grammars (Griemas, 1984/1966), text grammars (van Dijk, 1972), and story grammars (Rumelhart, 1975).

---

[3]This warning is quite different from that of the statistician who notes that (other things equal) analyses of data from homogeneous populations will afford statistics with small standard errors. Griemas's point is that one must assure the relevance of one's corpus to one's semantic model: "(A) model can be described only if it is already contained implicitly in the discursive manifestation of a semantic microuniverse" (Griemas, 1984/1966, p. 163).

In fields other than linguistics, social scientists have tended to be less interested in the form than in the content of texts' grammars. In analyses of text sequence this preference of content to form holds among social scientists who are not primarily linguists but who have orientations both qualitative (Abell, 1987; Heise, 1991) and quantitative (Danielson & Lasorsa, this volume; Namenwirth, 1973; Savaiano & Schrodt, this volume). In contrast to linguists' objective to reveal text structure as a sequence of distinct forms, in a semantic text analysis one generally presumes a single semantic form with varying content. Whereas linguists typically revise their semantic grammars to fit a relevant corpus, semantic text analysts use fixed semantic grammars to highlight relevant text.

## Phenomenal Versus Generic Highlighting of Text Structure

In a semantic text analysis, the researcher encodes only those parts of the text that fit into the syntactic components of the semantic grammar being applied. For example, a preliminary statement in a document from the *cahiers de doléances* that "The members of this guild have always honorably served our King" would quickly be recognized by the coder as not conveying a grievance and would accordingly be ignored. Likewise, Franzosi's semantic grammar does not lend itself readily to evaluative statements (e.g., a reporter's aside that the police had acted inappropriately during a strike). In such cases, the researcher does not experience the linguist's concern that the grammar might not fit the texts but instead notes that the semantic grammar highlights only text structures that fit the grammar (and presumably only those text structures that are relevant to the phenomenon under investigation).

The semantic grammar's highlighting role has methodological advantages when one's research objective is to analyze variations among the aspects of a well-defined phenomenon (e.g., the grievance or the labor dispute). By restricting encoding to text segments with relevance to the phenomenon of interest, such a *phenomenal semantic grammar* will save both time and expense. Yet the highlighting role works poorly when one's research objective requires a more *generic semantic grammar* for investigating the predominance of theme relations within randomly sampled text blocks that themselves do not correspond to specific, highly structured phenomena. In the former case, the researcher encodes only themes that are related according to a semantic grammar; in the latter case, the researcher encodes all data and investigates the conditions under which specific theme relations occur. Research questions posed, for example, in cultural indicators and media research lend themselves more readily to applications of generic than phenomenal semantic grammars: Is government depicted in totalitarian states' news media as the semantic subject (e.g., acting in the people's interests) but in democratic states' news media as the semantic object (e.g., affected by the people's wishes)? On prime-time television, do men utter fewer degrading self-references than women? Here the researcher is not interested in examining only relevant phenomena (be they government depictions or self-references) within a text population but rather in determining whether certain types of content are prevalent relative to all content in a population of texts.

## Surface Grammar's Highlighting of Ambiguous Text Structure

A generic semantic grammar is required to encode interrelations among themes within a domain of relatively unstructured texts (e.g., general content from news media or from prime-time television). The most obvious candidate for this semantic grammar is a S-V-O grammar to be applied to each clause in samples of such text.[4] In drawing inferences about the predominance of theme relations, the researcher could then treat either the clause or (collapsing data across clauses) the text block as the unit of analysis.

Both Gottschalk (1968, 1995) and Schrodt (1993) developed semantic text analysis methods that incorporate precisely this type of generic S-V-O grammar. Taking advantage of the fact that their methods encode surface-grammatical relations among themes, each has incorporated a parser into his software that identifies which of each clause's themes functions as which of the three syntactic components, subject, verb, and object. The Gottschalk–Gleser content analysis system outputs aggregate scores on individuals' psychological states (e.g., anxiety, hostility, etc.); Schrodt's KEDS program outputs unaggregated S-V-O tuples.[5]

Yet linguists have long argued that texts' intended meanings are not captured solely by their surface grammatical relations. Indeed, it is precisely this realization that led them to develop semantic grammars and to distinguish these grammars from more semantically ambiguous syntax grammars.

---

[4]The reader familiar with literature on semantic grammars will recognize a contradiction in terms when I refer to a clause's surface (or syntax) grammar as a type of semantic grammar. Semantic grammars were developed to map statements' unique meaning-as-intended and in so doing to avoid mapping superficial grammatical relations that could have many intended meanings. I return to this issue in the next section.

[5]Both Gottschalk and Schrodt take an instrumental approach to text analysis. According to Shapiro (this volume) instrumental text analyses treat the text as symptomatic of the phenomenon of interest (for Gottschalk, the individual; for Schrodt, the political event). Because coders are not required to divine clauses' intended meanings, the encoding of theme-relations can be largely automated with the help of parsing software. All other semantic text analysis methods discussed in this chapter are what Shapiro refers to as representational. That is, they are text analysis methods in which texts are encoded according to their sources' intended meanings.

For example, *He was abandoned* might either refer to a state of affairs (i.e., he was alone) or to a process (i.e., others had abandoned him). *She is a doctor* might be intended as descriptive (implying that she helps sick people) or judgmental (indicating that she is an achiever). In short, semantic grammars require the coder to take clauses' social context into account; syntax grammars do not.

Nonetheless, researchers may have legitimate reasons to base their semantic text analyses on syntax grammar. People often betray their mental states in the ways they phrase their discourse, making the words' surface phrasing more relevant than their intended meanings in making a psychological diagnosis (cf. Gottschalk, this volume). On the other hand, if one's analyses are of a sufficiently structured domain of texts (e.g., Reuters news service articles on international conflict), theme relations may follow sufficiently fixed formulae that their surface relations are nearly always unambiguous (cf. Savaiano & Schrodt, this volume).

Venturing beyond such cases, one finds syntax grammars fundamentally inadequate for addressing research questions that call for the analysis of words' intended meanings—a central tenet among functional linguists such as Halliday (1978, p. 192) and Winter (1994, p. 49). When clauses are embedded in texts that are unstructured enough for identical speech acts to serve different discursive functions (i.e., to have different intended meanings), surface grammatical relations cannot differentiate among these functions and thus cannot specify a clause's intended meaning(s).[6] Inferences about such text populations call for a generic semantic grammar that allows clauses to be encoded according to discursive function.

## A GENERIC GRAMMAR FOR SEMANTIC TEXT ANALYSIS[7]

It was Gottlob Frege (1959/1884) who first noted that the sentence, *x acts,* makes two assertions: "there is an x" and "x acts." That is, sentences of this form simultaneously describe a state of affairs and a process. This dual form is commonly expressed with the following notation:

$$(x)f(x)$$

---

[6]The assumption here is not that speech acts can serve only a single intended function. On the contrary, speech acts are often intended to affect others in ambivalent ways. The assumption is instead that in natural language each clause is uttered to function in an enumerable number of ways. Thus, a coder could in principle apply a semantic grammar to encode the same clause numerous times, each time according to a distinct function that the clause was intended to serve.

[7]Albert Baker's careful eye added greatly to the rigor and at times to the substance of the formalism developed in this section.

The first element in the form (namely, "(x)") may be expressed as "There is an x." The second element (namely, "f(x)") is read as "f(·) is a predicate involving x." If f(·) predicates acting, f(x) predicates x as acting. As I now formally argue, this rendering is ambiguous as a functional discourse form and as such cannot (without modification) serve as a basis for a generic semantic grammar. Researchers interested in encoding texts according to their intended meanings will have little use for grammars that afford semantically ambiguous mappings from text to meaning. My argument begins with a demonstration that a grammar's functional forms are semantically ambiguous (and thus of little value to these researchers) if they do not have unique semantic opposites.

## Semantic Opposition in Ordinary Discourse

This subsection provides the theoretical basis for a generic semantic grammar composed of four unambiguous functional forms (i.e., functional forms having unique semantic opposites). In it, two functional forms for descriptive speech are developed as components in a model of speech acts' intended meanings. The argument here is that in ordinary discourse a speech act's meaning consists of an unintentional, taken-for-granted component plus an intentional, asserted component. The unintentional component is neither denied nor asserted by the source but is simply assumed to be common knowledge. The intentional component's meaning is asserted (and, equivalently, its semantic opposite is denied) in the speech act. The ensuing discussion reveals a structure of linguistic ambiguity within ordinary discourse by showing that descriptive utterances admit of precisely two semantic opposites. This motivates a more formal specification in the next subsection of two unambiguous functional forms for descriptive speech acts. These are then supplemented by another two functional forms for judgmental speech acts.

A semantic opposite differs from a logical opposite in that it is the negation of the intended meaning, not the literal formal meaning, of a speech act. For example, consider the sentence, *Jerry went to the store.* Applying the (x)f(x) functional form, and setting x="Jerry" and f(·)="went to the store" yields "There is Jerry and Jerry went to the store." In formal Aristotelian logic, the sentence is rendered as follows:

$$\exists(\text{Phenomenon } x) \ \exists(\text{Process } p) \ [p(x) \wedge x=\text{"Jerry"} \wedge p=\text{"went to the store"}]$$

This statement reads, "There exists a phenomenon, x, such that (sic) there exists a process, p, such that p is predicated of x, x is 'Jerry', and p is 'went to the store'." Note that this statement has the following as its unique logical opposite:

∀(Phenomenon x) ∀(Process p) [~p(x) ∨ x≠"Jerry" ∨ p≠"went to the store"]

(I.e., for all phenomena, x, such that for all processes, p, p is not predicated of x or x is not "Jerry" or p is not "went to the store.") However, in analyses of ordinary discourse the semantic opposite of the sentence's intended meaning has a much narrower scope.

In ordinary discourse, the efficient functioning of natural language requires that both source and audience take much of the original Aristotelian expression's content for granted. That is to say, most elements of the expression will be assumed semantically invariant and thus superfluous to its intended meaning. There are four such elements.

- ∃(Phenomenon x) [x=•]—The speech act mentions physical and symbolic phenomena that are true to the audience's experiences. Thus, in ordinary discourse a loyal subject does not intend to communicate that the emperor's clothes exist when making references to their elegance. An emperor without clothes could not occur.

- ∃(Process p) [p=•]—The speech act relates phenomena in ways that are comprehensible to an audience fluent in the language of discourse. Thus, in ordinary discourse the source does not intend to communicate the existence of processes such as "going to the store." Discourse will be sidetracked when such processes require definition.

- p(x)—The source genuinely intends to communicate a process predicated on a phenomenon. That is, in ordinary discourse the source does not intend to communicate that a phenomenon and a process are being linked. Were the audience to begin attending to the appropriateness of the p on x link, the source's credibility could be called into question. Accordingly, the statement, "We Grecians offer the citizens of Troy a great wooden horse as a gift," was not understood by Laocoön as intended to describe an event but to link "Grecians" with "gift giving" in the minds of his fellow Trojans.

- ~(x≠"Jerry" ∧ p≠"went to the store")—The source intends to communicate relevant information. That is, in ordinary discourse the source does not intend communications that have uninformative semantic opposites. It is for this reason that the following could not be the semantic opposite of "Jodi ran away with a circus":

∃(Phenomenon x) ∃(Process p) [p(x) ∧ x≠"Jodi" ∧ p≠"ran away with a circus"]

If this were the semantic opposite of the source's intended meaning, "Jodi ran away with a circus" would comprise a denial that "Something 'other than Jodi' did something, which was 'something other than' running away with a circus"—a remarkably uninformative statement. When the audience discovers that such an uninformative denial was intended (e.g., as the source continues, "But the police made her bring it back"), a humorous departure from ordinary discourse results.

Thus, if the audience assumes the truth, comprehensibility, credibility, and relevance of the source's speech acts, the sentence, *Jerry went to the store,* has exactly two semantic opposites:[8]

$$\exists(\text{Phenomenon } x) \, \exists(\text{Process } p) \, [p(x) \wedge x \neq \text{"Jerry"} \wedge p = \text{"went to the store"}]$$

and

$$\exists(\text{Phenomenon } x) \, \exists(\text{Process } p) \, [p(x) \wedge x = \text{"Jerry"} \wedge p \neq \text{"went to the store"}]$$

Once the domain of a generic semantic grammar is restricted to ordinary discourse (i.e., to speech acts that the audience assumes true, comprehensible, credible, and relevant), the simpler $(x)f(x)$ notation can be substituted for expressions of Aristotelian logic. Accordingly, the functional forms of the two just-mentioned semantic opposites are as follows:

$$(x)f(\sim x) \text{ and } (x)\sim f(x)$$

When applied to the sentence, *Jerry went to the store,* the first form's transformation can be read as, "Something 'other than Jerry' went to the store," whereas the second transformation generates the semantic opposite, "Jerry did 'something other than' go to the store."

It is because of these dual semantic opposites that all sentences fitting the $(x)f(x)$ form are ambiguous. Differently put, the intended meaning of the sentence about Jerry depends on whether its function was to answer the question, "Who or what went to the store?" or "What did Jerry do?"[9] In the former case, the sentence functions to convey a description of a state of affairs; in the latter case, it functions to convey a description of a process.

---

[8]The audience's assumptions of truth, comprehensibility, credibility, and relevance have direct parallels with Habermas' (1979, pp. 1–68) discussions of validity claims that in ordinary communication are respectively true, comprehensible, truthful, and right.

[9]Of course, the sentence might instead have been intended to answer the question, "Where did Jerry go?" Or it might have been intended to answer more than one of these questions. The reader is referred to note 6 regarding this latter point. Regarding the former point: In addressing the where-did-Jerry-go question the sentence would function to convey a description of a state of affairs. Because this function is one of four being suggested in this chapter as the basis for a generic semantic grammar, it is a case perfectly consistent with the argument at hand.

## Four Unambiguous Functional Forms

What this rather lengthy illustration suggests is that a semantic grammar cannot yield unambiguous encoding of texts unless all its functional forms have unique semantic opposites. Let us assume that the discursive function of the sentence, *Jerry went to the store,* was to identify who or what was storebound. The following functional form provides a syntax for such descriptions of states of affairs:[10]

$$(x)a(x) \text{ with semantic opposite } (x)a(\sim x)$$

A fit between sentence and form might be read as, "There was (a storebound) Jerry," with semantic opposite, "There was no (storebound) Jerry."[11] If in a different context the discursive function of the same sentence were to convey a description of a process, the appropriate functional form would be:[12]

$$(x)^i p(x) \text{ with semantic opposite } (x)^i \sim p(x), i=0,1$$

The i-superscript is introduced here to acknowledge the optional role of the semantic subject in passive voice. Accordingly, if the semantic subject, Jerry, had not been named in the sentence being encoded, its rendering might be read as, "The store was gone to," with semantic opposite, " 'Something other than' going to the store happened."

Ambiguity is also present when a clause functions to convey a positive (or negative) judgment of a description's referent. For example, the sentence, *Chris makes charitable contributions,* may function to convey not only

---

[10]More formal renderings of $(x)a(x)$ and $(x)a(\sim x)$ are respectively $\exists(\text{Phenomenon } x)$ $\exists(\text{Attribute } a) [a(x) \wedge x=\text{"Jerry"} \wedge a=\text{"storebound"}]$ and $\exists(\text{Phenomenon } x) \exists(\text{Attribute } a) [a(x) \wedge x\neq\text{"Jerry"} \wedge a=\text{"storebound"}]$.

[11]Linguists commonly represent "being" and "becoming" as functions with two arguments, such that the content of one argument can be represented as being or becoming that of the other. Linguistic content analysis (Roberts, 1989) uses a functional form that renders descriptions of states of affairs as one of four, two-place predicates ("is an instance of," "becomes," "resembles," or "symbolizes"). When a two-place predicate is used, it is the posterior, not the anterior, argument that is negated in the clause's opposite. For example, it is semantically identical to assert that "Jerry went to the store" (with opposite "Jerry did 'something other than' go to the store") or that "Jerry was an instance of 'a storebound entity' " (with opposite "Jerry was not an instance of 'a storebound entity' "). In both cases, the sentence presumes Jerry's existence while functioning to convey a description of his storebound activity. If one encodes "Jerry" as the posterior argument in the two-place predicate, its rendering (i.e., "The storebound entity was Jerry" with opposite "The storebound entity was not Jerry") not only is semantically distinct from both other renderings but also functions to convey a description of a state of affairs and, identically, the answer to "Who or what went to the store?"

[12]Formal renderings of $(x)p(x)$ and $(x)\sim p(x)$ are respectively $\exists(\text{Phenomenon } x) \exists(\text{Process } p) [p(x) \wedge x=\text{"Jerry"} \wedge p=\text{"went to the store"}]$ and $\exists(\text{Phenomenon } x) \exists(\text{Process } p) [p(x) \wedge x=\text{"Jerry"} \wedge p\neq\text{"went to the store"}]$.

a description but also a positive evaluation of Chris (or possibly a positive evaluation of "making charitable contributions," if Chris is one of the speaker's heroes). For such cases, a functional form can be introduced that renders a positive judgment of a state of affairs as follows:[13]

$$(x)a(x)Q_a \text{ with semantic opposite } (x)a(x)\overline{Q}_a$$

In the former expression x's attribute, a, is assigned the positive qualifier, $Q_a$. In the latter expression the same attribute is assigned the opposite, negative qualifier, $\overline{Q}_a$. Thus, if the above sentence was solely intended to convey a positive judgment of Chris, its unique semantic opposite could be rendered as "Chris is a bad person (presumably by virtue of the egregious nature of those who contribute to charities)."

A formal representation of a positive judgment of a process can be rendered as follows:[14]

$$(x)^i p(x)Q_p \text{ with semantic opposite } (x)^i p(x)\overline{Q}_p, \ i=0,1$$

Here the i-superscript acknowledges that a state of affairs need not be explicit in such speech acts. (For example, one may assert, "Dancing on Sunday is immoral," without naming a particular dancer.) In the former expression, the process, $p(x)$, is assigned a positive qualifier, $Q_p$. In the latter expression, the same process is assigned the opposite, negative qualifier, $\overline{Q}_p$. Accordingly, if the sole intention of the speech act about Chris was to convey a positive judgment of his behavior, its unique semantic opposite could be rendered as "Chris's making of charitable contributions is immoral."

Note that in these last two judgmental functional forms, all elements except the quantifiers are semantically invariant. Differently put, in ordinary discourse the extent to which a speech act is intended to positively judge a process (or state of affairs) is the extent to which it is intended to deny a negative judgement of the same process (or state). If a speech act were intended to convey, "Chris is a good person," its intention would not be to deny that someone other than Chris is a good person but rather to deny

---

[13] Keeping with the earlier illustration, more formal renderings of $(x)a(x)Q_a$ and $(x)a(x)\overline{Q}_a$ are respectively $\exists$(Phenomenon x) $\exists$(Attribute a) $\exists$(EvalFunction $e_A$) [a(x) $\wedge$ x="Jerry" $\wedge$ a="storebound" $\wedge$ $e_A(a)$] and $\exists$(Phenomenon x) $\exists$(Attribute a) $\exists$(EvalFunction $e_A$) [a(x) $\wedge$ x="Jerry" $\wedge$ a="storebound" $\wedge$ $\overline{e}_A(a)$]. Here the function, $e_A$, assigns a positive (and $\overline{e}_A$ a negative) judgment to the attribute, a, contained in the set $A$.

[14] More formal renderings of $(x)^i f(x)Q_p$ and $(x)^i f(x)\overline{Q}_p$ are respectively $\exists$(Phenomenon x) $\exists$(Process p) $\exists$(JustFunction $j_P$) [p(x) $\wedge$ x="Jerry" $\wedge$ p="went to the store" $\wedge$ $j_P(p)$] and $\exists$(Phenomenon x) $\exists$(Process p) $\exists$(JustFunction $j_P$) [p(x) $\wedge$ x="Jerry" $\wedge$ p="went to the store" $\wedge$ $\overline{j}_P(p)$]. Here the function, $j_p$, assigns a positive (and $\overline{j}_P$ a negative) judgment to the process, p, contained in the set $P$.

that Chris is a bad person.[15] Likewise, if a speech act were intended to convey, "Dancing on Sunday is immoral," its intention is not to deny that activities other than Sunday dancing are immoral but rather to deny that Sunday dancing is moral.

In summary, when applying a generic semantic grammar to relatively unstructured texts, the coder's task is not one of identifying themes' surface grammatical relations but one of identifying each theme's role within the functional form(s) appropriate to its clause of origin. During the coding process such identifications can, of course, only be made after selecting the appropriate functional form, a selection that requires the coder to look beyond the clause. That is, the selection of functional forms requires that the coder understands both the source's intentions and the social context within which the clause appeared.

## Criteria for Selection Among Functional Forms

Understanding intentions requires coder intuition about the mental process that (by having uttered a clause) the source attempted to initiate in an audience.[16] The preceding discussion hints at four such intended mental processes: the recognition of a state of affairs, a perception or imagination of a process, a positive or negative evaluation of a state of affairs, and a positive or negative judgment (justification?) of a process.[17] Accordingly,

---

[15]Of course, "Chris is a good person" is a phrase that might be used in an attempt to communicate that someone other than Chris is a bad person (and "Dancing on Sunday is immoral" might be used to suggest that activities other than Sunday dancing are moral). In this, as in other paragraphs, phrases between quotation marks represent intended meanings, not direct quotations.

[16]In different contexts others have also held the premise that speech is motivated by a desire to affect one's audience's mental state: "A good writer or raconteur perhaps has the power to initiate a process very similar to the one that occurs when we are actually perceiving (or imagining) events instead of merely reading or hearing about them" (Johnson-Laird, 1970, p. 270). "The production of sound for the purpose of attracting attention *is* language, once we have reason to assert that 'attracting attention' is a meaning that fits in with the functional potential of language" (Halliday, 1978, p. 19).

[17]Rough parallels exists between these four types of intention and the classes some linguists have developed to capture the illocutionary (i.e., intended) force of speech acts (Austin, 1975; Searle & Vanderveken, 1985) or the structurally apparent features of an aspect grammar (Dowty, 1979). For example, among Austin's classes of performative utterances, "exercitives" and "behabitives" respectively function to convey descriptions and judgments of processes. (His "expositives" and "verdictives" have much rougher correspondence to the respective functions of conveying descriptions and judgments of states of affairs.) Dowty's "statives," "activities," "achievements," and "accomplishments" have clear parallels to the respective functions of conveying descriptions of states of affairs, descriptions of processes, judgments of states of affairs, and judgments of processes. Turning to functional linguistics, one might also draw rough parallels between Winter's (1994) two sets of basic text structures, "situation and evaluation" and "hypothetical and real" and, respectively, my "recognition and evaluation" and, less apparently, "justification and perception."

any matching of clause to functional form(s) requires that the coder weigh the relative plausibility of each of these four manners in which the clause may have been intended. By providing a framework for them to make such "judgments of subjective plausibility," the four functional forms provide coders with structure in their strivings to map sources' inherently ambiguous meanings into unambiguous code.

This structuring of the coding process has interesting parallels in Weber's (1973/1906, p. 290) recommendation that in their quest for the inherently elusive causes of past events, historical sociologists should guide their analyses by comparing numerous "judgments of objective possibility" (*objektiver Möglichkeitsurteile*). The idea here is that a causal understanding of history requires more than knowing the events that took place; it requires judgments about whether events would have taken place in the presence of various counterfactuals (i.e., "contrary-to-fact historical alternative(s) . . . conceptually and empirically quite close to the 'real past' "; Griffin, 1993, pp. 1101–1102). In his ETHNO program, Heise (1988, 1991) provides a structure for such counterfactual inquiry by requiring the user to identify causal links among the actions within a chronology. Similar analytic rigor is gained as coders (possibly under software guidance) are required to identify the functional form(s) judged most appropriate to the clauses in one's texts.

While weighing the relative plausibility of functional forms, the coder may judge the source not to have been sincere but instead to have attempted communication of irony, hyperbole, or understatement.[18] Interestingly, the coder's recognition of such discourse styles can only aid the coding process: Cases of hyperbole and understatement will usually suggest a clause's judgmental rather than descriptive intent. For example, *We have enough food to feed an army* may be used to convey a positive or negative evaluation of the amount of food on hand. Ironic, possibly sarcastic, speech acts must be encoded according to the semantic opposite of the functional form that would apply, were they to have been uttered in sincerity. For example, when said of a sputtering jalopy, the utterance, *It runs 'beautifully,' doesn't it,* should be encoded as a negative judgment of the jalopy's running (a process).

Finally, applying a semantic grammar requires that speech acts are understood in terms of their respective situational contexts. As always, these situational contexts are those within which the sources believed their speech acts would be interpreted. Invalid code will almost surely result when coders are insufficiently familiar with these contexts. However, even if the coder

---

[18]A source's intention to deliberately deceive its audience is unrelated to the coder's selection among functional forms. The semantic grammar proposed here only captures the meanings that sources intend to convey, not the pragmatics of why they opt to convey these meanings. Nonetheless, there is no reason why the coding of particular clauses might not be supplemented with identifiers that indicate the coder's suspicions regarding the genuineness of sources' intentions.

attained such contextual integrity in apprehending the source's intended meanings, these meanings may not have been those understood by their intended audiences. Little substantive import is likely to be found in an analysis of texts generated by sources who themselves were unable reliably to predict audience reactions (leaving their speech, one might say, little more than sound and fury). Moreover, encoding will be futile if the source's intended meanings (e.g., regarding preferred cookie recipes) are not relevant to the researcher's purposes (e.g., studying political attitudes).[19] Thus, the four functional forms are correctly applied within the source's situational context—a context hopefully familiar to both coder and audience, and relevant to both text population and research objectives.

**The Grammar**

This generic semantic grammar is a model of text (T), according to which text is a sequence of one or more clauses (C) separated by markers (&) that indicate subordination, coordination, and sentence boundaries:

$$T = C(\&C)^n, n \geq 0$$

Each clause in this sequence can be represented within its situational context (SC) according to one or more of the four unambiguous functional forms just introduced. Differently put, intention (I) is a function that maps ($\rightarrow$) clause–context pairs into a multiset comprised of subsets having one or more occurrences among recognition (R), perception (P), evaluation (E), and justification (J):

$$I(C_i, SC_{i-1}) \rightarrow MS_{\{R,P,E,J\}},$$
$$\text{where } MS \neq \{\}$$
$$\text{and } R = (x)a(x) \text{ with semantic opposite } (x)a(\sim x)$$
$$P = (x)p(x) \text{ with semantic opposite } (x)\!\sim\! p(x)$$
$$E = (x)a(x)Q_a \text{ with semantic opposite } (x)a(x)\overline{Q}_a$$
$$J = (x)p(x)Q_p \text{ with semantic opposite } (x)p(x)\overline{Q}_p$$

The restriction that this intention function have a single situational context as an argument assures the common ground (i.e., common assumptions made

<hr/>

[19] To determine the relevance of texts to a semantic grammar, one may begin by encoding a small representative sample from one's text population. If a phenomenal semantic grammar appears only to highlight a small proportion of the population, it follows that the unhighlighted proportion is not relevant to one's research. Of course, any text with identifiable clauses can be encoded using a generic semantic grammar. Yet, if application of a generic semantic grammar (or, for that matter, of software for representational thematic text analysis; cf. Popping, this volume) yields no common vocabulary among large segments of the population, these segments are likely to have little basis of comparison. In such cases, it is reasonable to consider whether one may have selected an inappropriate text population.

by the source regarding truth, comprehensibility, credibility, relevance, and evaluation and justification criteria) needed for a one-to-one mapping from clauses' surface representations to their appropriate functional forms.

Finally, situational contexts are continually updated by virtue of successive clauses' intended meanings. If $SC_0$ is the situational context at the beginning of one's text and $SC_i$ is the situational context after the ith clause, situation (S) can now be introduced as a function that takes the current clause's intention into account in transforming one situational context to the next:

$$S(SC_{i-1}, I(C_i, SC_{i-1})) = SC_i$$

To the extent that situational contexts (and rules for transformations among them) lack formal definition, coders' intuitions regarding these contexts and transformations will be necessary when this generic semantic grammar is used in encoding texts (cf. Shapiro, this volume).[20]

## APPLYING THE SEMANTIC GRAMMAR

For illustrative purposes, let us consider a hypothetical population of conversations that occurred over a one-year period within the personnel departments of two large American corporations. Each conversation is between a company representative and an employee at the close of the employee's probation period. The conversations invariably end with the hiring or firing of the employee.

Let us further assume that the corporate cultures within the two personnel departments are similar enough to assure a common situational context for all conversations (see note 19 regarding empirical tests for contextual similarity). A typical transcript (preceded by a short introductory paragraph) of such a conversation might look as follows:

> Joe *is* an employee at a bottling company. After a one-month probation period, Joe's performance *was* clearly inadequate. On two occasions he *was* found

---

[20]Given space constraints, only an abbreviated generic semantic grammar has been provided here. Not explicitly provided are types of clause coordination or subordination, types of questions, or types of modality. There is also no provision described for accommodating the speakers or audiences that typically accompany direct quotations. Moreover, all valences and qualifiers are (albeit without loss of generality) boolean in the presentation, ignoring the extent to which various types of attributes and processes may be exhibited as well as the strength of positive or negative judgments. The complete semantic grammar is implemented in the computer program Program for Linguistic Content Analysis, or PLCA (Roberts, 1989, 1991). (See Popping, this volume, for availability.) The following section illustrates the richness and potential of this fuller grammar.

asleep on the job. Because sleeping on the job *is* against company policy, Joe *had* to be fired.

Boss:   Joe, you *know* that it*'s* the end of your probation and that it *is* time for your evaluation. I *would* like you to know that although we *like* you as a person, we *will* not be able to retain you here as an employee. Your performance *has* simply not been up to our standards.

Joe:    Why? What *have* I done?

Boss:   You *remember* that you *were* found twice sleeping on the job?

Joe:    Yes. I *know*, but I *can* explain . . .

Boss:   Well, the second time that happened, the bottling machine *was* broken down for two hours before you *woke* up. That incident *brought* our productivity way down that week.

Joe:    But I *have* a family. What *am* I going to tell my wife?

Boss:   I*'m* sorry. Good-bye now.

## Encoding the Transcript

The generic semantic grammar developed in the previous section is at the heart of a quantitative text analysis method that I have somewhat presumptuously named Linguistic Content Analysis (LCA). Given the clause-specific relevance of the grammar, the method must be applied one clause at a time. "Clause" here has its usual sense, namely as a sentence or part of a sentence that contains an inflected verb and, optionally, a subject or object, plus all modifiers related to this verb, subject, and object. Because each clause contains an inflected verb, the first step in encoding the transcript is to identify each of its inflected verbs. To this end, each inflected verb in the transcript appears in italics.[21]

Let us begin by encoding sentences in the introductory paragraph. In the first sentence, Joe (a state of affairs) is described as falling into the class of a bottling company's employees. During the encoding process, phrases such as "Joe" and "a bottling company" are likely to be encoded as falling into more general thematic categories. Classifying "Joe" into the thematic cate-

---

[21]High coder reliability can only be assured if coders initially agree on what counts as a clause. For example, coders must follow explicit rules regarding cases of ellipsis, such as the one-word sentence, "Why?", in the transcript. In this context, the speaker clearly asks, "Why has my performance not been up to your standards?" Coding rules might be established to assure that isolated statements of "Yes" and "No" are coded as functioning to convey truth or lack of truth in another speaker's prior statement, but that the phrases "Hello" and "Good-bye" are better not treated as clauses but rather as delimiters of a conversation's beginning and end. Prior to locating inflected verbs, complicated constructions (e.g., "I would like you to know that . . .") may require the consistent application of rewrite rules (e.g., "I want to facilitate that you know that . . ."). A total of 26 clauses can be identified in the transcript once 3 clauses (gained by applying these coding rules) are added to the 23 clauses identified by the italicized verbs in the transcript.

gory "EMPLOYEE" and "a bottling company" into the category "THE COM-
PANY," the LCA functional form appropriate for this *recognition* (see note 11)
renders the sentence as "The EMPLOYEE is THE COMPANY's EMPLOYEE."

The second sentence conveys a negative judgment of Joe's performance.[22] Because business concerns are usually with outcomes (a.k.a. token
states of affairs) and not techniques (a.k.a. token processes) and because
the process-indicating gerund *performing* was not used, this clause is encoded as a judgment of a state of affairs—that is, as an *evaluation*. The syntax
for a negatively stated evaluation is "$(x)a(x)\overline{Q}_a$," and might be rendered as
"The EMPLOYEE's PERFORMANCE was of little value."

The third sentence is in passive voice and should be encoded as a
*perception* that describes the process of finding Joe asleep. The syntax for
a perception in passive voice is "$f(x)$". In this case, the sentence might be
rendered as "The EMPLOYEE's SLEEP was PERCEIVED."

The fourth sentence contains two clauses, the first of which is subordi-
nated to the second with the conjunction, *because*. This subordinate clause
conveys a negative judgment of the process of sleeping on the job and as
such should be encoded as a *justification*. The syntax for this negatively
expressed justification is "$f(x)\overline{Q}_p$". A corresponding rendering is "SLEEPING
is ethically wrong."

It is inevitable that some readers will disagree with some of the coding
decisions made here. (For example, in the second sentence above "Joe's
performance" may be considered a process rather than a state of affairs.)
On occasion, the coder may decide that a clause was intended to have more
than one meaning and that it should be encoded more than once (with each
coding assigned a weight equivalent to the proportion of its contribution to
the clause's overall meaning). Disagreements among coders are, of course,
the makings of poor interrater agreement. However, they are also grist in
the development of explicit coding rules (e.g., "Only noun phrases rendered
as gerunds will be considered processes in selections of functional form").
As it turns out, when coding rules have been conscientiously developed and
applied, coders are likely to attain consistently high agreement in LCA
encodings (cf. Eltinge & Roberts, 1993).

---

[22]To simplify presentation, the prepositional phrase at the beginning of this sentence as
well as other noun and verb modifiers from the transcript are ignored in the description of the
encoding process. In principle, there is no reason why in addition to subject-verb-object
relations arbitrary sequences of modifiers might not also be encoded, even if only according
to the surface grammatical syntax of the original text. However, in practice the number of
encoded modifiers is usually restricted to a manageable amount. To do this, the researcher
may choose to drop incidental modifiers from consideration or, when possible, to incorporate
them into the coding through the use of noun modifiers or more specific thematic categories.
For example, if it is critical for one's analysis to distinguish male from female employees, one
thematic category for "MALE EMPLOYEE" and another for "FEMALE EMPLOYEE" might be
created.

## LCA Translation and Retranslation

Text analysts have frequently depicted their work as a process of translation (Andrén, 1981; Franzosi, 1994). Yet in making their translations, semantic text analysts will want to avoid both the literal rendering of surface grammar and the paraphrasing of text. For example, when used idiomatically, *I'll stand by you in your misery* should not be encoded according to its surface grammar (i.e., as "I" and "you" having a relation of "standing together"). It would be equally inappropriate to paraphrase the idiom as "I assure you," despite the fact that the sentence is an assurance. In contrast, an LCA translation renders the clause's words according to the syntax of its appropriate functional form (i.e., not as a description of standing—a state of affairs, but as a description of assisting—a process). Thus, in a more accurate translation, the expression "to stand by" would be rendered as "to assist," leaving my relation to you being one of promised future assistance. That is, an acceptable translation would be, "I shall assist you."

The translation metaphor is not only apparent in linguistic content analysis; LCA encoding literally is a translation. Table 3.1 provides a translation of the entire transcript of Joe's interview, a translation according to one software implementation of the generic semantic grammar (see note 20). By generating ongoing translation of the text being encoded, LCA software affords the coder ready verification that the themes in the original text are related correctly according to the functional forms appropriate to their respective clauses. Yet the purpose of such semantic encoding is not merely to translate text into a sort of unambiguous pidgin English (a.k.a. LCAese).[23] Like all quantitative text analysis methods, LCA's encoding process is intended to produce a data matrix suitable for statistical analysis.

The translation in Table 3.1 is in fact a retranslation. That is, it is a direct translation of a data matrix and only indirectly a translation of the original text. Transparent to the user, the encoding process involves a translation from text to numbers (i.e., to an unambiguous matrix representation). The user is provided the retranslation to make the same kind of verification that developers of machine translation software use to check their routines: After translating the same text from one language to another, the translation is retranslated back to the original. If the retranslation closely resembles the original, the software's functionality is verified.

Unlike translation software, LCA software can automate the retranslation but not the translation process. Advances in the fields of linguistics and

---

[23]Although comprehensible to English speakers LCAese is not English but a language that unlike English, allows each of a speech act's intended meanings to be expressed in one and only one way. That is, unlike natural languages, LCAese is a language without ambiguity. As a consequence, users cannot legitimately disagree about the meaning of an LCAese expression, only about how well distinct LCAese expressions render the intended meaning(s) of a particular speech act.

TABLE 3.1

A (Re)translation of Joe's Interview According
to a Generic Semantic Grammar

---

The EMPLOYEE is THE COMPANY's EMPLOYEE.
The EMPLOYEE's PERFORMANCE was of little value.
The EMPLOYEE's SLEEP/UNCONSCIOUSNESS was PERCEIVED/CONSIDERED.
The EMPLOYEE was compelled to be DISCHARGED/FIRED,
because SLEEPING is ethically wrong
.

To the EMPLOYEE the EMPLOYER said, "
You RECOGNIZE/BELIEVE that [
there is not your PROBATION
and there is a JUDGMENT/EVALUATION of you
].
I want to ENCOURAGE/FACILITATE that [
you RECOGNIZE/BELIEVE that [
THE COMPANY will be not able to HAVE/CONTROL you,
although more positively THE COMPANY LIKES you
]
].
Your PERFORMING was technically inept.
"

To the EMPLOYER the EMPLOYEE asked, "
Why is it that my PERFORMING was technically inept?
How is it that I ACTED?
"

To the EMPLOYEE the EMPLOYER asked, "
Is it true that you RECOGNIZE/BELIEVE that [
your SLEEP/UNCONSCIOUSNESS was PERCEIVED/CONSIDERED
]?
"

To the EMPLOYER the EMPLOYEE said, "
There is a HONESTY/TRUTH(S).
I RECOGNIZE/BELIEVE,
although more positively I can DESCRIBE/REPORT
.
"

To the EMPLOYEE the EMPLOYER said, "
The MACHINE was of no value,
before you AWOKE
.
Your SLEEP/UNCONSCIOUSNESS DISCOURAGED/IMPEDED THE COMPANY's PERFORMANCE.
"

To the EMPLOYER the EMPLOYEE said, "
I HAVE/CONTROL a FAMILY.
How is it that I shall SPEAK/SAY to my WIFE?
"

To the EMPLOYEE the EMPLOYER said, "
I am lacking.
"

---

*Note.* The output in this table was generated by PLCA (MetaText, Inc.).

TABLE 3.2
An LCA Data Matrix Encoded from Joe's Interview

| Identifying information | Clause number | Sentence number | Depth in syntactic tree | Functional form (P=1, R=2, J=3, or E=4) | Type of subordination | Clause tense | Question? | Clause valence | Genitive of audience | Audience | Genitive of source | Source | Genitive of subject | Subject | Modal auxiliary verb | Main verb | Genitive of object | Object | Weight information | |
|---|---|---|---|---|---|---|---|---|---|---|---|---|---|---|---|---|---|---|---|---|
| GETTIN FIRED | 1 | 1 | 0 | 2 | . | 2 | 0 | T | . | . | . | . | . | . | . | 1 | 233 | 231 | C | 1.00 |
| GETTIN FIRED | 2 | 2 | 0 | 4 | . | 1 | 0 | VL | . | . | . | 231 | 231 | 19 | . | . | . | 231 | C | 1.00 |

74

| | | | | | | | | | | | | | | | | | | | | |
|---|---|---|---|---|---|---|---|---|---|---|---|---|---|---|---|---|---|---|---|---|
| GETTIN | FIRED | 3 | 3 | 0 | 1 | . | 1 | 0 | T | . | . | . | . | . | 21 | 231 | 16 | C | 1.00 | 1.00 |
| GETTIN | FIRED | 4 | 4 | 0 | 1 | . | 1 | 0 | T | . | . | . | . | 7 | 18 | . | 231 | C | 1.00 | 1.00 |
| GETTIN | FIRED | 5 | 4 | 1 | 3 | 6 | 2 | 0 | E- | . | . | . | . | . | 16 | . | . | C | 1.00 | 1.00 |
| GETTIN | FIRED | 6 | 5 | 0 | 1 | . | 2 | 0 | T | 231 | 232 | . | 231 | . | 22 | . | -110 | C | 1.00 | 1.00 |
| GETTIN | FIRED | 7 | 5 | 1 | 2 | OP | 2 | 0 | NI | 231 | 232 | . | . | 0 | 1 | 231 | 110 | C | 1.00 | 1.00 |
| GETTIN | FIRED | 8 | 5 | 2 | 2 | 3 | 2 | 0 | T | 231 | 232 | . | 232 | . | 1 | 25 | 231 | C | 1.00 | 1.00 |
| GETTIN | FIRED | 9 | 6 | 0 | 1 | . | 2 | 0 | T | 231 | 232 | . | 231 | 6 | 33 | 231 | 22 | C | 1.00 | 1.00 |
| GETTIN | FIRED | 10 | 6 | 1 | 1 | OP | 3 | 0 | NM | 231 | 232 | . | 233 | . | 22 | . | . | C | 1.00 | 1.00 |
| GETTIN | FIRED | 11 | 6 | 2 | 1 | OP | 2 | 0 | T | 231 | 232 | . | 233 | . | 52 | . | 231 | C | 1.00 | 1.00 |
| GETTIN | FIRED | 12 | 6 | 3 | 3 | 7 | 1 | 0 | T- | 231 | 232 | . | 231 | . | 26 | . | 231 | C | 1.00 | 1.00 |
| GETTIN | FIRED | 13 | 7 | 0 | 3 | . | 1 | 6 | T- | 232 | 231 | . | 231 | . | 19 | . | . | C | 1.00 | 1.00 |
| GETTIN | FIRED | 14 | 8 | 0 | 1 | . | 1 | 5 | T | 232 | 231 | . | 231 | . | 19 | . | . | C | 1.00 | 1.00 |
| GETTIN | FIRED | 15 | 9 | 0 | 1 | . | 2 | 3 | T | 231 | 232 | . | 231 | . | 73 | . | . | C | 1.00 | 1.00 |
| GETTIN | FIRED | 16 | 10 | 0 | 1 | OP | 1 | 0 | T | 232 | 231 | . | 231 | . | 22 | 21 | 16 | C | 1.00 | 1.00 |
| GETTIN | FIRED | 17 | 10 | 1 | 2 | . | 2 | 0 | T | 232 | 231 | . | . | . | 21 | 231 | 16 | C | 1.00 | 1.00 |
| GETTIN | FIRED | 18 | 11 | 0 | 1 | . | 1 | 0 | T | 231 | 232 | . | 231 | . | 1 | . | 100 | C | 1.00 | 1.00 |
| GETTIN | FIRED | 19 | 12 | 0 | 1 | 7 | 1 | 0 | V- | 231 | 232 | . | 231 | 6 | 22 | . | . | C | 1.00 | 1.00 |
| GETTIN | FIRED | 20 | 12 | 1 | 4 | . | 1 | 0 | T | 231 | 232 | . | 111 | . | 23 | . | . | C | 1.00 | 1.00 |
| GETTIN | FIRED | 21 | 13 | 0 | 1 | B | 1 | 0 | T | 231 | 232 | 231 | 231 | . | . | . | . | C | 1.00 | 1.00 |
| GETTIN | FIRED | 22 | 13 | 1 | 1 | . | 1 | 0 | T | 231 | 232 | . | 16 | . | 17 | . | 19 | C | 1.00 | 1.00 |
| GETTIN | FIRED | 23 | 14 | 0 | 2 | . | 2 | 5 | T | 232 | 231 | . | 231 | . | 34 | 233 | 235 | C | 1.00 | 1.00 |
| GETTIN | FIRED | 24 | 15 | 0 | 3 | . | 3 | 0 | T | 232 | 231 | . | 231 | . | 52 | . | 236 | C | 1.00 | 1.00 |
| GETTIN | FIRED | 25 | 16 | 0 | 4 | . | 2 | 5 | T | 232 | 231 | . | 231 | . | 74 | 231 | . | C | 1.00 | 1.00 |
| GETTIN | FIRED | 26 | 17 | 0 | 4 | . | 2 | 0 | - | 231 | 232 | . | 232 | . | . | . | . | C | 1.00 | 1.00 |

*Note.* The output in this table was generated by PLCA (MetaText, Inc.).

artificial intelligence remain insufficient to automate the coder's ability to recognize texts' intended meanings (cf. Shapiro, this volume). Thus, although potentially supported by various software amenities, the translation from words to numbers requires that coders make considerable use of both their intuition of the source's meanings and their knowledge of the situational context.

The purpose of LCA retranslation (i.e., from data matrix to LCAese) is to enable coders to verify whether their intuitions are accurately represented in a semantically unambiguous linguistic form that is grounded in the generic semantic grammar described above. LCA encoding requires more of coders than that they merely identify subjects and predicates; they must commit themselves to unambiguous encodings of ofttimes ambiguous linguistic expressions. By comparing original text to LCAese, one is able to evaluate whether the retranslation captures one's intuition that a clause was intended to communicate a description or judgment of a process or state of affairs.

Table 3.2 lists the data matrix from which the retranslation in Table 3.1 was generated. The first five columns of the matrix give identifying and sequencing information. Missing data are rendered as periods. The first clause (encoded in the first row of the matrix) is a recognition (code = 2) in present tense (code = 2), that is not a question (code = 0) and that functions to convey that one theme "is 'totally' an instance of" another (valence = T, verb = 1). The code for EMPLOYEE is 231 and that for THE COMPANY is 233. These codes, along with the LCA syntax for a recognition (again, see note 11), comprise sufficient information for LCA software to render the first clause as "The EMPLOYEE is THE COMPANY's EMPLOYEE." The three last columns indicate whether clause weights are fractions of sentence weights, what the base weight is for all clauses with the same identifying information, and what the clause weight is after taking a clause-specific weight and the other weight information into account. Other retranslations can be reconstructed via similar comparisons between the two tables.

## CONCLUSION

This chapter describes and then applies a text-encoding method for researchers who wish to draw probabilistic inferences about the prominence of semantically related themes within the clauses of a population of texts. Later in this volume Eltinge applies the method in documenting a recent decline in the odds that in a popular series of biology textbooks, science was depicted as a process of inquiry—a process evident, in part, in clauses with subject–verb relations between subjects such as "scientist" or "the reader" and verbs such as "think," "consider," "question," or "wonder." Because the method enables the researcher to encode all clauses in a sample of texts, it also enables inferences to be drawn about all clauses in the text population from which the sample was drawn.

Linguists have correctly noted that syntax grammars map themes' surface-grammatical relations, and thus afford only ambiguous indicators of texts' intended meanings. In contrast, the generic semantic grammar described here can be used to generate an unambiguous encoding of any clause with identifiable meaning(s). Once the coder has divined a clause's meaning, the clause's themes and theme relations are fit into the functional form appropriate to this meaning. The semantic grammar consists of four such unambiguous functional forms, each of which has a unique semantic opposite. In addition, the semantic grammar affords a sufficiently fine-grained mapping of text that the validity of the encoded data can be evaluated by retranslating them back into a semblance of the original.

If there is a central theme to this book, it is that in any study the best text analysis method is the one that most closely matches one's research question (cf. Roberts, this volume, chapter 16). My generic semantic text analysis method is no exception to this. If one's objective is to use texts as a source of information about relational characteristics of some well-defined phenomenon (e.g., the event, the grievance, etc.), a phenomenal approach to semantic text analysis may be more appropriate. If one is primarily concerned with theme occurrences (but not theme relations), thematic text analysis may provide a better match. If one's research question requires that text blocks be depicted as sets of interrelated themes, a network text analysis method may be best. The method presented here is for addressing research questions on how themes are related in relatively unstructured text populations—questions often of interest to students of culture and the media.

# 4

# NETWORK TEXT ANALYSIS: THE NETWORK POSITION OF CONCEPTS

Kathleen M. Carley
Carnegie Mellon University

Mental models can be abstracted from texts as a network of relations between concepts. Within these mental models different concepts play different roles depending on their position in the network. This chapter describes how to locate and empirically describe each concept's position in a mental model and how to construct composite empirical descriptions of the entire mental model. The measures and techniques for comparing texts using this framework are illustrated using data gathered from a study of undergraduates selecting a new tutor for their living groups.

Language is a chronicle of social knowledge that is predicated on the society's history, culture, and social structure (Cicourel, 1970; Vygotsky, 1962; White, 1992). Language contains within it societal choices about how to represent and interrelate concepts. Such choices frame the way individuals think about the world and so affect what actions individuals take. Thus, language affects behavior (cf., e.g., Cicourel, 1974; Cooley, 1902; Stryker, 1980). Language can be represented as a network of concepts and the relationships among them (Axelrod, 1976; Schank & Abelson, 1977; Sowa, 1984). This network can be thought of as the social structure of language or, equivalently, the representation of extant social knowledge. The social structure of language is related to the structure of action because these societal choices are embodied in the linguistic social structure.

Multiple techniques exist for extracting conceptual networks (cf. Carley, 1988; Carley & Palmquist, 1992; Kleinnijenhuis, de Ridder, & Rietberg, this volume). Such networks can be empirically analyzed, and the analysis may shed light on individual actions (Carley, 1986a; Carley & Kaufer, 1993; Kaufer & Carley, 1993b; Palmquist, 1990), political discourse (Kleinnijenhuis, de Ridder, & Rietberg, this volume), narratives, or scripts (Abell, 1984; Heise, 1991). This chapter builds on this prior work. I argue that:

- Language can be represented as a lossy-integrated conceptual network.[1]
- Each concept has a position in this network that can be characterized along several dimensions.
- Conceptual networks can be characterized by the distribution of concepts on this set of dimensions.
- Analysis of a society's language using these dimensions may provide insight into the use of language by members of the society to build consensus.

A network-based procedure for analyzing conceptual networks is presented. The procedure enables the researcher to characterize the structure of the conceptual network along a series of dimensions. These dimensions are independent of how the network was extracted and the source from which the network was extracted. The interpretation of the results (i.e., how concepts cluster along these dimensions), however, is dependent on both the method of extraction and the source of the network.

The proposed procedure for analyzing conceptual networks allows the researcher to locate the position of each concept in the conceptual network, classify concepts according to a taxonomy, and make predictions about action on the basis of the distribution of concepts in this taxonomy. The proposed procedure is then used to analyze the talk of a group of undergraduates at MIT. The results are used to illustrate the link between the social structure of language and action through an examination of the power of concepts to evoke consensus. The MIT data set includes information on the social language (i.e., social knowledge) and individual language about the topic of tutor (i.e., graduate resident) selection for a group of undergraduates in a single living group (Carley, 1984, 1986a).

This study is exploratory. The goal is not to explain the language of this particular group. Rather, the goal is to present a model of language as a social phenomenon and a procedure for using this model to look at the interrelations

---

[1]Lossy integration refers to an integration process in which information is lost, as when taking a moving average. A lossy-integrated network is one in which the relations between nodes change gradually over time through a moving average process. For language, the basic idea is that each person's language can be represented as a conceptual network. Social language can be represented as a composite network by combining (somehow) the networks of all individuals in the society at that point in time. Because individuals enter and leave societies, and because individuals can learn and evolve their personal networks, the network representing social language is lossy.

between language and action. The MIT talk is used purely as an illustration. Previously, the MIT talk was coded as a specific type of conceptual network—the cognitive network or mental model (Carley, 1984, 1986a). In such networks the meaning of each concept is captured by its network position (Carley & Palmquist, 1992; Carley, 1993; also see Fauconnier, 1985, and Johnson-Laird, 1983, for theoretical underpinnings). Using the proposed procedure these cognitive networks can be analyzed. However, the proposed procedure can also be applied to other types of networks. For example, this procedure could be applied to scripts or narratives where the relations between concepts represent story order or event sequences (Abell, 1984; Heise, 1991).

## DEFINITIONS

A conceptual network is characterized as a set of concepts and pairwise relations between them. Numerous schemes for representing conceptual networks exist in the literature. These schemes vary in the semantic grammars used for ascribing a relation among concepts (Franzosi, 1990a, this volume; Kleinnijenhuis, de Ridder, & Rietberg, this volume; Roberts, 1989, this volume). The specific scheme used in this chapter is grounded in map analysis (Carley, 1984, 1986a, 1993; Carley & Palmquist, 1992). Concepts, relationships, and statements are the basic network components of conceptual networks.

A *concept* is an ideational kernel—a single idea. Graphically a concept is represented by a circle (in Figure 4.1, for example, "Aria," "Cassi," "friends," "gives," "plays," and "toy" are all concepts). In cognitive networks (both at the individual and societal, or socioconceptual, levels), concepts are devoid of meaning except as they relate to other concepts.

A *relationship* links two concepts. Graphically a relationship is represented by a line connecting two circles. In Figure 4.1, the relationships are labeled as (a) through (i). Relationships can have a variety of properties, of which the only two that are important to this study are strength and directionality.[2] In sociocognitive networks the strength of a relationship indicates the degree of consensus—the extent to which members of the population agree that there is a relationship between these two concepts. In cognitive networks the

---

[2]Researchers have also included relationship type and sign as properties of relationships (see Carley, 1984, 1986a, 1988; Franzosi, this volume; Kleinnijenhuis et al., this volume; Roberts, this volume). In this chapter, all relationships are treated as of the same type (namely, a→b and/or b→a). If the researcher has multiple types, the procedures outlined in this chapter can be followed for each type of relationship separately. Although many approaches to coding texts allow for relationships to be both negative and positive, such an approach is not suggested when dealing with conceptual networks. The basic reason is that negated concepts may erroneously be interpreted as implying the opposite of positive concepts (e.g., that "not in love" has the opposite meaning of "in love"). To avoid making this assumption, which generally does not appear to hold, it is recommended that the researcher when generating the conceptual network use only positive relationships and separate positive from negative concepts.

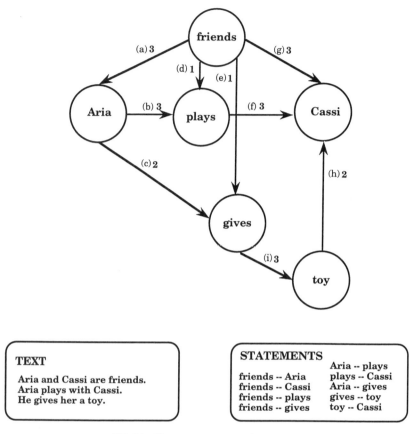

FIG. 4.1. Illustrative conceptual network.

strength of a relationship indicates the degree of emphasis, salience, implication, or belief—the extent to which the individual emphasizes or believes that the relationship between the two concepts holds. In Figure 4.1, for example, the strength of the relationship denotes the degree of inference that must be made to link the two concepts such that a "3" represents those relationships that are directly stated, "2" those relationships that can be inferred from syntax, and "1" those relationships that can only be inferred using tacit social knowledge not explicit in the text (cf. Carley, 1988).

A *statement* is two concepts and the relationship between them. Because relationships are directed, within a statement one concept is in the anterior position and one is in the posterior position. For example, in Figure 4.1, in the "Aria→plays" statement, "Aria" is in the anterior position, and "plays" is in the posterior position.

In conceptual networks, the relative network position of each concept can be measured along several dimensions. To define these dimensions six additional ideas are needed. *Vocabulary* includes the set of concepts in the conceptual network. To facilitate later discussions, let us represent the number of concepts in the conceptual network as N. The size of the vocabulary is N. The *focal concept* is the concept whose network position is being measured. To characterize the conceptual network completely, each concept in the vocabulary is in turn treated as the focal concept. Two concepts that occur in a single statement are said to be *directly linked* to each other. In graph representation, a concept is directly linked to those concepts to which it is linked by an arrow; "Aria" and "friends" are directly linked in Figure 4.1. An *indirect link* exists when two concepts do not occur in the same statement but are linked by a directed chain of statements. In graph representation, two concepts are indirectly linked when a path (following the arrows) exists between the two concepts with at least one intervening concept. In Figure 4.1, "Aria" is directly linked to "gives" and indirectly linked to "toy."

For a focal concept, its *local network* is the set of concepts to which it is directly linked. In Figure 4.1, the local network when "Aria" is treated as the focal concept includes the concepts "friends," "plays," and "gives" and the relationships (a) through (c). For cognitive networks, a concept's local network is the locally elaborated meaning of that concept. The *extended network* for a focal concept can be generated for each concept in the larger network by following the procedure illustrated in Figure 4.2 and described here. For cognitive networks, a concept's extended network defines the generative meaning of the concept.

In generating the extended network, relationship strengths are used. First, a cutoff is defined.[3] Those statements whose relationships have a strength greater than the cutoff are treated as definitives, defining what other concepts must be present. Those statements whose strength is less than the cutoff are treated as connectives, defining for co-present concepts what relationships must exist.

The process of generating an extended network for the focal concept uses a forward-chaining statement-inclusion method. The procedure begins with the focal concept. Then, using those definitives that have as their anterior concept the focal concept, a set of concepts (and the relationships) are added. This process is repeated, recursively, until no new concepts can be added. Then the connectives are used to fill in relationships between concepts in the extended network. In Figure 4.2, this procedure is followed for each of the concepts in the conceptual network in Figure 4.1, using the average strength as the cutoff. Not all concepts have an extended network (e.g., "Cassi" and "toy"). In cognitive networks, the extended network can be thought of as the

---

[3]The researcher can define the cutoff using any criteria. In the program CUBE, the default for the cutoff is the average strength of all relationships in the conceptual network. CUBE is written in C and can be obtained from the author. It is part of the MECA software package for encoding and analyzing maps.

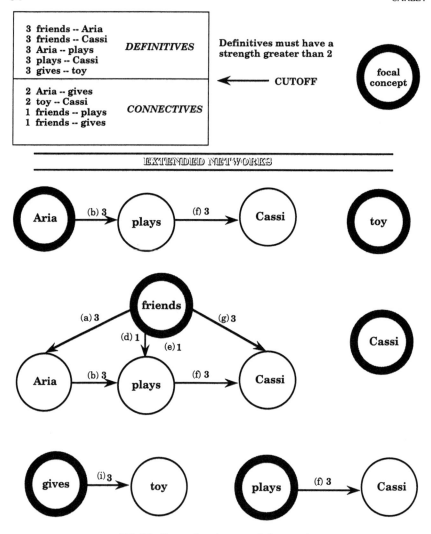

FIG. 4.2. Generating the extended network.

image that is most emphasized (in the individual's mental model) or most likely to be evoked (across all individuals in the society when the network is the sociocognitive network). The extended network provides insight into the train of thought and not just the direct inferences.

## DIMENSIONS

A concept's position in the conceptual network can be characterized along five connective dimensions: imageability, evokability, density, conductivity,

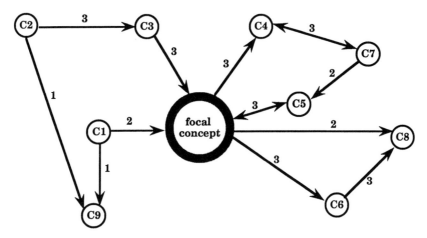

FIG. 4.3. Connective properties of concepts.

and intensity.[4] These dimensions have analogues at both the local level and the extended level. The dimensions can be thought of as measuring the connective properties of the concept, that is, as measuring the nature of each concept's connection to other concepts. In defining each of these dimensions, the abstract conceptual network in Figure 4.3 can be used. Each of these dimensions has a theoretical maximum. When analyzing data it is sometimes useful to consider a concept's absolute value on a dimension and at other times to consider its value as a percentage of the theoretical maximum. In Figure 4.3 the strength of the relationships is noted as 1, 2, or 3. A strength of 3 denotes a definitive.

*Local imageability* is measured as the total number of statements in the map that contain focal concepts in the anterior position. Graphically, this is the number of arrows going from the focal concept to other concepts. The local imageability of the focal concept in Figure 4.3 is 4. The theoretical maximum is $N - 1$, as the concept can have at most a relationship to all concepts other than itself.

*Local evokability* is measured as the total number of statements in the map that contain the focal concept in the posterior position. Graphically, this is the number of arrows going into the focal concept from other concepts. The local evokability of the focal concept in Figure 4.3 is 3. The theoretical maximum is $N - 1$, as the concept can have at most a relationship from all concepts other than itself.

*Local density* is measured as the total number of statements in the map that contain the focal concept in either the anterior or the posterior position.

---

[4]The program CUBE calculates, for each concept in the social vocabulary, the connective properties of that concept within a conceptual network coded as a map. The output from CUBE is a matrix of concepts by their position on each of the connective dimensions.

Local density is operationalized as the sum of local imageability and local evokability. The local density of the focal concept in Figure 4.3 is 7. The theoretical maximum is $2*(N-1)$.

*Local conductivity* is the number of two-step paths through the focal concept. Local conductivity is operationalized as local imageability times local evokability. The local conductivity of the focal concept in Figure 4.3 is 12. The theoretical maximum is $(N-1)^2$.

*Local intensity* is the strength of the focal concept's direct relationships to other concepts. This is measured as the fraction of the statements that contain the focal concept in either the anterior or the posterior position with greater than average strength. The local intensity of the focal concept in Figure 4.3 is 0.71 (5/7). The theoretical maximum for local intensity is 1.

*Extended imageability* is measured as the total number of concepts in the focal concept's extended network. The extended imageability of the focal concept in Figure 4.3 is 5. The theoretical maximum is $N-1$, as at most all other concepts can occur in the extended network.

*Extended evokability* is measured as the total number of concepts in whose extended network the focal concept occurs. The extended evokability of the focal concept in Figure 4.3 is 3. The theoretical maximum is $N-1$, as at most the focal concept can occur in all other concept's extended networks.

*Extended density* is measured as the total number of concepts that either occur in the focal concept's extended network or in whose extended network the focal concept occurs. Extended density is operationalized as the sum of extended imageability and extended evokability. The extended density of the focal concept in Figure 4.3 is 8. The theoretical maximum is $2*(N-1)$.

*Extended conductivity* is the number of pairs of concepts, such that neither of the two concepts are the focal concept, that are linked by at least one path through the focal concept. Extended conductivity is operationalized as extended imageability times extended evokability. The extended conductivity of the focal concept in Figure 4.3 is 15. The theoretical maximum is $(N-1)^2$.

*Extended intensity* is the strength of the focal concept's extended network. This is measured as the fraction of concepts that either occur in the focal concept's extended network or in whose extended network the focal concept occurs and that are strongly tied to the focal concept. The extended intensity of the focal concept in Figure 4.3 is 0.63 (5/8). The theoretical maximum for extended intensity is 1.

Let us pause and consider the conceptual bases of the three basic dimensions, density, conductivity, and intensity. Each of these dimensions can be thought of as measuring an aspect of the concept's communicative power. The communicative power of a concept is a multidimensional notion involving the extent of the consensus or shared meaning that occurs when a concept is used and the extent to which the use of the concept can affect social change. Concepts that are high in density derive communicative power from the wealth of other concepts to which they are attached. Highly dense concepts are likely to be used and thought about. Concepts that are high in conductivity derive their communicative power from their ability to tie groups of (otherwise largely disconnected) concepts together. Highly intense concepts derive their communicative power from the degree to which there is social consensus over their relations to other concepts.

## A GENERAL TAXONOMY

Using the dimensions of density, conductivity, and intensity, a taxonomy of concepts can be formulated that derives its power as a classification scheme by simultaneously "typing" concepts and providing a framework within which the evolution of concepts, and hence knowledge, relative to a specific task can be analyzed. This classification scheme categorizes concepts according to the potential role concepts play in communication. The identified types or classes of concepts are in effect ideal types, outliers whose position vis-à-vis the three dimensions defines the cube. Each type of concept has particular communication properties and may even have a characteristic label relative to the type of conceptual network. To facilitate the discussion of the data, these eight ideal types are labeled and described as though the conceptual network were a cognitive or sociocognitive network. The eight ideal types are ordinary concepts, prototypes, buzzwords, factoids, place-holders, stereotypes, emblems, and symbols. Within cognitive and sociocognitive networks, if language is a lossy-integrated network, then the utilization of concepts should change as their level of density, conductivity, and intensity changes.

One way of looking at this taxonomy is as differentiating concepts in terms of their embedded meaning. The network of concepts evoked by the focal concept can be thought of as its embedded meaning. Concepts with higher levels of embedded meaning are going to be more dense. Concepts with a more temporal meaning (i.e., likely to be evoked and to evoke) are going to be more conductive. Concepts with more historically developed networks (i.e., the network of concepts has arisen in response to historical events) are going to be more intense (Carley & Kaufer, 1993; Kaufer & Carley, 1993a, 1993b).

### Communicative Power and Network Position

One way of seeing the potential communicative power of concepts is to consider their relative position in this classification scheme. Let us consider the theoretical implications of a concept being extreme on one or more of these three dimensions.

*Type 1: Ordinary concepts.* Ordinary concepts are low on all three dimensions. Such concepts are isolated concepts within a system or network of concepts. Most concepts should be low on all three attributes. Ordinary concepts are used to define the critical or outlying concepts but are in themselves (relative to the discourse topic) of little importance. The use of ordinary concepts should neither generate nor inhibit consensus formation.

*Type 2: Prototypes.* Prototypes are high in density but low in conductivity and intensity. Prototypes are characterized by being connectively central but nevertheless perhaps of little import. Prototypes have an elaborate meaning that is not highly emphasized or agreed to. Such concepts should be handles for a set of ideas whose meaning (i.e., set of relationships to other concepts) has been affirmed historically but not to the extent that there is widespread consensus as to the existence or interpretation of these relationships. The movement from ordinary concepts to prototypes is a movement from the general and astructural to the historical and negotiable.

*Type 3: Buzzwords.* Concepts that are high in conductivity but low in both intensity and density are defined as buzzwords. Buzzwords are concepts that, relative to a particular topic, are highly utilized by individuals when discussing that topic. Such concepts have little meaning, and what meaning they do have is not particularly salient or socially shared. In a very loose sense, buzzwords are the result of individual belief or social consensus that a single idea should be important and highly relevant to the task at hand. The movement from ordinary concepts to buzzword is a movement from concepts that are very general and whose meaning is more a function of personal experience (i.e., little social or shared meaning) to concepts that are highly temporal and vogue. Buzzwords are very astructural in meaning (i.e., they have none) and are part of the more transient popular culture and not the stable long-term underlying culture. The movement from ordinary concepts to buzzwords is a movement from concepts that are atemporal to those that are temporal.

*Type 4: Factoids.* Factoids are defined as concepts that are high in intensity but low in density and conductivity. Such concepts have a narrowly ascribed meaning that is nonetheless highly salient or accepted. Within a general discourse community, such concepts are likely to be culturally shared identifications or trivia, such as dates: "1492," "1776." Trivia games rely on such concepts. Within a particular type of discourse community or a profession, such concepts are likely to be agreed upon definitions such as sociometric and demographic terms (e.g., age, sex). Such concepts underlie and serve to define many other concepts; however, as isolated concepts they have low levels of usefulness relative to any particular task. The movement from ordinary concepts to factoids is a movement from concepts with individual-ized meanings to concepts whose meaning is culturally embedded.

**Type 5: Place-holders.**  Place-holders are defined as high in density and conductivity and low in social consensus. Such concepts should be highly utilized. Place-holders, like buzzwords, admit the construction of consensus by producing a situation in which there is tacit consensus to an ill-defined entity, an entity whose formulation has not been socially consented to. Un-like buzzwords, place-holders serve as handles for a large set of ideas that bear some relationship to each other and are highly relevant to the task at hand. Place-holders and buzzwords should facilitate communication and pave the way for consensus formation and the resultant evolution of so-ciocultural knowledge. Their high level of usage implies tacit agreement that "x" should be important without social agreement as to what "x" means. The movement from ordinary concepts to place-holders is a movement from general meanings to highly task-relevant meanings. Place-holders have mean-ing; it's just highly negotiable.

**Type 6: Stereotypes.**  Stereotypes are defined as concepts that are high in intensity and density but low in conductivity. Stereotypes represent his-torical saliency or consensus to regularities perceived by members of the social unit. They should be highly structured images. Stereotypes should change slowly due to the low level of conductivity. Stereotypes can be thought of as highly consented-to prototypes. The movement from ordinary concept to stereotype is a movement from the astructural to the structural.

**Type 7: Emblems.**  Emblems are defined as concepts with high intensity and conductivity and low density. Emblems are concepts that are highly utilized relative to the task at hand but that have a very narrow, highly consented-to meaning. Emblems are useful communication tools as they admit instant identification. The movement from ordinary concepts to em-blems is a movement from concepts whose meaning is consented to only by the individual to concepts whose meaning is socially consented to.

**Type 8: Symbols.**  Symbols are defined as the sociocultural antithesis of ordinary concepts. Whereas ordinary concepts are low in all dimensions, symbols are high in all dimensions. One type of concept that acts as a symbol would be social roles. To the extent that this taxonomy holds, it should be possible to measure the level to which a particular role has become an accepted aspect of that social unit by measuring the degree to which the concept denoting that role is high in all three dimensions (either across all individual's cognitive networks or within the overall sociocognitive network). The movement from ordinary concepts to symbols is a movement from concepts with very general purpose and highly personal meaning and that are very astructural to concepts that are highly relevant to the task at hand, have strong social meanings, and are highly structured. The movement from ordinary concepts to symbols is a movement from a single conceptual entity to a sociocultural construct whose conceptual handle is relevant and highly embedded.

## ILLUSTRATIVE EXAMPLE

### Data Collection and Coding

The data were collected as part of a larger study on consensus construction (Carley, 1984) in which the language, social structure, and decision-making behavior of a group of undergraduates (all members of the same living group) were studied as they went through a process of tutor selection. For an overview of this study, refer to Carley (1986a). In this chapter, the concern is with the language used by the students to talk about tutors and tutor selection and how that language can be used to induce consensus.

As they went through this process, a variety of verbal information on what the students wanted in a tutor, how they thought about tutors, what they thought tutors did, the social history of tutors in that living group, and so on, was collected. Based on these data the language used by the students to talk about tutors was coded (Carley, 1988). These language data do not reflect the entire sociocultural environment and language of this group but only that part of their culture and language that relates to the tutor and the tutor selection process. Only a portion of the language data is used in this chapter—the general sociocognitive network. This illustrative network is coded from guided freeform interviews with four students (5% of the original sample) as well as from the sociohistorical records of the living group. (See Carley, 1984, Appendix 3, for more detail on these records.)

*Social Vocabulary.* The social vocabulary contains 210 concepts. Some concepts are single concepts (e.g., "gnerd"), whereas others are phrases (e.g., "fits in with hall"). Concepts are nouns or noun-based phrases. In most cases, the concepts are those actually used by the students. In some cases, however, they are paraphrases. The vocabulary is not complete in terms of the actual concepts used by the students. It is complete in terms of the set of general concepts needed to represent the perceptions about tutors forwarded by current and past residents of the living group. Roughly, this set of 210 concepts can be thought of as the set of concepts needed to engage in "tutor-talk."

*Socioconceptual Network.* In coding the sociohistorical records and interviews, each sentence, clause, or paragraph that contained tutor talk was coded as a statement using CODEMAP.[5] Details on the process of coding the socioconceptual network can be found in Carley (1988). Essentially, if two concepts occurred in the same sentence, for example, as subject and object, or if the two concepts logically followed one from the other within a paragraph, then a relationship was placed between those two concepts, from the first to the second, resulting in a single statement. The strength of each statement reflects the degree of agreement or consensus among members of the previous and current members of the living group that the two concepts are related and that when the anterior concept is used, the posterior is implied. Carley (1988) defined three strength levels (from high to low): definitives, logical connectives, and simple connectives. Definitives are statements where one concept defines the other, such that in the society in question, if the first concept is used the second is always implied. Logicals are statements where the concepts are logically connected, such that in the society in question, if the first and second concept are used the speaker intends a specific relation among them. Simple connectives are statements such that in the society in question, if the two concepts are used and the speaker has not specified an alternative relation, then the socially accepted relation between them is assumed. The socioconceptual network contains 1,214 statements, of which 275 are definitives, 837 are logical connectives, and 103 are simple connectives. Typical statements in this network are "someone who water fights encourages a fraternal atmosphere" and "someone who is older is lookupableto." In effect, the socioconceptual network can be loosely thought of as the set of sentences that have been and are commonly used by the students to conduct discussions about tutors. The result of the coding process is a single network with 210 concepts and 1,214 relationships among them.

## Statistics and Distributions

For the socioconceptual network, univariate statistics for each dimension are shown in Table 4.1. These statistics are based on treating each of the 210 concepts in the socioconceptual network in turn as the focal concept. On average each of the 210 concepts connects to (imageability) and is connected to (evokability) 6 other concepts, is involved in 12 statements (density), is the center of 42 paths (conductivity), and has an average intensity of each relationship of 1 (moderate). The average profile is far from the theoretical maximum (and the adjusted theoretical maximum). In other words, the socioconceptual network is very sparse.

---

[5]CODEMAP is an extended version of CODEF, which is described in Carley (1988). CODEMAP is part of the MECA software.

TABLE 4.1
Univariate Statistics for Sociocognitive Network

|  | Mean | Standard Deviation | Skew | Actual Maximum | Theoretical Maximum |
|---|---|---|---|---|---|
| Local network |  |  |  |  |  |
| Imageability | 5.78 | 7.46 | 3.39 | 52 | 209 |
| Evokability | 5.78 | 5.52 | 2.72 | 44 | 209 |
| Density | 11.56 | 10.17 | 2.41 | 67 | 418 |
| Conductivity | 41.99 | 90.69 | 5.43 | 780 | 43,681 |
| Intensity | 0.92 | 0.14 | −3.50 | 1 | 1 |
| Extended network |  |  |  |  |  |
| Imageability | 3.38 | 4.00 | 1.65 | 19 | 209 |
| Evokability | 3.38 | 8.03 | 4.21 | 66 | 209 |
| Density | 6.76 | 8.74 | 3.06 | 66 | 418 |
| Conductivity | 8.74 | 28.63 | 5.14 | 180 | 43,681 |
| Intensity | 0.47 | 0.35 | 0.30 | 1 | 1 |

Note. Averages are across the 210 concepts in the network, using each in turn as the focal concept.

In Figure 4.4 the distribution of tutor talk concepts across local density, local conductivity, and local intensity is shown. Concepts tend to cluster on all three dimensions. Within this community, most words are either highly imageable or highly evocable but are rarely both. There are concepts that do stand out on one or more dimensions and therefore hold a special place in the proposed taxonomy. These concepts have special communicative properties.

## Application of the Taxonomy

We would expect that were we to analyze all concepts in the English language for the American public that most would be ordinary concepts; that is, low on the three dimensions. As such, most concepts should play a fairly similar albeit unimportant role in terms of communication and consensus formation. On any one dimension, we would expect only a few concepts to stand out. For language about a specific topic, however, we might expect a different distribution, particularly given that researchers coding that talk may tend not to code most ordinary words such as *a, an,* and *the.* Nonetheless, the particular distribution of concepts for that talk should provide insight into the nature of the arguments being put forth by the speakers. Let us turn now to an examination of the MIT tutor talk.

Concepts in the socioconceptual network were classified into their requisite category using the following cutoffs. A density greater than or equal to 24 was considered high, a conductivity greater than or equal to 572 was considered high, and an intensity greater than 0.96 was considered high.

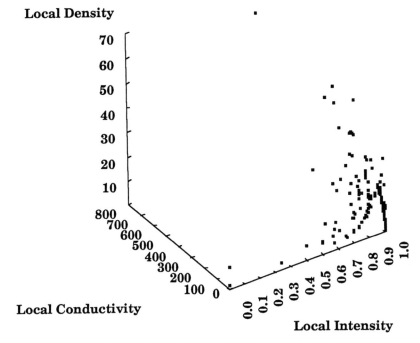

FIG. 4.4. 3-D projection of density, conductivity, and intensity at the local level.

Density and conductivity have a potential range based on the total number of concepts. However, most conceptual networks are quite sparse (i.e., very few concepts are connected to each other). Therefore, it makes sense to adjust behavior based on the achieved maximum. The cutoffs chosen here are .25 of adjusted maximums. For density the adjusted maximum is the sum of the actual maximums for imageability and evokability. For conductivity the adjusted maximum is the product of the actual maximums for imageability and evokability. These adjusted maximums are based on the assumption that potentially every concept can be connected as much as the most connected concept.

Given these cutoffs, most concepts in this socioconceptual network are either factoids or ordinary concepts (see Table 4.2). The high number of factoids is not particularly surprising given that this network represents knowledge used in making a decision. Factoids, which have a narrow but accepted meaning, allow individuals rapidly to describe similarities and differences between those items they are trying to decide upon. As such, factoids play a highly specialized but important communication role in decision-making processes.

The concept "car" is a typical factoid. In Figure 4.5, the local network for the focal concept "car" is shown. The arrows show the direction of implica-

TABLE 4.2
Number of Concepts per Category

| Category | D | T | I | Examples | N |
|----------|---|---|---|----------|---|
| ordinary concepts | L | L | L | finishing thesis humorous answer | 59 |
| prototypes | H | L | L | intelligence lookupableto | 5 |
| buzzwords | L | H | L | friendly* mature* | 0 |
| factoids | L | L | H | car bar hops | 133 |
| place holders | H | H | L | fits in gets along | 2 |
| stereotypes | H | L | H | gnerd hacker | 11 |
| emblems | I. | H | H | BS from MIT* | 0 |
| symbols | H | H | H | ex third easter* | 0 |

*Note.* Asterisks identify close examples that are near but do not fall into the corresponding cell using the specified cutoffs.

tion. The number on the line indicates the strength of the relationship. Whether the relationship is positive or negative is not indicated. Notice that this concept is rarely evoked and has a small image. However, there is high agreement. In particular, there is unanimous agreement that if the candidate has a car then he or she will encourage hall activities and that a car is a resource. If the students want to judge the candidates' ability to promote social interaction or encourage hall activities, they may well ask (and they did) whether the candidate has a car. If the candidate has a car, the students will tend to assume that the candidate will encourage activities within the living group. Factoids, given this small but highly consensual meaning, can be used in decision-making scenarios to narrow the field of choices quickly.

Consider the concept "hacker." The concept hacker is classified as a stereotype. In Figure 4.6, the local network for the focal concept "hacker" is shown. The arrows show the direction of implication. The number on the line indicates the strength of the relationship. Whether the relationship is positive or negative is not indicated. There are many things that the individual can do to be classified as a hacker and many things that a hacker will do. However, there is greater agreement on when an individual is a hacker than on what a hacker will do. For example, all students agree that someone who is interesting, sits in the lounge, and tells stories is a hacker, but not all students agree that hackers are interesting. In other words, among these students, being interesting is a sufficient but not a necessary condition for being a hacker. Consensus about whether a candidate is a hacker may be quickly achieved, but whether that translates into a good

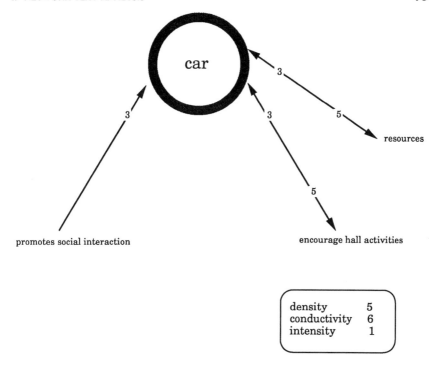

FIG. 4.5. Local network for the concept "car."

tutor candidate is ambiguous. Students in the living group may recognize only the agreement that the candidate is a hacker and so presume that there is agreement about the candidate as tutor, thus generating a false sense of consensus.

Consider the concept "gnerd." Gnerd is also classified as a stereotype; however, relative to hacker it is much closer to being a symbol. In Figure 4.7, the local network for the focal concept "gnerd" is shown. The arrows show the direction of implication. The number on the line indicates the strength of the relationship. Whether the relationship is positive or negative is not indicated. The concept "gnerd" almost serves as a symbol for this community as it has high density, conductivity, and intensity. Individuals labeled as gnerds play highly specialized social roles.

Labeling someone as a gnerd can have a particularly powerful negative effect on their chances of being a tutor, as "gnerd" is linked to two other stereotypes, "hacker" and "jerk." The negative link to hacker means that if the candidate is a gnerd then he or she is not a hacker. Gnerds are also considered jerks by some students. Thus, if a candidate is labeled as a gnerd, there can be strong ripples throughout individuals' cognitive models; however, these ripples have great variance across the community. "Hacker" produces similar ripples, but there is less variance in the ripples that are

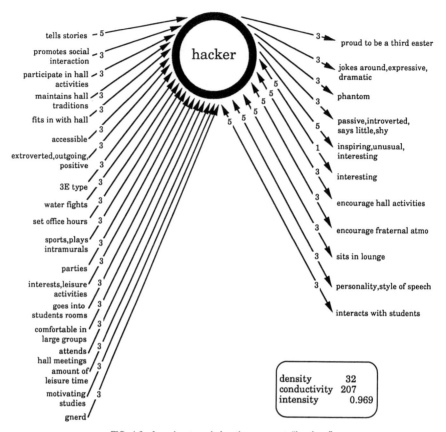

FIG. 4.6. Local network for the concept "hacker."

produced because the extended network for "hacker" is greater than that for "gnerd" for the community at large. In particular, "hacker" has higher extended imageability (18) than does "gnerd" (2). In consequence, presumptions of consensus by students when they label a candidate as a gnerd may be wrong, but similar presumptions based on labeling a candidate as a hacker are more likely to be correct. Stereotypes have great communicative power, but their power in affecting the decision-making process may be more a function of their extended position than their local position in the structure of language.

Figure 4.8 shows the conceptual network representing the consensus as to what was wanted in a tutor. No arrows are shown as all relationships are bidirectional. Whether the relationship is positive or negative is indicated by a solid or dashed line. The type for each concept is marked. This map is based on the intersection of all of the students' maps at the end of the tutor selection period. Each concept and all relationships shown were used by every student

FIG. 4.7. Local network for the concept "gnerd."

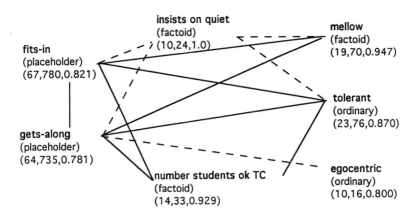

FIG. 4.8. Shared conceptual network for tutor.

in describing what they wanted in a tutor (Carley, 1984, 1986a). Each concept is annotated with information on its position in the typology and the local values for density, conductivity, and intensity. Two of the central concepts, "fits in" and "gets along," are place-holders. Although they have complex meanings, the meaning can not be agreed upon. The students can use these words with assurance that others will agree with them that the candidate should get along or fit in, without agreeing as to what this means. There are, however, three factoids that all students agree help to define what it means to fit in or get along: insisting on quietness, being mellow, and being "ok" from the perspective of many students. These factoids constrain the definition of the place-holders and provide the students with a common set of questions they can use to interrogate candidates, such that all students will agree on the meaning of the answers to those questions.

It is interesting to note that three of the four concepts specified by "gnerd" are major determinants of whether or not someone is chosen as a tutor due to their high levels of evokability. These concepts are "personality," "friendly, gets along," and "interacts with students." These three concepts are specified negatively by the concept "gnerd." Consequently, if a candidate is referred to as a gnerd then he or she is inferred not to have these traits and so does not meet the requirements for being a tutor.

## CONCLUSION

A procedure that allows the researcher to begin to relate the nature of language to action has been explored. A model of language was proposed. According to this model, language is a chronicle of social life formed through a lossy-integration process as knowledge is articulated during interactions. Under this model the concept in isolation is meaningless; hence, the smallest unit of meaning is the statement (i.e., two concepts and the relationship between them) or sentence. Representing language as a series of statements makes it possible to discover regularities in concepts' positions in conceptual networks. By using a set of simple dimensions it is possible to depict talk in a society or individual. Such an analysis can point to the communicative power of concepts. Simple analyses show that most concepts are ordinary (i.e., low on all dimensions). Those concepts that stand out on at least one dimension may have particular communicative significance; that is, they may engender consensus or miscommunication. The end result of the analyses is a taxonomy of concept usage, based on structural relationships, that describes the relationship of roles to stereotypes, historical prototypes, and so on.

From a methodological point of view, the argument is straightforward. Texts can be coded as conceptual networks. These networks can, depending on the coding scheme, represent mental models. Coding texts as mental models focuses the researcher on the analysis of meaning. Coding texts as networks allows the researcher to evaluate the texts in terms of the positional properties of the concepts. Examining concept positions focuses the researcher on the communicative power of the concepts. By analyzing language in terms of the positional properties of concepts collected relative to a particular social task, insight might be gained into aspects of the task that have to do with the evolution of social knowledge. The collection of a task-specific language and the subsequent analysis of it using connective and positional properties may also provide insight into the type of concepts used by the subjects to promote and maintain consensus and to communicate effectively.

This research illustrates an approach to studying the relationship between language and society. The methodology, although exploratory, is completely general. Because this work is exploratory, the ideas presented should be tested on other data sets. For example, one might test whether concepts' structural characteristics (i.e., their score on the various properties) are not fixed but dependent on the sociocultural environment and the task being performed.

We see some evidence for this hypothesis in the MIT study. Consider the set of concepts in the MIT data set that are referred to as stereotypes—"hacker," "gnerd," "phantom," and "expert." If all the language for the United States had been amassed, the structural properties of these concepts might change; for example, the concept "phantom" probably would not stand out as a stereotype. Along with this change in structural property comes a corresponding change in meaning. For example, for the United States as a whole, the concept "phantom" might have the dominant meaning "ghost"—that connection might be agreed to by nearly everyone. For Third Easters, in contrast, the dominant meaning is "someone who is never seen out in the hallway."

Another extension from this research would be to determine, for a specific task, whether or not the differences between the structure of an individual's language and the structure of the social language can be used to predict task-related behavior. An additional extension would be to determine whether there is a taxonomy for individuals' language that is similar to the general taxonomy located herein. Another extension would be to explore the evolution of concepts along the dimensions suggested. Palmquist, Carley, and Dale (this volume) show an evolution from the vague to the detailed. In the MIT study (Carley, 1986a, 1986b), there was an evolution from the general to the historically particular. See Kaufer and Carley (1993a) for further discussion of the evolution of meaning.

Language as social chronicle implicitly contains the socially accepted meaning or definitions of the various concepts in the social vocabulary.

Social meaning for a particular concept has been identified with various network measures—richness, imageability, and density. Which particular operationalization is the best is open to debate. However, the proposed model of language may provide a basis for a social theory of meaning. By defining meaning as the definition of a concept or as the network generated when a concept is used, then it follows that meaning is a constructed phenomenon. Another consequence is that the individual's meaning is different from the social or average meaning. All such meanings change over time. Therefore, meaning has a social reality external to any one individual; there may not be a single individual in the unit who ascribes to that definition in total. Coding texts as conceptual networks, and then analyzing these networks using the dimensions proposed herein, helps the researcher to examine the constructed nature of meaning, to determine the basis for individual and social differences in meaning, and to examine the relationship between concept usage and action.

# APPLICATIONS

# 5

# PERCEPTIONS OF SOCIAL CHANGE: 100 YEARS OF FRONT-PAGE CONTENT IN *THE NEW YORK TIMES* AND *THE LOS ANGELES TIMES*

Wayne A. Danielson
Dominic L. Lasorsa
University of Texas, Austin

This chapter illustrates a thematic content analysis in which theme prevalence is examined over time—in this case, during 100 years of front page news in *The New York Times* and *The Los Angeles Times*. The analysis reveals some major social and political changes in American society. These are trends that might go unnoticed over short time spans but that are clearly observable when a longer period is studied. Specific themes addressed include the rise and fall of Communism as a social threat; the perception of change in American society; the increasing importance of the executive branch of government; the ascendance of experts and professionals in American society; the rise of quantification in the social perception of reality; the general decline of the individual and the rise of the group; and the change from agriculture to manufacturing and information as the economic base of society. The chapter attempts to summarize and integrate the findings theoretically, and the predictive value of content analysis as an indicator of social change is assessed.

This paper has deep roots. In many ways it relates most strongly to the research of Lasswell, Lerner, and de Sola Pool (1952) undertaken at Stanford University in the early 1950s. The Lasswell group was then immersed in one of the first comprehensive and integrated series of content studies of mass communication. They were using a technique of quantitative semantics that they labeled content analysis.

Lasswell and his colleagues saw human beings as living mainly in a symbolic environment. Our physical environment as humans is basic, of course, but the environment that counts the most to us is the environment of words and images, the environment of meanings that surround us from our earliest moments of existence. Lasswell and his associates believed that these symbols, although they can be frozen and studied in the short term, are most meaningful if studied over long time periods so that trends or changes can be observed. Lasswell and his colleagues (1952) were interested in creating "models of symbolic behavior which will enable us to formulate and validate propositions about the mechanisms underlying the flow of symbols" (p. 78). They developed content analysis to study this flow of symbols.

> When it is desired to survey politically significant communication for any historical period on a global scale, the most practicable method is that of counting the occurrence of key symbols and cliches. Only in this way can the overwhelming mass of material be reliably and briefly summarized. By charting the distributions in space and time, it is possible to show the principal contours of . . . political history. (Lasswell et al., 1952, p. 16)

Lasswell, Lerner, and de Sola Pool made a concerted effort to map symbolic environments and to study changes in these environments. As director of research for the Hoover Institute at Stanford, Lasswell oversaw a series of studies under the auspices of a major research program entitled the *Revolution and the Development of International Relations* (or RADIR) project. The methods they used to study the flow of symbols are not unlike those many researchers use today: They sampled text over time. They established the reliability and validity of their coding techniques. They counted the occurrence of key symbols in political documents and in the press. They counted what they called themes (i.e., symbolic condensations of textual units). They applied statistical techniques to describe their findings.

Lasswell and his RADIR associates came to believe that newspapers were an especially apt source of data about the symbolic environment of most people.

> Newspapers appear regularly and frequently, in uniform formats. Also, they have a more or less explicit point of view. The press is mainly an information medium rather than an entertainment medium; and the most significant category on which the press regularly presents news and views is the political, including the ideological. As compared with such verbal flows as after-dinner speeches, golf-club stories, psychiatric interviews—all of which provide data symbols of great value—the press is both accessible and rich in the vocabulary of political ideology current among the elite of any given time. For these reasons the RADIR symbol studies concentrated on the press. (Lasswell et al., 1952, p. 17)

Noting that "politically significant symbols are usually concentrated in the front page or editorial page," Lasswell (1942, p. 14) suggested that analysts studying such symbols might limit their attention to such pages, depending on their particular objectives.

Finally, Lasswell noted that the coder who describes a given symbol needs to consider what amount of context is necessary for a symbol to be properly understood, and it is important to note that bigger is not necessarily better. Meaningful symbols often are made up of a single word or a simple phrase consisting of two or three words. An idea, which often is made up merely of the connection between two or more symbols, most often is embodied in a single sentence. Lasswell (1942) recognized that a map of the symbolic environment requires a judicious sampling of symbols, and he realized that one normally should need no more context than a sentence to understand the meaning of its words. "In general," he noted, "the analyst is directed to limit his attention to the sentence, coding it separately without reference to preceding or succeeding sentences" (p. 18). It should be kept in mind that Lasswell was suggesting criteria for the study of a prominent and enduring symbolic environment—the front page of the daily newspaper.

Although some other content analyses may require larger (or smaller) contexts to maintain what Weber (1990) called semantic coherence, one should consider carefully the costs and benefits associated with this important choice. Choosing a smaller context than necessary is likely to result in symbols improperly coded because of ambiguity or other semantic problems. The solution, however, is often not to err in the other direction. Although casting a larger semantic net may help the coder do a better job of representing the meaning of symbols, choosing a larger context than necessary is likely to result in cuts being made elsewhere in the study, such as in the size of the sample or in the complexity of the coding scheme. These tradeoffs should be considered carefully before a decision is made regarding the size of the context needed to code symbols accurately.

Restricting their context to the single sentence, Lasswell's researchers were able to analyze large corpora of texts to study an array of interesting topics from xenophobia in five major countries over the years 1890 to 1950 (Pool, 1951) to appeals to the masses in *The New York Times* from 1900 to 1949 (Pool, 1952). The work was difficult and was done almost entirely by hand. Only at the end of their complex and meticulous operations were the symbols transformed into numerical data on punched cards that could be run through a counter-sorter. Reading the Lasswell group's work today, one cannot help but be impressed not only by what they invented but by the audacity and energy with which they approached their task. To test even a simple hypothesis often took weeks or even months of labor. In one study 105,004 symbols were examined. As Lasswell, Lerner, and de Sola Pool (1952) noted, "It took over a year to analyze the data" (p. 53) and, "Without machine tabulation, analysis would have been impossible" (p. 63).

A decade after the Stanford group described their method for analyzing symbolic environments, a group of scholars at Harvard University began using the newly invented computer not just in the latter, statistical analysis stages of the process but in earlier coding stages as well. These scholars were able to employ computers to analyze linguistic information found in texts. Thus, the symbols themselves, as electronically coded, had become data, and content analysts found that throughout the entire content analysis process they could enlist the aid of a new, fast, and tireless coder that was perfectly reliable (Stone, Dunphy, Smith, & Ogilvie, 1966).

Since the pioneering work at Harvard, further developments in computer science and their consequent application in computer programs have helped automate the text analysis process to such an extent that today it is not just possible but practical to analyze massive texts. This chapter presents findings from five unpublished studies. The findings in each study were generated using GENCA, a computer software package written by Danielson (1988) that searches electronically stored text files for the occurrence of words and phrases contained in online dictionaries (see Popping, this volume, for availability). These dictionaries are similar in construction to those made by Lasswell, Lerner, and de Sola Pool in the 1950s. The results obtained are similar as well, as are the forms of statistical analysis and display. What is different is that the studies that took the Stanford group months to perform can now be completed in days. An error that might have meant weeks or even months of reanalysis can now be easily corrected and rectified in a retabulation that takes only hours or even minutes.

The studies reported in this chapter examine prominent and long-term flows of symbols in an attempt to document a century of social changes in the United States. By sampling the symbolic environment judiciously, the researchers in these studies hoped to discover particular patterns of change. The front pages of two prestige American newspapers, *The New York Times* and *The Los Angeles Times*, were examined over 100 years. These papers were selected for their size, longevity, and influence. *The New York Times* was founded in 1851, and *The Los Angeles Times* was founded in 1882. By the 1980s, the daily circulations of both papers surpassed 1 million, and the papers were highly regarded as newspapers of record in the United States.

A computer sampling program was used to sample text in the two papers for the period 1890 to 1989. Specifically, the program selected 10 days at random per year and 10 sentences at random from the front page of each of these days' edition of each paper. Sentences were typed into the computer by hand. Thus the data are from a stratified multi-stage cluster sample of 300 sentences per decade per newspaper, or 3,000 sentences for each paper, 6,000 sentences in all. With sentences averaging 25 words in length, the text includes about 150,000 words.

## RESULTS

By plotting the occurrence of the words *Communist, Communists,* and *Communism,* over the last 100 years, one gets a picture of the rise and fall of attention to Communism in the symbolic environment of the United States as reflected on the front pages of two leading U.S. newspapers. As Figure 5.1 shows, the symbolic flow of these terms rises and falls across the decades. The peak occurs in the 1950s, a time of great concern in the United States over domestic and international Communism. Notice how interest ebbs toward the end of the century, however. Even during the Vietnam War, the symbolic presence of Communism on the front pages was on the decline. Communism as a strong symbolic factor was already dying at a time when some American politicians were attempting to arouse concerns about a domino effect in Southeast Asia.

For those readers who lived through significant parts of the Communist era, the graph probably has a kind of face validity. Many will look at it and say, "Yes, that's the way it was" or "That's the way I remember it." The similarity of symbol flows in sentences taken on different dates in two geographically separated newspapers also argues for the validity of the technique. Other interpretations are possible, of course, but the close tracking of symbol frequencies in the two newspapers supports the notion that both were observing and reporting the same social phenomenon.

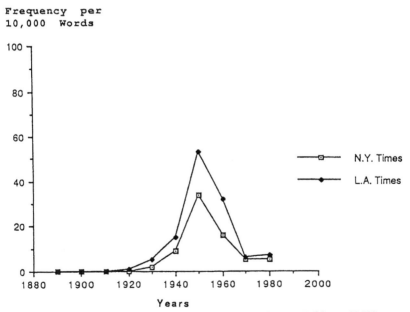

FIG. 5.1. Frequency of the words *Communism* or *Communist(s)* per 10,000 words.

Figure 5.2 deals with attention given in the newspapers to terms related to agriculture. In addition to showing the gradual decline in the frequency of agricultural terms in *The New York Times* and *The Los Angeles Times*, the graph also shows national figures for the percentage of the work force engaged in agriculture. The overall tracking of the external occupational measure with the symbolic measure offers additional evidence that symbol flows in the press can and do index some of the social changes taking place in U.S. society over broad stretches of time. Both symbolically and in fact, the United States in the time period studied was changing from an agricultural society to an industrial and information-based society.

These initial attempts to assess the validity of our text analysis method were encouraging. However, our studies turn toward symbolic representations of social change that cannot be checked so directly from memory or from government statistics.

Figure 5.3 tracks an interesting phenomenon involving the disappearance of people from the front page. This trend was first noted by White (1989) in her study of male and female references in *The New York Times* and *The Los Angeles Times*. White wanted to document the well-established notion that more men than women appear in the news, and she wanted to see whether references to women were on the increase in recent decades. Although the expected dominance of male references appeared as expected, the predicted gradual increase in female references did not seem to occur. Instead, both male and female references appeared to decline with the passage of time. Ghanem (1990) repeated the White study with a somewhat more inclusive

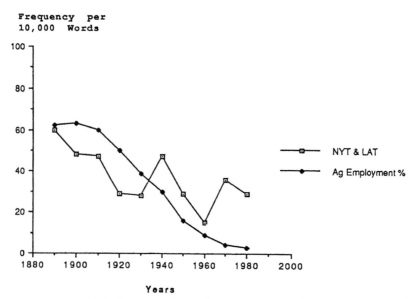

FIG. 5.2. Frequency of agricultural words per 10,000 words.

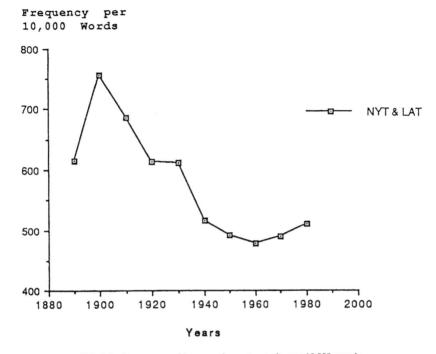

FIG. 5.3. Frequency of human element words per 10,000 words.

dictionary of what she called "human element" terms. The symbols in this dictionary referred both to men and women and to various relational words such as *husband, wife, son,* and *daughter-in-law.* Confirming White's findings, she found that such terms declined both in *The New York Times* and in *The Los Angeles Times* over most of the decades studied.

The disappearance of references to individuals from the flow of front-page symbols may be partly due to a growing tendency of the media to observe society not from the point of view of single persons but from the point of view of groups or "publics" or "masses" or other collective entities such as "consumers" or "viewers" or "voters." "Don't treat me as a statistic," we often hear people saying, but that may be precisely what is happening in front page depictions of American society. Ghanem (1990) took the notion of depersonalization a step further. She hypothesized that the decline in references to people as individuals over time would be paralleled by an increase in references to numbers generally. As Figure 5.4 shows, her hypothesis is supported. The frequency of occurrence of what she called "quantification words" increases as a function of time both in *The New York Times* and in *The Los Angeles Times.* Do the contrasting patterns shown in Figures 5.3 and 5.4 reflect a social world in which people as individuals are becoming less important and numbers more important?

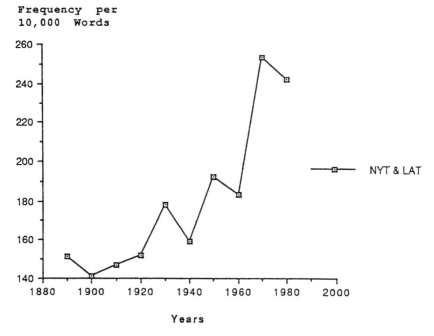

FIG. 5.4. Frequency of quantification words per 10,000 words.

Although the definitive answer to that question remains to be discovered, Figure 5.5 seems to show that the people who are referred to on the front pages of the two newspapers are increasingly people of power and influence. Figure 5.5 shows an increase in the use of terms that refer to experts and professionals, such as accountants and lawyers, nurses and doctors. Figure 5.6 shows an increase in the use of references to officials, such as elected office holders and government appointees. In a published analysis of our data set, Barker-Plummer (1988) found an almost linear increase over 100 years in verbs of attribution, such as *said* (by far the most common), *stated,* and *reported.* She argued that this corresponded to an increasing tendency of newspapers to rely for news on officials, particularly government officials, and to quote them as to the meaning of what was happening.

Closely related to the increase of references to experts and professionals is an increase, shown in Figure 5.7, in references to the president and the presidency over the century. In similar studies, O'Donnell (1989) found an increase in regulatory terms related to the federal administrative bureau-cracy, and Willats (1990) found an increase in terms related to the national government in general, whereas terms related to local government remained stationary or declined slightly. The sociopolitical world portrayed symboli-cally in all these studies is one in which attention increasingly seems to center

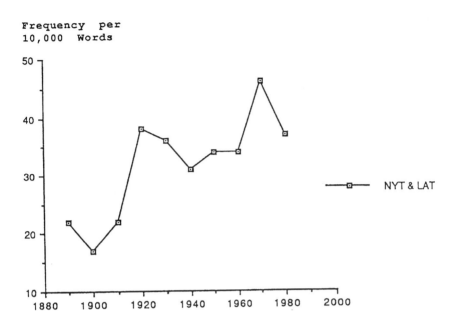

FIG. 5.5. Frequency of expert or professional words per 10,000 words.

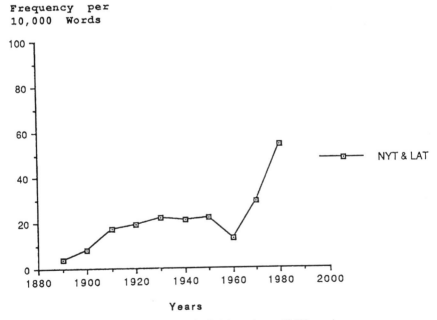

FIG. 5.6. Frequency of official words per 10,000 words.

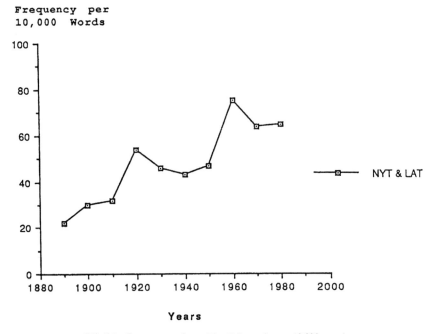

FIG. 5.7.  Frequency of presidential words per 10,000 words.

on central government, particularly the administrative branch, and more particularly on the occupant of a distant, almost mythical White House. Depictions of practical, day-to-day political activities on the local level are increasingly rare.

Johnson (1989) studied the perception of change itself. Figure 5.8 depicts the relative frequency over time of words such as *new*, *different*, and *innovative*. The figure shows change words are on the increase in both newspapers. Thus, the common perception that we live in a "sped-up" world is supported in the symbolic world of the press. The comforting, stable world of the past is gone. Increasingly, at least on the front pages of the two prestigious papers studied, we can expect the unexpected.

Finally, Figure 5.9 shows changes in the two papers regarding the distribution of words and phrases referring to religion and religious rituals. These terms include words such as *Christmas, funeral, marriage,* and *synagogue.* As the figure shows, a steady decline in such references has occurred over the century. The world depicted on the front pages is one increasingly devoid of people, places, and things religious. Rites, feasts, and other public displays once held to be sacred and central to the focus of the community have declined steadily, some transformed into secular rituals, others all but disappearing from the symbolic environment.

Frequency per
10,000 Words

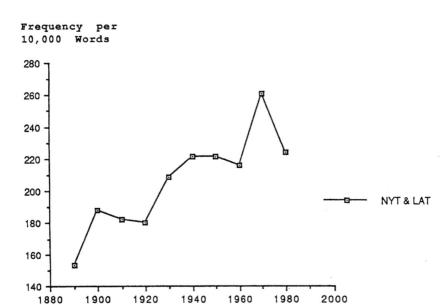

FIG. 5.8.  Frequency of change words per 10,000 words.

Frequency per
10,000 Words

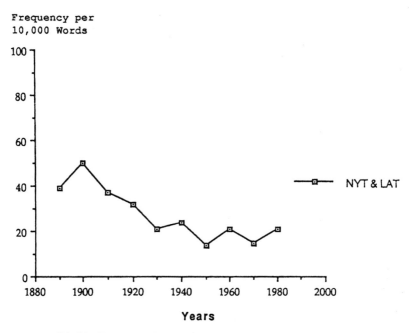

FIG. 5.9.  Frequency of religious or ritual words per 10,000 words.

## DISCUSSION AND CONCLUSIONS

As Lasswell, Lerner, and de Sola Pool would have expected, the flow of symbols through time does seem to reflect real social change. The flow of front-page symbols depicts a decrease in emphasis on the individual and an increase in emphasis on the group. It shows an increasing reliance on numbers to describe social reality. It shows power shifts from local to central government, particularly to the chief executive and to the regulatory bureaucracy. It increasingly relies on experts and officials (often anonymous) to tell us what is happening. It sometimes seems, indeed, that nothing happens until someone in authority says that it does. It depicts a world in which change, often bewildering change, has become a permanent feature. Finally, it depicts a world in which deeply held values, such as those associated with religious beliefs, are on the decline. It suggests a world, in short, that seems to be moving from what Toennies (1988) called *Gemeinschaft* (i.e., a community of persons closely knit by strong sentiments based on kinship and spirit) to *Gesellschaft* (i.e., a secular society loosely bound by impersonal interactions based on formal contracts and social functions).

The *Gemeinschaft–Gesellschaft* formulation is theoretically rich, and it has provided one of the most enduring interpretations of the direction and character of social change in the modern world. If our symbolic studies track, as we believe they do, some of the major social changes of the last century, Toennies' century-old theory seems to us to provide one of the most descriptive and integrative interpretations of the data we have observed.

Thus far we have assumed that news appearing on the front pages of two major U.S. newspapers reflects an important aspect of the symbolic environment of Americans living at the time of their publication and that the symbols used may serve to measure the substance of public attention. For most of the 19th and 20th centuries, the daily newspaper was the premier method for distributing news, but in the last few years that has gradually changed. Today, television is a mass communication channel with even greater penetration and influence. If Toennies were alive now, he probably would have recognized television, too, as providing an important representation of the symbolic environment. Were we not interested here in the U.S. symbolic environment for many years before the introduction of television, that medium might have been another excellent source of information about the flow of symbols in society.

It is also important to note that even if we accept the daily newspaper as a convenient repository of socially relevant symbols, newspapers themselves have changed over the last 100 years. Some changes in front-page news, therefore, may not be due to events directly related to the symbolic environment. For example, newspapers have moved toward a more sectionalized or departmentalized approach to the news. Thus, medical or science sections are popular today, and a story that might have appeared on the front page in times past today appears in sections such as these. For example, an observed decline in front-page medical terms may not represent a decline in public attention to medicine; it may in fact mean the opposite: Medical news is now so important that it gets its own section.

Similarly, the decline in religious ritual words in *The New York Times* and *The Los Angeles Times* noted in this chapter may be due in part to a more general and subtle change in the attitudes of editors and reporters. Over the years, both papers have become major players in American politics. Occasionally, their owners and employees have seemed to act not as observers of government but almost as if they considered themselves to be part of government. Thus, the difference in reporting about religion may in a way be attributable to papers imitating government and deliberately trying to avoid an undesirable mixing of church and state. As long as we keep such limitations in mind and recognize that some content changes may be due to developments unrelated to public attention, the symbols appearing on the front pages of these newspapers appear to serve us quite well in describing the symbolic environment Americans experienced in given eras.

Many hypotheses remain to be tested. Studies of changes in the key symbols and clichés of other societies would allow patterns of social change to be compared and contrasted around the globe. For example, it might be possible to determine whether the United States has become, as Toennies (1988) predicted nearly a century ago, "the most modern and *Gesellschaft*-like state" (p. 221). In addition, studies of the symbolic environment using contemporary versions of Lasswell's venerable method may give us additional insights into such grand sociological theories as those of Marx, Durkheim, Parsons, and their intellectual descendants.

With the completion so far of more than a dozen computer-aided textual studies of our data set, we are encouraged to think that we may be coming ever closer to the goal envisaged by Lasswell and his colleagues (1952) of creating "models of symbolic behavior which will enable us to formulate and validate propositions about the mechanisms underlying the flow of symbols" (p. 78). As more general and user-friendly content analysis programs emerge and as more texts are made available online, researchers undoubtedly will continue to find ingenious and ambitious uses for such programs and data. The studies reported in this chapter have tried to show that, just as scientific tools have helped us describe and explain the physical world we inhabit, they can now as well help us describe and explain the symbolic world in which we live.

# 6

# THE UNOBTRUSIVE MEASUREMENT OF PSYCHOLOGICAL STATES AND TRAITS

Louis A. Gottschalk
University of California, Irvine

This chapter describes a pragmatic measurement method of content analysis of verbal communications based on a combination of behavioral and conditioning, psychoanalytic, and linguistic findings. It derives its measures from the grammatical clause and the agent and recipient of the meaning of the clause's verb. To provide comparisons within and across individuals, scores obtained by this method are expressed in terms of a content-derived score per 100 words. Using this method, a group of scales have been developed on which intensive reliability and construct validity research have been done and for which there are normative scores for adults and children when the verbal samples are elicited by standardized and purposely ambiguous instructions. These scales include the Anxiety scale, Hostility Outward scale, Hostility Inward scale, Ambivalent Hostility scale, Social Alienation–Personal Disorganization scale, Cognitive Impairment scale, Depression scale, and Hope scale. Artificial intelligence software, written in LISP, has been developed and is capable of reliably coding these scales. Originating in the late 1950s, these scales have been applied to numerous psychosocial and biomedical problems. The method can accommodate any new content-derived dimension as long as it can be accurately defined and reliably coded.

The aim of this chapter is to familiarize readers with the origins and development of a method of measurement of psychological dimensions in children and adults through the analysis of the content and form of their verbal behavior. The method evolved originally in the late 1950s as a research tool and instrument (Gleser, Gottschalk, & Springer, 1961; Gottschalk, 1968; Gottschalk, Cleghorn, Gleser, & Iacono, 1965; Gottschalk & Frank, 1967; Gottschalk, Gleser, Daniels, & Block, 1958; Gottschalk, Gleser, D'Zmura, & Hanenson, 1964; Gottschalk, Gleser, & Springer, 1963; Gottschalk, Gleser, Wylie, & Kaplan, 1965; Gottschalk & Kaplan, 1958; Gottschalk, Kunkel, Wohl, Saenger, & Winget, 1969; Gottschalk, Mayerson, & Gottlieb, 1967; Gottschalk, Stone, Gleser, & Iacono, 1966, 1969; Gottschalk, Springer, & Gleser, 1961; Gottschalk et al., 1960). It has been used in this way for several decades (Gottschalk, 1979; Gottschalk et al., 1991; Gottschalk & Gleser, 1969; Gottschalk, Lolas, & Viney, 1986; Gottschalk, Winget, & Gleser, 1969; Lebovitz & Holland, 1983). Over this period of time, many clinical applications have become apparent and have been demonstrated, but these potential applications have not been broadly utilized. There are two major reasons for this limited application of the method. One reason is that the peer-refereed journals and books written on the research findings involving the method are not widely read by clinicians. The other reason is that using this method of measuring various psychological dimensions through verbal behavior analysis requires learning how to score the typescripts of spoken or written natural language up to level of interscorer reliability of 0.80 (among scorers who have established expertise using the method) to achieve maximal validity in any research enterprise. This latter problem has been resolved through the progressive development of computer-driven artificial intelligence software programs that are capable of scoring these verbal analysis scales with a reliability greater than .80 when computer scores are compared to those of expert human scorers (Gottschalk & Bechtel, 1982, 1989, 1993; Gottschalk, Hausmann, & Brown, 1975).

The procedure described in this article is the fruit of the amalgamation of different, some cognate, scientific disciplines and technical knowledge. Because these sciences and technical fields are, themselves, growing and evolving, one must expect that the methodological offspring of such modern and diverse scientific and technical fields is in a state of change and continuing improvement. I provide here information regarding recently completed or ongoing research involving new content analysis scales based on the content analysis methods. In addition, I report not only on past but also on new studies involving the application of these scales to clinical problems as well as to further construct validation research.

Norms on all scales have been established for adults and children from 5-minute verbal samples. These normative samples were elicited by standard instructions in which the subject was purposely given ambiguous directions to talk about any interesting or dramatic personal life experiences (Gottschalk & Gleser, 1969; Gottschalk, Winget, et al., 1969). Scale norms provide comparison values for verbal samples obtained in nonstandard ways.

## MAJOR INNOVATIVE CONTRIBUTIONS
## OF THE GOTTSCHALK–GLESER METHOD

The Gottschalk and Gleser (1969) method for the content analysis of verbal behavior has many advantages. It can measure any mental or emotional state or trait that can be clearly defined and categorized. It classifies content not simply by virtue of isolated words but also according to word combinations as they appear within clauses in meaningful and syntactical and grammatical relations with one another. It can content analyze the meaning of not only conventional dictionary-derived words, but also user-defined idiomatic and slang expressions that may not appear in ordinary dictionaries. It provides a means by which the frequency of occurrence of any content category can be corrected and stated for the number of words examined, namely, content category per 100 words. This calculation enables comparison of content analysis scores within an individual over time and across individuals. With respect to content analysis scores for affects such as anxiety and hostility, this method provides mathematical transformations of scores that make their frequency distribution parametric rather than skewed and nonparametric and permits the application of parametric statistical procedures for data assessment, if this is desired. Of potential use in clinical and research studies, norms are available for children and adults on all of the content analysis scales to be described here (Gottschalk, 1982; Gottschalk & Gleser, 1969). Cross-cultural studies have been carried out that indicate that most of these content analysis scales (especially the Anxiety and Hostility scales) have cross-cultural validity, as long as the English version of the scales has been accurately translated (Gottschalk & Lolas, 1989). Finally, computerized content analysis of the Anxiety, Social Alienation–Personal Disorganization, Cognitive Impairment, Depression, Hope, and three Hostility scales is now available (Gottschalk, Biener, et al., 1975; Gottschalk & Bechtel, 1982, 1989, 1993; Popping, this volume).[1]

## TOOLS AND PROCEDURES TO ASSESS
## PSYCHOLOGICAL STATES AND TRAITS

There are three behavioral or psychological methods of measuring psychological states or traits: self-report scales, behavioral rating scales, and scales derived from the content analysis of verbal behavior. A brief description and critical review of these methods is appropriate here.

---

[1]For illustrative purposes, the verbal categories associated with the Anxiety scale (Table 6.1), the Hostility Outward scale (Table 6.2), and the Social Alienation–Personal Disorganization scale (Table 6.3) are included in an appendix to this chapter.

## Self-Report Scales

Self-report scales are designed to give the subject an opportunity to describe subjective experiences. Scales derived from such self-reports may assess the magnitude of various psychological dimensions from direct reports of the occurrence of such mental events. The presence of psychological dimensions may be inferred indirectly from self-reports about somatic dysfunctions, general performance deficits, or more specific social or cognitive malfunctions.

The advantages of self-report scales are that they are easy to administer and their reliability is difficult to question, for no one except the self can accurately report the self's subjective experience. Moreover, the data derived from them can be readily scored and statistically manipulated. The disadvantages of self-report scales involve primarily their validity. Because the subject is describing personal feelings or behavior, his or her psychological defense mechanisms may obscure the assessment of the subjective state, or more serious psychopathological processes may grossly distort perspectives regarding self-appraisal. The subject's self-assessment may also be influenced by a desire to please the examiner or to appear socially desirable. Finally, the invalid assumption may be made that everyone is equally psychologically minded and competent to perceive and judge the quality and magnitude of personal mental events.

## Psychiatric Rating Scales

Psychiatric rating scales involve assessments of mental and behavioral dimensions made by a trained observer, usually a psychiatrist, clinical psychologist, psychiatric nurse, or social worker. The rater customarily has had some experience in measuring psychopathological phenomena and, in the better research projects, interrater reliability coefficients at an acceptable level have been obtained.

The advantages of rating scales, in contrast to self-report scales, are that the external observer, using a rating scale to assess a subject's mental processes, gains detachment and objectivity that may be deficient in a person evaluating the self. The disadvantages of rating scale procedures involve potential measurement errors and questionable validity. Rating scale users generally lack long-term familiarity with the individual they are rating and, thus, they may not correctly judge the emotional significance of some of the subject's behavior. The rater is obliged to make inferences regarding the mental states of the subject being observed, using a wide range of semantic, paralanguage, and kinesic cues. External raters, like self-reporters, are not free from systematic distortions. Definite biases regarding clinical interpretations can be introduced by the cultural background and the formal training of the trained rater. Also, different interviewers may evoke different emotional responses from the same subjects.

## Scales Based on the Content Analysis of Verbal Behavior

The psychological measurement method of verbal content analysis uses self-reporting in the form of natural (i.e., unedited) spoken language of the subject elicited by purposely ambiguous instructions requesting a 5-minute report of personal life experiences. Instead of constricting a person's responses to specific items, as is customary with mood and adjective checklists, such instructions aim to probe the immediate psychological reactions of subjects, somewhat similar to a projective test procedure, and to minimize reactions of covering up and guarding. Standardized instructions have been used, also, in order to be able to obtain personal data from individuals in a standard context so that the influence of demographic factors and personality variables can be explored and examined while holding relatively constant the influence of such variables as the instructions for eliciting the speech, the characteristics of the interviewer, the context, and the situation. Considerable data have been obtained on the possible effects of these noninterviewee variables (Gottschalk & Gleser, 1969). The verbal content analysis method uses the psychiatric rating scale procedure (or external observer) in the form of having built-in systematic and objective criteria for inferring and assessing the magnitude of various psychological states and traits. The theoretical foundation of the Gottschalk–Gleser content analysis method of measurement rests on a systematic combination of linguistic, behavioral conditioning, and psychodynamic perspectives. The method embodies the strengths of both the self-report and rating scale methods while minimizing the measurement errors inherent in both.

## RELIABILITY AND VALIDITY STUDIES USING THE GOTTSCHALK–GLESER METHOD

Details concerning the original validation studies on the Gottschalk–Gleser Anxiety and Hostility scales are systematically covered by Gottschalk and Gleser (1969). Construct validation research on the Anxiety scale is based on psychological, psychophysiological, psychopharmacological, and psychobiochemical criterion measures (Gottschalk & Gleser, 1969). For the Gottschalk–Gleser Hostility scales, the validation research is reviewed under the same headings (Gottschalk & Gleser, 1969).

For the Gottschalk–Gleser Social Alienation–Personal Disorganization scale, validation studies were organized differently from those involving the Gottschalk–Gleser Content Analysis scales for anxiety and hostility. Unlike the Gottschalk–Gleser affect scales, the Social Alienation–Personal Disorganization scale aimed to measure a psychological state that fluctuates relatively slowly and that is manifested to a considerable extent in observable behavioral variations. The empirical research was organized according to two major types: longitudinal studies measuring intraindividual variation over time in degree of social alienation–personal disorganization, and cross-sectional studies measuring interindividual differences in degree of social alienation–personal disorganization (Gottschalk & Gleser, 1969).

The Cognitive Impairment scale was developed empirically from a comparative study of verbal samples form various populations, ranging from normal individuals, medically ill patients, psychiatric outpatients, acute and chronic patients (Gottschalk & Gleser, 1964). From this and other studies (Gottschalk & Gleser, 1969), the content categories for social alienation–personal disorganization, a dimension characterizing the schizophrenic syndrome, were selected. In this comparative study, it was observed that although brain-damaged individuals obtained a score distribution on the total scale that was very similar to that of chronic schizophrenics, there were some verbal categories on which the two diagnostic classifications differed considerably. Subsequent research aimed to maximize the discriminatory capacity of the initial Cognitive Impairment scale verbal category items and their associated weights so that this scale would clearly distinguish patients with various degrees of cognitive and intellectual deficiencies from patients without these kinds of problems. Other research aimed to determine mean cognitive impairment scores found in mentally and physically healthy individuals (Gottschalk, 1976, 1984; Gottschalk & Gleser, 1969) and cognitive impairment scores one, two, or more standard deviations above these norms (Gottschalk, 1982, 1994; Gottschalk, Eckardt, Pautler, Wolf, & Terman, 1983).

Regarding other Gottschalk–Gleser content analysis scales, initial validation studies were reported for the Human Relations and Health–Sickness scales (Gottschalk & Gleser, 1969). New construct validation studies involving these and other content analysis scales can be found in Gottschalk (1979) and Gottschalk et al. (1986). Furthermore, in the process of the development of new content analysis scales, the Hope scale (Gottschalk, 1974) and the Depression scale (Gottschalk & Hoigaard-Martin, 1986), detailed reports of construct validation research are available elsewhere.


## RELIABILITY AND VALIDITY STUDIES
## IN NON-ENGLISH LANGUAGES

In 1980, Gert Schofer edited a book reviewing the theory and technique of the Gottschalk–Gleser method of measuring anxiety and hostility from the content analysis of speech. Then Koch and Schofer (1986) edited a collection of

29 separate reports of research in the German language testing the reliability and validity of the Gottschalk–Gleser Anxiety and Hostility scales. Other German researchers have applied the Gottschalk–Gleser content analysis scales to research in group psychotherapy (Tschuschke & MacKenzie, 1989; Volk & Tschuschke, 1982).

Lolas has been instrumental in translating and testing the Gottschalk–Gleser content analysis scales in the Spanish language (Gottschalk & Lolas, 1987, 1989; Gottschalk, Winget, Gleser, & Lolas, 1984; Lolas & von Rad, 1977). He and his co-workers have published many articles in Spanish language professional journals involving the use of the Gottschalk–Gleser content analysis scales (Gottschalk & Lolas, 1987). These journal articles support the construct validity of these content analysis scales.

The Gottschalk–Gleser method of content analysis has been used in other languages. For example, in an Italian study Pontalti and colleagues (1981) used the Gottschalk Social Alienation–Personal Disorganization scale to study the quality of the marital relationship in Italian couples. The same scale has been used in group psychotherapy research with a small sample of Yugoslavian-speaking patients (Morovic, Skocic, Skocic, & Buranji, 1990). D'Haenen and coworkers (1985) found that the Gottschalk–Gleser Affect scales did not distinguish between 32 French-speaking patients composed of a group with primary and another group with secondary depressive disorders.

## PSYCHOSOCIAL RESEARCH

Considerable psychosocial research has been carried out using this method. Only a brief overview is given here on such studies. Earlier studies examined the effects on the content of speech of the personality or sex of the interviewer (Gottschalk & Gleser, 1969) and effects on verbal content of the age of the subject (Gleser, Winget, & Seligman, 1979; Gottschalk, 1976, 1982; Gottschalk & Gleser, 1969). Even when interviewers use identical instructions to elicit speech, there may be significant interviewer effects. Moreover, children and adults give somewhat different content in response to identical methods of eliciting speech. For example, young children show higher cognitive impairment scores than aging adults, who have higher death anxiety scores than younger adults. Later studies examined the effects of ethnic, cultural, or racial factors (Gottschalk & Lolas, 1989; Gottschalk & Rey, 1990; Koch & Schofer, 1986; Uliana, 1979; Viney & Manton, 1975; Viney & Wang, 1987). In response to a standardized method of eliciting verbal samples, there are surprisingly minimal, if any, differences in affect scores obtained from normative North American, German, and Australian adults (Koch & Schofer, 1986; Viney & Manton, 1975).

This method has been widely applied to psychotherapy research (Gottschalk, 1987; Gottschalk, Fronczek, & Abel, 1993; Gottschalk, Mayerson, et al.,

1967; Kepecs, 1979; Lolas, Kordy, & von Rad, 1979; Lolas, Mergenthaler, & von Rad, 1982; Winget, Seligman, Rauh, & Gleser, 1979), not only in its psychodynamics, process, and assessment of outcome but also in the prediction of outcome. It has been applied to the prediction of relapse of schizophrenics (Gottschalk et al., 1988; Lebell, Marder, Mintz, & Mintz, 1990), effect of sensory overload on psychological state (Gottschalk, Haer, & Bates, 1972), measurement of depression (Gottschalk & Hoigaard-Martin, 1986), measurement of control and self-control (Shapiro & Bates, 1990), narcissism (Russell, 1990), and quality of life (Gottschalk & Lolas, 1992).

## BIOMEDICAL RESEARCH

The Gottschalk–Gleser content analysis scales have been widely used in many different kinds of biomedical research. It has been applied to the assessment of the relationship between emotions and their various physiological concomitants, such as electroencephalographic patterns (Gottschalk, 1955; Luborsky et al., 1975), skin temperature (Gottschalk et al., 1961; Gottlieb, Gleser, & Gottschalk, 1967), blood pressure variations (Gottschalk et al., 1964), or the effect of total and half-body irradiation (Gottschalk, Kunkel, et al., 1969) and of sensory overload (Gottschalk et al., 1972). It has been used to investigate the relationships between various biochemical concomitants of emotions, such as plasma lipids (Gottschalk, Cleghorn, et al., 1965; Gottschalk, Stone, et al., 1966) and localized cerebral glucose metabolic rate measured by positron emission tomography, while awake or dreaming (Gottschalk et al., 1991). The method has been heavily used in neuropsychopharmacologic research (Gottschalk et al., 1960; Gottschalk, Gleser, et al., 1965; Gottschalk, Biener, et al., 1975; Gottschalk, 1985). It has also been used to measure cognitive impairment with alcohol abuse, marijuana use, Alzheimer's disease, cerebral trauma, and other conditions (Gottschalk, 1994; Gottschalk et al., 1983).

## SUMMARY AND CONCLUSIONS

The content analysis method developed by Gottschalk and Gleser (1969) involves a pragmatic approach that aims to define the magnitude of the semantic message being conveyed by verbal communications. Based on a combination of behavioral and conditioning, psychoanalytic, and linguistic findings, it derives its measures from the grammatical clause, the smallest complete unit of verbal communication. In its evaluation of the meaning of the message being conveyed, it considers not only the nature of the predicate verb, that is, whether it involves a feeling, thought, or action, but also who is the subject and object, if any, of the verb. The method can be applied to written or spoken verbal communications, and has found applications (with other psychological measures based on content analysis) related to marketing, general business, and medical care as well as in the fields of psychiatry, psychology, sociology, and the humanities (cf. Gottschalk, 1995, for an annotated international bibliography of applications published between 1982 and 1992).

A group of scales measuring psychobiological states and traits have been developed based on the Gottschalk–Gleser content analysis method. To facilitate comparisons of scores within and across individuals, these scales all assess the dimension measured in terms of a score or index per 100 words. Scales that have undergone extensive reliability and validity research include content analysis measures of anxiety (i.e., total anxiety and six subscales), hostility outward (i.e., total, overt, and covert), hostility inward and ambivalent hostility (i.e., hostility directed to the self from external origins), depression (composed of seven subscales), social alienation–personal disorganization, cognitive impairment, and hope. (Normative scores for these scales are available for children and adults, and artificial intelligence software is available for scoring the scales.) The content analysis method introduced in this chapter also lends itself to the development of new scales, so long as the verbal categories constituting the scale can be clearly and reliably recognized and coded.

# APPENDIX

TABLE 6.1
Anxiety Scale

| Weights | Content Categories and Scoring Symbols |
|---|---|
| | A. Death anxiety—references to death, dying, threat of death, or anxiety about death experienced by or occurring to: |
| +3 | 1. Self. |
| +2 | 2. Animate others. |
| +1 | 3. Inanimate objects destroyed. |
| +1 | 4. Denial of death anxiety. |
| | B. Mutilation (castration) anxiety—references to injury, tissue, or physical damage, or anxiety about injury or threat of such experienced by or occurring to: |
| +3 | 1. Self. |
| +2 | 2. Animate others. |
| +1 | 3. Inanimate objects. |
| +1 | 4. Denial. |
| | C. Separation anxiety—references to desertion, abandonment, loneliness, ostracism, loss of support, falling, loss of love or love object, or threat of such experienced by occurring to: |
| +3 | 1. Self. |
| +2 | 2. Animate others. |
| +1 | 3. Inanimate objects. |
| +1 | 4. Denial. |
| | D. Guilt anxiety—references to adverse criticism, abuse, condemnation, moral disapproval, guilt, or threat of such experienced by: |
| +3 | 1. Self. |
| +2 | 2. Animate others. |
| +1 | 3. Denial. |
| | E. Shame anxiety—references to ridicule, inadequacy, shame, embarrassment, humiliation, overexposure of deficiencies or private details, or threat of such experienced by: |
| +3 | 1. Self. |
| +2 | 2. Animate others. |
| +1 | 3. Denial. |
| | F. Diffuse or nonspecific anxiety—references to anxiety or fear without distinguishing type or source of anxiety: |
| +3 | 1. Self. |
| +2 | 2. Animate others. |
| +1 | 3. Denial. |

TABLE 6.2

Hostility Directed Outward Scale: Destructive, Injurious,
Critical Thoughts and Actions Directed to Others

| Weights | Content Categories and Scoring Symbols |
|---------|----------------------------------------|
| | A. Hostility Outward, Overt Thematic Categories |
| +3 | 1a. Self killing, fighting, injuring other individuals, or threatening to do so. |
| +3 | 1b. Self robbing or abandoning other individuals, causing suffering or anguish to others, or threatening to do so. |
| +3 | 1c. Self adversely criticizing, depreciating, blaming, expressing anger, dislike of other human beings. |
| +2 | 2a. Self killing, injuring, or destroying domestic animals, pets, or threatening to do so. |
| +2 | 2b. Self abandoning, robbing domestic animals, pets, or threatening to do so. |
| +2 | 2c. Self criticizing or depreciating others in a vague or mild manner. |
| +2 | 2d. Self depriving or disappointing other human beings. |
| +1 | 3a. Self killing, injuring, destroying, robbing wildlife or flora inanimate objects, or threatening to do so. |
| +1 | 3b. Self adversely criticizing, depreciating, blaming, expressing anger or dislike of subhumans, inanimate objects, places, situations. |
| +1 | 3c. Self using hostile words, cursing, mention of anger or rage without referent. |
| | B. Hostility Outward, Covert Thematic Categories |
| +3 | 1a. Others (human) killing, fighting, injuring other individuals, or threatening to do so. |
| +3 | 1b. Others (human) robbing, abandoning, causing suffering or anguish to other individuals, or threatening to do so. |
| +3 | 1c. Others adversely criticizing, depreciating, blaming, expressing anger, dislike of other human beings. |
| +2 | 2a. Others (human) killing, injuring, or destroying domestic animals, pets, or threatening to do so. |
| +2 | 2b. Others (human) abandoning, robbing, domestic animals, pets, or threatening to do so. |
| +2 | 2c. Others (human) criticizing or depreciating other individuals in a vague or mild manner. |
| +2 | 2d. Others (human) depriving or disappointing other human beings. |
| +2 | 2e. Others (human or domestic animals) dying or killed violently in death-dealing situation or threatened with such. |
| +2 | 2f. Bodies (human or domestic animals) mutilated, depreciated, defiled. |
| +1 | 3a. Wildlife, flora, inanimate objects injured, broken, robbed, destroyed, or threatened with such (with or without mention of agent). |
| +1 | 3b. Others (human) adversely criticizing, depreciating, expressing anger or dislike of subhumans, inanimate objects, places, situations. |
| +1 | 3c. Others angry, cursing without reference to cause or direction of anger. Also instruments of destruction not used threateningly. |
| +1 | 3d. Others (human, domestic animals) injured, robbed, dead, abandoned, or threatened with such from any source including subhuman and inanimate objects, situations (storms, floods, etc.). |
| +1 | 3e. Subhumans killing, fighting, injuring, robbing, destroying each other, or threatening to do so. |
| +1 | 3f. Denial of anger, dislike, hatred, cruelty, and intent to harm. |

TABLE 6.3

Social Alienation and Personal Disorganization (Schizophrenic) Scale

| Weights | Content Categories and Scoring Symbols |
|---|---|
| | I. Interpersonal references (including fauna and flora) |
| |    A. To thoughts, feelings, or reported actions of avoiding, leaving, deserting, spurning, or not being understanding of others. |
| 0 |       1. Self avoiding others. |
| +1 |       2. Others avoid self. |
| |    B. To unfriendly, hostile, destructive thoughts, feelings, or actions. |
| +1 |       1. Self unfriendly to others. |
| $+\frac{1}{2}$ |       2. Others unfriendly to self. |
| |    C. To congenial and constructive thoughts, feelings, or actions. |
| −2 |       1. Others helping, being friendly toward others. |
| −2 |       2. Self helping, being friendly toward others. |
| −2 |       3. Others helping, being friendly toward self. |
| |    D. To others. |
| 0 |       1. Being bad, dangerous, strange, ill, malfunctioning, having low value or worth. |
| −1 |       2. Being intact, satisfied, healthy, well. |
| | II. Intrapersonal references. |
| +2 |    A. To disorientation—references indicating disorientation for time, place, person, or other distortion of reality—past, present, or future (do not score more than one item per clause under this category). |
| |    B. To self. |
| 0 |       1a. Physical illness, malfunctioning (references to illness or symptoms due primarily to cellular or tissue damage). |
| +1 |       1b. Psychological malfunctioning (references to illness or symptoms due primarily to emotions or psychological reactions not secondary to cellular or tissue damage). |
| 0 |       1c. Malfunctioning of indeterminate origin (references to illness or symptoms not definitely attributable either to emotions or cellular damage). |
| −2 |       2. Getting better. |
| −1 |       3a. Intact, satisfied, healthy, well; definite positive affect or valence indicated. |
| −1 |       3b. Intact, satisfied, healthy, well; flat, factual, or neutral attitude expressed. |
| $+\frac{1}{2}$ |       4. Not being prepared or able to produce, perform, act, not knowing, not sure. |
| $+\frac{1}{2}$ |       5. Being controlled, feeling controlled, wanting control, asking for control or permission, being obliged or having to do, think, or experience something. |
| +3 |    C. Denial of feeling, attitudes, or mental state of the self. |
| |    D. To food. |
| 0 |       1. Bad, dangerous, unpleasant or otherwise negative; interferences or delays in eating; too much and wish to have less; too little and wish to have more. |
| 0 |       2. Good or neutral. |

*(Continued)*

TABLE 6.3

*(Continued)*

| Weights | Content Categories and Scoring Symbols |
|---|---|
| | E. To weather. |
| −1 |     1. Bad, dangerous, unpleasant, or otherwise negative (not sunny, not clear, uncomfortable, etc.). |
| −1 |     2. Good, pleasant, or neutral. |
| | F. To sleep. |
| 0 |     1. Bad, dangerous, unpleasant, or otherwise negative, too much, too little. |
| 0 |     2. Good, pleasant or neutral. |
| | III. Disorganization and repetition. |
| |   A. Signs of disorganization. |
| +1 |     1. Remarks or words that are not understandable or are inaudible. |
| 0 |     2. Incomplete sentences, clauses, phrases; blocking. |
| +2 |     3. Obviously erroneous or fallacious remarks or conclusions; illogical or bizarre statements. |
| |   B. Repetition of ideas in sequence. |
| 0 |     1. Words separated only by a word (excluding instances due to grammatical and syntactical convention, where words are repeated, e.g., *as far as, by and by*, and so forth; also excluding instances where such words as *I* and *the* are separated by a word). |
| +1 |     2. Phrases or clauses (separated only by a phrase or a clause). |
| | IV. References to the interviewer. |
| +1 |   A. Questions direct to the interviewer. |
| $+\frac{1}{2}$ |   B. Other references to the interviewer. |
| +1 | V. Religious and biblical references. |

*Note.* The weights in this table are current but differ from those originally described in Gottschalk, Gleser, Daniels, & Block, 1958 (cf. also Gottschalk & Gleser, 1969; Gottschalk, Springer, & Gleser, 1961).

# 7

# LABOR UNREST IN THE ITALIAN SERVICE SECTOR: AN APPLICATION OF SEMANTIC GRAMMARS

Roberto Franzosi
University of Oxford

Semantic grammars provide powerful tools for the collection of narrative data. Semantic grammars organize text according to a fixed linguistic structure (e.g., Subject-Action-Object and respective modifiers). The relational structure of the grammar enables the analysis of text data using existing database technology (namely, relational DBMSs). This chapter illustrates the power of a linguistic approach to content analysis using data on Italian events of labor unrest. Data on 988 individual labor disputes were coded from 3,396 newspaper articles that appeared in an Italian newspaper during the first half of 1986. These data are used to compare peculiarities of labor unrest in the industrial and service sectors. None of these comparisons could have been made using aggregated strike statistics available from government sources.

Consider the following excerpt from a U.S. newspaper article on a service-sector strike within the French transportation industry:

PARIS, Oct. 20 (AP)—Air France canceled about 500 flights today as employees pressed ahead with a strike to protest the plans of the ailing state-run airline to cut jobs and wages. For the second consecutive day, the strike caused havoc at both of Paris's main airports . . . flights of all airlines at Orly Airport were halted at midmorning when hundreds of strikers marched onto the runways . . . Strikers tried to march onto runways at Charles de Gaulle, but were blocked by about 70 police officers. Union officials said scuffles broke out and about 10 protesters were detained. (Strike disrupts airports in France, 1993)

This newspaper account provides rich information on the actors involved (e.g., the strikers, the employer, the police) and the actions performed (e.g., the strikes, the demonstrations, the scuffles with police). These are familiar actors and familiar routines of labor relations. For all their familiarity, however, there are subtle novelties in these routines. New, for instance, are other actors, such as the stranded Air France passengers (i.e., the users of services withheld by the strikers). New is the role of the state, not so much in its law-enforcing role (via the police and the courts, all too present since the early times of industrialization) as in its new role as employer. Indeed, the state is often perhaps the main employer in the service sector (e.g., transportation, health care, education) in industrialized countries.

In official strike statistics—highly aggregated and based on raw counts of numbers of strikes, strikers, and hours lost—the Air France strike would simply end up as an extra tally in published records on numbers of strikes.[1] Lost would be the actors, the actions, and their characteristics. More to the point, lost would be our ability to understand labor conflicts as multiple-actor, multiple-action phenomena (Franzosi, 1995).

The problems with official, government-collected strike data are well known (Shalev, 1978), yet for some one hundred years strike research has almost exclusively been based on these data. On the one hand, the ready availability of official strike data has made it all too easy for scholars to rely on them. On the other hand, collecting richer and more disaggregated data may be very costly or may even provide inadequate data. For instance, the content analysis of narrative accounts of conflict events (e.g., from newspapers or police records) can potentially provide highly disaggregated data in time series form but at high costs and with serious validity problems (Markoff, Shapiro, & Weitman, 1974).

In this chapter I illustrate a linguistic approach to content analysis that applies semantic grammars to avoid some of the pitfalls of analyses based on aggregated event data. Semantic grammars organize text around a basic structure such as Subject–Action–Object and respective modifiers (e.g., time, space, type of actor, outcome, and reason). I used this S-A-O structure as a framework for encoding newspaper data on labor disputes in Italy during the period from January to June, 1986. The chapter begins by high-

---

[1]In most industrialized countries, strike statistics have been available since the second half of the 19th century. These statistics were first collected under the auspices of governments concerned with rising levels of working-class militancy. Typically, these official strike statistics provide information on the number of strikes, strikers, and hours lost. Occasionally (particularly in early times), they provide strike counts according to the reason given for striking (e.g., against layoffs, wage increases), level of negotiation (e.g., local, national), or presence of various organizations or of violence. As the number of strikes increased over time and as the strike became more and more institutionalized within the sociopolitical framework of capitalist societies (with strikes losing their original threat), much of the original detail of early statistics was lost. Modern strike statistics are typically highly aggregated and with little detail.

lighting the main characteristics of service sector conflict. Second, I describe the basic properties of the semantic grammar used in encoding the data. Next, an analysis of the data is performed. The paper concludes not only with some preliminary findings on differences between industrial and service sector conflict but also with confirmation that the findings could not have been produced by an analysis of official strike statistics.

## INDUSTRIAL VERSUS SERVICE SECTOR CONFLICT

In all industrialized countries during the late 1970s and 1980s, there was a sharp reversal in the 1960s trend of increasing labor militancy. Even in Italy, one of the most strike-prone Western countries, strike activity dropped to a postwar low in all manufacturing sectors including that of the traditionally highly militant metalworkers. However, during this same period levels of conflict in the service sector soared.

In this chapter, I examine five hypothesized consequences that the shift from industrial to service sector conflict has had on respective levels of state and public involvement in, social disruption from, and counter-cyclical prominence of labor disputes. First, the change in the location of conflict from the industrial to the service sector entailed a change in the nature of the two traditional actors involved in labor conflicts: workers and employers. Whereas industrial employment was predominantly male and blue-collar, service sector workers are largely white collar, with a high percentage of women, particularly at lower level clerical occupations. As for employers, in most Western countries the state has become the largest employer in the service sector (for comparative evidence, see Treu, 1987). Thus, whereas industrial workers work predominantly for private employers, service workers work for public employers (e.g., government agencies in the mail, transportation, health, and education industries). Furthermore, in its role as employer the state becomes a direct bargaining actor. Historically, the state has been backstage, only rarely intervening directly in labor disputes (either to repress, using its police and military forces, or to mediate). The state preferred to play an indirect role, regulating conflict through legislative means. In service disputes the state, as employer, has no choice but to play a more direct role.

Second, the change from industry to service sector in the location of labor disputes has dramatically increased strikes' disruptive power (i.e., their ability to inflict severe losses to the counterpart at minimal cost to strikers). This is a direct consequence of both the essential nature of the services provided (e.g., transportation, health care, etc.) and of the monopoly conditions under which most services are delivered. The more centralized and monopolistic a service is, the larger will be the number of users affected by a service strike. This disruptive potential transforms the service sector labor problem into a law and order problem. As a consequence, disruption is always intrinsic to service disputes, regardless of the intentions of the actors (Accornero, 1985; Pipan, 1989). Even when service disputes are located in the private sector, this potential for social disruption often forces the state to intervene.

This discussion on the actors involved and in the consequences of their actions leads to the following empirically testable propositions:

$H_1$:   More actors (such as the public and political authorities) are involved in service sector labor conflicts than in industrial sector conflicts.

$H_2$:   Workers' positional and disruptive power is higher in services than in industry.

Positional and disruptive power is a double-edged sword, however. Disruption will force quick settlements and concessions, but in the long run it may force the state to find regulatory solutions to the problem and may even turn the public against strikers. Given the inherently disruptive power of their actions, service sector unions have been caught in the dilemma of short- versus long-term gains: They can either use their disruptive power to press for short-term gains or moderate their actions in view of long-term institutional recognition. Service unions have become increasingly aware of their ambivalent position and have sought out various solutions. On the one hand, service workers and their unions have become increasingly inventive in implementing less disruptive but nonetheless effective forms of conflict (e.g., actions short of strike; Freeman, 1986).[2] On the other hand, unions have become more concerned with public opinion and the need to enhance public relations (Walsh, 1988). This leads us to the following, third hypothesis:

$H_3$:   Both highly disruptive actions and actions short of strike are more evident in service sector than in industrial sector labor conflicts.

Two corollaries to this hypothesis are as follows:

$H_{3.1}$:   Service sector unions will try to gain public sympathy by making universalistic demands (e.g., better services for the user).

---

[2]Actions short of strikes are common particularly among education and health care workers. Teachers often strike by refusing to give exams or to provide a choice of textbooks or by withholding work of commuter teachers only. Health care workers typically suspend some services (e.g., outpatient visits, laboratory tests, food services) or limit patients' admissions. Work to the rule (i.e., at the minimally required level) and the strict application of the paraphernalia of legal and trade regulations (some going back to the 1800s) remain customs workers' favorite tactic.

$H_{3.2}$:  Service sector unions will try to gain public sympathy by using public relations strategies (e.g., town meetings).

The industry-to-service shift in conflict also entailed a transition to a labor market that is less subject to the vagaries of the business cycle. Most service workers are public employees of local or central governments. The nature of the labor contract in the public sector has traditionally been quite stable. Furthermore, under Keynesian policies of full employment, governments have expanded public employment during recessionary periods.

In the industrial sector, however, the labor market has served historically as the main mechanism for the regulation of conflict. There is ample empirical evidence that strikes are least frequent when unemployment is high (cf. Franzosi, 1995, chapters 2 and 3). On the other hand, the lower dependence of public employment on the business cycle may make service workers relatively more willing to engage in collective actions during periods of economic dearth. In short, the change in the location of conflict from industry to services may have altered the nature of the relationship between strikes and the business cycle from pro-cyclical (industry) to counter-cyclical (services) (cf. Freeman, 1986; Fuchs, 1968, pp. 8, 167, 171, 181).

The fourth hypothesis is as follows:

$H_4$:  During periods of economic decline, there will be a higher number of strikes in service than in industry.

This hypothesis can be modified to consider the offensive versus defensive claims that workers make within the context of labor disputes. In particular, one might expect in poor economic times that the service sector will make offensive demands (i.e., claims upon resources that they currently do not control, such as higher salaries or more hirings). On the other hand, at such times industrial workers will be likely to make defensive demands (e.g., against plant closing, plant restructuring, and the privatization of firms belonging to state conglomerates). Thus, the last hypothesis is as follows:

$H_5$:  During periods of economic decline, there will be a higher proportion of offensive demands made in service than in industry; conversely, there will be a higher proportion of defensive demands in industry than in service.

Government strike statistics are of no help in testing these hypotheses. These statistics do not provide information either on the actors involved or on the type of actions performed, nor do they provide sector-specific data on the nature of the demands put forward. Thus, to test hypotheses on the differences between industrial and service sector conflict, one must get involved in primary data collection. Various methodological approaches are available, ranging from case studies to surveys. The approach I illustrate here uses newspapers as a source of data (Franzosi, 1987) and applies a linguistic variant of content analysis to these data. The following sections provide a brief introduction to this content analysis method and empirical tests of the hypotheses.

## DATA AND METHODS: SEMANTIC GRAMMARS
## AS CONTENT ANALYSIS SCHEMES

Several years back, Gurr (1974) wrote

> The essential research question is whether it is more appropriate to measure the *properties* of conflict such as its duration, intensity, scale, and impact, either in single events or at the national level; or to concentrate on the *incidence* of conflict, i.e., on the number of distinguishable events which occur. (pp. 250–251)

The question for Gurr was mostly rhetorical. In his mind, the answer was quite clear: Researchers "repeatedly and mistakenly . . . treat counts of conflict events as though they were conflict properties" (Gurr, 1974, p. 251). Few would dispute Gurr's claims that scholars involved in collective action research need to move away from event counts to event characteristics. Indeed, the question is not whether more empirical information is better than less information. The question is how richer data can be collected. How can one shift from event counts to event characteristics?

Traditionally, scholars involved in collective action research have used newspapers, police, or archival documents as sources of data and have relied on one or another form of content analysis as a data collection technique. Although content analysis has allowed researchers to go beyond official statistics on event counts and to collect information on event characteristics, it has also introduced many problems of its own (Franzosi, 1989b; Markoff et al., 1974). To overcome some of the problems inherent in the content analysis of texts, I have developed a linguistic approach to text analysis based on semantic grammars. Whereas syntax grammars map the surface structure of texts into grammatical categories, semantic (or text) grammars map the deep structure of a text into a limited set of functionally defined categories (cf. Halliday, 1970, 1978; van Dijk, 1972; Roberts, this volume, chapter 3). Semantic grammars work particularly well with narrative forms, including newspaper accounts of events and police or archival documents.

A semantic grammar consists of a template patterned after the canonical structure of a language. The basic structure used in my method is the <semantic triplet>, consisting of subject, action, and object with possible modifiers. The type and number of modifiers varies with the specific substantive application. For instance, in a semantic grammar for industrial conflict, the subject's modifiers might be <proper name of an individual>, <number of actors>, <type of actor> (e.g., skilled or unskilled, blue- or white-collar, if worker), and the <union> and <firm> involved. Possible <action modifiers> could be <type of action> (e.g., general, sit-down, wildcat, if strike), <reason for action>, <outcome of action>, <instrument of action> (e.g., stones, billy clubs, letters), and the <time> and <space> of the action. <Semantic triplets>, the basic building blocks of the grammar of data collection, can be further aggregated into higher level aggregates, such as <events> and <disputes>.

A linguistic approach to content analysis has several advantages over more traditional approaches (Franzosi, 1989a, 1990a, 1990b). In particular, it preserves the complex relations between parts of text (e.g., actors and their actions) and thus preserves much of the narrative flavor of the original text. Moreover, it produces more reliable data. Finally, despite the highly complex representation of information in semantic grammars, the relational properties of data collected using a semantic grammar make it possible to analyze words and their interrelations statistically (Franzosi, 1994).

Applying a grammar of this kind, the Air France newspaper clip would be coded as follows:

<subject> firm (<proper name> Air France <type of ownership> state run) <action> cancel (<time> today) <object> flights (<number> about 500); <subject> employees (<firm> Air France) <action> continue strike (<duration> two days <reason> job cuts <reason> wage cuts <outcome> havoc <outcome> passengers' disruption <space> Charles de Gaulle Airport <space> Orly Airport); <subject> strikers (<number> hundreds) <action> march (<space> runways, Orly Airport <outcome> flight halted); <subject> strikers <action> march (<space> runways, Charles de Gaulle Airport); <subject> police (<number> about 70) <action> block (<space> runways, Charles de Gaulle Airport) <object> strikers; <subject> ? police <action> detain <object> protesters (<number> about 10)

As the example shows, there is very little loss of information in going from the original newspaper narrative to the structured coding of the grammar. Much of the original text and also the text's linguistic interconnections have been preserved. It is a grammar of this kind that I used in collecting data from newspapers to test the propositions on service sector conflict. Exploiting the relational characteristics of the grammar, the data were encoded and prepared for statistical analysis using a relational database (Franzosi, 1994).[3] My encoding method was applied to all 3,396 articles on the 988

---

[3]PC-ACE (Program for Computer-Assisted Coding of Events) was used for data entry (Franzosi, 1990a). Written for MS-DOS, PC-ACE stores information in a hierarchical and relational rather than rectangular structure. For statistical analysis the relational information must be linearized into such a rectangular structure, however. See Popping (this volume) for availability.

industrial or service sector labor disputes that appeared in *L'Unità* (the Communist Party newspaper) between January and June of 1986.[4] In this chapter, I analyze data on these 988 disputes (405 in the service sector, 583 in the industrial sector).

## RESULTS

### The Actors

Table 7.1 provides a frequency distribution of the number of actors involved in industrial and service sector disputes. Although it is in the service sector that one finds labor disputes with the largest numbers of actors (even one with 16 distinct actors), differences between the sectors do not appear to be as stark as hypothesized in $H_1$. On the basis of the typical bilateral bargaining models of labor relations in industry, one would have expected most industrial disputes centered on workers (and their unions) and employers, with the occasional intervention of the police.

Why are so many actors involved in industrial labor disputes? The question's answer can be found by exploring the database for the identities of actors involved in industrial disputes with five or more actors. The results of these queries show that political parties, regional governments, and the central government become progressively more involved when industrial disputes entail more actors. In contrast, mostly local public authorities, such as the municipal government and municipal councilors, are drawn into such multi-actor labor disputes in the service sector. In contrast to the substance of $H_1$, the two sectors do not differ in how many but in which (esp. political) actors are involved in their labor disputes.

From the data of Table 7.1 it appears that both industrial and service sector disputes involve political authorities as central players in labor disputes. The role of political actors is confirmed by the data on the frequency distributions of the most common actors found in the database (see Table 7.2). Contrary to hypothesis $H_1$, however, state actors (both at the central and local level) are only slightly less likely to intervene in industrial disputes than in service disputes. Table 7.2 also shows, needless to say, that employers are much more likely to appear in the industrial sector than in services.

---

[4]Given the costs involved in using content analysis methodologies, I relied exclusively on one newspaper as a source of data. See Franzosi (1987) on the danger of relying on one source and on related problems of data validation. I chose *L'Unità* on the basis of extensive comparative analyses. In its coverage of labor disputes, *L'Unità* is preferable to other leading Italian papers in that it provides more and lengthier articles on labor conflict and on occurrences of conflict (disputes). *L'Unità* has 2 to 10 times more of such articles than *Corriere della Sera* and 4 to 10 times more than *Messaggero* and *La Stampa* (two other leading Italian papers).

## TABLE 7.1
### Frequency Distribution of Disputes by Number of Actors per Dispute

*Number of Actors per Dispute*

| Sector | 1 | 2 | 3 | 4 | 5 | 6 | 7 | 8 | 9 | 10 | 11 | 12 | 13 | 14 | 15 | 16 |
|---|---|---|---|---|---|---|---|---|---|---|---|---|---|---|---|---|
| Industry |  |  |  |  |  |  |  |  |  |  |  |  |  |  |  |  |
| N | 114 | 183 | 108 | 66 | 43 | 18 | 18 | 13 | 7 | 8 | 3 | 1 | 1 | 0 | 0 | 0 |
| % | 19.6 | 31.4 | 18.5 | 11.3 | 7.4 | 3.1 | 3.1 | 2.2 | 1.2 | 1.4 | .5 | .2 | .2 | 0 | 0 | 0 |
| Services |  |  |  |  |  |  |  |  |  |  |  |  |  |  |  |  |
| N | 97 | 104 | 87 | 39 | 27 | 12 | 8 | 8 | 8 | 5 | 2 | 5 | 1 | 1 | 0 | 1 |
| % | 24.0 | 25.7 | 21.5 | 9.6 | 6.7 | 3.0 | 2.0 | 2.0 | 2.0 | 1.2 | .5 | 1.2 | .2 | .2 | 0 | .2 |

TABLE 7.2
Frequency Distribution of Disputes by Most Common Actors

| Actors | Industry | | Services | | |
|---|---|---|---|---|---|
| | N | % | N | % | Δ |
| Employers | 422 | 72.4 | 174 | 43.0 | 29.4 |
| Workers | 394 | 67.6 | 289 | 71.4 | -3.8 |
| Trade unions | 373 | 64.0 | 261 | 64.4 | -0.4 |
| Political parties | 94 | 16.1 | 55 | 13.6 | 2.5 |
| Central government | 138 | 23.7 | 103 | 25.4 | -1.7 |
| Local government | 155 | 26.6 | 125 | 30.9 | -4.3 |
| Public/users | 22 | 3.8 | 77 | 19.0 | -15.2 |

In line with hypothesis $H_1$, the public appears as a typical actor in service disputes, whereas it has a negligible presence in industry.

The large number of disputes that involve political actors in both service and industrial sectors has a great deal to say about the much greater politicization of the Italian system of labor relations when compared, for instance, to the U.S. case. In particular, exploration of the data makes it clear that the potential for local disruption resulting from service disputes leads workers and unions to invoke the intervention of local authorities. Presumably, local authorities have a higher stake in the welfare of their fellow citizens for political, economic, and social reasons. Typical, for instance, is the case of health care and school workers whose unions put pressure on local town councils and mayors to intercede with higher level authorities (e.g., province, region, central government) or petition lower level institutions (e.g., commune, province, region) to put pressure on higher level institutions. The data contain many clear illustrations of the considerable disruptive power of service sector strikes—illustrations of disruption that typically affects the public more than the employer. For example, workers' actions are explicitly mentioned as causing disruption and inconveniences to the public in 52 service sector disputes (12.8%) and in only 4 industrial disputes (less than 1%). These observations are all consistent with an image of conflict's greater disruptive power in the service sector than in the industrial sector as hypothesized in $H_2$.

Table 7.3 shows a closer look at the nature of the political actors involved. The table displays the distribution of disputes by state level and function, when the state is a subject (i.e., an actor performing certain actions) and an object (i.e., the passive target of other actors' demands). The data show that the participation of political actors range the full gamut of state levels and functions. At the central level, it is representatives of the government, parliament, the ministries, and the judiciary who intervene in labor disputes. At the local level, it is regional, provincial, township, and municipal officials

TABLE 7.3
Frequency Distribution of Disputes by
State Actors' Role as Subject or Object

| | Subject | | | | Object | | | |
| | Industry | | Services | | Industry | | Services | |
| Actor | N | % | N | % | N | % | N | % |
|---|---|---|---|---|---|---|---|---|
| Central government | | | | | | | | |
| Government | 10 | 1.7 | 20 | 4.9 | 25 | 4.3 | 35 | 8.6 |
| Parliament | 5 | .9 | 10 | 2.5 | 2 | .3 | 9 | 2.2 |
| Ministries | 31 | 5.3 | 43 | 10.6 | 51 | 8.7 | 48 | 11.9 |
| Magistracy | 46 | 7.9 | 8 | 2.0 | 20 | 3.4 | 12 | 3.0 |
| Prefects | 6 | 1.0 | 14 | 3.5 | 10 | 1.7 | 16 | 4.0 |
| Local government | | | | | | | | |
| Region | 32 | 5.5 | 25 | 6.2 | 41 | 7.0 | 31 | 7.7 |
| Province | 13 | 2.2 | 6 | 1.5 | 9 | 1.5 | 5 | 1.2 |
| Commune | 69 | 11.8 | 53 | 13.1 | 39 | 6.7 | 54 | 13.3 |
| Municipal councilors | 45 | 7.7 | 57 | 14.1 | 22 | 3.8 | 30 | 7.4 |

who intervene. With the exception of the magistracy, all levels and functions of the state apparatus are somewhat more likely to intervene in service sector disputes.

## The Actions

Table 7.4 lists a wide array of actions that characterize the Italian system of labor relations. The high frequency of employers' offensive actions from layoffs to temporary layoffs, plant closings, and plant restructuring bears witness of the industrial relations climate in Italy during the mid-1980s. The labor market in the service sector does not appear to have been hit as hard by the economic crisis of the 1980s, however. This is in line with arguments related to $H_4$ and $H_5$ about the counter-cyclical nature of service economies or, at least, of public employment. The smaller percent of contract agreements reached in services shows that the machinery for the settlement of disputes is less effective in services (i.e., in the public sector) than in industry (i.e., in the private sector). The relatively high percentage of service disputes with the action "criticize" also confirms the greater difficulties and the more contentious nature of labor relations in the public sector.

For Italian workers the strike remains the most typical form of collective action, along with mass meetings and demonstrations. Although 41.0% of the service disputes involve a strike, only 23.2% of industrial disputes result in a strike, just as hypothesis $H_4$ states would occur in economic hard times such as those experienced by Italians in 1986. Also, in these times only 3.3%

TABLE 7.4
Frequency Distribution of Disputes by Most Common Actions

| Action | Industry | | Services | | Δ |
|---|---|---|---|---|---|
| | N | % | N | % | |
| Temporary layoff | 77 | 13.2 | 7 | 1.7 | 11.5 |
| Plant closing/restructuring | 73 | 12.5 | 12[a] | 3.0 | 9.5 |
| Layoff | 80 | 13.7 | 29 | 7.2 | 6.5 |
| Contract agreement | 108 | 18.5 | 53 | 13.1 | 5.4 |
| Mass meeting | 163 | 28.0 | 114 | 28.1 | −0.1 |
| Demonstrate | 67 | 11.5 | 50 | 12.3 | −0.8 |
| Claim making | 19 | 3.3 | 35 | 8.6 | −5.3 |
| Act short of strike | 2 | 0.3 | 30 | 7.4 | −7.1 |
| Criticize | 95 | 16.3 | 126 | 31.1 | −14.8 |
| Declare strike | 73 | 12.5 | 111 | 27.4 | −14.9 |
| Strike | 135 | 23.2 | 166 | 41.0 | −17.8 |

[a]All of these 12 disputes are in the oil industry.

of industrial disputes involved offensive claim making, whereas that figure rises to 8.6% in services, a finding consistent with $H_5$.

Further support for hypothesis $H_5$ can be found in Table 7.5. Whereas the vast majority of industrial disputes center on defensive demands (e.g., against layoffs, against wage cuts, against plant closing), the majority of service sector disputes center on offensive demands (e.g., improvement of service quality, more hirings). It appears that the general climate of adverse economic conditions of the mid-1980s did not affect the bargaining position of service workers. The demands of these workers do not reflect fear of job losses. In fact, service workers asked for more hirings rather than fewer layoffs.

The nature of workers' demands in the two sectors mirrors closely the large number of management's offensive actions in industry—layoffs, plant closing, and restructuring—and the low number of the same type of actions in services. No doubt, the economic crisis of the 1980s hit industrial and

TABLE 7.5
Frequency Distribution of Disputes by
(Defensive or Offensive) Type of Demand

| Type of Demand | Industry | | Services | | Δ |
|---|---|---|---|---|---|
| | N | % | N | % | |
| Defensive | 538 | 92.3 | 350 | 86.4 | 5.9 |
| Offensive | 287 | 49.2 | 293 | 72.3 | −23.1 |
| Contract renewal | 82 | 14.1 | 83 | 20.5 | −6.4 |
| Agreement | 43 | 7.4 | 20 | 4.9 | 2.5 |

service workers differently. It is this different bargaining position in the labor market that explains service workers' higher propensities to make claims and to strike, as highlighted in Table 7.4.

A close analysis of the nature of demands or the reasons given for the dispute also sheds further light on some questions left unanswered by the analyses to this point: Table 7.1 leaves unresolved why in the industrial sector there are so many distinct participating actors. Given that mostly political actors enlarge the scope of industrial disputes, what reasons do local political authorities and state actors have to intervene? The answer to these questions lies in part in the politically charged nature of labor relations in Italy. Also, in part it depends on the specific historical climate of the mid-1980s, with industrial workers and unions on the defensive. Whereas all service sector disputes involving five or more actors entail offensive demands, in industry all but a handful are defensive. Political authorities intervene in those industrial disputes at various levels and in various functions. Individual members of parliament and local political authorities intervene to protect jobs threatened by plants closing in their political districts. Different ministries intervene in industrial disputes centered on the privatization of state-owned firms, in their role as employers. Judges intervene in industrial disputes either to investigate corruption charges in the process of privatization or to protect workers whose jobs are under threat through plant restructuring and plant closing. It is, indeed, the magistracy that shows a higher rate of intervention in industrial disputes versus service disputes, contrary to all other state actors.

Returning to Table 7.4, one finds actions short of strike to be more likely in the service sector than in industry (7.4% vs. 0.3%). This use of actions short of strike among service workers provides support for hypothesis $H_3$, according to which service sector workers will enhance their public image by moderating the disruptive power inherent in their actions.[5] Exploration

---

[5]From the available evidence it would appear that the public's reaction to the disruption is mixed, sometimes in protest (even violently) against strikers, sometimes in solidarity with them. Such solidarity seems to be more likely when people have alternative sources for the services interrupted by strikers. On October 4, 1986, for instance, shoppers, particularly younger ones, willingly accept the strikers' invitation to boycott many Standa supermarket stores in Rome. However, when strikers operate in a monopoly (or near monopoly) regime, the public may be less sympathetic. Thus, during the strikes for the renewal of health care workers' collective contract (e.g., at Forlanini hospital in Rome on January 24, 1986), patients and their families protested against strikers. Similarly, truck drivers violently protested at state borders against the disruption caused by customs workers' work-to-the-rule strike. Nonetheless, even when strikers operate in a monopoly (or near monopoly) regime, the public can be an ally, particularly in local disputes when a sense of community exists between workers and public. See Walsh (1988) for more on the relation between trade unions and the media in the public sector.

of the database provides further support along these lines related to hypothesis $H_{3.1}$. Specifically, 10.4% of the service sector disputes (versus 0.3% in industry) found workers and their unions justifying their actions and demands universalistically as "striking to achieve better and more efficient service for the user." State school teachers, municipal kindergarten teachers, and state health workers always make reference to the poor quality of services as part of their grievances. Public solidarity was invoked on similar grounds by SIP (the national telephone company) workers in a 1986 strike. On April 2, 1986, striking workers at Enel (the national electric company) demanded the public's right to information on service quality.

Usually, workers on strike use leaflets in their interaction with the public, but during a strike by sanitation workers in Florence in April 1986, the three main unions (CGIL, CISL, and UIL) set up telephone hot lines to answer questions from users. Similarly, during the strikes for the renewal of health care workers' national contract, doctors held informal meetings with patients and their families to explain their grievances and to defend their strike strategies. Thus, we have evidence in support of hypothesis $H_{3.2}$, on the unions' use of public relations strategies.

## CONCLUSIONS

I have provided evidence in this chapter that service sector conflict has characteristics that clearly set it apart from traditional industrial conflict. I began the chapter by developing and testing a set of formal hypotheses, using data obtained by applying a semantic grammar to articles that appeared in early 1986 in an Italian newspaper. The findings show that labor disputes in both industrial and service sectors are multiple-actor, multiple-action phenomena. These similarities notwithstanding, the findings highlight remarkable differences in the patterns of conflict in the two sectors: During economic downturns, strikes, actions short of strike, and workers' offensive demands are considerably more likely in the service sector than in the industrial sector. The results provide strong evidence for the relative disruptive power of service workers, for the involvement of the public in service disputes, and for the counter-cyclical nature of service sector conflict. Contrary to expectations, the data do not support a clear dichotomy in the role of political actors in industrial versus service sector disputes. In part, this is due to the generally politicized nature of labor relations (whether industrial or service) in Italy. In part, the social disruption caused by the deep economic crisis of the 1980s—with its trail of plant closing, industrial restructuring, downsizing, layoffs, and privatization of state-owned firms—forced political authorities to intervene at various state levels and in various state functions *even* in industrial disputes.

In conclusion, the statistical analyses presented in this chapter clearly show the substantive advantages of abandoning traditional strike data based on event counts, in favor of new data based on event characteristics. In terms of the text analysis theme of this collection, the analyses show the advantage of the formal application of semantic grammars in the quantification of narrative data.

## ACKNOWLEDGMENTS

The research presented in this chapter is part of a larger project on industrial conflict in Italy that has received funding from Confindustria, Consiglio Nazionale delle Ricerche (progetto strategico "Il conflitto e le relazioni di lavoro nel prossimo decennio"), Formez, Intersind, the National Science Foundation (grant # NSF SBR 94-11739), and the University of Wisconsin-Madison.

# 8

# ENVIRONMENTAL CHANGE AND CONFLICT: ANALYZING THE ETHIOPIAN FAMINE OF 1984–1985

Scott Savaiano
Philip A. Schrodt
University of Kansas

Event data analysis is used to study political behavior by coding various types of interactions—for example comments, meetings, protests and uses of force—from media reports. In the past, event data were created by human coders, a process that was slow, expensive, and error prone. Automated coding, in contrast, is inexpensive, completely consistent, and has been shown to be comparable in reliability to human coding. This chapter demonstrates the use of machine-coded event data in a study of the Ethiopian civil war and famine. Data on Ethiopian internal conflict and foreign policy are coded from Reuters newswire reports. Regression analyses that combine event data with data on food production and refugee movements show that internal conflict appears to have had little effect on refugee movement but did affect Ethiopia's foreign relations with Somalia and Sudan.

Scholars and environmentalists have for some time theorized that the effects of human activity on the environment, both global and local, may lead to threats to security such as armed conflict and war. Much of the literature on the subject, however, addresses this in very general terms, such as how environmental change and resource competition build tensions and threaten security at the systemic level of analysis (Homer-Dixon, 1991, 1994). This chapter restricts its scope to the more specific questions: How are environmental stress, refugee movements, and internal conflict interrelated, and what influence do they have on international conflict?

The chapter begins with a brief review of literature concerning environmental change and conflict. After describing the environmental and political situation in Ethiopia during the 1980s and early 1990s, two hypotheses are introduced regarding the interrelations among the environment and internal as well as international conflict. Our analysis tests these hypotheses using archival and text-based event data on Ethiopia during the period. The chapter concludes with a discussion of the implications of computerized text analysis for the study of issues such as conflict.

## ENVIRONMENTAL CHANGE AND CONFLICT

In recent years there has been increasing concern about the possible linkages between environmental stress and violent conflict. For example, Durham (1979) examined the possibility that population pressures and transboundary migration contributed to the 1969 Soccer War between El Salvador and Honduras. Although the war was caused by multiple factors, Durham's in-depth case study made a strong argument for including environmental changes as contributing causal variables.

Porter and Ganapin (1988) studied the complex interaction of environmental and political variables that contributed to the ongoing civil insurgency in the Philippines. Population growth and the severe degradation of agricultural land due to farming practices and deforestation fueled popular support for the Marxist insurgency operating among the peasantry. Other studies linking environmental stress and conflict include research on water issues in the Middle East (Gleick, 1992; Lowi, 1992), the impact of environmental pressures and economic problems on conflict scenarios in China (Goldstone, 1992; Smil, 1992), and the roles played by population migration and land pressure issues in fueling conflict in Bangladesh and Assam (Hazarika, 1993; Suhrke, 1993).

This newer research on environmental change and acute conflict is characterized by the emphasis it places on how environmental change influences acute conflict indirectly, by causing or exacerbating various social and political factors that contribute to increases in tension and violence (Homer-Dixon 1991, 1994). Studying the role of physical factors in this way means, for example, that the researcher should look at how declines in agricultural productivity (i.e., a social problem) that are caused in part by drought or deforestation (i.e., environmental change) figure into the broader history of a society's economic development. This socioenvironmental story can then be related to the historical development and causes of tensions among groups in that society or between societies and how they may have been exacerbated by the economic decline associated with environmental stress.

## THE ETHIOPIAN CASE

From early 1983 until mid-1985, the rains that fall biannually in northern Ethiopia and most of the surrounding Sahel region consistently failed to appear. This drought was an important but not the sole contributor to one of the most severe famines in modern African history. In fact, it seems likely that the drought was a necessary but not sufficient cause of famine in Ethiopia in 1984–1985, because both an ongoing civil war and the Ethiopian government's resettlement policies were also important causes of famine (cf. Cliffe & Davidson, 1988, chap. 8).

This government-sponsored campaign of controlled population resettlement and "revillagization" was escalated at the time of the famine. The Mengitsu regime claimed the resettlement policy was intended to alleviate the chronic overpopulation of northern Ethiopia that had caused the famine. However, many observers both inside and outside of Ethiopia claim that these programs had political aims, given the government's targeting of rebel-held areas of the country as the most "overpopulated," and therefore the most in need of "relief" through depopulation. Efforts to induce participation in the resettlement programs during the famine years often took the form of withholding food aid to small towns and villages in rebel areas. Those peasants unlucky enough to enter the larger cities looking for food were seized and shipped to their new "homes" (i.e., collective farms) in the south. Resentment among the Tigrayan and Eritrean peasantry against the government ran high as a result of these policies and transformed itself into support for the two popular rebel insurgencies in its northern provinces, the Eritrean People's Liberation Front (EPLF) and the Tigray People's Liberation Front (TPLF) (cf. Clay & Holcomb, 1986; Giorgis, 1989, chap. 10).[1]

Support for this contention comes from interviews conducted by the organization, Cultural Survival, with refugees who fled in 1985 into Sudan and Ethiopia from the famine and the repressive government policies associated with it.[2] Cultural Survival interviewers reported, "Virtually all of those interviewed claimed that as a result of the past year's events, they were now much more willing to assist the TPLF in whatever way they could" (Clay & Holcomb, 1986, p. 55). Furthermore, seizures of property by the Dergue to feed the Ethiopian army during the famine years also led to peasant defections to the TPLF. One respondent said, "There are many villages who had oxen taken by the Dergue. These people often join the TPLF" (Clay & Holcomb, 1986, p. 61). Families and sometimes entire villages moved into TPLF-controlled areas rather than be resettled by the Ethiopian government (Clay & Holcomb, 1986, p. 116).

Yet the famine and refugee problems may themselves have played a causal role.[3] For example, the famine may have increased civil violence

---

[1] Ethiopia has a long history of rebellion against government authority (cf. Harbeson, 1988). The longest standing rebellion, the Eritrean armed resistance, was waged from 1961 to 1991.

[2] See Kaplan (1988, pp. 106–110) for a (favorable) discussion of the reliability of these interviews.

[3] Most Ethiopia studies focus on how military conflict contributed to the starvation. We explore the role famine may have played in intensifying the conflict. See Semait (1989) for a treatment sympathetic to our own.

indirectly as the insurgent fronts responded to government famine policies that were apparently intended to starve or depopulate regional insurgency strongholds. The TPLF and EPLF developed relief agencies that helped large numbers of environmental refugees flee into Somalia and Sudan in search of international food aid.[4] The Eritrean Relief Agency (ERA) and the Relief Society of Tigray (REST) organized the exodus of over 200,000 Tigrayans and Eritreans into neighboring countries. Many more fled as a result of fear that they would be forced into a government resettlement program (Clay & Holcomb, 1986, pp. 101–128). These agencies also helped with the distribution of international food and medicine in the refugee camps established along the borders.

This humanitarian effort seems to have led to increased support for the rebels among the Tigrayan and Eritrean peasantry. It also defused Ethiopian government policy that could have been damaging to the rebel cause and molded the rebel groups into more effective fighting organizations. The relief activities in the Sudan afforded the rebels safe havens outside Ethiopian territory (critical to the coordination of the armed struggle) and increased their contact with the outside world.

Despite the massive outmigration of environmental refugees from Ethiopia to neighboring Sudan (Ahmed, 1989; Kimberly & Kimberly, 1991), there is little evidence of violence between the refugees and the people they encountered after crossing over into Sudanese territory. This lack of conflict between refugees and host populations is likely due to the fact that most of the Ethiopians arriving in the Sudan were literally starving to death and thus were easily isolated from indigenous populations in refugee camps run by international agencies.

Nonetheless, the large numbers of Ethiopians interned in the Sudan may have been a source of tension and conflict between the Ethiopian and Sudanese central governments. The majority of those who fled famine in Ethiopia left the country not only to seek food aid that they could have received in Ethiopia but also to elude government relocation policies and thereby aid (at least symbolically) the rebel insurgent groups. The majority of the refugees residing in Sudan were Tigrayan and Eritrean. Thus, their presence in Sudan could have been a source of tension with the Ethiopian government even if it was not a problem for those in direct contact with the refugees.

More generally, the Ethiopian civil war provides an opportunity to test the internal–external hypothesis, according to which the internal conflict and the external policies of a country are either positively or negatively

---

[4]See Suhrke (1993) for a useful discussion of the distinction between environmental refugees of the sort found in the Sudan and Ethiopia and economic migrants who are usually responsible for instances of local conflict involving population movements.

linked. This issue has been extensively studied in the quantitative international relations literature (see Levy, 1989, and Zinnes, 1976, pp. 159–175, for reviews of this literature). The test discussed in this chapter regards the impact of the drought and Ethiopian internal conflict on relations between Ethiopia and two of its neighbors, Sudan and Somalia. Either a positive or a negative relationship could be politically credible: If the relationship were positive, then the environmental and political stress within Ethiopia caused it to become more bellicose toward its neighbors, following the pattern that Blainey (1988) called the scapegoat hypothesis, where "rulers facing internal troubles often start a foreign war in the hope that a victory would promote peace at home" (p. 291). A positive relationship might also be explained by the refugee-linked spillover of the internal domestic and environmental problems into the international realm. A negative relationship, in contrast, would indicate that internal problems made Ethiopia less able to pursue its long-standing dispute with its neighbors because of the constraints imposed by the government's finite diplomatic and economic resources (see Blainey, 1988, pp. 87–96).

In summary, this analysis explores two general issues. First, to study the linkage between environment and political behavior, we look at correlations between variables measuring internal conflict, famine, and refugee movements. Second, to explore the internal–external hypothesis for this case, we use those three measures as independent variables to predict Ethiopia's foreign policy toward Somalia and Sudan.

## DATA

To estimate the strengths of these interrelations statistically, measures of famine, refugee flow, and conflict are required. Information on the first two variables was obtained from international agencies. Measurements for the third were gleaned by quantifying the texts of news reports.

Data on food production levels in Ethiopia from 1982 to 1992 are from the UNO's *Food and Agricultural Organization (FAO) Annual Report*. Data on transboundary refugee flows are from the United Nations High Commissioner on Refugees' (UNHCR) *Annual Budgetary Reports*, which describe in a fair amount of detail the composition of the refugees in each country. The UNHCR data provide annual measures from 1982 to 1992 of total Ethiopian refugees residing in the Sudan.[5] Food production and refugee levels, as well

---

[5]Obviously some amount of estimation is involved in all cases of crowd counting like this; the methods used by UNHCR are described in detail in the opening sections of the budgetary reports.

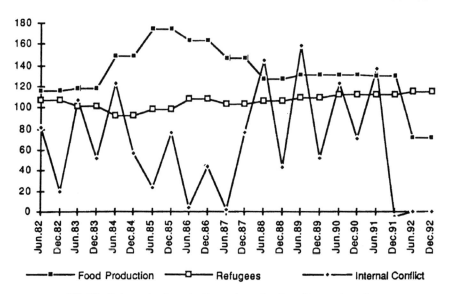

FIG. 8.1. Data on food production, refugee level, and internal conflict.

as the levels of internal conflict in Ethiopia derived from newswire reports, are shown in Figure 8.1.

Political event data were used to measure internal and international conflict (Merritt, Muncaster, & Zinnes, 1993; Schrodt, 1994). Widely used in quantitative international research, these data are generated by assigning nominal codes to news reports of political interactions such as meetings, grants of aid, accusations or denials, and armed conflict. In this study, we are interested in each instance of an interaction between the Ethiopian government and either the rebel groups, Somalia, or Sudan. Figure 8.2 depicts the international conflict data used in our analysis.

The texts under analysis were drawn from the Nexis archive of the Reuters news service, using the Boolean search term "Ethiopia" (i.e., any story containing the word *Ethiopia* or its derivatives was included in the data set). The data set includes all events for the years 1982 to 1992. Only the first sentence of each article was encoded, under the premise that an article's lead sentence summarizes its key points. The following are a few examples of Reuters leads from 1985 that are contained in our data set.

*August 27.* Ethiopian troops have retaken the strategic towns of Barentu and Tessenaye in Eritrea from Eritrean People's Liberation Front (EPLF) rebels following a fierce battle Sunday, sources in the capital Addis Ababa said today.

*October 30.* Ethiopian Foreign Minister Goshu Wolde today accused President Reagan of misrepresenting the situation in Ethiopia in a "despicable manner" in his recent speech at the United Nations.

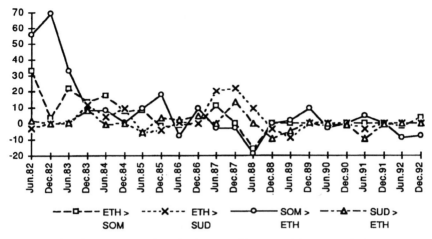

FIG. 8.2. International conflict between Ethiopia and Somalia or Sudan.

*December 9.* Sudanese officials expect another 200,000 Ethiopian refugees to flood across the border from Tigray after another poor harvest there.

In the past, event data were compiled by individuals, usually students, working from hard-copy news reports, such as those in *The New York Times* and *The Times of London*, or in chronologies such as *Facts on File*. This task was usually too time-consuming and expensive for an individual researcher, and even when funding was available, assembling a large event data set required months of work that had to be closely monitored for high intercoder reliability.

For this project we compiled event data using machine coding.[6] The machine coding system does some simple parsing of news reports—for example, it identifies the political actors, recognizes compound noun–verb phrases, and determines the references of pronouns—and then uses a large set of verb patterns to determine the appropriate event code.

A sparse parsing approach can be used to code event data because event data, as originally defined by international relations researchers (Azar & Ben-Dak, 1975; Burgess & Lawton, 1972; McClelland, 1968; Munton, 1978), depends only on the basic Subject-Verb-Object structure of an English sentence, with the verb determining the event category. Parsing of the first of the Reuters leads would first identify a set of proper nouns and verbs or verb–object combinations (in pointed brackets) in the lead.

---

[6]The program used was the Kansas Events Data System, or KEDS (Gerner, Schrodt, Francisco, & Weddle, 1994; Schrodt, Davis, & Weddle, 1994; Schrodt & Gerner, 1994). Although KEDS currently runs only on the Macintosh, a Windows version is under development. See Popping (this volume) for availability.

*Ethiopian* troops <have retaken> the strategic <towns> of Barentu and Tessenaye in *Eritrea* from *Eritrean People's Liberation Front* (EPLF) rebels following
a fierce <battle> Sunday, sources in the capital *Addis Ababa* <said> today.

The program first looks for a simple *noun*$_1$ <verb phrase> *noun*$_2$ combination,
in this instance, *Ethiopian* <have retaken towns> *Eritrea*. The verb phrase
corresponds to a use of force, which is code 223 in the standard World Events
Interaction Survey (WEIS) coding scheme (McClelland, 1976); the first noun is
the source of the action and the second is the target. If this basic structure is
not found, the program looks for other common patterns. For example, the
target might occur prior to the verb phrase, or a passive voice construction
might lead to the reversal of the source and target. Verbs occurring after the
initial S-V-O construction are ignored, though if the sentence were compound,
the first verb after the conjunction would also be coded.

This approach to machine coding is dependent on the fact that most
newswire leads have a relatively simple grammatical structure. For example,
in almost all leads the source of an action is the first noun in the sentence
and, consistent with the standard pyramid style of journalistic writing, the
lead sentence succinctly summarizes the entire article. Consequently, the
machine coding accuracy is comparable to that of the student coders used
in most event data coding projects, around 80% to 90% (Bond, Bennett, &
Vogele, 1994; Gerner et al., 1994).

In addition to being inexpensive, machine coding also provides a high
degree of consistency because a phrase always generates the same code.
Although this will occasionally cause problems when a phrase occurs in an
unusual context, such errors are relatively infrequent and are more than
compensated by the absence of "drift" in the interpretation of coding rules
during the coding of a large number of news reports by multiple coders. In
this study we used a dictionary of about 3,000 verb patterns and 700 political
actors originally developed for coding Middle Eastern events using the WEIS
coding system. These dictionaries were customized slightly to deal with
additional events and actors that occur only in the Ethiopian context. Bian-
nual conflict/cooperation scores were then generated based on how words
in the dictionary were grammatically related in the Reuters leads.[7]

## RESULTS

Our analysis examines relations among food production, refugee movements, and conflict (both internally, with rebel forces, and externally, with
Somalia and Sudan). In the first of two analyses, we consider the synergistic

---

[7]In our analysis we use the negative of the cooperation/conflict scale proposed by Goldstein
(1992) because virtually all the interactions in our data involve conflict, and it is easier to
visualize these data in terms of positive levels of conflict rather than negative levels of
cooperation.

interrelations among Ethiopian famine, internal conflict, and the outmigration of refugees. As previously discussed, relations among these three are
likely to be reciprocally interrelated. Here we explore the relative strengths
of these interrelations.

In the second analysis, we study the effect of food production, internal
conflict, and drought (as reflected in low food production) on international
relations between Ethiopia and two of its neighbors, Sudan and Somalia, to
study the internal–external hypothesis for the Ethiopian case. First, however, consideration must be given to methodological issues related to the
time-series nature of our data.

Because the event data are daily reports, whereas the U.N. food production and refugee reports are annual, aggregation was required. To reduce
the autocorrelation in the U.N. variables while preserving some of the detail
of the event-based conflict measure, we used a 6-month aggregation of the
total conflict reported in the previous 6 months. Moreover, there is likely
to be a delay between the occurrence of the independent variables and the
increase in the refugee levels, so we looked at a number of different lags in
those variables.

Delayed responses are likely for two reasons. In the case of food production, the initial effects of drought will be ameliorated by food stocks remaining
from earlier harvests. In the case of both food and conflict, a significant delay
can also be expected between the time people leave their homes and the time
they show up in the UNHCR refugee data. Many of the refugees were traveling
on foot, and they were also likely to have stopped at a number of intermediate
points before crossing the international boundary into Sudan.

Figure 8.3 shows the zero-order correlations between various lagged or
leading pairs among food production, refugee level, and internal conflict. Here
one finds a clear pattern of significant negative correlations between lagged
food production and refugees, going back about two years. There is no
significant leading correlation. The remaining two relations, in contrast, show
no significant lagged or leading correlations. Based on this pattern, the
refugee movement appears to have had primarily environmental rather than
political origins. Finally, and contrary to our expectations, there is no statistical evidence that the famine affected the level of conflict within Ethiopia.[8]

The second part of our analysis suggests that internal conflict may have
an effect on international conflict, however. Table 8.1 gives the results of
multiple regressions in which the dependent variables are indicators of
conflict from Ethiopia directed to Somalia or Sudan. The lagged international
conflict variable is the lagged value of this dependent variable. Reciprocal
international conflict refers to conflict directed from Somalia or Sudan to

---

[8]The lack of association between internal conflict and either food production or refugee
level is a finding that also holds in partial associations among the three variables.

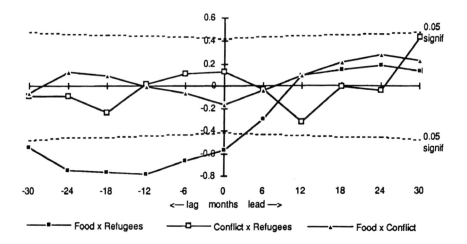

FIG. 8.3. Lagging and leading correlations among refugees, food production, and internal conflict.

Ethiopia, a variable found by Goldstein and Freeman (1990) to be a strong predictor among event data. The refugees, internal conflict, and food production variables are the same as described previously.[9] Season is a dummy variable coded 1 for the January–June data points and 0 for the July–December points. This last variable was added after an examination of the residuals indicated an alternating pattern that may be due to seasonal differences in military activity, as evident in Figures 8.1 and 8.2.[10]

This model fits the interactions with Somalia and Sudan equally well, and the coefficients are generally of similar signs and magnitudes. This consistency suggests that the model is capturing some aspects of the overall foreign policy of Ethiopia. The results are largely supportive of a model arguing that internal political and environmental stress distracted Ethiopia and thereby reduced its conflict with its neighbors, rather than supporting the scapegoat theory. That result is consistent with Blainey's anecdotal analysis, which also found little support for the scapegoat theory despite that theory's popularity in the informal literature.

---

[9]Because, like the refugee data, only annual food production data are available, 12- and 24-month lagged values are included to reduce the level of collinearity among the independent variables. Because the conflict data are aggregated over the previous 6 months, each actually incorporates a lag of up to 6 months.

[10]Having first acknowledged that the Durbin–Watson statistic loses accuracy once lagged values of the dependent variable appear in the right-hand side of a regression equation, it may nonetheless be instructive to note that in the absence of the season indicator, the statistic's value for the Somalia model increases from 2.00 to 2.67, indicating the distinct possibility of negatively autocorrelated error.

TABLE 8.1
Results of the International Interaction Models

|  | to Somalia | | to Sudan | |
|---|---|---|---|---|
| Lagged international conflict | 0.02 | (0.14) | 0.37 | (2.92)** |
| Reciprocal international conflict | 0.48 | (5.08)*** | 0.76 | (3.81)** |
| Refugees | 0.00 | (−0.39) | 0.01 | (2.22)* |
| Internal conflict | −0.06 | (−3.13)** | −0.03 | (−2.33)* |
| Food production | −0.83 | (−3.30)** | −0.52 | (−2.75)* |
| Food production, lagged 12 months | 0.73 | (2.70)* | 1.13 | (4.25)*** |
| Season | 4.65 | (2.63)** | 1.69 | (0.82) |
| $R^2$ | .85*** | | .84*** | |

*Note.* $N = 20$. In parentheses are $t$ statistics associated with coefficients.
*$p < .05$. **$p < .01$. ***$p < .001$.

As expected, reciprocal interactions are a strong positive predictor in both models, and lagged international conflict is significant for Sudan, though not Somalia. Both internal conflict and lagged food production are associated with a decrease in the amount of conflict Ethiopia directed externally. The refugee variable is significant only for Sudan, which is not surprising because the data recorded only refugees crossing into Sudan. As noted earlier, the refugees in Sudan were probably freer to support the EPLF and TPLF rebels than they had been in Ethiopia, which most likely increased tensions between Ethiopia and Sudan.

The one anomalous result is the significant negative coefficient on contemporaneous food production. The sign of this coefficient proved quite stable in alternative formulations of the model and does not seem to be due to collinearity. The bivariate correlations of food production with the two dependent variables are weak and negative (−0.39 for Somalia and −0.29 for Sudan; neither is significant at the 0.05 level) so the positive relation appears to be due to some sort of complex association with the remaining variables.

## CONCLUSION

Research on environmental change and conflict must always face the complicated interplay of a variety of causal forces that often do not interact in a strictly linear fashion. The researcher's task is to discern the various processes that cause conflict and to strive to tell a complete and convincing story. Environmental changes, like the Ethiopian drought and the famine and refugees it created, were by no means the only influential factors at work during the Ethiopian civil war. This study has analyzed the relative importance of a few of these variables in one of the longest struggles for independence ever undertaken.

This study has demonstrated the potential of computerized text analysis as a means of enhancing our ability to apply statistics in investigations of issues related to conflict and the environment. News service reports provide an admittedly imperfect record of conflict, because they are influenced by censorship, the proximity of reporters to the conflict, editorial attention spans, competing stories, and other factors. Nonetheless, valid measures of conflict can be developed out of these reports. Because the purpose of statistical analysis is to detect a signal amid noise, the imperfect nature of the journalistic record does not preclude useful analysis.

Wire service reports can now be acquired inexpensively through data services such as Nexis and Dialog. Reports of political events can also be obtained from specialized hard-copy sources through optical character recognition (cf. Gerner et al., 1994). Once texts describing political activity are in machine-readable form, machine coding methods allow them to be coded quickly and inexpensively. We can now evaluate a large set of hypotheses that were previously inaccessible to statistical studies due to the costs of coding textual sources using human coders.

Although we used the standard WEIS event coding scheme in this study, our method is flexible in that it allows the development of new coding systems that reflect new theoretical concerns. Because our hypotheses dealt with traditional issues of conflict, the WEIS coding system was sufficient. In contrast, had we specifically been interested in refugee issues, which traditional event coding schemes do not code in detail, we could have modified the coding dictionaries and easily developed a specialized set of event codes, much as we modified dictionaries to include words corresponding to the rebel groups unique to the Ethiopian situation. In short, computerized coding allows us both to acquire data that were unavailable before and to ask questions we could not ask before.

## ACKNOWLEDGMENTS

Our thanks to Phillip Huxtable and Shannon Davis for helpful comments. The development of the KEDS machine coding program was supported by National Science Foundation grant SES90-25130 and by the University of Kansas General Research Allocation 3500-XO-0038.

# 9

# ASSESSING THE PORTRAYAL OF SCIENCE AS A PROCESS OF INQUIRY IN HIGH SCHOOL BIOLOGY TEXTBOOKS: AN APPLICATION OF LINGUISTIC CONTENT ANALYSIS

Elizabeth M. Eltinge
Texas A&M University

In the early 1960s science educators emphasized the importance of teaching science not as a body of facts but as a process whereby knowledge is generated. In this chapter, an analysis is performed of depictions of scientific inquiry within the introductory, genetics, and leaf-structure chapters of the 1956, 1965, 1977, and 1985 editions of the Holt series, *Modern Biology*. Random samples of sentences from these 12 chapters were encoded using linguistic content analysis. The resulting data were used to measure the occurrence of "science as inquiry" within a clause. Inquiry was most prevalent in the 1965 edition, which was written when educators placed greatest emphasis on textbook depictions of science as inquiry. Inquiry was also prevalent in introductory chapters, the place where the scientific method itself tends to be discussed, and in chapters covering genetics, an area in which considerable scientific inquiry, and discovery, has occurred since mid-century.

The science textbook has been for many years the most dominant influence over what is taught in high school science classrooms. Classroom activity is predominantly guided, organized, and restricted to what is contained within the science textbook (Harms & Yager, 1981; Helgeson, Blosser, & Howe, 1977; Stake & Easley, 1978). Teachers' questions generally focus on the information contained in the textbook, and students are trained to seek the "right" answers in textbooks. As a consequence, science, as presented in classrooms, is often limited to the facts and concepts included in the textbook.

However, science is much more than a collection of facts. Over half a century ago Crowell (1937) chastised science teachers who had forgotten that science is "a method of thinking," and "have concerned themselves unduly with the teaching of facts, to the neglect of science as a method by which the pupil can solve his own problems" (p. 525).[1] Moreover, many writings on science education over the past 30 to 40 years have emphasized the goal of "bringing students to a state of scientific inquiry." Numerous educators have argued that teaching science as inquiry presents a more realistic view of science than teaching science as a collection of facts (Herron, 1971; Tamir, 1985; Welch, Klopfer, Aikenhead, & Robinson, 1981). Teaching science as inquiry may also help students to assimilate more scientific knowledge as they grow and mature.

Despite all the rhetoric, very few studies have been conducted that evaluate the extent to which textbooks portray science as inquiry. In fact, there are few studies of any kind in which science textbooks or science curricula have been analyzed (Good, 1993). In its analysis of depictions of science as inquiry within biology textbooks, this study might well be thought of as a pioneering effort in this respect. Before I proceed with a description of the study, let us first consider the meaning of "science as inquiry," as well as changes since mid-century in the emphasis that science educators have placed on scientific inquiry.

## SCIENCE AS INQUIRY

Terms such as "scientific inquiry," "the nature of inquiry," and "inquiry skills" have appeared frequently in science education literature, particularly during the curriculum movement of the early 1960s. Despite the importance science educators have placed on science as inquiry, little evidence exists that this importance was incorporated into teaching practice (Herron, 1971; Hurd, Bybee, Kahle, & Yager, 1980; Tamir, 1983, 1985), leaving a gap between educational research and practice. This gap is particularly evident in the discrepancy between goals as stated in the science education literature and those as issued by state education agencies, whose directives teachers are compelled to follow. The goal statements issued by state education agencies tend to be content-oriented rather than inquiry-related (Welch et al., 1981). Moreover, teacher training has been found to better prepare teachers to teach facts than to teach inquiry (Duschl, 1986).

Part of the reluctance to address the issue of inquiry could be a confusion as to what is actually meant by "inquiry." In work connected with the

---

[1]In fact, Crowell (1937) may have been the first to implicate the textbook in this regard, "because science textbooks probably determine to a large degree what topics shall be taught and the method by which they are taught" (p. 525).

Biological Science Curriculum Study (BSCS) Curriculum, Schwab (1962) portrayed teaching science as inquiry as consisting of two parts: teaching by inquiry and science as inquiry. Respectively, these parts represent the process and the product of what might occur in a science classroom. Teaching by inquiry involves the means by which the students gain knowledge. It includes the development of the so-called inquiry skills, such as the abilities to identify and define a problem, to formulate a hypothesis, to design an experiment, to collect, analyze, and interpret data, and to draw meaningful conclusions. Thus, teaching by inquiry is exemplified by hands-on, experiential laboratory activities that encourage students' creativity.

Science as inquiry deals with the realistic depiction of science. Science is both a collection of facts and a method by which those facts are obtained. The scientific method of inquiry shows science as being fallible, self-corrective, and progressive rather than infallible and conservative. It is skeptical rather than dogmatic and is constantly undergoing change (Lampkin, 1951). When viewed as a process of inquiry, science is seen not as the final truth about the world but rather as the most adequate account of the world at any given time (Connelly, Whalstrom, Finegold, & Elbaz, 1977). Of the two parts, Schwab (1962) argued that the second part, science as inquiry, is more important in science education. Despite the importance of textbooks in science education and the prominence of the image of science as inquiry in science education literature, most research has investigated teaching by inquiry (e.g., Tafoya, Sunal, & Knecht, 1980; Tamir & Lunetta, 1978, 1981; Tamir, Nussinovitz, & Friedler, 1982), rather than science as inquiry (Herron, 1971; Tamir, 1985). This latter science-as-inquiry aspect is the focus of this study.

## EDUCATORS' EMPHASIS ON SCIENTIFIC INQUIRY

The launching of the satellite Sputnik by the Russians on October 4, 1957, provoked fear in the United States that the Russians would become superior to the Americans in science and technology. This fear produced a demand for more rigorous school curricula, particularly in the areas of mathematics and science. As a result, several federally funded national curriculum projects were started in mathematics and science. These national curriculum efforts were seen as a radical departure from conventional patterns, particularly in the development of the major theme of science as a process of inquiry (Schwab, 1963). Three programs were developed in high school biology by the BSCS, a nationally funded effort that brought together a mixture of scientists and educators with the common goal of improving biology education in the United States. Three series of textbooks arose from these programs called the BSCS blue, green, and yellow versions—materials that have had a profound influence on biology education (Grobman, 1969;

Hurd et al., 1980). Since the development of these curricula, there have been no movements of a similar magnitude in biology education.

During the 1970s and '80s dissatisfaction with the discipline-centered science curricula of the 1960s grew. It was argued that the purpose of science education should not be solely that of creating more scientists and engineers through exposure to science as inquiry but in helping students to cope in an increasingly technological society. The interface of science, technology, and society emerged as a focus of education, along with all the moral and ethical issues it entails (Hofstein & Yager, 1982). Science became viewed as value-laden and no longer as a value-free search for truth.

During the last half of this century, biology programs have generally been structured on five goals: biological knowledge, scientific methods, social issues, personal needs, and career preparation. Changes in science education over the past few decades have not so much been changes in these five goals as they have been changes in the relative emphasis placed on each. The goal of achieving biological knowledge has traditionally received the greatest emphasis. The goal of depicting science as a method of inquiry was emphasized in the 1960s but received less emphasis in the 1950s and 1980s. It was replaced in the 1980s and 1990s with the goal of social issues, despite the fact that this goal has not always come to be reflected in science textbooks (Chiang-Soong & Yager, 1993; Hickman & Kahle, 1982; Hurd et al., 1980).

## DATA

Biology was selected because it is the science course most frequently taken by high school students; for many students, it is their only high school science course (Stuart, 1982). Among high school biology textbooks, the most prominent have been the BSCS yellow and green versions and the Holt *Modern Biology* series. The Holt textbook has been one of the best-selling high school textbooks since 1945 (Grabiner & Miller, 1974; Helgeson et al., 1977; Lowery & Leonard, 1978). The Holt series was selected because, unlike the BSCS series, it was well established from the mid-1960s through the 1980s—the historical period of interest in this study.

The object of this study is to trace the extent to which science was treated as a process of inquiry in the Holt series of biology textbooks over a period during which such treatment received various levels of endorsement in the science education literature. Nine editions of *Modern Biology* were published from 1956 to 1985. The analysis is of texts from the 1956, 1965, 1977, and 1985 editions of the series (Moon, Mann, & Otto, 1956; Otto & Towle, 1965, 1977, 1985). These editions were selected to afford intervals of roughly 10 years over a 30-year time span. Of the remaining five editions, the 1981 edition was selected for reliability analyses.

A blocking design of three subject areas within each of the four editions was used. The three subject areas were strategically selected to represent hypothesized contrasts in the treatment of science as inquiry. The first subject area is the material found in the introductory chapters. The introductory chapters all describe what the subject of biology is and how it fits into the realm of science. These chapters were selected to provide global descriptions of how the authors view biology and science as well as a basis for exploring their approaches to the image of science as inquiry.

The second subject area is genetics. This is an area in which there have recently been many major scientific advances, such as in the knowledge of gene structure and in the control of genetic expression. It was hypothesized that this area would have the highest potential for depictions of science as an active, ongoing process of inquiry.

The final subject area is leaf structure and function. This material tends to be very descriptive in nature. Accordingly, it was hypothesized that this subject area would be least likely to contain imagery of science as a process of inquiry and more likely to portray science as a collection of facts.

Every sentence within each of the twelve blocks (viz., 4 time periods by 3 subject areas) was numbered one to N and a 20% random sample of the sentences was collected. Only sentences in the main body of the text were included. Excluded from analysis were chapter introductions, figure and picture captions, marginal notes, chapter summaries, and end-of-chapter questions. Each sampled sentence was assigned an identification code that uniquely identified its source (i.e., edition, subject area, page number, etc.). A total of 813 sentences containing 1,350 clauses were encoded.

The selected sentences were encoded using linguistic content analysis (Roberts, 1989, 1991). Encoding was done with the aid of PLCA (Program for Linguistic Content Analysis).[2] Prior to coding, the blocks were randomly ordered, and year of publication was masked. It was impossible to mask the subject area because of the contextual clues that the sentences provided. Sentences within the blocks were coded in the order in which they appeared in the text. This sequential order within chapters was used because it afforded contextual clues during the coding process in the representation of sentences' intended meanings. That is, the advantages of validity offered by within-chapter sequential coding were deemed more valuable than any additional benefits that might have been gained with a totally random ordering of sentences for coding.

## Linguistic Content Analysis

In a linguistic content analysis (LCA) the unit of analysis is always the clause. Thus, LCA affords probabilistic inferences about all clauses in a population of texts when applied to randomly sampled clauses. A clause is defined as

---

[2]Versions of PLCA have been written for both MS-DOS and Windows 95. See Popping (this volume) for availability.

any sentence or portion of a sentence that includes an inflected verb and, optionally, a subject, object, and related modifiers (e.g., "Go!" is a clause). After a clause has been identified, it must then be classified according to the intent of the clause's source, as judged by the coder (Roberts, 1989, p. 154ff).[3] The user has four types of intention from which to select: perception, recognition, justification, or evaluation.

The most frequently occurring clause type, the perception, describes an activity. Examples of perception clauses are "A scientist performs experiments," "Refer to Figure 3," and "A green plant grows toward the sunlight." The second most common type of clause is a recognition clause—a clause that classifies a phenomenon as belonging (or not belonging) in a category. Examples of recognition clauses are "Biology is a science," "A starfish is actually not a type of fish," and "Glucose is a sugar."

The other two types of clauses, justification and evaluation, are rare in descriptive writing such as that in textbooks. A justification clause judges the goodness or badness of an activity. Examples of justification clauses are "Drunk driving is wrong" and "It is good to clean your microscope." Evaluation clauses judge how well a phenomenon fits (or does not fit) into a category. Examples of evaluation clauses are "Pasteur is recognized as being a brilliant scientist" and "When considering observable genetic traits, blood type is a good example."

The selection of clause type is fundamental to linguistic content analysis. It is also one of the strengths of the technique in that it helps remove much of the ambiguity that is inherent in communication. To determine a clause's type, the researcher must try to grasp the intent of the writer based on the clause's context and on knowledge of the clause's subject matter.

The importance of context in determining clause type is well illustrated in the following example from Roberts (1989, pp. 165–166): Ambiguity inherent in the clause, "John bought that book," is revealed when one notes how its clause type changes with its context. For example, the clause is a perception (i.e., a description of a process) when the context is "We both went to the store. Then John bought that book." This is a descriptive accounting of an activity that occurred. An example of a recognition clause (i.e., a description of a state of affairs) is "I'm trying to figure out what he spent his allowance on. Oh yes, John bought that book!" Here, the purchasing of the book falls into the category of "what John spent his allowance on." An example of a context within which the clause is a justification (i.e., a judgment of a process) is "I pointed out that he might be arrested if he stole it. Fortunately, John bought that book." Here, the phrase is intended to communicate that the purchasing of the book was the right or appropriate thing

---

[3]Given this interpretive role of the coder, LCA is correctly understood as taking a representational approach to the analysis of texts (cf. Shapiro, this volume).

to do. An example of a context within which the clause is an evaluation (i.e., a judgment of a state of affairs) is "John is an excellent cook. From all the cookbooks in the store, John bought that book." Here the phrase is used to communicate that the book is a very good cookbook. Clearly, the coder must look beyond phrases' syntactic forms in obtaining valid representations of their intended meanings (cf. Roberts, this volume, chapter 3).

Once a clause's type has been inferred, the user fits words from the clause into the semantic grammar appropriate to this type. The more practice one has in applying the coding technique, the more one's knowledge of the subject matter, and the less unambiguous one's text, the more valid and reliable will be one's selections of clause types. Fortunately for this study, ambiguities are much less common in descriptive texts or in texts intended to convey specific information than in other forms of written text, such as folktales, poetry, or transcripts of conversations (Kelly & Stone, 1975, p. 32; Roberts, 1989, p. 166). All the clauses in this study were either perceptions or recognitions. There were no justification or evaluation clauses.

In addition to selecting from among clause types, the coder records verb tense and valence (e.g., positive, occasional, negative, etc.). When applicable, the clause's question type (e.g., why, how, etc.) and use of a modal auxiliary verb (e.g., can, ought, etc.) are also encoded. Direct quotations can be coded to indicate the source (i.e., writer or speaker) of a clause and this source's audience. Moreover, relations among clauses can also be encoded as relative clauses, conjunction-linked clauses, or proxy clauses (i.e., clauses that stand proxy for the subject or object of a superordinate clause, as does "plants require carbon dioxide" in "Botanists know that plants require carbon dioxide.").

The detail afforded in an LCA-mapping of text allows the coder to obtain a correspondingly detailed reconstruction of each encoded sentence. For example, an encoded version of the sentence, "How do scientists follow the scientific method when they wish to explore new ideas?" is given the following on-screen reconstruction by PLCA: To the READER the AUTHOR said, "How is it that the SCIENTIST USES a SCIENTIFIC METHOD, if the SCIENTIST wants to INVESTIGATE a THOUGHT/IDEA?" This reconstruction capability allows the coder to make face validity checks during the encoding process itself.

Four general coding rules were established. The first rule dealt with the use of the speaker and audience codes. If a clause was phrased as a question or a direct command, or contained one or more of the words *we, you,* or *us,* then the speaker of the clause was coded as the author and the audience was coded as the reader. Otherwise the speaker and audience codes were not used. These codes were later used as indicators of the author's involvement of the reader with the text's content.

The second rule addressed the treatment of verbs. Verbs are a pivotal element in the coding process. Because a clause must contain an inflected verb, locating the inflected verbs in a sentence is the first step in identifying its clause(s). A sentence's verbs were only used to identify separate clauses if they had either distinct meanings or distinct subjects, objects, or modifiers. Otherwise, multiple inflected verbs identified only a single clause for the coder. For example, in the phrase, "the scientist tested, then reported her theory," the verbs *tested* and *reported* have two distinct meanings, as becomes evident when they are classified into different verb categories (i.e., respectively into INVESTIGATE and DESCRIBE/REPORT). This phrase would have been coded as two separate clauses. In the phrase, "the child hopped and skipped around the room," the two verbs *hopped* and *skipped* denote rather similar actions, would both be classified into the same verb category (e.g., MOVE), and would have been assigned to this category within a single clause.

A third rule was that all adverbial information, including that conveyed by many gerunds and in most prepositional phrases, was dropped during the coding process. Accordingly, gerunds were not used as a basis for identifying clauses. For example, the phrase, "the researcher investigated the effects of the virus while controlling for environmental factors," would be coded as a single clause, "the researcher investigated the effects of the virus." There is some loss of information due to this rule, just as with any coding process. Generally, the rule applied here was that if the author did not consider the text important enough to devote an inflected verb to it, the information was not important enough to code.

A final rule involves restriction in the size of the coding dictionary. Biology textbooks have a very large vocabulary, particularly of nouns, and it would have been unduly laborious to use a separate category for every noun that appeared. Instead, certain noun groupings were established for the many technical and scientific nouns that appeared in the text. These noun groupings were for PLANT SCIENCE WORD, ANIMAL SCIENCE WORD, GENETIC SCIENCE WORD, MINERAL SCIENCE WORD, and SCIENCE WORD. These were words that one might find listed in a glossary. Examples of words falling respectively into these five science word categories are *photosynthesis, epidermis, genotype, parenchyma,* and *heterozygous.* Less technical words (e.g., *bean plant, food, fish*) were classified into more generic categories such as PLANT, NUTRIENT, and ANIMAL. Further details about the coding process can be found in Eltinge (1988) and Eltinge and Roberts (1993).

### The Measurement of Inquiry

Once coding was completed, an LCA data matrix was downloaded and used to develop a measure of inquiry. Tamir (1985) provided the basis for my development of an operational definition of science as inquiry. Table 9.1 lists Tamir's 23-item categorization scheme for classifying sentences as narrative

TABLE 9.1
Indicators of Science Expressed as Inquiry

1. Information is presented as tentative and incomplete.
2. Doubts are raised; validity is tested.
3. Controversial opinions are presented.
4. History of ideas and of discoveries is described.
5. One scientific method is implied.
6. Different scientists use different methods.
7. Facts depend on guiding conceptions of scientists.
8. Names of researchers are mentioned.
9. Personal and social background of researchers are described.
10. Contribution of technology to research is described.
11. Questions are raised.
12. Problems are formulated.
13. Hypotheses are formulated.
14. Predictions are made.
15. Observations and measurements are described.
16. Data are presented.
17. Data are interpreted; conclusions are drawn.
18. Experiments are described.
19. Explanations are presented.
20. Assumptions and limitations are mentioned.
21. Tables are presented and interpreted.
22. Graphs are presented and interpreted.
23. Pictures/drawings are presented and interpreted.

*Note.* Adapted from P. Tamir (1985, p. 91).

of inquiry.[4] According to this scheme, a sentence is classified as narrative of inquiry when it presents conclusions in the framework from which they arose and were tested. Some of the items in Table 9.1 are simply observations of isolated grammatical events and do not rely on linguistic relations among words in clauses (e.g., when a clause is formulated as a question [item 11] or when it refers to research [item 8], tables [item 21], graphs [item 22], or illustrations [item 23]). Accordingly, clauses formed as questions or those containing names of researchers or references to tables, graphs, or illustrations were classified as inquiry clauses. Clauses relating histories of ideas and discoveries (item 4) or the background of researchers (item 9) were identified by noting if they were set in the past tense. Yet like the previously mentioned criteria, the use of past tense in identifying inquiry clauses still does not take linguistic interrelations among the words into account.

On the other hand, the relational information afforded by linguistic content analysis can be used in denoting inquiry indicators for most of the

---

[4]In Tamir's study, the chapter was the unit of analysis, and tally marks were recorded for each of the 23 items found within it. The maximum number of marks used was two. That is, once an item had appeared twice in a chapter, any additional appearances were not recorded.

remaining items on Tamir's list. For example, a clause was considered indicative of inquiry when *scientist* was its subject and *think* (or *consider, contemplate,* etc.) its verb. When a scientist thinks about something or considers alternatives, the objects of his or her thoughts and considerations are "presented as tentative and incomplete" (item 1). Likewise, "doubts are raised" (item 2) whenever a scientist is said to "question" (or "wonder") about something. Clauses that contained a scientist as the subject of such an inquiry verb or that referred to the reader as the potential subject of an inquiry verb were identified as inquiry clauses. Only four of the categories (items 3, 5, 10, and 20) were deemed too general to be assigned a specific LCA operationalization in this study.[5]

## RESULTS

The dependent variable in this study indicates the presence or absence of inquiry in a clause. Logistic regression analysis allows one to use continuous or discrete variables in estimating the natural logarithm of the odds of the occurrence (versus nonoccurrence) of dichotomous dependent variables such as this (cf. Agresti, 1990). Parameters estimated in a logistic regression analysis can be interpreted in much the same manner as those from a linear regression analysis, except that the units of the dependent variable are the log odds of an occurrence (here, of inquiry).

Table 9.2 lists the estimated log odds that science was portrayed as inquiry between pairs of historical or substantive contexts.[6] Standard errors are listed in parentheses next to their respective parameter estimates. When reading these equations, it is important to note that the constant represents a baseline with which to compare all other parameter estimates. In this case, the baseline estimates the log odds of inquiry within the 1956 introductory chapter. Other estimates are deviations from this baseline.

Keeping in mind that parameter estimates represent deviations from the baseline of 1956 (after correcting for any marginal effects due to subject area), one notes that after rising slightly in 1965, the log odds of inquiry in 1977 dropped back to almost the same level as 1956, then dropped well below that level in 1985. Thus, the highest level of inquiry was in 1965, the lowest was in 1985, with 1956 and 1977 levels remaining about the same at slightly lower than the peak level.

---

[5]The intra- and interreliability of the encoding process was high, with kappa statistics of around 0.9 (Eltinge & Roberts, 1993). The measure also demonstrated certain aspects of content validity in that clauses of a factual nature were not classified as inquiry clauses.

[6]Differences in inquiry among historical and substantive contexts were each statistically significant at the .001 significance level.

TABLE 9.2
Parameter Estimates for Logistic Regression Model of Inquiry

| Variable | Estimate | Standard Error |
|---|---|---|
| Constant | 0.77 | 0.17 |
| 1965 versus 1956 | 0.18 | 0.18 |
| 1977 versus 1956 | −0.01 | 0.18 |
| 1985 versus 1956 | −0.59 | 0.20 |
| Genetics versus introduction | −0.46 | 0.14 |
| Leaf structure versus introduction | −2.31 | 0.19 |

Like those associated with publication year, estimates related to subject areas must be interpreted as deviations from the model's constant (viz., the 1956 introductory chapter). The parameter estimates associated with genetics chapters and leaf structure chapters were −0.46 and −2.31, respectively. This indicates that introductory chapters had the highest log odds of inquiry of all the subject areas. The log odd of inquiry was lower in the genetics chapters and substantially lower in the leaf structure chapters.

## DISCUSSION

The modest rise from 1956 to 1965 in the level of inquiry in the Holt series of high school biology textbooks suggests that Holt may have been responsive to the concerns of science educators in the 1960s. The educators' influence may also have occurred indirectly as the writers of the Holt series mimicked the content of the BSCS textbooks with which they were competing. This may have played a role in Holt's decision to break its tradition of releasing new editions at 4-year intervals when it released its 1960, 1963, and 1965 editions immediately following the 1960 publication of pilot versions of the BSCS textbooks. Yet the 1956 to 1965 rise in inquiry level is not significantly large and may simply be due to sampling error.

In contrast, the analysis provides strong evidence that the level of inquiry dropped dramatically from the three early time periods to 1985. Because facts are much easier to teach and factual knowledge is much easier to test than is the student's understanding of scientific process, part of this drop could have been a response from the publishers to the requests and desires of classroom teachers (Duschl, 1986; Herron, 1971; Hurd et al., 1980). On the other hand, the post-1960s decline in the level of inquiry may also have resulted as competition from BSCS textbooks waned, when their founding goals (i.e., the emphasis on science as inquiry) gradually lost favor (Conference on Goals for Science and Technology Education Grades K–12, 1983; Hurd et al., 1980). In other words, inquiry content in the Holt series may have been increasingly displaced by content intended to meet newer science education goals related to applications of science in society (Bybee, 1985; Hickman & Kahle, 1982; Hofstein & Yager, 1982; McConnell, 1982).

The analysis also showed inquiry to be highest in the introductory chapters, lower in the genetics chapters, and very low in leaf structure chapters. The difference in level of inquiry between genetics and leaf structure was anticipated. Due to the high level of scientific activity in the area of genetics during this century, the treatment of genetics material was expected to reflect an active, growing scientific process. In contrast, a relatively inert subject such as leaf structure was expected (and found) to lend itself comparatively less to a demonstration of science as a process of inquiry. Although not anticipated at the outset, it appears that the high level of inquiry in the introductory chapters resulted because authors introduced the process of science (including historical background and the steps of the scientific method) in these chapters, with the remaining chapters focusing primarily on the products of science.

Within the context of this book, the purpose of this chapter is as an illustration of linguistic content analysis. LCA was applied to measure scientific inquiry in a series of high school biology textbooks. The text analysis methodology of the study is more rigorous than can be found anywhere else in the science education literature. Unlike previous textbook analyses, it affords the researcher more precise measures than counts of end-of-chapter questions, figures, and graphs. Moreover, by restricting subjective judgments to the assignment of clauses to one of four types of intention, it avoids the gross subjective impressions required to classify entire paragraphs into highly generalized categories.

# 10

## APPLICATIONS OF COMPUTER-AIDED TEXT ANALYSIS: ANALYZING LITERARY AND NONLITERARY TEXTS

Michael E. Palmquist
Colorado State University

Kathleen M. Carley
Thomas A. Dale
Carnegie Mellon University

This chapter describes a methodology for representing mental models as maps, extracting those maps from texts, and analyzing and comparing the maps. Drawing on a computer-based cognitive mapping procedure developed by Carley (1986a, 1988; Carley & Palmquist, 1992), we illustrate the methodology with two analyses—one of 27 works of science fiction in which robots play a significant role, the other of students' understanding of class material during a course on academic writing. Results indicate that by the 1980s robots were portrayed much more positively than they were prior to the 1940s. Evidence is also provided that during the semester students gained consensus in their understanding of academic writing. The chapter concludes with a discussion of potential applications of the methodology.

In this chapter, we describe and discuss two studies that employ computer-aided text analysis. The first study explores depictions of robots in 27 works of science fiction published between 1818 and 1988 (Dale, 1991). The second study explores the growth of shared knowledge about writing among students in an introductory college composition classroom (Carley & Palmquist, 1992; Palmquist, 1990). The two studies share a number of similarities. Both employ computer-aided text analysis. Both develop their concept lists, or dictionaries, empirically (i.e., based on concepts actually found in the texts under analysis). Both employ independent raters to assess the reliability of human judgments concerning coding of concepts and statements (or pairs of related concepts). Both employ statistical tests to explore trends in the data.

Despite these similarities, the two studies differ in important ways. The robot study is an analysis of literary texts (specifically, plays, short stories, and novels), whereas the writing study is an analysis of student interviews and written journal entries. In addition, the writing study includes a comparison of observable behaviors (i.e., student interaction) with data drawn from texts, whereas the robot study deals almost entirely with data drawn from texts. Finally, the two studies differ in that only one specifies how concepts are related in the texts. The robot study defines six types of relations between a single central concept *robot* and more than 400 other concepts in a concept list. In contrast, over 200 concepts are considered in the writing study, but the types of relations among those concepts are left undefined. The similarities that extend across the two studies allow us to generalize about how computer-aided text analysis might be applied in other research contexts. In turn, the differences provide us with examples of the different uses to which computer-aided text analysis might be put.

## STUDY ONE: DEPICTIONS OF ROBOTS IN SCIENCE FICTION

This study analyzed 27 works of science fiction by 20 authors (for a more complete discussion of this study, see Dale, 1991). In each of the selected plays, short stories, and novels, robots play a significant role. The texts ranged from Shelly's *Frankenstein* and Capek's *R.U.R.* to Asimov's *The Robots of Dawn* and Anthony's *Robot Adept*, with particular attention paid to texts published during the past five decades. In all, 30 robots are depicted in the texts.

The texts were selected using a three-step process. First, an electronic database search of the holdings of Hunt Library at Carnegie Mellon University was conducted using the terms *Science Fiction* and *Robot$*, with the *$* denoting a wild-card character. Second, the results of the search were screened to produce a preliminary set of 65 texts that matched the search criteria. Finally, the researcher selected a subset of 27 texts on the basis of their representativeness and, to a lesser extent, on the relative importance of the author. Mary Shelly's *Frankenstein*, for instance, was selected because it is one of the first literary works that explores the implications of creating an artificial being. Several of Isaac Asimov's works were selected because he is both a seminal science fiction writer and a writer well known for using robots as central characters in his stories. Because no attempt was made to create a random sample of works of science fiction in which robots played significant roles in the plot, we present the results of this study strictly as a demonstration of the ways in which such texts can be analyzed, rather than as generalizable findings.

Our analysis of these texts was designed to explore whether we could measure differences in attitudes exhibited toward robots by authors writing at different times. To pursue that goal, six questions were addressed. Do the types of robots that authors describe (e.g., android, metallic humanoid) change over time? Do the features of robots change over time? Do the actions in which robots engage change over time? Do the emotions that robots exhibit change over time? Do the attributions that characters in the play, short story, or novel make to the robots change over time? Does the overall depiction of the robots in each work of fiction (i.e., positive or negative) change over time?

## Method

*Grouping the Texts.* To determine whether attitudes toward robots changed over time, the texts were placed into three groups. The two dividing points were chosen in light of two important milestones in the U.S. space program. The first, 1960, marks the beginning of the decade in which the United States, spurred first by the Soviet success of Sputnik and then by John Kennedy's challenge to send a mission to the moon by the end of the decade, firmly committed itself to the space race. The second point, 1969, marks the successful lunar landing of Apollo 11. The 1960s is seen as a pivotal decade not only for the development of the U.S. space program but also for the national self-image of the United States as a high technology culture. Using 1960 and 1969 as demarcation points, the 30 maps of robots can be grouped into one group of 12 robots in texts written before 1960, one group of 6 robots in texts written between 1960 and 1969, and one group of 12 robots in texts written from 1970 to 1988.

*Creating the Concept List and Relationship Types.* Cognitive maps are networks of statements, where each statement consists of a pair of related concepts. Thus, prior to encoding statements, one must determine the concepts and relations according to which texts are to be encoded. The concept list and relationship types for this study were developed empirically; that is, they were established during and after the texts were read rather than prior to reading the texts. (For a more complete discussion of issues related to creating concept lists, see Carley & Palmquist, 1992.) Following an initial reading of the texts, six types of relationships were established: (1) the type of robot in each text (e.g., "Robot <IS OF THIS TYPE> metallic nonhumanoid"); (2) the features each robot possessed (e.g., "Robot <HAS FEATURE> eyes"); (3) the actions each robot engaged in (e.g., "Robot <DOES ACTION> walking"); (4) the emotions each robot experienced (e.g., "Robot <HAS EMOTION> anger"); (5) attributions made to each robot by characters in each text (e.g., "Robot <HAS CHARACTERISTIC ATTRIBUTED BY CHARACTER> pride"); and (6) the author's apparent attitude toward each robot, ranging from very negative to very positive (e.g., "Robot <IS EVALUATED BY AUTHOR> positive"). In all, the researcher coded 412 concepts as being related in one of these six ways to the robots in the set of texts.

**Creating Maps.** To answer each of the research questions, the texts were coded and subsequently analyzed using MECA, or Map Extraction Comparison and Analysis.[1] One researcher coded the entire set of texts, producing maps of 30 robots (three texts contained two major characters who were robots; the others contained one). A second researcher coded a subset of three texts. Using signal-detection analysis (Lindsay & Norman, 1972, pp. 664–682) agreement between the two raters was 97.5% for concepts and 97.0% for statements.[2] False alarms (defined as instances in which the second rater coded a concept or statement as being present when the first rater had not coded it as being present) were 15.1% for concepts and 40.4% for statements. The high false alarm rate for statements reflects the tendency of the second rater to create more detailed maps of each text. For the three texts, the total number of statements coded by the second rater exceeded that of the first rater by roughly 25% to 40%.

After the coding was completed, a separate set of four coders ranked the emotions and character attributions identified by the primary coder. The various emotions and attributions were ranked as either negative, neutral, or positive. These rankings afforded the three-level ordinal measure on these variables used in subsequent statistical analyses. Average simple agreement among the raters was 80.8%.

**Creating Modified Maps Using SKI.** Because the goal of this study was to represent the depictions of each robot as accurately as possible, a software program, SKI, was used to make implicit statements explicit. SKI accepts two files as input, a map file and what might be termed an implicit knowledge file. A fairly simple illustration may clarify the manner in which SKI operates. Imagine that the implicit knowledge file contains a statement amounting to "if something has ears then it can hear." Then, if a map file contained the statement that a robot has ears, SKI would add two additional statements: if a robot has ears then a robot can hear, and a robot can hear. When creating modified maps, SKI adds concepts and statements that explicate the implicit knowledge. SKI does not delete concepts. It can add concepts and add relations among existing or new concepts, thus creating statements.

---

[1]MECA is a collection of 15 text analysis programs. The programs can run on UNIX workstations, many IBM personal computers or clones, and Apple Macintosh computers (Carley, 1986a, 1988, 1993; Carley & Palmquist, 1992). For availability, see Popping (this volume).

[2]To increase comparability of statements across texts, a number of explicit concepts were coded as synonyms. For instance, the explicit concepts "annihilated" and "destroyed," as in "the robot annihilated the humans," were coded as "attack."

Although SKI cannot overcome gross coder error, it can overcome some of the most frequent coder errors, such as neglecting to fully specify all implied statements in the text. The modified maps generated by SKI are thus larger than those generated by novice coders. SKI-modified maps tend to be closer to maps coded by individuals who are experts in the domain from which the texts are selected. Carley (1988) described SKI in detail and demonstrated how its application to texts coded by novices actually improves the coding so that it more closely resembles coding by experts.

A comparison of agreement on features of robots between unmodified and SKI-modified maps indicates that the modified maps allow more common features to be identified (see Table 10.1). Similar results were obtained for emotions, actions, and character attributions. Because of this, the subsequent analyses are based on maps modified using SKI.

***Analyzing Maps.*** After each map had been modified by SKI, all maps were analyzed statistically and depicted graphically. To prepare the maps for statistical analysis, software was used to produce data matrices for each map in which the rows were either concepts or statements and the columns were the names of the other maps. The cells in the data matrices indicated whether or not each concept or statement was found in that map. Summary matrices

TABLE 10.1
Robot Features by Period

| | Pre-1960s (12 texts) | | 1960s (6 texts) | | Post-1960s (12 texts) | |
|---|---|---|---|---|---|---|
| Unmodified maps | | | | | | |
| | Hear | (12) | Hear | (4) | Hear | (10) |
| | Memory | (9) | Memory | (3) | Memory | (12) |
| | Voice | (10) | Voice | (4) | Voice | (10) |
| | | | Circuits | (5) | Circuits | (10) |
| | | | Consciousness | (4) | Consciousness | (10) |
| SKI-modified maps | | | | | | |
| | Brain | (12) | Brain | (6) | Brain | (12) |
| | Face | (10) | Face | (4) | Face | (10) |
| | Hear | (12) | Hear | (4) | Hear | (12) |
| | Intelligence | (12) | Intelligence | (6) | Intelligence | (12) |
| | Memory | (9) | Memory | (3) | Memory | (12) |
| | Senses | (12) | Senses | (4) | Senses | (12) |
| | Sight | (9) | Sight | (3) | Sight | (9) |
| | Voice | (11) | Voice | (4) | Voice | (10) |
| | Eyes | (9) | | | Eyes | (9) |
| | | | Circuits | (5) | Circuits | (10) |
| | | | Consciousness | (4) | Consciousness | (10) |

*Note.* The numbers in parentheses indicate the number of maps in which each feature is present.

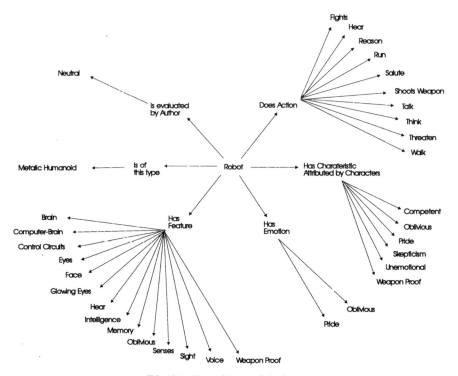

FIG. 10.1. Map of "Arm of the Law."

were subsequently produced in which the rows were individual maps and the columns were variables indicating the total numbers of concepts and statements in each map, the intersection of concepts and statements across the set of maps, the number of concepts and statements in each map not found in each of the other maps, and the number of concepts and statements that were unique (i.e., not found in any of the other maps) to each map.

Maps were also depicted graphically. A modified map of Harry Harrison's short story, "Arm of the Law," is presented in Figure 10.1. To read the map as a series of statements, begin at the central concept, "robot," read a phrase such as DOES ACTION as the relationship between robot and another concept, and read one of the concepts linked to DOES ACTION by a line as the second concept. The arrow on each line indicates the direction in which the statement should be read. For example, you could read "Robot <DOES ACTION> Fights" as a statement meaning that the robot in "Arm of the Law" fought. In a more detailed map, concepts such as "fight" might be linked to still other concepts, such as the person or thing being fought, the type of weapons (if any) used in the fight, and who won the fight. The reader should note as well that a map of a longer text, such as Robert Heinlein's novel, *The Moon is a Harsh Mistress*, would be more detailed than the map of "Arm of the Law."

## Results

Comparisons of Figures 10.2, 10.3, and 10.4 indicate only one trend across the three time periods in robot types, features, or actions. Over time, fewer authors depicted robots as nonmetallic humanoids, and more authors depicted robots as metallic humanoids. This trend is mirrored by the presence of one feature, circuits, in the second and third periods that does not appear in the first period.

Clearer trends over time can be seen in the emotions that robots exhibit during the three periods, the attributions made to robots by characters in the texts, and the overall evaluations of robots by the authors of the texts. In general, the characterizations of robots in texts written after the 1960s are more positive than those written prior to or during the 1960s. In the texts written prior to 1960, consensus exists only on the emotions "disdain" and "fear" and on the character attributions "disdain," "fear," "formidable," and "intelligent." In the 1960s, the emotion "disdain" is joined by "anger," whereas "fear" is not present, and the character attribution "disdain" is joined by "anger" and "pride," but "fear" is not present. In the 1970s and 1980s, "fear" is present but is counterbalanced by the more positive emotions of "loyalty," "trust," and "friendship," emotions that authors do not attribute to robots in the first two periods. Similarly, in the 1970s and 1980s, the character attribution "fear" is present but is counterbalanced by the

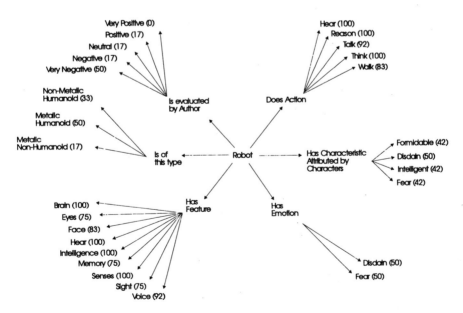

FIG. 10.2. Map of pre-1960s texts. In parentheses are percentages of texts in which statement occurs.

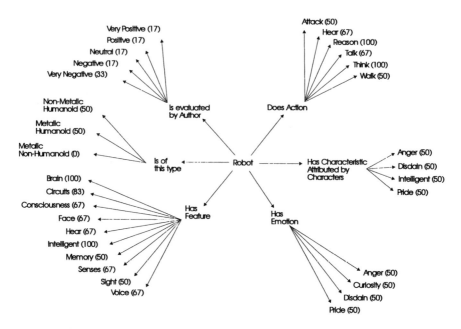

FIG. 10.3. Map of 1960s texts. In parentheses are percentages of texts in which statement occurs.

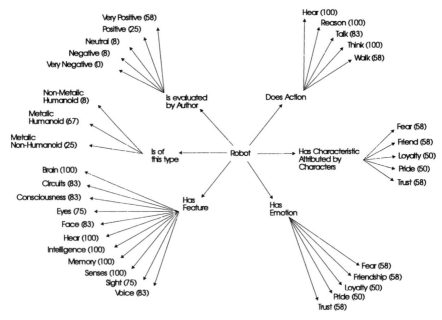

FIG. 10.4. Map of post-1960s texts. In parentheses are percentages of texts in which statement occurs.

more positive character attributions of "loyalty," "trust," and "friend," qualities that characters do not attribute to robots in the first two periods.

Statistical analysis mirrors these trends. Positive and negative robot emotion, character attribution, and author evaluation scores were calculated for the modified map of each text, the first two of which were based on rankings by four raters. Table 10.2 presents the results of three analyses of variance that showed significant differences among the three time periods in the mean percentage of science fiction texts in which positive emotions were exhibited by robots and in which positive attributions were made by characters. The table also lists the mean author evaluation score. The mean scores for positive emotion statements, character attributes, and author evaluations were significantly higher for texts written in the 1970s and 1980s than for the other two periods.

A Pearson correlation between the percentage of positive emotion statements and publication year (excluding *Frankenstein*, which was published in 1818 and which served as a strong outlier) also indicated a significant positive trend ($r = .468, p < .01$). As publication year grew more recent, the percentage of positive emotion statements increased. Similarly, a Pearson correlation between the percentage of positive character attribution statements and publication year (again excluding *Frankenstein*) also indicated a significant positive trend ($r = .380, p < .05$). As publication year grew more recent, the percentage of positive character attribution statements increased.

## Discussion

**Results.** These results illustrate change over time in the depictions of robots by the authors in this set of texts. Although the actions and features of robots have remained relatively constant during the periods studied, robots' emotions, characters' attributions, and authors' evaluations have shifted

TABLE 10.2
Temporal Changes in Statements Indicating Robot Emotions,
Character Attributions, and Author Evaluations That Are Positive

|  | Pre-1960s (12 texts) | 1960s (6 texts) | Post-1960s (12 texts) | F |
|---|---|---|---|---|
| Robot emotions | 28.1 | 29.5 | 55.0 | 6.25** |
|  | (20.9) | (24.1) | (17.8) |  |
| Character attributions | 26.4 | 27.5 | 47.1 | 3.58* |
|  | (18.7) | (20.7) | (21.9) |  |
| Author evaluations | 2.0 | 2.7 | 4.3 | 11.43*** |
|  | (1.2) | (1.6) | (1.0) |  |

*Note.* Robot emotions and character attributions are in percentages; author evaluations are means on a 5-point scale with 1 being very negative and 5 being very positive. Standard deviations are in parentheses.

$*p < .05. **p < .01. ***p < .001.$

from largely negative to largely positive. By the 1970s and 1980s, robots were considered capable of inspiring loyalty, trust, and even friendship within their human counterparts.

Because the texts were not selected randomly, however, we cannot generalize these findings to depictions of robots in science fiction in general. Despite this limitation, these results suggest that a more ambitious investigation of texts in which robots play a significant role might reveal changes over time in writers' presentation of robots and, by implication, of changes over time on a societal level.

**Method.** This study provides a relatively straightforward example of how computer-aided text analysis can be used to conduct map analysis. However, at least two issues related to the use of the methodology are worth noting: the inherent threats to reliability and validity entailed by the use of human coders and the data reduction problem. First, the use of human raters to code the texts (as opposed to machine coding, which carries with it another set of challenges) raises questions about the reliability and validity of that coding. Although the interrater reliability reported in the study is at an acceptable level (i.e., over 80% agreement), analysis of the results indicates some anomalies. For instance, based on the 1960s texts our analysis of the maps indicates that three of the robots have vision, yet only two robots are listed as having eyes. The explanation for this apparent discrepancy lies in the manner in which the robot in Heinlein's *The Moon is a Harsh Mistress* "sees." Essentially, the robot is a mainframe computer that sees through video cameras. We might question whether those cameras should have been listed as eyes, and we might ask what difference exists between the video cameras and an analogous light sensor in a metallic humanoid robot. Because a human coder could reasonably choose one of several answers in this situation, this is a case in which human coding can lead to a great deal of ambiguity.

The use of human raters also introduces problems related to inconsistency in the level of analysis as a coder moves from one text to another. Particularly when dealing with a large set of texts, it is possible to have judgments being made in a qualitatively different manner at the beginning and end of coding a set of texts. This issue can be dealt with to some extent by using multiple coders and by making more than one pass through each text. However, it is difficult, when using human coders, to ensure that texts are coded in precisely the same manner.

The nature of text analysis also necessarily entails some data reduction. The amount of information provided by a statement that a robot possesses a certain feature or exhibits a certain emotion cannot be expected to provide the same amount of information conveyed by an author's careful development of a character or a scene. For instance, a statement that is coded

"Robot <DOES ACTION> Attack" does not indicate who was attacked, why they were attacked, or how they were attacked. Map analysis would be able to indicate that the same statement occurred in two or more texts, but it would not be able to indicate, unless it were explicitly coded as such, that in one case the attack occurred because the robot was defending someone whereas in another case the robot was running amok. The data reduction problem can, to some degree, be alleviated by careful and comprehensive coding of a given text. However, it seems unlikely that researchers will always want to create highly detailed maps of a particular text. For the majority of researchers, it seems that at least some data reduction is inevitable.

## STUDY TWO: LANGUAGE AND LEARNING IN A UNIVERSITY WRITING CLASSROOM

A common problem in writing instruction is lack of a shared set of terms for discussing writing. Students are often uncertain, for instance, about the meaning of terms such as *voice* or *tone*, and writing instructors often express dismay about students' misunderstanding of important terms such as *revision*. When teachers suggest that a student revise a draft, for instance, they typically want their students to rethink global issues such as audience, purpose, or structure. Students, on the other hand, often interpret a suggestion to revise a paper as a need to check spelling, punctuation, and word choice. This kind of mismatch between intention and understanding can significantly reduce the learning that takes place in a classroom.

This study explores the evolution of a shared lexicon about writing among the 16 students and teacher in one semester-long writing course (for a more complete description of the study, see Palmquist, 1990). The purpose of the course was to introduce students to academic writing. Specifically, students were taught that academic writing involved reading, interpreting, and responding to arguments. One expectation of this study was that, as the semester progressed, students and teachers would develop a shared understanding of key concepts and the relations between pairs of these concepts (i.e., within statements). To determine whether that expectation was met, maps of students' mental models of writing at the beginning and end of the semester were created and analyzed. These maps were compared both with each other and with a map of the instructor's mental model of the course content. Four questions were addressed. As the semester progressed, did student maps become more similar to those of their teacher? As the semester progressed, did student maps become more similar to those of their classmates? Which concepts and statements were used by at least half the students at the beginning and end of the semester? Was student interaction positively associated with similarities among student maps?

## Data and Method

*Data Collection.* Students were interviewed at the beginning, middle, and end of the semester. They also submitted writing journals in which they discussed key concepts in the course, among them the purpose of research writing. The teacher was interviewed at the beginning of the semester. Class sessions were observed, and key concepts used during discussions and lectures were noted.

In-class interaction was tracked through classroom observation notes and records of computer-based interactions among students during a once-weekly meeting in a computer classroom. Interactions were summarized using a grid for each week of the semester. The weekly grids were subsequently summarized into a single grid, each cell of which contained the total number of in-class interactions between each pair of students during the semester.

To track out-of-class interaction, students were asked to indicate (on a form administered each week) classmates with whom during the past week they had discussed course-related matters outside the classroom. Each interaction sheet consisted of a space for the student to write his or her name, a list of all students in the class, and a line following each name in the list. Students were asked to indicate the number of meetings they had with each classmate and to note briefly what they discussed during each meeting. The interaction sheets were distributed to students 13 times during the semester. The weekly interaction sheets were coded using a grid for each week of the semester. These weekly grids were subsequently summarized into a single grid representing the total reported interactions among each pair of students during the semester. For a more detailed discussion of the methods used in this study, see Palmquist (1990, 1993).

*Creating the Concept List.* The concept list was established using an empirical approach. UNIX utilities were used to identify frequently occurring words and phrases in the interview transcripts, student journals, and transcriptions of the classroom observation notes. Terms and phrases found in at least 25% of the interviews or journal entries were added to the concept list. Terms and phrases that were used in at least three class sessions were also added to the concept list. In addition, key terms and phrases that were used in the textbook were added to the concept list.

*Creating Maps.* Maps were created for each student interview transcript and each student journal. A map was created for the instructor based on interviews, analysis of the textbook, and classroom observation notes. Each map was created using a two-step process. First, using the query/replace utility in a word processing program, terms and phrases in the concept list were marked in the text files (e.g., the term *write* was replaced with ___*write*). Second, the text files were printed and, using software in the MECA suite, maps were created for each text. A primary rater coded all texts analyzed in the study, and a second rater coded 10% of the interview transcripts and journal entries. Interrater reliability was calculated using signal-detection analysis (Lindsay & Norman, 1972). For the interview transcripts, interrater agreement was 95.5% for concepts and 70.7% for statements, with false alarms for the second rater of 6.5% and 38.6%, respectively. For the journal entries, interrater agreement was 93.1% for concepts and 65.5% for statements, with false alarms for the second rater of 5.8% and 33.8%, respectively.

Unlike the maps created in the robot study, no relationship types were defined in this study. Statements simply indicated that two concepts were related in some way. This procedure was followed primarily because this was an exploratory study of learning in an ill-defined domain. It seemed likely, based on previous research efforts, that students would provide relatively imprecise descriptions of their efforts to learn about writing. As a result, the choice was made to focus primarily on the use of concepts and the extent to which (although not the manner in which) those concepts were related.

*Analyzing Maps.* Analysis of the maps was conducted in a manner similar to analysis in the robot study. Maps were analyzed statistically and depicted graphically. A sample student map is depicted in Figure 10.5. Statistical measures of interest include the intersection of concepts (i.e., the number of concepts that any two maps have in common) between each student map and the instructor map and between each pair of student maps; the intersection of statements (i.e., the number of statements that any two maps have in common) between each student map and the instructor map and between each pair of student maps; the mean intersection of concepts between each student map and all other student maps; and the mean intersection of statements between each student map and all other student maps.

## Results

The results presented in Table 10.3 indicate significant increases in a series of one-tailed tests in the intersection of concepts and statements between student maps and the instructor map and significant increases in the intersection of concepts and statements among student maps. The only test that did not indicate a significantly larger intersection was the nonsignificant increase ($p = .07$) for the intersection of concepts between student and instructor maps in the journal entries.

As might be expected, given the increases in the intersections of concepts and statements across student maps, several concepts and statements were

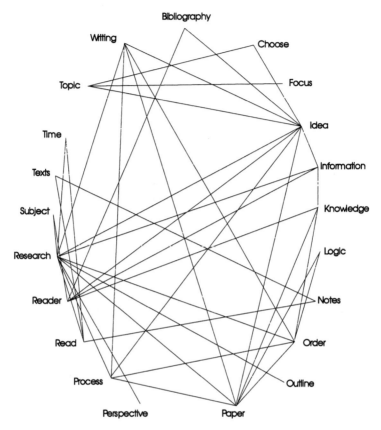

FIG. 10.5. Student map of first journal entry: "How and for what purpose(s) do you write a journal entry?"

used by more students at the end of the semester than at the beginning. As Table 10.4 indicates, concepts such as "analysis," "contribution," and "line of argument," which were used by less than 10% of the students in the first round of interviews, were used by over 60% of the students in their final interviews. Similarly, five statements found in at least 50% of the student maps based on the end-of-semester interviews were not present in any of the maps based on the first round of interviews. It is clear, however, that this growth in shared concepts and statements was not simply additive. Although a number of new concepts entered the lexicon of the classroom, several concepts that were used by a majority of students at the beginning of the semester saw substantial declines in use during interviews at the end of the semester (e.g., "outline," "organize," "notes," and "library"). Similarly, several statements were found in fewer maps at the end of the semester than at the beginning.

TABLE 10.3
Concept and Statement Intersections at Beginning Versus End of Semester

| | Beginning of Semester | End of Semester | t |
|---|---|---|---|
| Intersections between student and instructor maps | | | |
| | Concept intersections | | |
| Interviews | 13.1 | 27.4 | 5.82*** |
| | (3.7) | (9.6) | |
| Journal entries | 21.1 | 25.6 | 1.57 |
| | (5.5) | (7.8) | |
| | Statement intersections | | |
| Interviews | 5.8 | 40.3 | 5.19*** |
| | (4.3) | (25.5) | |
| Journal entries | 29.7 | 73.5 | 4.07*** |
| | (16.5) | (32.3) | |
| Intersections between student and classmates' maps | | | |
| | Concept intersections | | |
| Interviews | 11.6 | 19.5 | 7.09*** |
| | (2.3) | (4.1) | |
| Journal entries | 13.6 | 23.0 | 6.17*** |
| | (2.2) | (4.8) | |
| | Statement intersections | | |
| Interviews | 28.4 | 37.3 | 3.08** |
| | (6.0) | (12.3) | |
| Journal entries | 25.9 | 45.5 | 4.44*** |
| | (6.7) | (15.4) | |

*Note.* Standard deviations are in parentheses below percents.
*$p < .05$. **$p < .01$. ***$p < .001$.

To determine whether student interaction was positively associated with similarities among student maps, the number of interactions between each pair of students over the semester was compared with the number of concepts and statements each pair had in common at the end of the semester. Total interactions and shared concepts and statements were represented by data matrices in which the rows and columns were students and the cells were either total interactions per pair of students or the intersection of statements or concepts. The matrices were compared using the quadratic assignment procedure, which compares the corresponding cells of two matrices and, accounting for row and column effects, produces a $z$ score indicating the probability that the two matrices covary. (For more information on use of the quadratic assignment procedure, see Hubert, 1987.) In addition to producing a probability score, the quadratic assignment procedure also indicates the direction (positive or negative) of the association between the matrices. It does not, however, indicate the strength of the association. Our analysis produced two significant positive associations between student interaction and shared concepts and statements ($z = 1.85$,

TABLE 10.4
Percentage of Concepts and Statements Mentioned
in Interviews at Beginning Versus End of Semester

| Concepts | Semester | | Statements | Semester | |
|---|---|---|---|---|---|
| | Begin | End | | Begin | End |
| organize | 56 | 25 | notes–research | 69 | 13 |
| outline | 50 | 38 | source–writing | 63 | 13 |
| knowledge | 56 | 44 | paper–topic | 50 | 19 |
| library | 75 | 44 | notes–paper | 50 | 31 |
| notes | 88 | 44 | notes–writing | 69 | 31 |
| source | 75 | 44 | research–source | 75 | 31 |
| argument | 6 | 50 | information–writing | 75 | 38 |
| books | 69 | 50 | library–research | 69 | 38 |
| solution | 13 | 50 | analysis–summary | 0 | 50 |
| subject | 44 | 50 | author–paper | 0 | 50 |
| talking | 38 | 50 | information–research | 88 | 50 |
| thinking | 44 | 50 | problem–writing | 6 | 50 |
| articles | 19 | 56 | author–summary | 0 | 56 |
| group | 6 | 56 | author–writing | 19 | 56 |
| issue | 19 | 56 | idea–writing | 56 | 56 |
| important | 44 | 63 | issue–research | 6 | 56 |
| line of argument | 0 | 63 | problem–research | 13 | 56 |
| topic | 100 | 63 | read–research | 44 | 56 |
| contribute | 0 | 69 | research–topic | 94 | 56 |
| difference | 44 | 69 | topic–writing | 81 | 56 |
| information | 88 | 69 | author–research | 13 | 63 |
| approach | 13 | 75 | contribute–research | 0 | 63 |
| newness | 19 | 75 | idea–research | 56 | 63 |
| point | 44 | 75 | newness–research | 13 | 63 |
| synthesis | 13 | 75 | research–summary | 25 | 63 |
| problem | 19 | 81 | analysis–synthesis | 6 | 69 |
| analysis | 6 | 88 | paper–writing | 88 | 69 |
| author | 19 | 88 | paper–research | 94 | 75 |
| find | 75 | 88 | summary–synthesis | 0 | 75 |
| read | 75 | 88 | research–writing | 100 | 100 |
| summary | 31 | 88 | | | |
| paper | 94 | 94 | | | |
| idea | 69 | 100 | | | |
| research | 100 | 100 | | | |
| writing | 100 | 100 | | | |

$p < .05$, and $z = 1.89$, $p < .05$, respectively, in one-tailed tests). However, these associations were found only between out-of-class interactions and shared knowledge in the written descriptions of research writing. No significant associations were found between out-of-class interaction and shared knowledge in the student interviews. Nor were significant associations found between in-class interaction and either type of shared knowledge.

## Discussion

*Results.* This study illustrates how text analysis can be used to track the development of a shared lexicon. As the semester progressed, the mean number of concepts and statements shared between student maps increased, as did the mean number of concepts and statements that student maps shared with the instructor map. The study also illustrates how data derived from this form of text analysis may be associated with observable behaviors, in this case student interaction. Finally, the study calls attention to the dangers of assuming that growth in shared concepts and statements is additive. In this study, several concepts and statements that appeared in at least half of the student maps at the beginning of the semester appeared in fewer maps at the end of the semester.

*Method.* As was the case in the robot study, this study underscores potential problems associated with relying on human judgment. In this study in particular, the agreement between raters on statements in each text was low (65% to 70%). This study also calls attention to a loss of information associated with data reduction. Because the types of relations between the concepts in this study were not specified, it is impossible to reconstruct accurately the texts from which they were drawn.

As we noted previously, this study is exploratory. The choice not to define relationship types was a direct result of not being sure that similarities between texts would be found if these similarities required matching relationship types as well as concepts. Had it been possible to recode the maps of each text easily (in effect, to do a finer grained analysis), this choice might not have been made. As software for computer-aided text analysis becomes more sophisticated, it seems likely that the tradeoffs in this study will be less common. However, for the time being, logistic constraints often require the text analyst to make a large number of self-restricting choices (Carley, 1993). Software developments in the near future may alleviate many of these restrictions (Bechtel, this volume).

## GENERAL DISCUSSION

The two studies in this chapter demonstrate how researchers can empirically analyze shifts in meaning, definition, and intent by focusing on both concepts and the relationships among concepts. In both studies graphical and statistical devices are used to address research issues. In this way, the approach allows the researcher to move back and forth between qualitative and quantitative analysis.

Currently, it is quite difficult to analyze maps. Indeed, our ability to code complex maps far outstrips our ability to compare and analyze these maps. Complex maps may have multiple types of relations, uni- and bidirectional relations, and variable strengths on the relations (e.g., Kleinnijenhuis, de Ridder, & Rietberg, this volume). Such complexity differentiates and gives power to the coding scheme. However, current statistical techniques for analyzing maps are most reliable and most highly developed for simple maps. Future research needs to address the statistical comparison of more complex maps.

The simplest map has all relations of the same type—relations that are either uni- or bidirectional and that are either present or not. Maps coded in this way can be described as binary graphs. Comparison and analysis techniques for binary graphs are fully developed. For maps coded in this way, the hamming metric can be used for determining the extent of similarity. For a set of such maps, it is possible to locate the central map (as was done in the writing study) and to estimate its sampling distribution (Banks & Carley, 1994). This is comparable to locating the mean and standard deviation for a variable. These statistics can be used to test hypotheses about differences among classes of maps. For example, with respect to the robot study, these statistics make it possible to test whether the cultural perception of robots has shifted significantly over time. The significant trend from negative to positive attitudes toward robots was evaluated in analyses of single statements. The Banks and Carley technique would allow the researcher to simultaneously focus on all statements in each map.

Aside from the methodological issue that statistical techniques for complex graphs are limited, there is also a theoretical issue: What theoretic purpose does this greater complexity serve? Clearly, with more complex coding schemes the ability to regenerate text from code is increased (Roberts, this volume, chapter 3). Further, such complexity may have diagnostic value at the individual level (Gottschalk, this volume). However, the greater the complexity of the coding scheme, the lower the likelihood that two maps will appear similar. This issue was described earlier as a tradeoff between validity and data reduction. Specifically, the more data are reduced, the more coder agreement is enhanced, but, quite likely, the less valid will be one's encoded data and the less likely these data can be accurately reconstructed into a semblance of the original text. The rule of thumb seems to be that the researcher should only opt for the degree of complexity required to answer the research question at hand.

There is a final cautionary note, however. Interrater reliability varies negatively with the complexity of the coding task. We found great differences among coders in their willingness and ability to make inferences and to generalize. Moreover, coders are more similar in their treatment of concepts than they are in their treatment of statements. This suggests that applications of map analysis must tailor coder training to increase interrater reliability with respect to statements. We see three possible avenues worth exploring: development of a (possibly hierarchical) theory of concept relations (cf. Roberts, this volume, chapter 3), development of computer-aided procedures that decrease reliance on human coders (cf. Popping, this volume), and further development of tools like SKI that make explicit implicit relations and so augment human coding by focusing on the missed relations.

The two studies we have presented illustrate the power of using maps to analyze and compare mental models. Even simple maps admit empirical analysis and make it possible to address detailed questions about shifts in meaning. Further, map analysis allows us to address learning in terms of the structure and the content of what is learned. We can ask, with these maps, do mental models become more complex or more integrated over time? Under what conditions do novice mental models become more like expert models? What is the content of this change? With map analysis, we can thus focus not only on concept usage but also on meaning and shifts in cognitive structure.

# 11

# REASONING IN ECONOMIC DISCOURSE: AN APPLICATION OF THE NETWORK APPROACH TO THE DUTCH PRESS

Jan Kleinnijenhuis
Free University Amsterdam

Jan A. de Ridder
University of Amsterdam

Ewald M. Rietberg
Free University Amsterdam

This chapter discusses a method for relational content analysis that is based upon the idea that the explicit or manifest content of a text can be depicted as a network consisting of relations between meaning objects. To map the content of a text into a network, texts are parsed into nuclear sentences, each of which connects one meaning object to another. The network representation enables the formulation of inference rules that reveal implicit or latent content. In addition to providing a rigorous description of text content, network analysis also provides a foundation for various significance tests, for example, for differences over time or between implicit and explicit content. The chapter concludes with an application of network text analysis to economic news, which shows the decline of Keynesianism in the Dutch press.

   Usually texts convey more than explicit messages. Part of their meaning is expressed between the lines. In fact, ordinary users of language are quite sophisticated interpreters of unspoken and unwritten meanings. Whereas explicit meanings can be understood by employing the author's and audience's common knowledge of the grammar and semantics of a language, implicit meanings can often be inferred from explicit information within the text by employing the author's and audience's application of inference rules.

The method for text analysis described in this chapter allows not only for an analysis of the manifest content of texts but also for an analysis of their latent content (i.e., the content that can be logically inferred from the manifest content). The first section of the chapter describes concepts and coding procedures for unraveling (i.e., parsing) a text into a list of so-called nuclear sentences. This list of nuclear sentences can then be used to construct a network representation of the analyzed texts. The next section describes procedures, derived from the field of network theory, for representing explicit meaning as well as for inferring implicit meaning. The balance of the chapter is devoted to describing an application of this method within a content analysis of Dutch economic news coverage between 1968 and 1984.

## THE ENCODING OF MANIFEST CONTENT

Philosophers such as Ludwig Wittgenstein have suggested that the manifest content of a text can be represented as a list of elementary assertions, or *nuclear sentences*, each connecting one meaning object to another (cf. Wittgenstein, 1973/1921, par. 3.144). Osgood, Saporta, and Nunally (1956) were the first to develop explicit coding instructions to assure that the list of "atomic sentences" would be reliable. They also introduced mathematical formulae for rendering political language according to Heider's (1946) psycho-logic, a logic subsequently made more rigorous by Abelson and Rosenberg (1958). It was Holsti (1966) who first used the computer in an attempt to automate this approach. From a different starting point, Axelrod (1976) originated a similar two-place predicate coding scheme to exhibit authors' cognitive maps, which would be predictive of future actions. Amidst these developments, Abelson (1968) was able to show the logic of the underlying psycho-logic to be partially nonsensical and surely incomplete. The next section presents a consistent set of rules for logical inference—rules that meet Abelson's early critique. It is here that we introduce the structure of a nuclear sentence.

### The Structure of a Nuclear Sentence

The grammar of a human language enables authors to combine many nuclear beliefs in one complex sentence. The text analysis method presented here relies on the reverse ability of the audience (or, more important, the coder) to unravel complex sentences. A formal method is described here for mapping the logic of texts' nuclear sentences.[1]

---

[1]Ideally, we should describe the precise linkage between the structure of nuclear sentences and the possible surface structures of sentences in a language, for example, starting from Dixon's functional description of English grammar (Dixon, 1991). However, such an enterprise would go beyond the scope of this chapter.

TABLE 11.1
Structure and Illustrations of Nuclear Sentences

| Author: (!) | (Quoted Source: (!)) | (IF | $i$-object $i_f$-object | / predicate / predicate | / $j$-object / $j_f$-object | THEN) |
|---|---|---|---|---|---|---|
| John: | | | Anna | / doesn't like (-) | / Frank | |
| John: | Maureen: | | Anna | / has made eyes at (+) | / John | |
| John: | Frank:! | | Anna | / ought to love (+) | / Frank | |
| John: | | IF | Anna | / has made eyes at (+) | / John | THEN |
| | | | John | / can date (+) | / Anna | |

Original text:
John said, "Anna doesn't like Frank. According to Maureen, its John that Anna has made eyes at. From what Frank told me, Anna ought to love him—that is, Frank. But if Anna has made eyes at John, he's the one who can date her."

*Note.* Column headings list nuclear sentences' optional components in parentheses.

A nuclear sentence is defined as a two-place predicate connecting an $i$-object (i.e., its agent or subject) with a $j$-object (i.e., the object influenced or implied by the $i$-object).[2] Optionally, the authorship of a two-place predicate can be attributed to a quoted or paraphrased actor. Two types of quotes are distinguished: the *say-quote* (denoted by :) and the *order-quote* (denoted by :!). In an order-quote, the quoted or paraphrased actor orders, wishes, or desires what the nuclear sentence signifies; in a say-quote no such order, wish, or desire is indicated. Furthermore, an author may use an IF-clause to specify under which condition the two-place predicate holds. Table 11.1 illustrates the core of nuclear sentence structure.[3]

## The Two-Place Predicate

Almost any relation established by a two-place predicate can be ranked on a positive–neutral–negative axis. For example, "$i$ / enhances / $j$" is a positive connection, whereas "$i$ / inhibits / $j$" establishes a negative connection. "To enhance" is a positive predicate, because $j$ (e.g., unemployment) will be influenced positively, which means that there will be more ups, more prominence, more fortune, or more success for $j$. Note that it is not relevant whether

---

[2]When sentences are in passive voice, the $i$-object is the indirect object, not the subject. For example, in "Mary received a letter from John," not Mary but John is the $i$-object. $i$'s activity should always be more relevant for the success of what the two-place predicate describes than $j$'s activity.

[3]The optional quotes and conditions in Table 11.1 are treated only briefly here. Other options not included in Table 11.1 but suggested by the theory of functional grammars (e.g., Dik, 1981; Dixon, 1991) are not discussed here. This chapter's focus remains on the core of the nuclear sentence.

success for $j$ is desired by other actors or normatively desirable according to the author (e.g., as "success" for unemployment would unlikely be).

We use the word *quality* to label the degree of positivity or negativity of a predicate. The quality of a predicate takes values along the range [−1 . . . +1], where −1 denotes *extremely negative* and +1 *extremely positive.* Moreover, the quality of a nuclear sentence can be dampened by its ambiguity. Nuclear sentences are normally assumed to be unambiguous (ambiguity = 0). However, when they include double-edged complements (e.g., "overly intelligent") or chance words (e.g., "probably attractive"), nuclear sentences are coded as ambiguous ($0 \leq$ ambiguity $\leq 1 -$ [quality × quality]).

The quality of a predicate does not exhaust its full meaning (Abelson, 1968). Obviously, both "to kiss" and "to give $25" are positive predicates, but the activities these predicates refer to are not interchangeable in social life. To capture somewhat more of the substance of relations between $i$- and $j$-objects, predicate types are also encoded.

## Meaning Objects and Predicate Types

Both the $i$- and $j$-object are *meaning objects*—objects that can be classified into a few abstract types. Various types of meaning objects include *actors*, such as individuals, collectively acting groups, organizations, and institutions (e.g., President Clinton, the Supreme Court, the United States); *states*, more or less concrete products of human action or interaction (e.g., "President Clinton's plan for health care reform," "Amendment 5 to the U.S. Constitution," "Irangate," "Communism"); *variables* (e.g., the level of inflation, the level of employment) and *attributes* (e.g., dichotomous variables such as "being president of the United States"); *values* (e.g., doing good, doing what is desirable); and *realities* (e.g., the economic reality in the Netherlands in 1984).

The last two object types are in need of a further clarification. A value is a meaning object that an author uses to evaluate another meaning object. According to the author, the evaluated meaning object has an effect on the value. President Clinton's evaluation (simplified here), "The current health care system is endangering lives," suggests that the "current health care system" has a negative effect on a value (namely, the preservation of human lives). Our approach does not distinguish among evaluations involving different types of values but rather lumps all values under one meaning object labeled *Ideal* (i.e., "good"). By this token, Clinton's evaluation could be coded as "Clinton: health care system / is endangering lives (-¾) / Ideal." Note that Ideal can only occur as a $j$-object.

A reality encompasses everything that happens within itself. Many different realities may be distinguished by an author (e.g., Ronald Reagan's world in 1981, the world our children will live in), but in almost every discourse explicit references are made to the author's reality. Obviously President Clinton's sentence, "This new world has already enriched the lives of millions of Americans," should be coded as "Reality / has already enriched (+) / Americans." The same coding also applies to sentences in which Reality is not explicitly stated, such as "The lives of millions of Americans have already been enriched." If an author proclaims an actor's success (+) or failure (−), a state's appearance (+) or disappearance (−), or a variable's increase (+) or a decline (−) but makes no attribution to a specific *i*-object, then Reality is to be coded as the *i*-object. Note that Reality is never coded as a *j*-object.

Different types of meaning objects correspond loosely to qualitatively different types of predicates. Although predicate types may be defined for assignment to nuclear sentence types that frequently occur in one's texts, we describe only five types of predicates that are directly relevant to the research at hand. Illustrative sentences are (often loosely) derived from President Clinton's 1993 State of the Union Address.

- *EVA* predicates are used to evaluate a meaning object (e.g., "The current health care system is endangering lives" is coded as "Clinton: health care system / is endangering lives (-¾) / Ideal").
- *REA* predicates relate a *j*-object to the author's reality (e.g., "The lives of millions of Americans have already been enriched" is coded as "Clinton: Reality / has already enriched (+) / Americans").
- *ACT* predicates are used to code actions (e.g., "We are reducing our budget deficit" is coded as "Clinton: Clinton / are reducing (−) / budget deficit").
- *CAU* predicates are used to code causal relations between pairs of variables (e.g., "The reduction of the deficit will increase savings" is coded as "Clinton: national debt / reduction increases (−) / savings").
- *AFF* predicates may be used to code an affective relation between two actors (e.g., "I salute George Bush for his half-century service" is coded as "Clinton: Clinton / salutes for his service (+) / Bush"). AFF predicates may also be used to code an affective relation from an actor (as *i*-object) toward a variable (as *j*-object). For example, "We will insist on fair trade rules" is coded as "Clinton: Clinton / will insist on (+) / fair trade."

Finally, it should be noted that one verbal phrase may be encoded as multiple nuclear sentences. The statement "The increasing debt is responsible for the decline in national savings," for example, should be encoded as two nuclear sentences of REA type ("Reality/+/debt," "Reality/−/savings") and one nuclear sentence of CAU type ("debt/−/savings"). The statement "unemployment is too high" gives rise to one REA type ("Reality / exhibits high (+) / unemployment") and one EVA type ("unemployment / is too (−) / Ideal"). However, such detailed coding may come at a cost to lowered intercoder agreement.

## Increasing Coder Reliability

Coding a text according to the method presented here takes effort and time. The coding task is complex, and detailed coding instructions are required (e.g., Azar, 1982; Kleinnijenhuis & Rietberg, 1991a). Nevertheless, careless errors and elaborate coding will decrease reliability among as well as within coders. A few ways to reduce the amount of work and to increase the reliability are discussed here. Most of our recommendations have been tested in reliability research (Kleinnijenhuis, 1990, pp. 299–309; Kleinnijenhuis & Rietberg, 1991b).

Coders' attention must be directed by a list of well-defined and intuitively clear meaning objects as they aggregate words into general categories of meaning objects. If the researcher's starting point is curiosity (e.g., "What's in here?"), then the texts to be analyzed should be inductively searched for meaning objects. If the starting point is a research question (e.g., "What's in here with respect to $X$?") and answering the research question requires the analysis of many texts by many coders, then extensive pretests should be conducted to find a good match between the research question at hand, the meaning objects specified thus far, and the levels of abstraction in the texts to be analyzed.

Coders must also be given a clear set of predicate types. Generally, one's substantive research questions should guide the selection of the smallest possible number of types of relations to be coded. In conflict-and-cooperation research, for example, Azar (1982) found only relations between actors to be relevant. The fewer (and more mutually exclusive) the predicate types, the greater intercoder agreement is likely to be.

The method presented here uses the nuclear sentence as the recording unit. However, such fine-grained data can be aggregated and analyzed using the paragraph, book, or other text block as the unit of analysis. Data from a sample of events or of a series of events (possibly discussed in multiple texts) might be aggregated into event networks (e.g., Azar, 1982). Likewise, nuclear sentences can be assembled into cognitive networks (e.g., Carley, this volume). Although aggregation will not reduce coders' systematic prejudices, the higher the level of aggregation, the more likely coders' random errors will be smoothed out of the aggregate-level data.

Many coding errors can be prevented by using a specialized computer program to validate the completeness and consistency of codings. Many errors can be detected by the text analyst, if software is used that confronts one's common sense interpretation of the text with the logical implications of one's codings.[4] In this way errors can be detected, and coders can be retrained during the coding process itself.

---

[4]Many of the advantages listed here are afforded by CETA, a software package developed by Jan A. de Ridder (1994a, 1994b) specifically for encoding texts for the type of network text analysis illustrated here. The program was used to generate the data analyzed in this chapter. See Popping (this volume) for availability.

## INFERRING THE LATENT CONTENT OF TEXTS

Before explaining rules for inferring latent content from aspects of indirect paths between objects, we must first consider methods for preprocessing IF–THEN statements and say-quotes. To interpret a source's IF–THEN statements, the propositional calculus prescribes that coded sentences attributed to that source should be searched for nuclear sentences satisfying or denying the IF part. Whenever the IF part is satisfied, the THEN part is added to the list of nuclear sentences as an unconditional nuclear sentence. However, when the search for satisfaction or denial of the IF part renders nothing, the THEN part is added as an unconditional nuclear sentence with weakened quality and high ambiguity.

An order-quote may be interpreted as a set of two conditional evaluations. The sentence, "President Clinton should reduce the budget deficit," may be interpreted not only as the IF–THEN sentence, "IF President Clinton / ACT reduces (−) / the budget deficit THEN President Clinton / EVA acts appropriately (+) / Ideal," but also as the IF–THEN sentence, "IF President Clinton / ACT increases (+) / the budget deficit THEN President Clinton / EVA acts inappropriately (−) / Ideal."

Statements of neutral actors are presumably impartial and can be trusted, whereas statements of partial actors are indicative of their position. Accordingly, say-quotes attributed to actors who are neutral according to the source are added as unquoted nuclear sentences attributed to the source. On the other hand, an evaluative say-quote attributed to an actor who is partial according to the source is added as an unquoted affective nuclear sentence connecting the quoted actor with the object of evaluation. Thus, evaluations by quoted partial actors are treated according to the rule $s: q: i$ / EVA-connection / *Ideal* $\Rightarrow s: q$ / AFF-connection / $i$. Following this logic, the say-quote in the *Washington Post*, "Clinton: current health care system / is endangering lives (−) / Ideal," gives rise to the unquoted nuclear sentence, "Clinton / attributes endangerment of lives to (−) / current health care system."[5]

### Direct and Indirect Relations

Because an object of a first nuclear sentence may be the subject of another, a text may be considered as a concatenated network with subjects and objects as vertices (i.e., nodes, points) and predicates as directed edges (i.e., arcs, arrows). Whereas the direct relations in the network (i.e., links) represent the literal content of the text, psychologists such as Heider (1946) and Osgood, Saporta, and Nunally (1956) purported that the indirect relations (i.e., chains,

---

[5]The preprocessing of say-quotes is further complicated when latent evaluations by quoted actors are considered according to the inference rules discussed here. The rules to infer whether a quoted actor is neutral or partial according to a source are not treated here.

paths) represent inferences that might be drawn by reasonable, sophisticated users of a language. Unfortunately, these early authors treated predicates as if they were symmetric or applied inconsistent inference rules. The inference rules presented here are based on those discussed by Van Cuilenburg, Kleinnijenhuis, and de Ridder (1986, 1988).

These inference rules take the world of one author or the world of one quoted author as the point of departure. As a first step, all nuclear sentences that have the same $i$- and $j$-objects are combined in parallel, thus rendering the $ij$-links.

Let's define $f_{ij}$ as the frequency of $i$'s link toward $j$ and $q_{ij}$ as the averaged quality of this link. Equation 1 defines $f_i$ as the relative frequency of nuclear sentences of $i$ toward other meaning objects (i.e., the "outdegree" of $i$).

$$f_i = \sum_j f_{ij} \tag{1}$$

We define in equation 2 the base, $b_{ij}$, of the $ij$-link as the number of nuclear sentences of $i$ toward $j$ as a proportion of the total number of nuclear sentences of $i$ toward other meaning objects. The base, $b_{ij}$, can be interpreted as the importance of the relation of $i$ toward $j$ from the point of view of $i$.

$$b_{ij} = \frac{f_{ij}}{f_i} \tag{2}$$

An acyclic or elementary path $\mu$ from $i$ toward $j$ is a sequence of directed relations $\{u \rightarrow v\}$, in which $i$ is the initiator, $u$, of the first relation $\{u \rightarrow v\}$, $j$ is the target, $v$, of the last relation $\{u \rightarrow v\}$, each relation's target, $v$, is the initiator, $u$, of the next relation within the sequence, and not one initiator, $u$, or target, $v$, appears more than once in the sequence. As defined in equation 3, the base, $b_{ij}^{\mu}$, of an acyclic path $\mu$ from $i$ toward $j$ represents the importance (i.e., base) of this path from $i$'s point of view, given the importances of the links within the path.

$$b_{ij}^{\mu} = \prod_{\{u \rightarrow v\} \in \mu} b_{uv} \tag{3}$$

The frequency, $f_{ij}$, of a path from $i$ toward $j$ is defined in equation 4 as the product of the base of this path and the outdegree of $i$.

$$f_{ij}^{\mu} = b_{ij}^{\mu} f_i \tag{4}$$

The quality of the $ij$-relation for a single acyclic path, $\mu$, is denoted as $q_{ij}^{\mu}$. Given a value range of $[-1 \ldots +1]$ to express the quality of separate links, the multiplication operator is used in equation 5 to define $q_{ij}^{\mu}$ as the product of the qualities of the links that constitute path $\mu$.

$$q_{ij}^{\mu} = \prod_{\{u \to v\} \in \mu} q_{uv} \tag{5}$$

Multiplication represents the idea of *transitive evaluative transfer*: If $Z$ is evil, and $Y$ causes $Z$, then $Y$ causes evil to occur. However, this idea has been criticized by Abelson (1968). Types of links having an unsure effect on the state of the $j$-object, such as AFFection links, make the quality of a path hard to interpret. The idea of evaluative transfer is also dubious in the case of "scarce" meaning objects. If $A$ wants to build a coalition with $B$, and $B$ with $C$, but a minimum coalition of only two actors suffices, then $A$ and $C$ may be rivaling for the scarce affection of $B$. Contrary to the idea of transitivity, $A$ may thus not be "on $C$'s side." Our solution is to circumvent Abelson's critique by only inferring evaluative transfer among types of links for which $j$-objects clearly change due to the activities and processes described by the predicates. When paths' predicate types consist solely of links of the types REA, ACT, CAU, and EVA, their interpretation is straightforward in the light of evaluative transfer. These are the only predicate types for which we trace the directed relations within acyclic paths.[6]

In a dense network the number of paths between two actors increases exponentially with the number of actors. Bundling all separate paths (of length greater than 1) may be useful to keep track of latent content. This is because a path of at least length 2 is needed for latent content to be inferred. The frequency, $F_{ij}$, of a bundle of paths is defined in equation 6 as the sum of the frequencies of the separate paths.

$$F_{ij} = \sum_{\mu} f_{ij}^{\mu} \tag{6}$$

The quality, $Q_{ij}$, of a bundle of paths is defined in equation 7 as the weighted mean of the qualities of the separate paths. Paths are weighted by their frequency.

$$Q_{ij} = \frac{\sum_{\mu} f_{ij}^{\mu} q_{ij}^{\mu}}{\sum_{\mu} f_{ij}^{\mu}} \tag{7}$$

---

[6]The program, CETA, offers the possibility not only to compute aspects of paths but also to exclude paths with links of specified types from these computations.

The degree of divergence is defined in equation 8 as the variance among the qualities of separate paths. The paths are weighted again by their frequency.[7]

$$D_{ij} = \frac{\sum_{\mu} f_{ij}^{\mu} (q_{ij}^{\mu} - Q_{ij})^2}{\sum_{\mu} f_{ij}^{\mu}} \tag{8}$$

In sum, inference rules apply only once nuclear sentences have been combined in parallel into a network (via a generalized summation operator). Within separate paths, links between meaning objects are combined serially (via a generalized multiplication operator). Bundles are created by combining paths in parallel (via a generalized summation operator). Once this has been done, it can be proven that the definitions given here of the base and quality of nuclear sentences, as well as of links, paths, and bundles, are consistent with the requirements of a path algebra (Carré, 1979, pp. 84–85; de Ridder, 1994a, pp. 109–116). As a fortunate consequence, the orders of parallel and serial computations do not alter values of the various measures presented here.

Let us consider the manifest information in a text to be those links in a network prior to the application of inference rules. If the starting point of transitive evaluative transfer applies, then bundles generated according to the formerly specified inference rules represent the text's latent content.

## AN APPLICATION: ECONOMIC DISCOURSE IN DUTCH NEWSPAPERS, 1968–1984

This illustration of network text analysis uses data from a research project on economic news coverage in Dutch newspapers between 1968 and 1984 (Kleinnijenhuis, 1990). In the Netherlands, approximately 80% of the adult population reads a newspaper regularly. The two newspapers in our analysis represent roughly 10% of the total readership market share. *De Volkskrant* and *NRC Handelsblad* are the most popular newspapers among the highly educated. *De Volkskrant* is an outspoken left-wing newspaper. *NRC Handelsblad*, emerging from a fusion between two conservative-leaning liberal newspapers, holds the most intellectual image.[8]

---

[7]Van Cuilenburg, Kleinnijenhuis, and de Ridder (1986, pp. 91–95) provide a somewhat more complex formula to compute the variance within chains. This measure of ambiguity takes into account ambiguities both within and between nuclear sentences that are linked in a particular chain.

[8]A content analysis of newspaper orientation on a left–right scale (left = −1, right = +1) reveals that in 1983–1984 the score of *NRC Handelsblad* was −0.10 and the score of *De Volkskrant* was −0.39 (Kleinnijenhuis, 1990, p. 115).

The method for content analysis described here has been applied to samples of economic articles in the two newspapers from the months September and October of the even years in the period 1968–1984. In the Netherlands, economics is most newsworthy in September and October. In September the Dutch government coalition presents its economic forecasts, budget estimates, and major policy proposals for the subsequent year. The Lower House of the Dutch Parliament discusses these forecasts, estimates, and proposals in October.

Texts were assembled from the newspapers using a snowball sampling procedure. Whenever a newspaper devoted one of its editorials to economics or economic policy, all newspaper reports and commentaries with respect to economics and economic policy from the same day and the preceding day were included in the sample. The coding scheme included a variety of meaning objects. Eight political actors (e.g., the government, political parties, employer unions) and 29 economic variables (e.g., employment, interest rate) were included, as well as the abstract meaning objects Ideal and Reality.

Texts were coded by 18 students from different disciplines (e.g., economics, political science, law, linguistics). Coder reliability was assessed for a small sample of the news articles ($n = 109$ were independently coded twice). It turns out that the coding procedure did well to detect which issues (i.e., relations between meaning objects) were at stake. Although not as good, the reliability in the coding of the quality of relations is sufficiently high for one to be confident in tests of hypotheses. Krippendorff's $\alpha$ (interval level) for the frequency of a bundle (i.e., for $F_{ij}$ scores) was 0.82 and for the quality of a bundle (i.e., for $Q_{ij}$ scores) was 0.57 (Kleinnijenhuis, 1990, pp. 306–309). A total of 14,241 nuclear sentences were coded (*De Volkskrant*, 6,811; *NRC Handelsblad*, 7,430).

## The Example: The Return to (Neo-)Classicism

The 1968–1984 period is an interesting one from an economic point of view. In the early 1970s the economic boom of the 1960s waned. The 1980s saw the severest economic recession since the big depression of the 1930s. Also during this period there was a loss in the authority of the Keynesian doctrine that the government could cure temporary imperfections of the market. The late 1970s and 1980s saw an increasing popularity of theories (e.g., monetarism, neoclassicism, supply-side economics) that claimed the ineffectiveness of Keynesian demand management. Because economic news presumably plays an important role in establishing the cognitive map of decision makers, it is interesting to investigate whether new fashions in economic theory were reflected in economic news. New modes of economic thought are expected to slip into economic news as brute causal assertions on a commonsense level rather than as direct renderings of economists' esoteric journal-bound statistical methods (Klamer, 1984).

What type of causal reasoning would be expected in the news given our hypothesis of a return to (neo-)classicism? According to the laissez-faire, classical view of economics the processes of employment and wealth would operate naturally in terms of their own built-in mechanisms without any necessity for the government to intervene. Unemployment could be banned by lowering wages, which would cause an increase of profits and investments in labor (wages/−/profits; profits/+/investments; investments/+/employment, thus wages/−/employment). An increase in public spending would lead to a finance deficit but not to an increase in employment (public spending/+/finance deficit; public spending/0/employment).

According to Keynesianism, government expenditures can alleviate unemployment by increasing demand for government-purchased products (cf. Samuelson, 1967). Business investments would not depend primarily on profits (profits/0/investments) but on effective demand for the goods to be produced. Public spending and high wages could stimulate effective demand (public spending/+/employment; wages/+/employment).

## A Network Representation of Changes in Newspaper Coverage

Figure 11.1 depicts two selections from the economic outlook of *NRC Handelsblad* and *De Volkskrant*, one from 1968 until 1976 ($n_1$ = 881 nuclear sentences) and one from 1978 to 1984 ($n_2$ = 1,025 nuclear sentences) respectively. The omitted year, 1977, can be seen as a turning point in Dutch politics. In 1977 the left-wing coalition government was succeeded by a series of right-wing coalition governments, whose policy rhetoric centered on "clearing the rubbish" created by this left-wing government. Although leftist ideas became popular in the Netherlands in the late 1960s and early 1970s, it was not until 1973 that a left-wing coalition government headed by the social democrat, Joop den Uyl, came into office. Figure 11.1 exhibits the qualities ($q_{ij}^\mu$) of the links between eight meaning objects that played a major role in the controversies of the 1970s between the neoclassical view of economics and Keynesianism: government, public spending, the finance deficit, wages, profits, investments, employment, and the Ideal.

The figure for 1968–1976 displays a mixture of classical and Keynesian arguments. According to neoclassical thought, the newspapers maintain that an increase of public spending will increase (+.7) the finance deficit; an increase in wages will diminish (−.7) employment, because high wages will diminish (−.7) profits, whereas increasing profits would have increased (+.7) employment because profits will lead (+.3) to higher investments, which in turn will increase (+.3) employment; high public spending is evaluated slightly negatively (−.2).

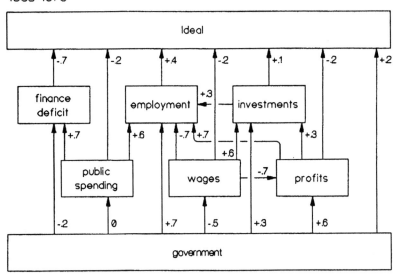

1968-1976

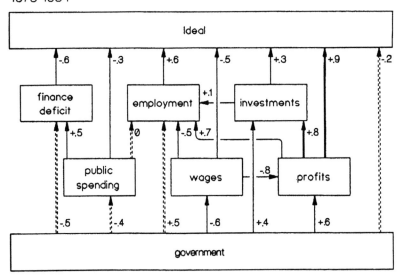

1978-1984

Legend: the numbers represent the 'quality' (directional thrust) of a relationship

──────▶ Quality did not change significantly as compared to 1968-1976

━━━━━▶ Quality significantly more positive than in 1968-1976

∙∙∙∙∙∙∙▶ Quality significantly more negative as compared to 1968-1976

FIG. 11.1. Changes in the economic outlook of the Dutch press, 1968–1984.

Elements of the Keynesian mode of economic thought are present also. Public spending will contribute (+.6) to full employment, and because an increase in wages (and associated demand for products) stimulates investments (+.6), which in turn increase (+.3) employment, high wages may indirectly create employment. High profits are not necessary for a healthy economy but are evaluated slightly negatively (−.2).

In the figure for 1978–1984 a dashed line means that the quality of a relation has decreased significantly in the expected direction ($p < .05$ in one-tailed tests) as compared to 1968–1976, whereas a thick line means that the quality of a relation has increased significantly in the expected direction. Because the quality of a link is defined as the mean quality of the nuclear sentences that build up the link, the question of whether a relation changed significantly or not can be judged using a $t$-test for the equality of means.[9] The figure shows that elements of Keynesian thought are nearly absent for 1978–1984. Public spending will not contribute (0) to full employment, higher profits will contribute enormously (+.8) to higher investments, and profits are extremely desirable (+.9). No mention is made of wages' stimulation of investments.[10]

The links between the government and the economic variables show that in the period 1978–1984 the government was depicted as pursuing less Keynesian policies than in the period 1968–1976. According to the two elite newspapers, the government tried harder in the latter period to reduce public spending (0 to −.4) and to reduce the finance deficit (−.2 to −.5) than in the 1978–1984 period. The figure for 1978–1984 illustrates that the government pursued good policies according to newspapers: The chains (i.e., indirect relations) between the government and the Ideal are all positive. Moreover, journalists appear to have agreed by and large with the neoclassical economic theory that underlay government policy.

## Chain Reasoning and Latent Content

In the previous section attention was paid solely to manifest content. The analysis was restricted to links (i.e., direct relations) between meaning objects. However, Figure 11.1 may also be used to trace the meaning objects that are indirectly connected in the elite newspapers. The principle of transitivity states that every indirect relation from $i$ toward $j$ amounts to a chain argument that provides an implication about $i$'s relation with $j$. If a newspaper

---

[9]For example, the sample for the period 1968–1976 contained 361 nuclear sentences with direct evaluations of the government, with a mean quality of 0.16 and a sample variance of 0.55. The sample for the period 1978–1984 contained 476 nuclear sentences with a mean quality of −0.19 and a sample variance of 0.41. This results in a $t$-value of −7.39 ($df = 835$, equal variances assumed), which implies that the elite newspapers came to evaluate government as significantly more negative.

[10]The quality of this link could not be computed because no nuclear sentences in 1978–1984 linked wages to investments. It is for this reason that Figure 11.1 does not display the link during this latter period.

writes that a high employment rate is desirable whereas investments contribute to employment (investments/+/employment rate/+/Ideal), then this implies that higher investments are desirable (investments/+/Ideal). Of course, this chain argument would be invalid when investments have major undesirable side effects (e.g., investments/+/environmental pollution/−/Ideal). Even in the case of multiple effects, the direct relation from investments to the Ideal should correspond with the (weighted) mean of the expectations based on separate chain arguments, provided one reckons with all effects and side effects of investments considered in the texts to be analyzed.

We expect that the quality of a direct relation does not differ significantly from the mean quality $(Q_{ij})$ of the corresponding bundle or chain arguments, weighted by their frequency. Chain arguments can be used to expose texts' latent content—content that normally corresponds to the manifest content reflected in directly observed links. In the absence of such correspondence, the reader might find explicit information to contradict conclusions inferred from chain arguments.

$T$-tests can be used to test the hypothesis that the quality of the links depicted in Figure 11.1 does not differ significantly from the mean quality of chain arguments. Indeed, this is the case for most relations depicted in the 1968–1976 period. Table 11.2 lists the four exceptions to the hypothesis. Based on chain arguments derived from the news of the two elite newspapers in the 1968–1976 period, one can only faintly infer that the government promoted business profits and employment (the mean quality of chains is +0.1 in both cases). One cannot infer that the government did anything to reduce wages; it may even have promoted increases in wages (+0.1). One cannot infer that high wages are a major cause of unemployment (−0.2 as compared to −0.7). Each of the four differences is interesting, but here we concentrate on the divergence between the manifest news that the government wanted to increase employment (+0.7) and the latent news derived from chain arguments that the government promoted employment only faintly (+0.1).

TABLE 11.2
Significant Differences Between Manifest and Latent Content, 1968–1976

| Nuclear Sentence | | Quality of Link $(q_{ij}^u)$ | Mean Quality of Chains $(Q_{ij})$ | df | t |
|---|---|---|---|---|---|
| i-object | j-object | | | | |
| government → business profits | | +0.6 | +0.1 | 30 | 3.66 |
| government → employment | | +0.7 | +0.1 | 173 | 9.18 |
| government → wages | | −0.5 | +0.1 | 20 | 3.96 |
| wages | → employment | −0.7 | −0.2 | 8 | 3.09 |

*Note.* All $t$-values are significant at the .05 level in two-tailed tests using separate variance estimates. $Q_{ij}$ is computed based on chains that exclude the direct $ij$-link.

Consistency theory argues that journalists will strive for consistent news because they are sophisticated and involved readers of their own news (Wicklund & Brehm, 1976). In the end an inconsistency between the latent and manifest content of economic news (that is, divergence between direct and indirect relations) will predispose journalists to adopt a more parsimonious economic outlook that does not suffer from the earlier inconsistencies. In keeping with consistency theory, news will show long-run changes in links (i.e., direct relations) or changes in chain arguments (i.e., indirect relations) that reflect greater consistency.

Both types of changes occur in our data. Journalists described the government's dedication to full employment less positively in 1978–1984 than in 1968–1976. The quality of the direct link from government to employment decreased significantly (cf. Figure 11.1). Parallel to this is the finding that Keynesian chain arguments in the newspapers had faded away almost completely by the later period. For instance, the one 1968–1976 chain argument (i.e., indirect relation) that was inconsistent with this positive influence of government on employment disappears entirely. In the 1968–1976 period, readers were told that the Dutch government played a negative role (−0.5) in how employment is increased (+0.3) via investments that are stimulated by higher wages (+0.6). Because investments were supposed to increase employment, the policy of the government to reduce wages allegedly had diminishing employment as a side effect. In the period 1978–1984 this could no longer be inferred from the news because no mention was made of wages' stimulation of increased investments. Thus, consistency theory appears useful as a means for explaining the disappearance of Keynesian chain reasoning from elite newspapers in the period 1978–1984. Although Keynesian theory commends policies for overcoming economic recession, when the Dutch economic recession appeared, the theory was the first victim.

## DISCUSSION

This chapter provides an illustration of network text analysis. Like other relational content analysis methods, it involves the coding of connections between meaning objects, in this case, connections and meaning objects as intended by their author(s). The text analysis method described here allows the encoding of both manifest and latent content, whereby latent content is content that could be inferred by any reasonably sophisticated user of language from statements manifest in texts.

In an analysis of economic news coverage in the Netherlands during the period 1968–1984, a shift was found away from Keynesian economic imagery to a more consistent neo-orthodox view of government in the Dutch economy. For all but four pairs of meaning objects, manifest and latent depictions corresponded closely. One of these four rated the effect of government on employment negatively "between the lines" (i.e., latently) at a time in 1968–1976 when it was simultaneously rated positively in manifest statements. By 1978–1984 the newspaper journalists had completed their shift from such inconsistencies to a consistently neo-orthodox view of government, although included in this view was a modestly attenuated depiction of the government's positive role in enhancing employment.

## ACKNOWLEDGMENTS

This research was sponsored by a grant from the Netherlands Organization for Scientific Research (NWO 430-130/224).

# 12

# COMPUTER PROGRAMS FOR THE ANALYSIS OF TEXTS AND TRANSCRIPTS

Roel Popping
University of Groningen

This chapter provides an annotated list of computer programs currently available for quantitative text analysis (i.e., for drawing statistical inferences from samples of texts or transcripts). Elsewhere, Tesch (1989, 1990) and Weitzman and Miles (1995) have compiled comprehensive lists of contemporary software for the analysis of qualitative data. In her listings, Tesch arranged programs on a dimension that ranges from the highly impressionistic and holistic treatment of data to the systematic organization and management of discrete text elements (cf. Tesch, 1989, p. 143). The programs listed here tend to exemplify the latter end of this range.

Each of the programs discussed here allows the user to download a data matrix suitable for statistical analysis. That is, each program was designed for (or at least affords the possibility of) encoding randomly sampled blocks of text. Of course, it is inevitable that the list is incomplete. This is true, in part, because it only contains text analysis software that I was able to identify through published sources. Moreover, descriptions of the software are necessarily dated because they refer to (possibly superseded) versions as described in these sources. Finally, the list is restricted to programs that run on microcomputers (i.e., PCs and Macintoshes)—The General Inquirer is excepted, due to the historical role it has played in the evolution of quantitative text analysis methodology.

The list is annotated with a short description of each program, tailored to the needs of the researcher who must select software for use in a specific project. In particular, descriptions are given of the type and amount of user input that is necessary to create a specific type of output. Programs are classified according to their *instrumental or representational orientation* toward text and *thematic, semantic, or network depiction* of text. Programs based on an instrumental orientation involve the user only in minimal preprocessing of text (cf. Bechtel, this volume). Beyond this, the user merely feeds text in and gets information out. Programs based on a representational orientation require more user input to divine the texts' intended meanings. (See Shapiro, this volume, for more on the instrumental vs. representational distinction.)

Software for thematic text analysis yields data matrixes, each column of which corresponds to a single theme (or concept) and each cell of which contains (for each row or corresponding text block) the count or occurrence for the theme of its corresponding column. Semantic text analysis software yields data matrixes, each column of which corresponds to a specific syntactic component within a semantic grammar and each cell of which represents the theme that comprises the syntactic component of its corresponding column. (In contrast, instrumentally oriented semantic text analysis software commonly outputs scale scores for each randomly sampled text block, after semantic information has been incorporated internally into scale computations.) Although existing network text analysis software downloads a broad range of numeric matrices, the type of data matrix most appropriate for the statistical analysis of a sample of network-encoded text blocks has one row for each text block and cells containing data on the network characteristic to which the matrix's respective column corresponds. (See Roberts, this volume, chapter 16, for more on matrices appropriate for thematic, semantic, and network text analysis methodologies.)

The following information is presented about each program: its name (and version), a short description, citation(s) where the program is described (if possible, a contribution to a journal or book, and not the program's user manual), system requirements,[1] and the vendor. For completeness, I have included a more abbreviated listing of some qualitative text analysis programs, grouped according to the main activity for which they were developed. Within each section, programs are listed in alphabetic order.[2]

## THEMATIC TEXT ANALYSIS SOFTWARE WITH AN INSTRUMENTAL ORIENTATION

### GENCA (General Content Analyzer)

*Description.* The program allows researchers to build a dictionary in which thematic constructs are defined in terms of words and phrases that are searched for in text. For example, occurrences of the concept "gender"

---

[1]Unless otherwise specified, programs running under MS-DOS need at least 640 KB memory and should be run from a hard disk.

[2]To the best of my knowledge no network text analysis software with an instrumental orientation currently exists. For this reason, no corresponding section for such software is included.

might be identified by searching text for male words (*he, his, son, father, boy, man,* etc.) or female words (*she, her, daughter, mother, girl, woman,* etc.). The program outputs a summary of hits for each dictionary term employed and for occurrence totals (expressed as raw frequencies of hits and as percentages of total words in the text). If multiple dictionaries are employed in the analysis of a single text, the program outputs a decision on which dictionary captures the text's dominant domain of discourse.

**Reference.** Danielson and Lasorsa (this volume).

**Operating system.** MS-DOS and Macintosh.

**Vendor.** Wayne Danielson; 10407 Skyflower Drive; Austin, TX 78759; USA.

## The General Inquirer III

**Description.** The General Inquirer is one of the oldest systems for text analysis. It consists of a collection of interdependent batch-oriented programs. The system classifies texts' words into content categories according to the list of words-within-categories in its dictionary. The system produces a file of the frequency of occurrences within each of the dictionary's categories and a file of the sequence of occurrences of coded items. The program is succeeded by TextPack (described later).

**Reference.** Anonymous (1989).

**Operating system.** Mainframe IBM (PC version under development).

**Vendor.** ZUMA (Zentrum für Umfragen, Methoden und Analysen); P.O. Box 12 21 55; D 68072 Mannheim; Germany. E-mail: zuell@zuma-mannheim.de.

## InText 3.0

**Description.** Using a language-independent dictionary of thematic constructs and a set of text blocks, both specified by the user in advance, the program counts the frequency of occurrences of these constructs within each block of text. A search entry in the dictionary can be a word (or word part), a word sequence, or a word combination. The program downloads a data matrix and an SPSS setup for this matrix. SPSS can be executed from inside the program. The program indexes texts in various ways conducive to qualitative text analysis. The program contains an interactive coding reliability coefficient and several indices for readability. The program allocates protocol files for ambiguous, negated search entries or uncoded text units.

**Reference.** Klein (1991).

**Operating system.** MS-DOS, with versions tailored to different processors.

**Vendor.** SBS; Rheinlandstrasse 5; D 07743 Jena; Germany.

## MCCA (Minnesota Contextual Content Analysis)

**Description.** The MCCA program uses verbatim transcriptions of text. No special spacing or precoding is necessary. Output consists of two sets of normed scores: context scores (i.e., indicators of relative focus on traditional, practical, emotional, and analytic social contexts) and idea emphasis scores (i.e., indicators of relative emphasis on idea categories). These are displayed in various ways (e.g., cluster plots). The program generates a data matrix of idea emphasis scores for each text block. Also provided are data on specific words' contributions to idea emphasis. MCCA is currently on a Cyber mainframe at the University of Minnesota, and also runs in a PC environment.

**Reference.** McTavish and Pirro (1990).

**Operating system.** Mainframe Cyber and MS-DOS.

**Vendor.** Don McTavish; P.O. Box 120695; New Brighton, MN 55112; USA.

## Micro OCP

**Description.** This is the version of the Oxford Concordance Program for the personal computer. The program is batch oriented and produces word lists and concordances (i.e., key-word-in-context output) in a variety of languages and alphabets.

**Reference.** Hockey and Martin (1987).

**Operating system.** MS-DOS.

**Vendor.** Oxford Electronic Publishing; Oxford University Press; Walton Street; Oxford OX2 6DP; UK.

## TextPack V 5.0

**Description.** TextPack is a collection of interdependent utilities designed to perform frequency counts of words, key-word-in-context lists, key-word-out-of-context lists, comparison of vocabularies, cross-references, procedures for iterative dictionary construction, etc. The program produces a file of the frequency of each code in the dictionary and a file of the sequence of occurrence of coded items in the source text. The utilities are batch oriented, reflecting their earlier development on mainframe computers. Although Textpack was intended to be a successor to the General Inquirer, it cannot do many things that the Inquirer does. In particular, it does not handle many of the Inquirer's dictionaries, especially those using disambiguation. For this reason, ZUMA continues to distribute both software packages.

**Reference.** Olsen (1989).

**Operating system.** MS-DOS.

**Vendor.** ZUMA (Zentrum für Umfragen, Methoden und Analysen); P.O. Box 12 21 55; D 68072 Mannheim; Germany. E-mail: zuell@zuma-mannheim.de.

## SEMANTIC TEXT ANALYSIS SOFTWARE WITH AN INSTRUMENTAL ORIENTATION

### Gottschalk–Gleser Content Analysis Computerized Scoring System

**Description.** The goal of this program is to quantify the quality and intensity of writers' and speakers' psychological states (e.g., anxiety, hostility, cognitive impairment) as made manifest in their clauses or sentences. The program uses a parser for mapping a subset of English. Each clause is assigned a weight on the basis of its verb (or action) and the noun phrases that function as initiators and recipients of this action. These weights are then combined into text-block-specific scores that measure the psychological states of each text or transcript's source (i.e., its author or speaker). The program generates a data matrix with each of these source's scores on the scales selected. The program can also provide data on word frequencies, on occurrences of the various psychological-state-related phrases, on average scores across text blocks, and on the extent to which sample scores deviate from the norms for each scale.

*Reference.* Gottschalk and Bechtel (1989).

*Operating system.* MS-DOS (15 MB disk space); Windows (8 MB memory, 20 MB disk space).

*Vendor.* Louis Gottschalk; Department of Psychiatry and Human Behavior; College of Medicine; University of California, Irvine, CA 92717; USA.

### KEDS 0.5B2 (Kansas Events Data System)

*Description.* KEDS is a system for coding of international event data based on pattern recognition among subject–verb–object triplets. The program is primarily designed to work with short news articles. The program contains a simple parser and employs a knowledge base of verb patterns to determine the appropriate event code. The program downloads subject–verb–object relations ordered on a time scale.

*Reference.* Schrodt (1993).

*Operating system.* Macintosh, with at least 2 MB memory (Windows version under development).

*Vendor.* Philip A. Schrodt; Department of Political Science; University of Kansas; Blake Hall; Lawrence, KS 66045; USA.

## THEMATIC TEXT ANALYSIS SOFTWARE
## WITH A REPRESENTATIONAL ORIENTATION

### ATLAS/ti (Archive for Technology, the Lifeworld, and Everyday Language)

*Description.* ATLAS/ti is a text interpretation program for the purpose of theory construction based on the grounded theory approach by Glaser and Strauss (1967). The program enables the integration of primary texts, text passages, codes, and memos into hermeneutic units. It has hypertext functions on primary texts. The program allows the user to construct a theory based on impressions gained as the texts are explored. This theory can then be represented as a network. Several types of network relations (i.e., types of links or arcs) are build in, and user-defined relations are also possible. ATLAS/ti also allows the examination of users' various interpretations of the text under analysis. Users' memos can be embedded in the text, clustered into families, and then contrasted according to these users' strategies of text interpretation. Although the program has greatest utility for qualitative text analysis, it can download a data matrix in which cells indicate the occurrence or nonoccurrence of user-defined codes for each text block (or quotation).

*References.* Muhr (1991); Weitzman and Miles (1995).

*Operating system.* MS-DOS, 80386 processor, 4 MB memory, and a mouse are required.

*Vendor.* Thomas Muhr; Trautenaustrasse 12; D 10717 Berlin; Germany.

## FlexText 1.0

*Description.* This program was written initially for the content analysis of open-ended responses to interview questions. The investigator defines and labels themes (or concepts) interactively by tagging and classifying multiple word or phrase occurrences from within concordance (or key-word-in-context) windows. Concordances can be constructed (and, thus, data can be encoded) either while perusing individual text blocks or while scanning a list of word frequencies. For any displayed concordance, the user can obtain additional contextual information immediately by accessing the entire text in which it appeared. The program downloads a data matrix and an SPSS setup for this matrix. The cells in the data matrix contain within-text-block frequencies of concept occurrences.

*Reference.* Sly (1991).

*Operating system.* MS-DOS.

*Vendor.* Albert L. Baker; 2325 Van Buren Avenue; Ames, IA 50010; USA.

## Kwalitan 4.0

*Description.* Not designed for quantitative text analysis, the program was written to perform qualitative interpretive analysis according to Glaser and Strauss's (1967) grounded theory approach. The program allows the user to split texts into scenes that are differentiated in terms of codes or key words. During execution the program provides data on codes currently attached to the scenes, together with the frequencies of codes within scenes. Scenes can be called up on-screen, based on a code (or combination of codes) attached to them. Logical operators are available to generate search profiles. During analysis, codes can be combined or subdivided. The program can download a data matrix of within-scene occurrences of the codes.

*References.*  Peters and Wester (1990); Weitzman and Miles (1995).

*Operating system.*  MS-DOS.

*Vendor.*  iec *Pro*GAMMA; P.O. Box 841; NL 9700 AV Groningen; the Netherlands. Phone: +31 50 3636900. Fax: +31 50 3636687. E-mail: gamma.post@gamma.rug.nl.

## Text Base Alpha

*Description.*  This program was developed for interviews but can handle any kind of textual data. Texts are encoded interactively. The user assigns codes after demarking the beginning and end of code segments. Codes can be added and deleted during the coding process. The program performs frequency counts and can download a data matrix containing frequencies of code occurrences within each text block.

*Reference.*  Tesch (1990).

*Operating system.*  MS-DOS.

*Vendor.*  Qualitative Research Management; 73425 Hilltop Road; Desert Hot Springs, CA 92241-7821 USA. Phone: +1 (619) 329-7026. Fax: +1 (619) 329-0223.

## SEMANTIC TEXT ANALYSIS SOFTWARE
## WITH A REPRESENTATIONAL ORIENTATION

### PC-ACE (Program for Computer Assisted Coding of Events)

*Description.*  PC-ACE is a data entry program based on a semantic grammar for historical events. The grammar organizes textual data around an actor–action–object (with numerous modifiers) relational structure. The program combines a front-end program with a relational database management system. The database can produce a data matrix of occurrences of relations among actors, actions, etc. within each event under study.

*Reference.*  Franzosi (1990a).

*Operating system.* MS-DOS.

*Vendor.* Roberto Franzosi; University of Oxford; Department of Applied Social Studies and Social Research; Barnett House; Wellington Square; Oxford OX1 2ER; England. Phone: +44 1865 270325. Fax: +44 1865 270324.

## PLCA (Program for Linguistic Content Analysis)

*Description.* PLCA is a program for interactively encoding the intended (as opposed to the more ambiguous surface grammatical) relations among words within clauses. Subject–verb–object (and modifiers) relations are encoded according to the unambiguous semantic grammar appropriate to one of four types of intention. Once encoded, the program reconstructs sentences on screen by translating their encoded form into a sentence that the user can verify for coding accuracy. The program can download a data matrix (and SPSS setup) that provides subject–verb–object relations in each clause, along with an indicator of which of the four types of intention the relations reflect (plus data on valence, tense, modal auxiliary verb, subordination, question type, speaker, audience, and so on). The Windows 95 version allows key-word-in-context interactive encoding of data and the downloading of theme-occurrence as well as LCA data matrices. The technique is useful for comparing strategies of communication in different sociohistorical settings and for measuring shifts in public opinion. The objective is to estimate the probability that specific classes of statements occur.

*Reference.* Roberts (1989).

*Operating system.* MS-DOS (version 2.2) and Windows 95 (version 3.0).

*Vendor.* iec *Pro*GAMMA; P.O. Box 841; NL 9700 AV Groningen; the Netherlands. Phone: +31 50 3636900. Fax: +31 50 3636687. E-mail: gamma.post@ gamma.rug.nl.

## NETWORK TEXT ANALYSIS SOFTWARE WITH A REPRESENTATIONAL ORIENTATION

### CETA 2.1 (Computer-Guided Evaluative Text Analysis)

*Description.* CETA 2.1 has roots in Osgood, Saporta, and Nunnally's (1956) evaluative assertion analysis. The program allows the user to parse text interactively and to derive from already encoded nuclear sentences (subject–verb–object triplets) additional nuclear sentences that are not explicitly stated but are logically implied by the text. Nuclear sentences can also be encoded according to the positive or negative evaluative meanings connoted by their verbs. After nuclear sentences are encoded, data can be generated on interconnections among meaning objects within a network of interrelationships—a network that consists of nodes (i.e., meaning objects) and links (i.e., semantic relations). The program can download a data matrix (and SPSS setup) with cells containing a variety of measures related to the links between pairs of meaning objects within a network. The ultimate goal is make comparisons among networks for the purpose of revealing fundamental differences in the underlying structures of various texts. The program is tailored for comparing propositional content among texts sampled from distinct social contexts.

*Reference.*  Van Cuilenburg, Kleinnijenhuis, and de Ridder (1986).

*Operating system.*  MS-DOS.

*Vendor.*  iec *Pro*GAMMA; P.O. Box 841; NL 9700 AV Groningen; the Netherlands. Phone: +31 50 3636900. Fax: +31 50 3636687. E-mail: gamma.post@gamma.rug.nl.

## MECA (Map Extraction, Comparison, and Analysis)

*Description.*  MECA is a set of programs to analyze the cognitive maps of individuals or groups. Relations among themes (or concepts) are assumed to represent mental models or cognitive maps that reside in individuals' minds. The program facilitates the parsing of text into statements (i.e., into subject–verb–object triplets with verb-valence modifier) and the assignment of words and phrases to concepts. The user begins by identifying and encoding concepts and the types of relations that exist between pairs of concepts. Once encoded, data can be displayed graphically as clusters of partially interlinked concept-nodes. These displays can be of unions (i.e., knowledge shared among groups) or intersections (i.e., knowledge on which consensus exists between groups) of statements among groups of individuals. The program is particularly useful for doing text analysis research on group consensus and dissent.

*Reference.*  Carley and Palmquist (1992).

*Operating system.*  MS-DOS, Macintosh, UNIX.

*Vendor.*  Kathleen Carley; Department of Social and Decision Sciences; Carnegie Mellon University; Pittsburgh, PA 15213; USA.

## QUALITATIVE TEXT ANALYSIS SOFTWARE

This section includes programs for more qualitative analyses of texts. Programs are only mentioned here by name. For each program, reference is given to a source of information (frequently, Tesch, 1990, or Weitzman and Miles, 1995). Each program is grouped under a heading that (albeit roughly) describes its main objective. Most of these programs are unable to download a data matrix suitable for drawing statistical inferences.[3] In many cases the complete text comprises a single unit of analysis, leaving the program's utility clearly unrelated to the formulation of statements of statistical probability.

### Theory Builders

These are programs primarily for building theories, in general based on conceptions from grounded theory construction.

**AQUAD.**  Also a hypotheses tester (Tesch, 1990; Weitzman & Miles, 1995).

**ArchiText.**  (For information, contact BrainPower, Inc.; 30497 Canwood Street; Suite 201; Agoura Hills, CA 91301; USA).

**COPE.**  (Cropper, Eden, & Ackermann, 1990).

**HyperRESEARCH.**  (Hesse-Biber, Depuis, & Kinder, 1991; Weitzman & Miles, 1995).

**NUD*IST.**  (Tesch, 1990; Weitzman & Miles, 1995).

**QCA.**  (Weitzman & Miles, 1995).

### Code-and-Retrieve Programs for Descriptive and Interpretive Analysis

These are programs that enable the user to attach codes to segments of text and to search for (and assemble) text segments that have been coded in a certain way. For a detailed treatment, see Tesch (1990, pp. 150ff).

**ETHNOGRAPH.**  (Tesch, 1990).

**GATOR.**  (Tesch, 1990).

---

[3]It must be acknowledged that some qualitative text analysis programs are able to download data matrices with text-block-specific frequencies of word counts (e.g., see Hesse-Biber, Depuis, and Kinder, 1991, regarding HyperResearch). However, in each case this feature appears to be tangential to the primary purpose of the software.

*HyperQual2.* (Tesch, 1990; Weitzman & Miles, 1995).

*Martin.* (Weitzman & Miles, 1995).

*MAX and WINMAX.* (Kuckartz, 1994; Weitzman & Miles, 1995).

*QUALPRO.* (Tesch, 1990).

*TAP.* (Tesch, 1990).

## Text Base Managers

These are special purpose database programs that do not use predefined fields of fixed length but that allow information of unlimited length to be entered.

*askSam.* (Tesch, 1990; Weitzman & Miles, 1995).

*Concordance.* (Tesch, 1990).

*DISCAN.* (For information, contact P. Maranda; NCI Inc.; Québec; Canada G1R 4B1).

*Folio VIEWS.* (Weitzman & Miles, 1995).

*FYI 3000 Plus.* (Tesch, 1990).

*Metamorph.* (Weitzman & Miles, 1995).

*Orbis.* (Weitzman & Miles, 1995).

*Sonar Professional.* (Weitzman & Miles, 1995).

*STRAP.* (For information, contact T. Snelgrove and L. Presutti; Centre for Computing in the Humanities; University of Toronto; Toronto; Canada).

*Tabletop.* (Weitzman & Miles, 1995).

*TACT.* (Hawthorne, 1994).

*TextCollector.* (Tesch, 1990; Weitzman & Miles, 1995).

*WordCruncher.* (Tesch, 1990; Weitzman & Miles, 1995).

*ZyIndex.* (Tesch, 1990; Weitzman & Miles, 1995).

**Other**

*ETHNO.* (Tesch, 1990). For studying concepts and their logical connections and for discovering systems of rules that govern action.

*Inspiration.* (Weitzman & Miles, 1995). For making network-type diagrams.

*MetaDesign.* (Weitzman & Miles, 1995). For making network-type diagrams.

*Pertex.* (Bierschenk, 1991). For perspective text analysis: detects structural relations in texts via cluster analysis.

*RELATUS.* (Alker, Duffy, Hurwitz, & Mallery, 1991). For graphically representing story grammars.

*Sage.* (Colby, Kennedy, & Milanesi, 1991). For process structure analysis.

*SeeSoft.* (Eick, 1994). Database for graphically displaying text.

*SemNet.* (Weitzman & Miles, 1995). Semantic network builder.

*SHAPA.* (Sanderson, James, & Seidler, 1989). For protocol analysis.

*WordNet.* (Miller, 1990). For grouping English synonyms.

PART

# III

# PROSPECTS

CHAPTER

# 13

# THE FUTURE OF CODERS: HUMAN JUDGMENTS IN A WORLD OF SOPHISTICATED SOFTWARE

Gilbert Shapiro
University of Pittsburgh

Since the introduction of computers, there have been prodigious efforts to eliminate human judgments entirely from such fields as language translation, information retrieval, and content analysis, not always with much success. Researchers point to two advantages to purely machine procedures: they are more cost effective, and are more (indeed, they are completely) reliable. But these advantages are purchased at the cost of *validity,* a price many, if not most researchers find too high. This, I propose, is the major reason that content analysis has declined over the past 15 years, from a flood to a trickle. It seems to many social scientists that content analysis enables us to measure, with perfect reliability, variables neither we nor our publics want to know anything about. We seem to face a dilemma: human coders are expensive and of questionable reliability, but they provide us with the opportunity to freely specify the meanings in the text we seek to categorize, while available machine procedures, while efficient and reliable, require that we restrict our research to particular theoretical orientations or accept far-fetched and bizarre interpretations of text as indicative of the variables we are truly interested in. In this chapter, I will discuss new methods of using coders as human instruments along with computers in a two-stage procedure that shows promise of avoiding the worst penalties of pure machine analysis as well as the precomputer use of coders.

As a historical sociologist, I find it impossible to begin a discussion of the future of coders without a look at their past.[1] During the heroic age of

---

[1]Many of the ideas in this chapter were developed in my collaborative work with John Markoff (Shapiro & Markoff, in press). Although at this time, it is impossible to separate our distinct contributions, he is in no way to be held responsible for errors in this presentation.

content analysis (that is, before computers), coders were, of course, all we had. In the tradition of Lasswell (Lasswell, Leites, & Associates, 1949), they were used to count symbols; in the tradition of Murray (1938) and McClelland (1961; McClelland, Atkinson, Clark, & Lowell, 1953), to identify needs and themes in communications. Most clearly in the latter case, coders were regarded as surrogate scientists. Surely, if Murray or McClelland had an infinite amount of time and patience they would prefer to read all the documents themselves and make their own professional judgments of the presence of needs or themes. The coder was an unfortunate economic necessity, a second choice, and a source of error. For this reason, extensive efforts were made by the researchers to control the coder's judgments, or to convince themselves and their colleagues that they had done so, by the development of definitions of code categories that were to have the scientific status of operational definitions. The objective was to develop a coding manual so detailed and specific as to effectively eliminate the influence of human judgment in the coding process. For the same reason, it was important to keep the coding categories simple so that the instructions could, in effect, be performed by clerks, despite the inherent complexity of any translation of theoretical hypotheses into language expectations. The human content coder, conceived as a surrogate scientist, was tolerable only if he followed the detailed rules of observation laid down by the researcher. On a number of occasions, McClelland claimed that his written instructions to coders constitute operational specifications defining his categories: "Ideally, the judge simply 'points to' an identifiable phrase and classifies it according to a scoring definition as belonging in a category, just as he might classify a movement of a rat as a 'right turn' or a certain visual image under the microscope as a 'red blood corpuscle' " (McClelland, 1958, p. 32).

When we examine the coder instructions themselves, however, we find this claim far from justified. The coder is provided only with general guides and illustrative examples. The coder gets nothing resembling the exact conditions (which must be language specifications) under which he or she is supposed to isolate some portion of text and classify it in a given category. For example, in scoring for the need for achievement, one is supposed to seek indicators of "competition with a standard of excellence," which is defined as follows:

> One of the characters in the story is engaged in some competitive activity (other than pure cases of aggression) where winning or doing as well as or better than others is actually stated as the primary concern. Wanting to win an essay contest, or an apprentice wanting to show the master that he, too, can fix the machine, are typical examples. (McClelland, Atkinson, Clark, & Lowell, 1958, p. 181)

What in the world is a "competitive activity (other than pure cases of aggression)"? And how do we decide when a particular concern is "primary"?

Any of the other instructions to coders could be cited to illustrate the same point. They all provide a very incomplete form of guidance to the coder, who must exercise his capacity for complex, intuitive, semantic judgments in assigning text to categories. He certainly does not merely follow explicit rules. The analogy between the judgment that some text indicates a "pure case of aggression" and the judgment that a rat turned to the right is nothing short of ludicrous.

Largely out of despair at the difficulties of getting surrogate scientists to execute the incredibly complex instructions that would serve as operational definitions of semantic categories like the need for achievement, the world of content analysis has recently been dominated by efforts to eliminate the human coder. Today, it is common for those engaged in computerized content analysis and for the more general social science public to regard computerization as a norm. Implicitly or explicitly, the use of human coders is regarded as obsolete, at best a temporary expedient pending the solution of programming problems or an indulgence for a graduate student lacking the resources for a proper study. As an option, therefore, the use of coders is more frequently ignored than seriously discussed in the scientific dialogue.

## REPRESENTATIONAL VERSUS INSTRUMENTAL ANALYSES

Two very different models of computerized content analysis are available: special purpose programs using the tools of artificial intelligence to attack the complexities of natural syntax and general purpose systems of computerized content analysis, with little or no use of artificial intelligence methods and much less elaborate attention to the complexities of syntax and context. I discuss in much more detail the contribution of the general purpose programs; the application of artificial intelligence to content analysis is in its infancy, so that, although I look at the kinds of content analyses to which it has been successfully applied, any estimate of its ultimate potential would be premature.[2]

The most important and the most widely applied general purpose computerized system for content analysis is the General Inquirer (Stone et al., 1966). This system moved the art far beyond the mere counting of individual words in a heroic effort to capture at least some of the subtleties and complexities of natural language. It retrieves sentences (or, with the aid of hand-coding, clauses) on the basis of the presence of boolean functions of

---

[2]For achievements and limitations as of 1988, see van Cuilenberg, Kleinnijenhuis, and de Ridder (1988).

words listed in a dictionary (i.e., a list of words or phrases associated with theoretical concepts of interest).[3]

The authors of the General Inquirer sought to do away with all doubts regarding the reliability with which rules of coding are followed. Unlike the human judge of meaning, the computer is, for all practical purposes, a perfectly reliable instrument. They also wished to impose a discipline upon content analysts. As a field of scientific work, content analysis requires full operational specification. "In content analysis research prior to the computer, it was often difficult to determine exactly how the investigator translated hypotheses stemming from his theory into measurement procedures. Judgments were often intuitive, making replication impossible" (Stone et al., 1966, p. 69). Another objective was to reduce the cost and the tedium associated with coding (Stone et al., 1966, pp. 30, 62, 187, and 345).

In the 1966 volume, *The General Inquirer*, the results of sixteen studies were described. None of these studies provided a representational approach to the texts under analysis; i.e., there was no attempt to classify, tag, or retrieve the intended meanings of the authors. In some cases, the researchers sought to measure the concentration of attention in documents, as indicated by the frequency of words within various word classes or by the co-occurrences of words. Most of the studies approached the language of a text as a collection of psychological or psychiatric symptoms, indicative of personality structures, underlying motivations, or mental illnesses. Such studies, whether measuring the concentration of attention or some psychological traits, have been called instrumental, in contrast with representational studies, which seek to measure the intended meanings of the authors of texts.

The methodological problems for content analysis posed by the occasional presence of deception in human communications initially gave rise to a distinction by Mahl (1959) between representational and instrumental uses of language by the source of the communications studied, and to corresponding modes of content analysis. Following his lead, the other participants in the Allerton House conference (Pool, 1959) took up the issue as central. Osgood (1959) (among others), however, uses the term *representational model* in a somewhat different way, to stand not for the guileless expression of the communicator's views but for the attempt on the part of the analyst to represent the structure of thought found in the communication, rather than some other characteristic of the source or audience. Although Osgood's derivation of the model from the vocabulary of behavioral

---

[3]The system provides for multiple complex forms of analysis. The researcher can specify the order in which these various elements occur in the sentence. Idioms—word sequences with a distinct aggregate meaning—can be treated as if they were single words. Provision is made for preliminary hand coding, to distinguish homographs. Computer routines eliminate such word endings as the plural "s" and the past tense "ed." A given sentence may be retrieved or counted if the previous sentence meets specified conditions.

psychology is rather intricate, his summary is simple enough: "This, of course, is merely a more formal way of saying that words 'express' the ideas of the speaker and 'signify' ideas for the hearer" (p. 39). The distinction between analyses that are representational in this sense and those that are instrumental is crucial to an understanding of the strengths and limitations of the computerized content analysis methods hitherto available.[4]

As conventionally understood, the normal role of the source of a communication is to express views, beliefs, attitudes, values or ideas that are held, whereas the normal role of the receiver of a communication is to discover precisely what meanings are intended by the source. This latter task is also what a representational content analysis seeks to do. Those who approach the language behavior of the source instrumentally, as so many symptoms from which unconscious or unacknowledged characteristics are to be inferred, are engaged in so different an enterprise that they will have little use for the kinds of models or research tools that are necessary for the proper comprehension of the message that was intended. Those whose conception of their role is representational will not be satisfied with the solutions found by those with instrumental orientations. In particular, those who seek seriously to meet the requirements of operational specificity by the development of coding rules that can be translated into computer programs invariably work with an instrumental orientation to text.

Frequently, this instrumental orientation is unexceptionable, particularly when the system is used by clinical psychologists for the proper pursuit of their trade. For example, Maher et al. (1966) cannot be faulted for their use of such instrumental analyses to discover grammatical differences between documents judged to be "thought disordered" and those judged to be normal. The actual content of the documents, in the representational sense of the ideas their authors intended to communicate, need not enter into consideration in a research design that seeks to explore symptoms of cognitive breakdown. There are, however, other times when a psychological approach fails to exhaust the interesting alternatives. For example, we never learn from Dunphy's (1966) report on a study of self-analytic groups whether the members regard the group leader as excessively or as insufficiently directive, nor from Holsti (1966) what were the issues on which China and the Soviet Union agreed or disagreed, only where their communications stood on the dimensions of affect, strength, and activity.

Of course the conventional response to such complaints is correct: Everything depends upon what the researcher wants to find out. However, in such

---

[4]The concept of instrumental analysis enables us to discuss research on characteristics of texts unknown to or unacknowledged by their source without recourse to the mysterious near-oxymoron *latent content*. It is also a broader concept, including, for example, studies of the attention given to different subjects that may or may not be known to the source or conceptualized as a part of the unconscious mind.

cases, we cannot be sure whether the researcher has chosen the General Inquirer as an appropriate instrument to pursue an authentic psychological orientation or has chosen a psychological orientation because it permits a plausible application of the instrument. If content analysis is restricted to instrumental orientations to text, only such studies will be performed, and, in effect, the choice of a psychological orientation will be made by the discipline simply because it can be operationalized in this manner. This is a disturbing possibility. Namenwirth and Weber (1987, p. 195) expressed distress at a decline of content analytic studies in recent years, so extreme that they see it as "virtually abandoned" by social science in this period. I suggest that this decline might be a symptom of the disillusionment of the research community with procedures that trade the validity of measurements for increased reliability. Researchers seeking to be state of the art are offered the possibility of measuring with perfect reliability variables that they are not interested in knowing about at all.

Apart from its contribution to the trivialization of research objectives, the limitation of pure machine techniques of content analysis to instrumental orientations to text would seem to be unexceptionable, so long as no claims are made that representational analyses have been achieved. In at least one case, however, such a claim is clearly made. Namenwirth and Brewer (1966) claimed to reveal the degree of consensus or agreement to be found in the editorials in four "elite newspapers" of the West: *The New York Times*, *The London Times*, the *Frankfurter Allgemeine Zeitung*, and *Le Monde*. Because they measure only the attention to various issues, however, the researchers' measure of consensus—the differential concern with categories—is, in my view, of very questionable validity. Simply because two newspapers both discuss military affairs does not mean that they agree. Indeed, the subject may monopolize their editorial pages because they and their nations are engaged in a great strategic debate.

To what extent does the General Inquirer in fact liberate us from the unreliability and expense of human coders? Its dictionaries are supposed, in principle, to derive from theories (Stone et al., 1966, p. 139). The insistence that dictionary construction ought to be based upon theory seems clearly based upon a model of content analysis in which words are objects that are observed by the scientist much as flowers are observed by botanists. However, as Stone (1966) has acknowledged, "Unfortunately, although our social scientific theories may lead us to the concepts we wish to study, we lack an adequate theory of language to direct us in finding the alternative signs that express a particular concept. In a situation where something is to be said, there is no theory to tell us what words will be used to say it" (pp. 9–10). This modesty of the founder is not always reflected in his followers: Goldhamer (1969, p. 343) described the Inquirer dictionaries not just as deriving from theory but as operationalizing theory in fact (not only in the ideal).

The judges engaged in constructing a dictionary are described as drawing "upon their collective experience as language users in deciding which meaning should be regarded as most common and which tags should be chosen to make the best representation of . . . meaning" (Stone et al., 1966, p. 154). The elimination of subjective, intuitive judgments of meaning from content analysis, then, has been very incomplete in the General Inquirer. The difference between the work of the general inquirers and the coding normally performed by traditional human coders is not that the former eliminate intuitive judgments of meaning but rather that in constructing a dictionary they render them wholesale. In a study of the Icarus complex, an obsession with flight, for example, the attribution of Icarian tendencies on the basis of the use of a word, such as *leap,* is performed collectively, in the process of dictionary construction, for all authors using the word in all contexts. There are of course advantages—economy, for one—in such a procedure, but there are also disadvantages, of the sort the transformational linguists alert us to: The coder dealing individually with documents can judge the same words quite differently, depending upon their contexts. One can leap to a conclusion, during leap year.[5]

The most impressive special-purpose computerized content analysis system mobilizing the techniques of artificial intelligence is in the work of Louis Gottschalk, Robert Bechtel, and associates. Because this work is the subject of a chapter of this book, it will not be described in detail here. For the purposes of this chapter, it is important to note that the objectives of Gottschalk are clearly instrumental in character. He aims at the measurement of psychological states and traits, such as anxiety, hostility, social alienation, hope, and cognitive impairment—characteristics of the person not at all intrinsic to the intended meaning of the communications analyzed.[6]

## CODING VERSUS SCALING

It appears that representational content analysis continues to require the use of human coders. In the computer era, however, the coder can be

---

[5]Furthermore, the enormous expense of dictionary construction at least significantly reduces the advantage of efficiency in pure machine methods over the use of human coders, unless dictionaries are reused. Such reuse presumes that later research is in the same language, with similar documents and research objectives. There is a serious danger here that materials and research problems will be chosen that fit these requirements, particularly by researchers such as graduate students with limited access to research resources.

[6]The evidence of the validity of these measures is impressive. The achievements to date of this group for instrumental purposes surely demonstrate the importance of further research on other applications of artificial intelligence methods to the study of text. One limitation must be noted: Thus far, every field of study has required new and extremely costly program development, which tends to cancel the advantages of economy in the elimination of human coders.

conceptualized in an entirely new way and consequently can be assigned an entirely different role in the research process. If a coder is viewed not as a surrogate scientist but as a research instrument, we need not struggle with the impossible problem of explicating the full complexities of the natural language rules governing the assignment of text to a code category.[7] The coder is then subject to the requirements that govern all instruments: the measurable criteria of reliability and validity. Like many other scientific instruments, a coder can be a black box; the researcher may have no idea of the language rules, the internal circuitry that governs the coder's behavior, but if the coder provides reliable and valid outputs for known inputs he or she is a useful instrument of research. In this view, the manual of instructions given to coders is not a collection of operational definitions but merely one of many tools used in the training of the coders, a process that is understood as the fashioning of the instrument.

This conceptualization of the coder as an instrument is particularly appropriate to a new division of labor between the coder and the analyst and between the human and the machine that has already been instituted in some pioneering work. The kinds of coding systems that are constructed, the definition of the coder's function in the research process, and the coder's training and evaluation, are profoundly affected by the coder's new association with computer processing. In this approach, the tasks that were generally performed by human coders before the advent of the computer are now broken down into two steps. One, conveniently called coding, is the peculiar province of the coders, for which they are particularly qualified and for which they have been specifically recruited and trained. The other, called scaling, is performed later by an analyst, a scientist, or scholar, who may or may not be the originator of the study, equipped with an electronic computer along with the required computer programs. The coder's task, in this division of labor, is no longer to interpret the text within a conceptual framework provided by the researcher in order to judge its status on each of the theoretical variables that enter into the research design. The coder is charged with a more modest duty: an act of translation, ideally a many-to-one transformation from the natural language of the document to the artificial language of the code. In accordance with the view of coders as instruments and not as surrogate scientists, they are assigned the tasks that can be effectively performed by virtue of their competence in the natural language rather than (as formerly) tasks of theoretical interpretation that were always more properly the province of the director of the research or other professional scholars.

Coders clearly are regarded as instruments recording what they, as competent language users, understand as the contents of newspapers and other

---

[7]The position we take here regarding the coder as an instrument is also affirmed by Franzosi (1989a, p. 267). See also Markoff, Shapiro, and Weitman (1974, pp. 35–38).

accounts of events in such work as that of Tilly (1981, 1986), Franzosi (1987), and Olzak (1989b). It is also the basic methodology of a study of the grievances of the French Revolution—a study that I review here to illustrate the principles of a two-step content analysis, using the coder as a research instrument, with a division of labor between coder and analyst.[8]

## AN ILLUSTRATION

The *cahiers de doléances* are well-known lists of grievances drawn up during the Convocation of the Estates-General in 1789 and frequently used by historians in less than systematic fashion over the past two centuries. More than 40,000 eligible individuals, status groups, corporations, and territorial entities, including craft guilds, rural parishes, towns, and *bailliages* (local judicial districts) drafted and approved lists of grievances or demands to serve, roughly speaking, as mandates for the delegates to the national convocation of the Estates-General in Versailles in May. The *cahiers* vary significantly in their length, their tone, the range of subjects covered, their mode of expression, as well as actual opinions.

Any quantitative study of such a mass of documentation must depend heavily upon a coding scheme. Ours utilizes a human coder as an intermediary between the text and a computer. In the construction of the code, our objective was to translate every grievance in the documents into a language that is convenient for computer analysis. We attempted to capture as much as possible of the concrete meaning (as distinguished from the analytical significance) of the text in its coded representation.

The code for a given demand consists of a designation of the subject of the grievance (ordinarily an institution or problem area, such as the church's finances, or the salt tax) and a code for the predicate, which consists of the action (for example, the abolition or reform of the subject) and an optional object, which is sometimes required to complete the meaning of the demand.[9] Finally, there might be qualifications, for which there are codes for conventional remarks[10] as well as a provision for free text recording.[11]

---

[8]A more thorough description is available in Markoff et al. (1974) and Shapiro and Markoff (in press).

[9]My reference to the subject of a grievance is not intended as a grammatical statement (e.g., as the actor within a semantic grammar [cf. Roberts, this volume, chapter 3]). Instead, it refers more generally to a grievance's subject matter.

[10]Codes include COND, meaning the demand is conditional, the exact conditions recorded in the free text field; ALT, the action demanded is one alternative among others; LO, the demand is focused on the local community rather than the province (PV) or the nation (NA).

[11]If the rarely used negated actions are counted, the code has 91 standard actions, 1,227 institutional subjects, 76 standard objects, and 45 conventional remarks code categories. Because there are frequently demanded actions that are relevant only for particular subjects, the standard actions are supplemented by 286 special action codes.

The action codes are usually simple, common verbs of the sort to be found in grievances and demands in many historical situations. Some are relatively precise, such as "reestablish," "abolish," "maintain," "equalize," or "simplify," whereas others must be extremely vague if they are to capture faithfully the diffuse character of some of the texts. For example, we have a code for the demand that somebody merely "do something about" the subject. The optional object code usually is required when some particular aspect of the subject is the concern of the demand. For example, "Abolish venality of office in the judiciary" would be coded with the code for "venality" as the object, along with that for "judiciary" as subject and "abolish" as action.

The code for the subject of the grievance, its institutional or problem area, is somewhat more complex: It is organized as a four-level hierarchy. I illustrate the hierarchical principle by showing those sections of the code that are required to encode the demand that the *gabelle* (i.e., the salt tax) be standardized (i.e., subject to the same rate and administrative rules throughout the country). The full code reads: G TA IN GA ST, meaning Government, Taxation, Indirect Taxes, Gabelle, Standardize. To begin with, the Level 1 category of "Government" is chosen from a list of major institutional categories of 18th-century France:

| | |
|---|---|
| 0 | MISCELLANEOUS[12] |
| 1 | GENERAL |
| C | CONSTITUTION |
| E | ECONOMY |
| G | GOVERNMENT |
| J | JUDICIARY |
| R | RELIGION |
| S | STRATIFICATION SYSTEM |

"Government" is broken down into the following Level 2 codes:

| | |
|---|---|
| G 0 | GOVERNMENT, MISCELLANEOUS |
| G 1 | GOVERNMENT, GENERAL |
| G AA | ADMINISTRATIVE AGENCIES |
| G FI | GOVERNMENT, FINANCES |
| G KI | THE KING |

[12]In any position of the hierarchy, or even in the action or object fields, a "0" or miscellaneous code refers to a grievance that does not fit any of the categories provided. In the present instance, the first hierarchical level, it would mean a grievance neither constitutional nor economic nor governmental, nor referring to the judiciary, religion or stratification. A "1" is very different: It refers to a general grievance, which falls under all or (at least, diffusely) most of the categories provided.

G MI          MILITARY
G RL          REGIONAL AND LOCAL GOVERNMENT
G TA          GOVERNMENT, TAXATION

G TA, Taxation is then divided at Level 3 into categories as follows:

G TA 0        GOVERNMENT, TAXATION, MISCELLANEOUS
G TA 1        GOVERNMENT, TAXATION, GENERAL
G TA AD       TAX ADVANTAGES
G TA DA       DIRECT TAX AGENCIES
G TA DI       EXISTING DIRECT TAXES
G TA IA       INDIRECT TAX AGENCIES
G TA IN       EXISTING INDIRECT TAXES
G TA NT       NEW TAXES
G TA TA       TAX ADMINISTRATION

Finally, G TA IN, Indirect Taxes, is divided into the following relatively concrete Level 4 coding categories:

G TA IN 0     EXISTING INDIRECT TAXES, MISCELLANEOUS
G TA IN 1     EXISTING INDIRECT TAXES, GENERAL
G TA IN AI    AIDES
G TA IN CD    CENTIEME DENIER ACCESSOIRES
G TA IN CU    CUIR, TAXES ON LEATHER
G TA IN DC    DROITS DE CONTROLE
G TA IN DD    DROITS DOMANIAUX
G TA IN DF    DROITS SUR LA FABRICATION
G TA IN DJ    DROITS JOINTS AUX AIDES
G TA IN ES    DROITS D'ENTREE ET DE SORTIE
G TA IN FE    FER
G TA IN GA    GABELLE
G TA IN HU    HUILES
G TA IN IN    INSINUATION
G TA IN OC    OCTROIS DES VILLES
G TA IN OF    CENTIEME DENIER DES OFFICES

A major advantage of this kind of hierarchical organization is that it facilitates the analysis of grievances at multiple levels. We can study, for example, the frequencies of grievances on the specific subject of the *gabelle* or, just as easily, on the more general category of indirect taxes, or on taxes in general, or even demands relative to government, whether they have to do with taxes or not. The analyst, however, is not restricted to the use of the hierarchy in constructing scales comprising Boolean functions of the codes. If an analyst wishes to study grievances related to impositions of financial burdens upon peasants, for example, he or she can retrieve or count the demands relative to taxation along with those on the subject of the ecclesiastical tithe and seigneurial dues.[13]

The coder's role is to read the text and translate it into this artificial language. It is important to note the fabulous variety of expressions by which the natural language may communicate the same essential meaning. For example, the demand for the standardization of the *gabelle* might be expressed as follows:

- The *gabelle* should be standardized.
- The salt tax should be made equal throughout the realm.
- It is unfair that the tax on salt should be higher in some provinces than in others.
- We are obliged to pay indirect impositions on salt from which other communities in the nation are excused, and this is unacceptable.
- Our community is in a condition of great distress, due to the unfair discrimination it suffers at the hands of the tax collectors. They extract from us many taxes, including the *gabelle*, which exceed the requirements imposed upon other regions.
- The burden of an obligatory payment to the government for the salt required to sustain our life and that of our animals is particularly distressing because others in France are excused from all or part of that obligation.

This list could go on endlessly. Although no computer program can reduce such a variety of surface structures to the single meaning represented by our code,[14] it is demonstrably possible for a competent human user of the natural language (such as the reader) to do so. This is a job for coders. The question of the historical or theoretical significance of such a demand is to be decided by the analyst at the second stage of the two-step process. For example, the grievance may be regarded as one of many on the subject of the particular tax or some broader class of taxes, or it might be regarded as one of many indicators of a demand for homogenization of national institutions or a manifestation of an abstract commitment to the principle of *égalité*.

---

[13]This facility, of course, assumes the availability of highly flexible computer programs for use in analysis, which is not a trivial consideration.

[14]Note that the idea of a tax on salt is not necessarily expressed by any single term or even one of a small number of terms, and, for the programmer, the idea of standardization is even more elusive.

This new division of labor between coder and analyst implies the use of concrete, inductive codes rather than abstract, theoretical codes. The coder supplies the analyst with a dataset holding, in the ideal, the same concrete meanings to be found in the original documents but in a language that can be readily manipulated by the researcher (given the appropriate computer programs) to measure the theoretical variables of interest. Such a code must necessarily have a vast number of categories. The richness of the code results from the desire to capture the concrete meaning of the original document. The mastery of such a large code is substantially facilitated by its organization in a hierarchical structure, and, in this era of inexpensive desktop computers, the code can be provided on a screen in a series of hierarchical menus, relieving the coder and the analyst of the requirement of memorizing a large system or frequently referring to a paper code manual.

Once coding is complete, researchers or other analysts are able, by means of computer programs, to create scales or scores that reflect the conditions in the documents that they interpret as representing the concepts they wish to measure. Technically speaking, a good scaling program permits complete freedom to specify any Boolean function of the coded data, whose satisfaction would lead the computer to take a specified action. Most commonly, the computer is asked to retrieve or identify the records that satisfy the function, to change those records in some way, or to add a constant to a counter in order to find the frequency of the condition in some set of records. In the process of scaling, retrieval is particularly useful when the researcher is in doubt regarding the appropriate theoretical interpretation of some class of grievances (such as demands that are somehow qualified). Doubts tend to disappear when the decision is fed by a retrieval of particular cases.

It would clearly be impossible to tell the computer what to do with every possible code combination. Although, for any given problem, most of the code combinations can be ignored, the richness of the vocabulary does, nevertheless, frequently impose a heavy burden on the researcher who seeks to include within the scaling instructions every grievance that is actually relevant to his or her interests. This burden is the other side of the coin, the price paid for the advantages of a concrete code and the division of labor this method offers. Giving code a mnemonic character and organizing it in a hierarchy substantially reduces this burden. Another device for reducing the burden of scaling is the establishment of pre-scales, classifications of code categories that are of general utility (such as positive and negative actions). Interactive microcomputer programs can appreciably reduce the work and the error in scale construction. Following the semantic structure of the coding unit, the various coding options can be displayed, and choices can be reduced to the click of a mouse button. Scaling problems (such as the exclusion of demands with some recorded qualifying conditions) that might otherwise be overlooked can be automatically raised for review.

## CONCLUSION

Two final points concerning the representational analysis of texts. First, it is of great importance that such a procedure produces a data file, the coders' output, that is no more committed to one theoretical orientation, hypothesis, or intellectual interest than was the original set of documents. For historical studies, this is particularly important because it enables multiple researchers to explore the data from different perspectives and with different theoretical orientations. Second, the question of whether representational analyses can, in principle, be performed by digital computers (or some other machines) in the distant future is an entertainment. Before five o'clock, working researchers engage in science, not science fiction, and to do such science requires, for the foreseeable future, the use of coders as human instruments.

# 14

# DEVELOPMENTS IN COMPUTER SCIENCE WITH APPLICATION TO TEXT ANALYSIS

Robert Bechtel
GB Software

Quantitative analyses of textual materials have benefitted from computing technology as long as that technology has been available. In fact, some of the earliest computers were designed specifically to support text analysis for code breaking during World War II (Kahn, 1967; Winterbotham, 1974). Computers can be used to enrich text analysis in two ways. Their speed, compared to completely manual analysis, enables a larger volume of material to be processed in support of a particular analysis, or an identical volume to be processed in less time. Also, their consistency can improve the reliability and accuracy of measurements over purely manual methods. In combination, these advantages not only offer improvements over existing manual processes but can permit researchers to consider analyses that would be impractical or impossible if performed manually.

Despite the long history of computing technology support to text analysis, the computing techniques exploited for text analysis have tended to lag behind the current capabilities of the technology. Although this gap reflects a healthy conservatism in technique selection, the primary reason for delay in computing technology application is that researchers in text analysis are not, in general, computer specialists. Computing technology is a tool of the discipline, rather than its focus. The limited time and resources available to researchers tend to be spent in their domain of interest rather than on staying "up to speed" on the latest advance in computing.

This chapter provides an overview of current computer technology with potential applications to text analysis. Of course, it is not possible in a single chapter to provide a complete guide to even one, let alone all, areas of computer science with such potential. Instead, the focus here is on identifying some techniques and hardware that may be relatively unfamiliar to text analysis researchers.

## FOUR STAGES IN THE ANALYSIS OF TEXT

Text analysis can be viewed as a four-stage process. First, text is collected in either written or spoken form. If the original material is spoken, it is typically transcribed to written form. Second, texts must usually be preprocessed to simplify subsequent analysis or to enable various research goals. For example, a large corpus may be sampled to reduce the size of the material to manageable proportions. Other examples of preprocessing include replacement of proper names to preserve anonymity and annotation with information on pauses or inflection.

The third stage involves extracting items of interest from the preprocessed texts. Extraction may be of explicit content (e.g., specific words, phrases, or references), implicit content (e.g., any latent material gleaned from a text within which it does not explicitly appear), or a combination of these. Finding occurrences of a particular name would be extracting explicit content. Finding occurrences of references to a particular political office by finding names of specific officeholders would be extracting implicit content. Notice that extracting implicit content requires additional information beyond that found in the text itself, such as a list of all individuals who have held a particular office. Inference rules must be applied to extract implicit content from textual and extratextual information.

In the fourth stage an analysis of the extracted data is performed. When probabilistic inferences are to be made, this analysis will involve the application of some statistical procedure. After this, conclusions are drawn about the topic of interest (e.g., about some attribute of the original text, such as its author, its intent, or the author's state of mind).

Developments in computer science and engineering have applications in each of these four stages. Yet developments in statistical software (related to the fourth stage) are in no sense specific to text analysis. Accordingly, this chapter focuses on developments with specific applicability to the collection, preprocessing, and extraction of text data.

## COLLECTION

Perhaps surprisingly, one of the more difficult and time-consuming aspects of content analysis is the capture of material in a form amenable to further analysis. Spoken material is commonly recorded and transcribed to written form. Written material may already be in a usable form but more often must at least be copied, if not rekeyed. In both cases, intent to use computational methods to support analysis requires that the material be placed into a machine-readable format.

Word processors have made text manipulation much easier in just the past few years. The ability to correct mistakes in transcription easily and to control printed output formats have caused the almost complete eclipse of the typewriter, with the added benefit that material captured through a word processor is in machine readable form. Word processors are a current, widely used technology.

Other, less common technologies offer opportunities in data capture to replace human labor with computer power. For already existing printed materials, scanning and optical character recognition (OCR) can offer direct conversion to machine-readable form. The conversion is a two-step process. In the first step, scanning, an image of the original page is created in the computer memory or on disk. The second step, OCR, extracts text from the page image.

Scanning can be accomplished in several ways but is usually done by a scanner—a device specially designed for this purpose. Although most scanners are designed to work on flat paper originals in notebook paper or smaller size, versions are available that can accommodate larger formats, transparencies, and bound materials. Automatic sheet feed mechanisms make it much more convenient to deal with larger quantities of material.

The computer image produced by a scanner is made up of a collection of numbers, each representing a specific tiny area of the input page (typically one three-hundredth of an inch or less on a side). The value stored for each picture element, or pixel, indicates the brightness (and possibly the color) of that spot on the original page. In the simplest form, the only possible values are 0 and 1, representing dark and light. Because there is a one-to-one mapping between the numbers in the computer and the pixels on the page, and because the numbers themselves are a pattern of bits, the computer representation is often referred to as a bit-map, or as a bit-mapped image. Because most text is black on a white background, a scanner that produces either monochrome or gray-scale is usually sufficient. As a rule, color scanners can be configured to produce monochrome or gray-scale output as well, which is ordinarily more suitable for character recognition. Scanners are hand-held, desktop, or commercial-grade, distinguished according to their successively increasing cost, speed, and quality of output.

Although a scanned bit-mapped image itself is in machine-readable form and can be printed out in a form of high-technology copying, it must be converted into a collection of text characters to be useful for content analysis. OCR software performs this conversion. The simplest technique is template matching, where the OCR program has a small bit-map for each character (i.e., a template) and simply tests to see which of these templates is the closest match to the input bit-map. However, any deviation from the ideal (as represented in the templates) will cause problems for recognition. Because most inputs will display problems such as slight skewing of the text from perfectly horizontal, variations in size, variety in typefaces or fonts, and image degradation introduced by copying or the scanning process itself, the simple technique is unlikely to be successful except under very highly constrained circumstances. Even under the best of conditions, it can be hard to distinguish between some characters (e.g., the letter *O* and the number *0* [zero]). Sophistication can be added to the template approach, for example, by allowing "fuzzy" matches or template rotation, but the technique remains sensitive to the degree with which the templates are an accurate representation of the characters found in the source.

Rather than attempting direct bit-map matches, an alternative approach to OCR extracts features from the bit-map and matches these features against feature templates. Although the features will vary among implementations, typical features include characteristics such as number of (near) vertical and horizontal lines, number of loops or closed areas (e.g., there are two loops in a capital *B* but only one in *D*), and relative line position. Each character to be recognized is represented as a list of features, and that feature list is compared against the stored feature template for the character set. As with bit-map matching, the closest match wins. Whereas features matching may enable one to eliminate some options out of hand, bit-map matching affords no such elimination.

Most commercially available OCR software uses a combination of template and feature techniques to recognize characters within the bit-mapped image produced by scanning. Moreover, some commercial packages allow users to "train" the software on previously unrecognized symbols so their performance can be improved over time.

OCR accuracy is sensitive to the quality of the input image. Poor quality originals (for example, multiple generation copies) will degrade recognition, as will misalignment and noisy backgrounds. Newsprint frequently causes lower accuracy. Although specialized software is available to compensate for some of these problems, the current commercial state of the art in OCR is between 95% and 99% accuracy in recognizing individual characters from clean copy. Although impressive, this still means that about one character in every 100 (or roughly one character in every twenty words, in English) will be incorrectly recognized. Thus, proofreading is still an essential step when scanning and then using OCR. Use of a spelling checker can help speed up the process because most errors will result in nonwords in the output.

Most readily available OCR software is restricted to the modern Roman alphabet and may require additional options or more expensive versions to handle diacritical marks within the Roman character set. Even high accuracy OCR software has trouble dealing with ornate or decorative fonts. Although less readily obtained, there is OCR software for Cyrillic, Hebrew, and Arabic character sets and maybe for other alphabets as well. Scanners and OCR software are available for most common personal computer platforms and for some Unix workstations.

Recently, character recognition has started to extend from printed to handwritten material. To a limited extent, handprinted characters can be recognized, so long as the recognition software can "watch" as the characters are formed. Such software is feature-based and needs features about stroke order and direction to perform acceptably. Moreover, the recognition is currently limited (in commercial systems) to handprint as opposed to cursive handwriting, and the software usually comes bundled as part of an overall hardware and software system rather than being separately installed and portable between computers. Research is progressing rapidly, however, and may well make automated conversion of handwritten materials into machine readable form practical by the end of the decade.

Automated support for language translation may be useful in preparing materials available only in one language for analysis by a tool or technique involving methods specific to another language.[1] The state of the art in commercially available machine translation software can be generally characterized as useful at an initial rough-draft level. Existing machine translation software is highly dependent on the vocabulary available and tends to reflect a literal interpretation of the input materials. Although most packages offer a fully automated translation option, the resulting output is seldom of sufficient quality to provide reliable or sophisticated insights into the content or structure of the material.

Instead, machine-aided translation can be useful as a time-saving aid in preparing translations for later analysis. Most commercially available translation packages support an interactive approach in which the software will propose a translation of a phrase or sentence, interacting with the user to resolve ambiguities and create a consistent and meaningful translation. Frequently, translation software packages enable the user to extend the translation vocabulary, and some permit definition of new syntactic structures or semantic relations as well so that the overall performance of the system can be improved over time. The improvement is particularly notable when translating texts in a restricted topic area.

Of course, even sophisticated machine translation software is of no use if the language pair in question is not supported. At present in the United States, the primary commercial emphasis is on translation between English and three dominant European languages: Spanish, French, and German. Russian is

---

[1]Of course, for translations (whether human or machine prepared) to be useful, the language-specific analysis technique must be shown to be valid for translations as well as for texts in the original language.

available, though less supported, and experimental or limited systems are in place for other European languages such as Norwegian and on a very limited (and expensive) basis for Japanese. European vendors address non-English language pairs but have generally found a smaller market.

Once captured, the text needs to be stored. Storage duration may vary from application to application. The original text must be available not only for subsequent steps in the analysis process but also for later comparisons among various analysis techniques or between old and improved versions of a familiar technique.

In general, the most common form of medium- to long-term storage for computers is the fixed (or hard) magnetic disk. At this writing a single fixed disk for desktop and workstation computers typically has a capacity in the range from about 100 million characters to about 8 billion characters. Both absolute capacity and capacity per unit cost are constantly growing, so these numbers are likely to be outdated quickly. If more space is needed, magnetic tape and optical media offer higher capacities in removable form. The tradeoffs compared to fixed disks are that tape provides significantly slower access because of its inherently sequential nature and that optical media can be slower and tend to have higher initial acquisition costs.

Text is frequently stored on disk as a file containing a simple sequence of characters. If the text is input through a word processing program, the file may also contain information about formatting, printing, and similar extratextual information regarding the function of the text as opposed to its appearance or format. At a later stage, processing programs may need to distinguish between the extratextual information and the base text to avoid confusion and improper processing.

In the past decade, an effort has been mounted to define a consistent means of marking or tagging text with extratextual information, typically regarding the function of the text as opposed to its appearance or format. This effort has resulted in an international standard, called the Standard Generalized Markup Language or SGML (Bryan, 1988; Smith, 1992). In theory, SGML-annotated documents are independent of presentation medium. Like the text formats of many word processors, SGML incorporates additional information into the original text, leaving the text analyst to remove or ignore this markup during the collection stage.

In more demanding environments, textual material can be stored in a database system. The details of database systems, their benefits and costs, are beyond the scope of this presentation, but many sources discuss these topics in detail (Date, 1995; Frost, 1986). Briefly, database systems provide structure for information storage and data integrity enforcement mechanisms (e.g., controlled access), and they may afford input for already created data-manipulation tools. All these features may be desirable in a large-scale text processing application.

The advantages of database technology for text applications are so great that some vendors have developed what are referred to as document management systems—systems that offer database features tailored specifically to text and related materials. These systems are oriented to large collections of documents and usually treat the entire document as the unit of storage. Documents in such systems may contain nontextual material such as charts, graphics, audio and video segments, and the like.

Each document is uniquely identified and is indexed for quick retrieval. Systems' indexing features may require that the user provide key words to be used as the index value or select index keys from the input text. The indices are used for rapid retrieval of documents rather than sentences, for example. Some document management systems are integrated with scanning and OCR capabilities to provide an end-to-end solution. Most document management systems can store, index, and retrieve documents in virtually any word processor format, but not all can distinguish between the base text and extratextual material in some word processor files.

## PREPROCESSING

In some text analyses no preprocessing is performed, leaving all extraction to be performed on the original text. Yet once text has been collected and stored, the text analysis process may proceed to a preprocessing stage. Preprocessing may be a bit of a misnomer; such steps involve modification of the original input and thus may have a flavor of extraction about them. For example, a typical preprocessing step may remove punctuation from the original text, which in some sense extracts the nonpunctuation content from the sample. However, unless the analysis is concerned with a topic in which punctuation plays a role (e.g., the relative frequency of commas versus parentheses for setting off clauses), this extraction is not germane to the analysis and so is not part of the extraction step.

Other possible preprocessing steps are less seemingly extractive. Many analysis programs convert all input text to a standard case (either upper or lower), which is more a translation than an extraction. Probably the most common preprocessing step in a computer-based analysis system is removal of extratextual material introduced by the text collection process, such as formatting codes added by a word processor. Preprocessing can be summarized as all those modifications made to the original text to prepare it for presentation to the central extraction process.

Of particular relevance to preprocessing are techniques developed in formal language theory. Formal language theory is based on the premise that the legal strings (i.e., words, sentences, utterances) of a language can be recognized and generated from a structural description of the language (i.e., a grammar) and a base set of tokens (i.e., a lexicon). The insights and algorithms of formal language theory have been honed on computer languages and provide a range of tools that can be very useful in manipulating text.

At the lowest level, consider the problem of breaking an input text into individual words so that an extraction system can have words (rather than raw text) as input. At first glance, this seems trivial, at least in English: A word is a sequence of one or more alphabetic characters whose edges are marked (or delimited) by spaces. Of course, there are nonalphabetic characters, including punctuation marks, which are also delimiters, so we need to deal with them. Some words seem to include nonalphabetic characters (e.g., *1st, it's, computer-oriented,* etc.). Yet the problem is not as simple as it might appear at first. Assuming that one can arrive at a reasonable definition of "word," the problem of applying the definition to the input remains. Even if considerable effort were expended in writing a computer program to do this, changes in the definition of "word" would likely require considerable recoding of the program to take into account various counterexamples to the definition that may arise.

Exactly this same type of problem is faced by compilers (i.e., computer programs that translate code written in a high level language such as C or Pascal into the executable form understood by the computer). The recognition of tokens within a body of high level code is facilitated by special programs called lexical analyzer generators—programs that write token-recognition computer programs based on a designer's rules for determining what is and is not a token. Perhaps the most widely known of these is Lex (Aho, Sethi, & Ullman, 1986), which is supplied as a utility with most versions of the UNIX operating system.

Lexical analyzer generators can be used to do more than identify text segments (e.g., word boundaries). With enhancements added by researchers in information retrieval (IR), they can be used to filter texts by rejecting selected terms and expunging them from the text. In IR, this capability is often used to ensure that commonly occurring words such as articles and prepositions are not used as index items. By filtering these words out before the text is passed to the indexing routine, less work is done in indexing while making the resulting index more useful.

Having a list of words rather than an undifferentiated string of characters is usually a step in the right direction. However, even at this point unnecessary complexity may remain in the partially processed text. If, for example, a researcher is interested in detecting references to computers, at the least it would be desirable to ignore the distinction between singular and plural forms, and it might be helpful to collect all verb forms (e.g., computed, computing, computes, etc.) in a single count as well. Once again, specialized code can be written for the cases of interest, or techniques for what is termed "stemming" can be borrowed from computational linguistics (CL) and IR.

Although they use roughly the same approaches, CL and IR have different goals, and so there are some differences in the details of stemming algorithms between the two fields. CL programs identify linguistically meaningful stemming points to use in separating prefixes and suffixes from the root form. In comparison, authors of IR software are more concerned about speed and consistency, making them relatively less accommodating of certain exceptional cases. Thus, although an IR-oriented stemmer such as Porter's (1980) algorithm may occasionally make linguistic errors, it executes very quickly and will always make the same errors in the same way.

Stemming is one of a number of conflation processes that replace a variety of tokens in the input with a single token in the output. A more extreme form of conflation would be the replacement of synonyms or near synonyms with a selected meaning token, perhaps the head word in a thesaurus entry. Applications that do this in a rapid, accurate manner most likely draw on CL techniques and require an extensive lexical database relating (stemmed or whole) words to each other on the basis of their meaning. WordNet, a long-term research project at Princeton University, has developed just such a lexical database for a subset of English.

Some forms of extraction may require more information about the structure of the input than a word list can provide, even in conflated form. Structure above the level of individual words or tokens is the domain of syntax in language and of parsing techniques from both formal language theory and CL. Again, the differing goals of these computer science subdisciplines lead to some differences in the algorithms they offer and in the resulting output.

As its name suggests, formal language theory is concerned with languages having precisely defined structural characteristics. Computer languages fall into this category, for example. Yet substantial portions of human natural language behavior can also be described in the formal terms amenable to processing with the tools of formal language theory. Analogous to lexical analysis generators' identification of token-level structure, syntax analyzers based on formal language theory identify phrase-, clause-, or sentence-level structure: Given a set of rules that describe a variety of linguistic structures, these tools generate programs that are capable of mapping input token lists into a structural definition. A companion to the Lex tool mentioned earlier, YACC (Yet Another Compiler Compiler) is the canonical tool in this area (Aho et al., 1986). As with Lex, there are many alternatives to YACC, each with features that offer variations on the theme (Parr, Dietz, & Cohen, 1990; QCAD Systems, 1987).

Substantial portions of human natural language behavior are subject to formal analysis and definition. However, no one has yet offered a formal definition of all of any naturally occurring human language. For this reason, CL researchers have devised parsing techniques that go beyond those of formal language theory in flexibility and robustness, though typically at the cost of execution speed. Natural language analysis techniques currently include augmented transition networks, dependency grammars, word expert parsers, and generalized phrase structure grammars (Allen, 1995). To be sure that the features of the parsing approach complement the goals of the text analysis research, expert advice should be sought before incorporating a CL-based parser into one's text analysis tools.

## EXTRACTION

The extraction process is the stage in which the characteristics of interest in the text are distinguished from the background and projected into a data matrix for later statistical analysis. The term *extraction* implies that items are being removed from the input text, with the remaining material discarded afterward. This image is appropriate, but details can vary from analysis to analysis. In some analyses it is sufficient to count occurrences or even to note presence or absence of literal words or phrases. In others, it may be necessary to extract information on systematic relations among words and phrases. Moreover, it may be that the material extracted does not appear directly in the input text at all but is generated by drawing inferences from the input (cf. Kleinnijenhuis, de Ridder, & Rietberg, this volume).

During the extraction process, patterns are matched to words or phrases in each text block that has been sampled. Patterns in the (possibly preprocessed) input material are detected and matched against a target set of patterns—patterns that correspond to theoretical concepts around which the researcher has constructed some hypotheses. Two artificial intelligence (AI) technologies that are widely used to implement pattern matching are production systems (Harmon & King, 1985) and neural networks (Simpson, 1990). Although these technologies have occasionally been presented as in conflict, growing experience has shown that they tend to be complementary, in that each tends to show strengths where the other has weaknesses. For example, production systems are facile at handling symbolic information but are less efficient at managing continuously varying values such as those found in signals or images. On the other hand, neural nets are very well suited for continuous variables like those found in signal processing but are less adept at coping with symbolic inputs, usually requiring a translation of symbols into some sort of value representation.

On this basis alone, it would appear that production systems would be well suited to the extraction phase because the input can reasonably be expected to be symbolic. Yet neural nets have proven to be invaluable when the patterns to be detected or matched are difficult or impossible to specify except by example. Working from examples, a neural net can be trained to find desired features in an input. However, a neural net without training cannot make useful distinctions, so the trainability feature is both an asset and a liability.

The appropriateness of one technology over the other is largely dependent on the researcher's ability to specify a priori what text information is to be extracted. Production systems require an up-front, explicit specification of the patterns to be matched, usually given in terms of features. Although the specifications required by a production system can be learned using other mechanisms, they can also be provided directly by a designer or researcher. In most text analyses, the researcher will be able to specify the patterns to be matched in the input and thereby bypass the neural net training stage. On the other hand, a neural net is a more appropriate mechanism for extraction when the precise nature of the patterns to be detected is not known, but when the researcher can provide numerous exemplars of the desired qualities. In such situations the trainability of neural networks may be enough of an advantage to outweigh their difficulties in handling symbolic data.

During execution, a production system's interpreter applies rules to data in a working memory. Each rule has two parts, a condition and an action. The condition of the rule is a pattern specification that is matched against the contents of working memory. When the condition successfully matches something in working memory, the rule is said to be triggered. Once triggered, a rule may fire, meaning that it carries out its action. Details differ from implementation to implementation, but usually such a rule-action sequence changes working memory by adding, deleting, and/or modifying content. Other actions, such as input, output, or invocation of other programs, are also possible.

When a production system is adapted for the extraction stage in a text analysis, one rule must be written for every pattern that is to be detected. The conditions of these rules specify the patterns to be found, and the actions indicate the material to be extracted. Once text is placed in the working memory, the rule interpreter is invoked to apply the rules until all possible matches have been found and their corresponding rules fired.

Production systems are useful not only for finding and noting specific patterns in the input text but also for drawing inferences from the explicit content about implicit content that may itself form the basis for further extraction. For example, a production system might contain a group of rules, each of which has as its single condition a word indicating some type of familial relationship (e.g., mother, father, cousin, etc.). Let's assume that each of these rules has an identical conclusion, namely to "note familial relationship." Moreover, assume that in a similar fashion a second group of rules notes workplace relationships such as "boss" or "assistant." A special rule could be added to this production system, with conditions to "note familial relationship" and "note workplace relationship" and with action to "note balanced concerns." This rule would fire whenever both familial and workplace relations co-occur, without the need to provide explicit rules that list every possible combination of all familial and workplace relations. Much more sophisticated combinations are possible, including tests on frequency of occurrence and other characteristics inferred from the input.

Production systems have a long history in artificial intelligence. Like many other tools and techniques, they began in formal language theory as a form of language recognition mechanism (Hopcroft & Ullman, 1969). They were adopted and enhanced by AI workers with a cognitive science orientation and were used to model a variety of cognitive tasks (Klahr, Langley, & Neches, 1987). Production systems are most closely associated with the work on human cognition done by Newell and Simon at Rand Corporation and later at Carnegie Mellon University (Rychner & Newell, 1979). The technology was adapted to form the basis of what have come to be known as expert systems (Hayes-Roth, Waterman, & Lenat, 1983)—computer applications that were at the heart of a boom in artificial intelligence during the 1980s. The boom has subsided, but it produced a number of excellent production system tool kits that can be obtained and readily adapted to text analysis tasks (cf. Carley, 1988). Among the most widely used of these tool-kits is CLIPS, developed by NASA and widely available through the Internet (for example, at the Carnegie Mellon Artificial Intelligence Archive). The Prolog programming language (Clocksin & Mellish, 1984) provides a form of production system as part of its basic operation.

## SUMMARY

Since its inception, computer science has been a resource for text analysts. The application of computer-based tools and techniques to the analysis process continues but has yet to exhaust their vast potential for all phases of text analysis, from initial text collection through preprocessing and extraction to final statistical analysis. Recent developments in office automation systems as well as in data base management, language theory, and artificial intelligence offer opportunities to expand both the potential and rigor of text analyses.

# 15

# TEXT ANALYSIS AND NATURAL LANGUAGE DATABASE SYSTEMS

Albert L. Baker
Iowa State University

Text analyses must ultimately be based on quantified, or quantifiable, representations of the information in verbatim texts. This basis is similar to that for any database system, except that with general purpose database systems the source of the quantified or quantifiable information is not verbatim text but rather information more directly representable as a table. There are interesting parallels between the theory of database systems, which focuses on data models and query languages, and the development of systems for use in formal text analysis research. After a brief introduction to abstract data models, I use this formalism to describe data models and query languages for general purpose relational database management systems. The formalism is then used to develop analogous *content models* for three types of quantitative text analysis: thematic, semantic, and network. Insights are also given regarding the types of query languages that can be applied to each content model. These content models and query language characterizations delineate the types of queries available to researchers via each of the three approaches. Commonalities across the methods' content models suggest their potential synthesis into an integrated content model for text analysis research.

Every text analysis involves building a database. In fact, there are many parallels between traditional relational database systems and the kind of databases that are constructed when texts are encoded in text analysis. These parallels become particularly evident when one compares the data models of database systems with the content models developed in this chapter. Recent developments in software specification afford a succinct approach to formally defining data models (Coleman, 1991; Guttag & Horning, 1993; Jones, 1990). In this chapter I apply these specification techniques to develop formal definitions of the content models appropriate to each of the three text analysis methods described and illustrated in this book (i.e., thematic, semantic, and network text analysis). This formalization of the content models demonstrates that each text analysis method corresponds to a distinct data model. By formally specifying each method's content model, I provide insight not only into the methods' inherent distinctions but also into the possibilities and limits of the types of queries that can be used to extract quantitative results.

Figure 15.1 presents a simplified view of the text analysis process. There are two steps in the process: constructing a model of the content of the source text and subsequently using the content model to generate data. For example, in thematic text analysis the content model could be "the count of each unique word" in a block of text. Based on this model, a list of the 20 most commonly used words, the total number of unique words, or the number of occurrences of a particular word could be generated.

The view of the text analysis process depicted in Figure 15.1 has a natural parallel in relational database systems. In a relational database system the data model is always a table of tuples. In an employee database each tuple corresponds to the information for a single employee. This "set of tuples" data model determines the types of queries that can be posed in a relational database system. Figure 15.2 provides a depiction of the process of constructing and querying a relational database.

Prior to developing formal content models for the different types of text analysis, I introduce the notation used to compose these models. This formal modeling technique is then used to define the relational data model and to characterize the potential and limits of query languages for relational databases. The next section is then devoted to formally defining the three content models. In conclusion, I discuss possibilities for synthesis of the content

FIG. 15.1. Simplified text analysis model.

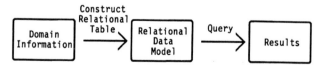

FIG. 15.2. Simplified view of a relational database management system.

models in the development of more comprehensive text analysis support tools.

Before considering the details of the formal modeling technique, two key points should be stressed. First, a formal model should be thought of as a specification or defining vehicle. Although the user of a relational database can conceptualize what is going on in terms of sets of tuples, the implementation will actually require complicated file organization, and other procedures. Second, the appropriateness of a particular abstract model has more to do with informal expressiveness than mathematical rigor. Although every discrete mathematical domain can be specified entirely in terms of integers, this does not imply that one should do so in practice. The goal is formal models that are intuitively appealing to the system's users.

## INTRODUCTION TO ABSTRACT DATA MODELING

This section contains a brief introduction to the discrete mathematical structures that are to be used in developing data models. These structures have a proven track record for the specification of software systems in general (Gerhart, 1990; Guttag & Horning, 1993). Moreover, they are contained in a number of the formal software specification languages that are used to make software development a more rigorous engineering activity (Coleman, 1991; Delisle & Garlan, 1990).

There are two general categories of discrete mathematical structures for providing abstract models of database systems: simple primitive types and structured primitive types. The modifier *primitive* is used to emphasize that these structures are intrinsic to the model-building language. Simple primitive types are not (readily) selectable into component parts. Structured primitive types are "container" types in that they are composed of other types.

### Simple Primitive Types

Only three simple primitive types are needed to develop the models in this chapter. These are *integer, boolean,* and *char.* Integers are the positive and negative integers plus zero. Booleans only take a value of true or false. The simple primitive type char represents any finite collection of symbols. For the content models in this chapter, this set is composed of the usual printable characters.

### Structured Primitive Types

The following structured primitive types are found in a number of modeling languages (Baker & Riley, 1993; Jones, 1990; Spivey, 1988; Wahls, Baker, & Leavens, 1994).

**Set.** The values of the structured primitive type, set, are finite mathematical sets. Note that all the elements in this type, set, are themselves of the same type (e.g., all integer, all boolean, etc.) and that there is no inherent notion of the order of elements in a set. The only distinguishing characteristic is set membership. A set is well-defined if, for every value in some universe, one can always determine whether the value is or is not in the set. To model something as a set, one has to name the thing being modeled and provide a type for each of its elements. The following statement defines a type, RelationalModel, and defines it as a set of elements of type, RowType.

set of RowType                                      RelationalModel

Further, if r1, r2 and r3 are of type, RowType, then an instance, rm, of RelationalModel can be denoted

rm = {r1, r3, r2} // Recall that elements' order[1]
                  // is unimportant.

Although numerous operations are defined for structured primitive types, only a subset of these is required in this chapter. For the type, set, the most important operator is set builder.

{ ( XType x ) | P(x) }

This is read, "The set of all values, x, of type, XType, such that the assertion, P, holds." Because this operation refers to all of the x's that satisfy P, it precisely defines a particular set (as long as P is well defined for all values of XType). The only other set operator required in this chapter is the "is an element of" operator, $\in$. The expression $x \in S$ is true if and only if x is an element of the set, S.

**Sequence.** Values of the structured primitive type, sequence, are finite mathematical sequences. Sequences are like sets in that all the items in a particular sequence are of the same type. However, order is a distinguishing feature of sequences. For example, content models for text analysis may depict text as a sequence of words.

sequence of Word                                   TextType

So if we let w1, w2, w3, and w4 represent (not necessarily distinct) words, then an instance, t, of type, TextType, is denoted

---

[1] In this formal notation, all text that follows a "//" is merely a comment.

t = < w1, w2, w3, w4 >

As another example, the order of characters in a word is not arbitrary. Thus, a *string* can be modeled as

sequence of char                                     String

However, in this chapter string values are denoted using quotation marks rather than the angle-bracket notation.

**Tuple.** This structured primitive type is different from the first two in that the components of a tuple do not have to be of the same type. However, the type and name of each component of a tuple must be specified. Suppose that we are modeling a relational database of employees, where for each employee we store the employee's name, address, and salary. A declaration of such a tuple would be

```
tuple (
        string      Name,
        string      Address,
        integer     Salary )
                           EmployeeRec
```

A specific instance, e1, of type, EmployeeRec, might be represented as follows:[2]

e1 = ("Lois Lane", "123 Main Street", 35000)

Finally, an operation is needed for selecting a particular component of a tuple. For example, if e1 is an instance of the type, EmployeeRec, then the Name component of e1 is referenced

Name(e1)

This collection of abstract primitive types provides an expressive foundation for modeling problem domain information structures in a variety of areas, including relational databases and the three types of text analysis. A formal language for defining (or specifying) operations over these abstract models is also needed. Query languages are just such classes of operations—operations that, in this case, are performed on data models. Formal logic

---

[2]This notation for tuple constants relies on the order in which the components of EmployeeRec were declared. For example, "Lois Lane" is assumed to be the value for the Name component.

provides a concise language for specifying operations. Only three logical operators are needed in this chapter:

- Logical "and" ($\land$): The expression, A $\land$ B, is true if and only if both A and B are true.
- Logical "or" ($\lor$): The expression, A $\lor$ B, is true if and only if either A is true, B is true, or both A and B are true.
- Logical implication ($\Rightarrow$): The expression A $\Rightarrow$ B is true if and only if B is true or A is false.

Two standard quantifiers are also needed:

- Universal quantifier ($\forall$): The expression, $\forall$( XType x ) [ P(x) ], is true if and only if for every value x of type, XType, the predicate, P, is true.
- Existential quantifier ($\exists$): The expression, $\exists$( XType x ) [ P(x) ], is true if and only if there is at least one x of type, XType, such that the predicate, P, is true.

## THE RELATIONAL DATA MODEL AND QUERIES

Examples in the preceding section have taken all anticipation out of the relational model. Any database can be modeled as a set of tuples. The names of the components of the tuple are its attributes. Let us consider the following example as a basis for illustrating queries on relational databases.

```
set of Student                          SeminarDB
tuple (
        string          Name,
        string          Major,
        string          EMailAddress,
        boolean         PaperDone,
        integer         VisitCount      // student's number
                                        // of visits during
                                        // office hours.
                        )               Student
```

What follows is a specific instance of a SeminarDB.

```
Course =    { ("Joe", "History", "jblow@nostate.edu", False, 0),
            ("Mary", "Psychology", "msmith@nostate.edu", True, 3),
            ("Phil", "Education", "prock@nostate.edu", True, 0),
            ("Kathy", "Geology", "klink@nostate.edu", True, 1)
            }
```

Most current relational database systems support Structured Query Language (SQL), a standardized language for expressing queries over the relational data model. In such a system one could, for example, construct a query to list the subset of all the tuples with their PaperDone components equal to True. Using the set-builder notation, the query can be expressed formally as

Q1 = { (Student a) | a ∈ Course ∧ PaperDone(a) = True }[3]

The logical operators defined in the preceding section can be used to specify a subset with prespecified values on more than one attribute. For example, query Q2 defines the subset of all students whose Name component is 'Mary' or whose PaperDone component is True.

Q2 = { (Student a) | a ∈ Course ∧
( Name(a) = "Mary" ∨ PaperDone(a) = True ) }

One can use any combination of the logical operators, ∧, ∨, and ⇒, and the quantifiers, ∀ and ∃, to define a particular subset of the set of tuples. Also note that because the result of a query is itself just a set of tuples, queries can be applied to the results of queries.

Although SQL notation differs from the formal model notation just illustrated, the isomorphic relation between the notations is well established (Date, 1995). The only additional pertinent feature of both notations is their ability to define a new tuple type out of the components of the tuple type of the original model. For example, a new tuple type could be defined as

```
tuple (
    string              Name,
    boolean             PaperDone )
                                    NeedsTweak
```

A query could then be defined to return a set of tuples from this new tuple type:

Q3 = { ( NeedsTweak nt) | ∃ (Student a) [ a ∈ Course ∧
PaperDone(a) = False ∧ nt = ( Name(a), PaperDone(a) ) ] }[4]

---

[3]The query can be read as, "The set of all tuples, a, of type, Student, such that a is an element of the set, Course, and the tuple component, PaperDone(a), is True."

[4]This query can be read as, "Build the set of all elements, nt, of the type, NeedsTweak, such that there exists an element, a, of type, Student, such that a is the set, Course, and a's paper is not done, and the Name component of nt is the Name component of a, and the PaperDone component of nt is the PaperDone component of a."

## CONTENT MODELS FOR TEXT ANALYSIS

Models for each of the three text analysis methods requires both a model of the text and the corresponding content model. Thus, the top level for each method would have the form

        tuple (
            MethodText          theText,
            MethodModel         coding)
                                                MethodTextAnalysis

Whether one substitutes "Thematic," "Semantic," or "Network" for "Method" in the form, the task of providing a model for the text (i.e., for "MethodText") remains reasonably straightforward and only peripherally relevant to the focus of this chapter.[5] More central to this presentation is each method's content model (i.e., the model for type, MethodModel).

### The Thematic Content Model

In a thematic text analysis, text is viewed as a set of text blocks (e.g., paragraphs from different books, separate responses to an open-ended question, or transcribed words uttered within distinct focus groups). Within each block, the text is considered a sequence of words. It will be convenient in building the thematic content model to assume that the text blocks have unique IDs (e.g., of type, TextBlockIDType) and some block-specific descriptive information (e.g., of type, AttributeValue).

At the top level the content model for a thematic content analysis is a set of themes. Each theme is modeled as a name and a set of its instances.

        set of Theme                            ThematicModel
        tuple (
            string              name,
            set of Instance     occurrences )
                                                Theme

"Instance" is, in turn, modeled as a text block ID, an indicator of the instance's thematic category, plus an indicator of its location in the text.

        tuple (
            TextBlockIDType     inTextBlock
            InstanceCategory    instCat

---

[5]In each of the three text models standard closed-ended information can be associated with particular units of text (e.g., a sentence). These units can be modeled as tuples, where each such tuple is a description of the corresponding unit of text.

TextLoc                    location )
                                                    Instance

Each instance of a theme is either a general instance or a phrase instance. A general instance assigns a thematic category to an entire text block. It is like any other generic information associated with an entire text block, except that a general theme instance reflects the coder's subjectively derived decision that the category fits the text block as a whole. A phrase instance is an occurrence of a phrase within a text block.

(General, Phrase)                              InstanceCategory

A phrase is modeled as an offset from the beginning of the text and a phrase length, both in number of words. Unlike general instances, phrase instances are modeled as a contiguous subsequence of words from the text.

```
tuple (
    integer         offset,
    integer         length )
                             TextLoc
```

The model for phrase occurrences is important. It allows that phrases can trigger thematic categories even when they overlap in arbitrary ways. For example, in a three-word sequence of text the first two words can trigger one theme, and the last two words can trigger another.

There are numerous software systems that support thematic text analysis based on words or phrases that are preclassified in a dictionary as occurrences of themes (see Popping, this volume, for a list of programs that support such an instrumental approach to thematic text analysis). In such systems, every occurrence of a preclassified word is considered an instance of the theme. Even allowing for rather complex phrase patterns,[6] this approach nearly always leads to some inaccuracies in the coding of text. Phrases that should be counted as instances of particular themes may be missed, and phrases may be incorrectly treated as triggers.

For illustrative purposes, suppose that three individuals were asked two open-ended questions as part of a course evaluation: What one single suggestion would you make to the course instructor to improve the course? What single thing about the course should not change? Moreover, assume that the respondents and their answers are as follows:

---

[6]The thematic content model could be extended to include a collection of theme patterns, each consisting of a theme name and a set of phrase patterns, which could include ellipses, involve root-word strategies, and so on. Such a collection of theme patterns would reduce the number of software-generated coding errors somewhat. In general, theme instances can accurately be identified only through manual checking of phrases in context.

Student ID: 103          Gender: Male          Grade: B

Question 1:   More practical examples. Less theory.                    Blk1

Question 2:   The extra problem sessions.                              Blk2


Student ID: 105          Gender: Female          Grade: B+

Question 1:   Switch texts. The Smith text was over my head.
              I mostly studied from my lecture notes.                  Blk3

Question 2:   Professor Jones was usually available for
              questions outside of class.                             Blk4


Student ID: 107          Gender: Male          Grade: C

Question 1:   Too mathematical. Would rather do more
              programming.                                            Blk5

Question 2:   Emphasis on specifications. I see now that we
              need to do better early in the software
              development process.                                    Blk6


What follows is an instance of the formal content model generated in a thematic text analysis of the data in this example.

{ // Every thematic content model is a set of tuples of
// type, Theme.

( "Increase Practical Emphasis",

{ // Each theme contains a set of occurrences.

( Blk1,       // This represents an occurrence in text
              // block, Blk1.

Phrase,       // This occurrence is triggered by a
              // particular phrase.

(1, 3)        // The triggering phrase starts with the
              // first word in Blk1 and contains three
              // words.
),

( Blk1, Phrase, (4, 2) ),
( Blk3, Phrase, (5, 5) ),
( Blk5, Phrase, (1, 2) ),
( Blk5, Phrase, (6, 2) )

} // end of occurrences of theme, "Increase Practical
// Emphasis"

), // end of "Increase Practical Emphasis" theme

( "Change Text",
{ ( Blk3, Phrase, (1, 2) ),

```
      ( Blk3, Phrase, (5, 5) ),
      ( Blk3, Phrase, (11, 6) )
    }
  ), // end of "Change Text" theme

  ( "Outside Support",
    { ( Blk2, Phrase, (2, 3) ),
      ( Blk4, Phrase, (2, 4) )
    }
  ), // end of "Outside Support" theme

  ( "Explained Response",
    { ( Blk3, General, (?, ?) ),   // With general instances,
                                   // the values of the
                                   // location tuple are
                                   // irrelevant.

      ( Blk6, General, (?, ?) )
    }
  ), // end of "Explained Response" theme

  ( "Specification Focus",
    { ( Blk6, Phrase, (1, 3) ),
      ( Blk6, Phrase, (8, 11) )
    }
  ) // end of "Specification Focus" theme
} // end of theme content model
```

Although the thematic content model supports themes with both General and Phrase instances, particular themes are unlikely to have both types because of fundamental differences in the judgments required in identifying each. Whereas General instances call for global judgments regarding relatively large portions of text blocks, Phrase instances are directly tied to specific, relatively brief sequences of words.

Note also that the thematic content model does not support meta-themes (i.e., themes composed of other themes). An example of a meta-theme would be " 'Female' as 'Aggressor,' " where 'Female' and 'Aggressor' are themselves two distinct themes.

This discussion is, in part, intended to provide insight into query possibilities. Recall that the data model for a relational database is just a set of tuples, where each component of a tuple corresponds to a particular attribute. The content model for thematic text analysis can be mapped to the relational model in three steps. First, one-to-one relations are established between text blocks and corresponding tuples (i.e., rows) in the relational model. Second, variable names in the relational table (i.e., column labels or tuple component names) are generated from either descriptor names or themes. Third, for each text block the values for one tuple (i.e., cell values) in the relational model are

TABLE 15.1
Relational Data Model for the Thematic Text Analysis Illustration

| Student ID | 103 | 103 | 105 | 105 | 107 | 107 |
|---|---|---|---|---|---|---|
| Quest # | 1 | 2 | 1 | 2 | 1 | 2 |
| Gender | M | M | F | F | M | M |
| Grade | B | B | B+ | B+ | C | C |
| Theme 1: Increase Practical Emphasis | 2 | 0 | 1 | 0 | 2 | 0 |
| Theme 2: Change Text | 0 | 0 | 3 | 0 | 0 | 0 |
| Theme 3: Outside Support | 0 | 1 | 0 | 1 | 0 | 0 |
| Theme 4: Explained Response | 0 | 0 | 1 | 0 | 0 | 1 |
| Theme 5: Specification Focus | 0 | 0 | 0 | 0 | 0 | 2 |

*Note.* The usual representation of relational tables is with attributes as columns, not as rows. It has been inverted here to conserve space.

generated as follows: For each block-specific descriptor, let the value of the corresponding tuple component be the descriptor's value; for each theme, let the value of the corresponding tuple component be a count of the number of instances of that theme in the text block.

Table 15.1 illustrates the product of such a mapping with the relational data model generated from the content model for the above thematic text analysis. Given such a transformation, the queries possible on the relational data model define exactly the class of queries that can be used to generate data for a thematic text analysis. Informally stated, this class consists of queries for selecting subgroups of text blocks according to their descriptive attributes or theme occurrences as well as for generating arbitrary statistical results.[7] For example, a subset of tuples could be selected from the table based on the values of any tuple components, or the values of particular columns could be summed for particular groups to differentiate the number of mentions of each theme by males versus females.

## The Semantic Content Model

The linear nature of text is a significant source of ambiguity. Consider, for example, each of the following ambiguous phrases:

*deep blue sea*
*the umbrella by the lamp near the door*

In the first phrase, it is unclear whether the color or the water is deep; in the second phrase, it is unclear whether the umbrella or the lamp is near the door. As previously discussed, the content model for thematic text

---

[7]Although SQL is quite general, it will prove less computationally efficient than statistical software for addressing most complex quantitative queries.

analysis does not support meta-themes in which grammatical relations among themes are taken into account. It is with semantic text analysis that both themes and theme relations are encoded.

Informally, the data model for a semantic text analysis is a tree. A tree is a restricted directed graph, consisting of nodes and arcs between nodes, in which there is a unique root node with no arcs into it, each node may have zero or more child nodes, each child node has exactly one parent node, and no node may be its own descendant. One example of a tree is the following parse tree for a prepositional phrase in a context free grammar (cf. Chomsky, 1957):

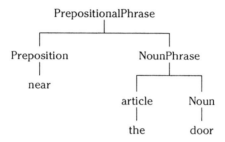

Even without specifying the meaning of the arcs in the semantic data model, one can see how the nonlinear representation in a tree can serve to distinguish among possible interpretations of our two ambiguous phrases:

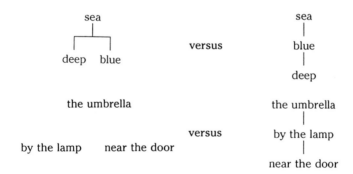

Like the other two text analysis models, the semantic data model has both a model for text and the content model. The text model for semantic text analysis requires that text be viewed as a sequence of sentences.[8] Like

---

[8]Actually, text could also be modeled here as a sequence of clauses (cf. Roberts, this volume, chapter 3). Because one clause can contain another, some ingenuity will be required to represent clauses as a linear sequence. Because it does not detract from our conclusions about queries based on the semantic model, the simpler view of text as a sequence of sentences can be assumed without loss of generality.

text blocks in the thematic model, sentences in the semantic model can have attribute descriptors associated with them. For example, in the semantic model each sentence can have its text-block ID as descriptor, allowing for delineation of text into blocks as well as its primary delineation into sentences.

Whereas the text model for semantic text analysis is a sequence of sentences, its content model is a sequence of semantic trees in which the nth tree corresponds to the nth sentence.

    sequence of SemanticTree                    SemanticModel

The central issue for the semantic data model is what the nodes and arcs of these trees represent. In almost all instances the arcs in a semantic tree correspond to the "is made up of" relation used in parse trees.

One possibility for the nodes in a semantic tree is to allow the leaves of the trees to represent words and the nonleaf nodes to represent syntactic structures, much as in a traditional parse tree. Another useful possibility is to allow the leaves to represent themes, requiring that all words be encoded according to nonoverlapping thematic categories (with general themes disallowed). In developing a semantic content model I assume that leaves represent words and that trees' arcs all represent the same (e.g., "is made up of") relation.

    tuple (
        NonLeaf              root,
        sequence of Node     children)
                                            SemanticTree

A node can either be a leaf, representing a word, or a nonleafs representing a syntactic category (e.g., direct object).

    (NonLeaf, Leaf)                          Node

    tuple (
        SyntacticCategory     cat,
        sequence of Node      children)
                                            Nonleaf

    Word                                     Leaf

The syntactic categories appropriate to a particular semantic text analysis will depend on the semantic grammar being used by the researcher (Roberts, this volume, chapter 3). Moreover, if there is sufficient correspondence between semantic and surface grammars, parsing software may assist the coder in the task of matching words and phrases to the syntactic categories of one's semantic grammar (Gottschalk, this volume; Schrodt, this volume). The greater the distinction between semantic and surface grammars, the more limited the progress in natural language processing technology toward the illusive goal of automatic encoding in the semantic content model.

What follows is one part of the semantic content model for the course evaluation data presented previously. A tree is represented graphically, prior to its description in the formal model notation. I have added words and phrases in parentheses to complete ellipses in the responses. I have also made some simplifying assumptions about semantic categories and semantic tree structure, assumptions that do not detract from the ensuing discussion of queries over the semantic content model. The student's evaluation, "More practical examples" (Blk1), is modeled

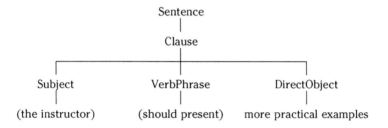

Note that each nonleaf node in the tree is modeled as a tuple consisting of a semantic category and a sequence of child nodes. Because we are omitting parts of the semantic tree, we use ellipses (. . .) to denote the missing parts in the formal content model.

```
( Sentence,
  < ( Clause,
      < ( Subject . . . "the instructor" ),
        ( VerbPhrase . . . "should present" ),
        ( DirectObject . . . "more practical examples" )
      >
    )
  >
)
```

Because the thematic content model can be mapped directly to the relational data model, there is a well-developed theory of the nature of queries for the thematic content model. There is no such well-developed theory for queries over trees. However, one can envision the formalization of the queries for the semantic content model as based on partial trees (i.e., trees with some components specified and with others to be retrieved, labeled "???" here). The queries, "retrieve all things that were too mathematical" and "how many things were too mathematical," might both be based on a partial tree of the form:

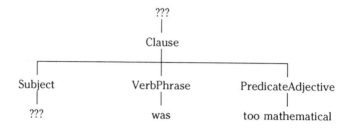

This partial tree could also be used to obtain a partial solution to the query, "Were there things that were too mathematical that should not change?"

Semantic content models that use themes as leaves in semantic trees profit from even greater generality of the partial trees used in queries. For example, one might have encoded a theme "too abstract" that would be triggered by the phrase occurrences "too mathematical," "too theoretical," and "too formal." Thus the following partial tree could be used to retrieve every occurrence in the text in which something was too abstract, precluding the particular ways that "too abstract" is expressed from impeding the query:

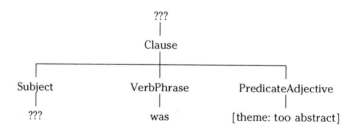

Thus, there is potential for synthesizing thematic and semantic text analysis—a point to which I return in my concluding remarks.

Tree pattern matching queries present tremendous opportunities for text analysis. Once text has been encoded according to the appropriate semantic grammars, queries like the following might be posed: "Are there contradictions to 'A is a B'?" (i.e., "Are there occurrences of 'A is not a B'?"); "Who praised Mary?", "How many times is John referred to as acting (i.e., as the subject of active verb clauses), relative to the number of times John is acted on (i.e., as the object of active verb clauses)?" It is significant to note that each of these queries could be answered in a thematic text analysis, as long as a decision is made a priori to encode the themes "A is a B," "A is not a B," "X praised Mary" (which would involve identifying all Xs, so that a separate theme could be encoded for each), "John is actor," and "John is acted on." In contrast, with a semantic text analysis the relations of interest need not be known at the time the text is encoded. It is exactly this feature that highlights the considerable potential of semantic text analysis.

## The Network Content Model

Like the text model for thematic text analysis, the text model for network text analysis is represented as a set of text blocks, each with a unique ID. Unlike thematic text analysis, however, network text analysis generally requires relatively large text blocks. This is not to imply that thematic text analysts do not analyze large text blocks such as political speeches and party platforms; they do (Namenwirth, 1973; Weber, 1990). Instead, the implication is that, whereas thematic text analyses can be performed on relatively small text blocks such as the sentence (e.g., Danielson and Lasorsa, this volume), relatively large text blocks are required for a text analyst to build networks of substantial complexity (cf. Kleinnijenhuis, de Ridder, & Rietberg, this volume).

In contrast to the semantic content model, which is based on a type of restricted directed graph (i.e., the tree), the network content model is based on an unrestricted directed graph. Research on unrestricted directed graphs for representing meaning dates back to the 1960s, when semantic networks were first developed. This work has continued particularly in conjunction with research on domain knowledge representation (Allen, 1995). Of particular importance to text analysis is the insight from semantic network research that such networks allow the researcher to represent meaning drawn directly from the text and at least some of the domain knowledge that provides a context for text understanding.

Although trees are adequate for depicting the semantics of individual clauses and sentences, they provide no clue as to the meaning of clause constituents. For example, in the clause *the bat is broken*, a tree representation of "the bat" as subject, "is" as verb, and "broken" as predicate adjective gives no clue to the meaning of "the bat," "is," and "broken." Yet in a semantic network "bat" may be associated with other phrases such as "baseball" and "wood or aluminum," and "broken" may be associated with "nonfunctioning."

Figure 15.3 depicts a simple, informal network representation of "the bat is broken." Like all semantic networks, each arc in this representation is labeled (between parentheses) according to the relationship appropriate to its associated pair of nouns. Both "bat is broken" and other domain knowledge are represented. Researchers in computational linguistics offer strong arguments that without such domain knowledge, natural language text cannot be parsed with an accuracy that approaches that of a native speaker (Allen, 1995). For this reason, the network content model offers considerable potential for text analysis.

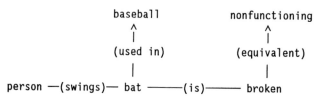

FIG. 15.3. A network representation of "the bat is broken" with domain knowledge.

The more that domain and implied knowledge are incorporated into one's network (e.g., via such software systems as CETA and SKI), the less direct and obvious is the correspondence of the network content model and the original text. At present there are no programs for automatically generating networks from blocks of text (i.e., there are no programs for instrumental network text analysis; cf. Popping, this volume). The content model presented below is general enough to capture network constituents both that are triggered by specific phrases and that are inferred from either domain knowledge or coder intuition.

The network content model associates one network with each text block.

> set of Net                    NetworkContentModel

Each net consists of the ID of the corresponding text block, a set of nodes that usually represent noun-like themes, and a set of labeled arcs between nodes.

> tuple (
>     BlockIDType          id,
>     set of NodeType      nodes,
>     set of ArcType       arcs )
>                                              Net

Each node is modeled as having a unique ID and a mnemonic node label. The node ID is helpful in the model for arcs. The label roughly corresponds to the name of a theme in the thematic content model. Each node can represent either domain knowledge or a theme inferred by the coder from the text, or it can represent specific theme occurrences (i.e., phrases) in the text.

> tuple (
>     NodeIDType           nodeID,
>     string               nodeLabel,
>     Represents           reps,
>     set of Location      textOccurs )

                                                         NodeType
( DomainKnowledge,
  CoderInference,
  Phrase )                                               Represents

If a node represents domain knowledge or a coder-inferred theme, then no other information need be associated with the node. If a node represents a theme that is triggered by occurrences of particular phrases, then the node must include information on these phrases' locations in the text block. As in the thematic content model, locations of phrases in text are modeled as an offset and a length in the text block associated with the network containing the node.

    tuple (
        integer            offset,
        integer            length )
                                        Location

    Arcs in the network content model can represent a variety of relations among nodes. Moreover, arcs can be related to the text in the same manner as nodes. This follows because arcs, like nodes, represent themes grounded in domain knowledge, coder inference, or specific phrases. The model for arcs need only add the name of the relation, the source node, and the destination node.

    tuple (
        ArcIDType          arcID,
        RelationName       rn,
        NodeIDType         fromNode,
        NodeIDType         toNode,
        Represents         reps,
        set of Location    textOccurs )
                                        ArcType
        string                          RelationName

Of course, in arcs within any actual instance of type, Net, each fromNode ID or toNode ID must be a nodeID among those in the set of nodes. Like nodes, arcs that represent domain knowledge or coder-inferred themes will have empty sets of locations.

    Consider the following block of text, Blk7, that contains two responses from the course-evaluation example.

    More practical examples. Less theory. Too mathematical.
    Would rather do more programming.

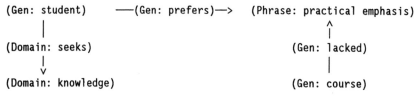

FIG. 15.4.  Semantic network for Blk7.

Figure 15.4 gives a graphical representation of a simple semantic net that represents the information in this text block. The net contains four nodes and three arcs. The node representing the phrase-triggered theme, Practical Emphasis, actually represents four occurrences of the theme in the text block. This aggregation of one theme's occurrences into a single node (and the resulting lack of one-to-one correspondence of nodes or arcs to theme occurrences) is fundamental to network text analysis methodology. A more formal rendering of this instance of the type, Net, is now provided using the notation of abstract models.

```
{ // Every network content model consists of a
  // set of tuples of type, Net.

  ( Blk7,    // Each net is modeled as a tuple whose first
             // component is a block ID.

    { // The second tuple component represents
      // the set of nodes.

      ( Node1,     // Each node is modeled as a tuple.
        "student",
        General

        { }          // For a node representing a general
                     // theme (or domain knowledge), the
                     // set of locations is empty.

      ),           // end of model of the net's first node

      ( Node2,
        "Practical Emphasis",
        Phrase,

        { // The phrase triggered theme represented by
          //  this node has four occurrences.

          (1, 3),  // The first phrase occurrence starts
                   // with the first word and contains
                   // three words.
          (4, 2),
          (6, 2),
```

```
        (11, 2)
      }

    ), // end of "Practical Emphasis" tuple

    ( Node3, "the course", General, { } ),
    ( Node4, "knowledge", Domain Knowledge, { } ),

  }, // end of the set of nodes

  { // start of the set of arcs

    ( Arc1,      // Each arc is modeled as a tuple.
      "prefers",

      Node1,
      Node2,
      General,
      { }
    ),

    ( Arc2, "lacked", Node3, Node2, General, { } ),
    ( Arc3, "seeks", Node1, Node4, DomainKnowledge, { } )

  } // end of the set of arcs
  ), // end of Blk7 Net

  ( Blk8, // start of another Net

      .

      .

      .

  ) // end of last Net
} // end of network content model
```

Although the network content model does have appeal in that it represents text as an interrelated whole into which domain knowledge can be incorporated, the lack of restrictions on the network structure, relative to the thematic and semantic content models, makes it more difficult to identify patterns in the network text representation systematically. Although one could represent a set of networks using the relational model,[9] this representation would not be of intuitive value. The relational encoding of a network and the subsequent use of queries on the relational model would be both complicated and computationally intractable.

There is no well-developed theory for queries in arbitrary networks like there is for queries of relational databases. Moreover, it is unclear what analogue to partial-tree queries within the semantic content model one

---

[9]For each net, the corresponding relational model consists of two sets of tuples, the first representing the set of nodes and the second representing the set of arcs.

might find for queries within the network content model. One possibility would be to construct queries of the form

    Node   —(relation)—   Node

in which one of the constituents is empty. Using the course evaluation example, the query

    [General: the course]   —[General: has property]—   ???

would retrieve all the properties that students identified with the course. However, the unrestricted character of the network content model is not exploited in this type of query. If one denotes the relation name as the root of a binary tree, the source node of the relation as the left subtree, and the destination node as the right subtree, then the more restricted semantic content model suffices for representing this type of query.

On the other hand, the network content model is required when one wants to identify relations among nodes that are not directly connected. For example, consider an instance of the network model in which the only relation is the "is a" relation. As a simple example, consider the domain knowledge that could be represented for "student":

    [theme: student]   —is a—   [theme: person]   —is a—   [theme: mammal]

Accordingly, every phrase that triggers the theme, student, corresponds to something that is a person. Everything that is a person is a mammal. With the "is a" relation, however, the further inference can be drawn that such phrases correspond to things that are mammals. This inference is legitimate given the transitivity of the "is a" relations. When themes' relations are transitive, a more general type of query becomes possible. Examples of transitive relations are "effects" (as in cause and effect), "heats," and "surrounds." On the other hand, "loves" is not transitive. That Mary loves John and John loves Carol does not imply that Mary loves Carol.

If some of or all the relations in an instance of the network model are transitive, it become possible to construct queries such as, "Retrieve all things that are mammals," a query that can be expressed using the formal language developed earlier for abstract data modeling.[10] Many other types of queries are also possible: Are there strongly connected components in a

---

[10]The precise expression of this query calls for the use of recursive abstract functions. For the purpose of this chapter, the benefits of such an exercise are not worth the costs of developing the required formalism. However, it is significant that a formal language can be used to define the nature of possible queries over the network content model. The formal language bounds the class of all possible queries.

net (i.e., are there subgraphs that are more tightly intrarelated than they are to the rest of the directed graph)? Are there simple cycles in the network and what do they represent?

It is important to note that the type of nodes and arcs used in an instance of the network model can have a direct bearing on the reliability of the construction of the instance. If each node and each arc in an instance of the network content model represents explicit occurrences of phrases of a particular theme, then it is possible to audit the correspondence of the instance of the network content model to the text. Instances of the network content model composed of nodes and arcs representing general themes or domain knowledge would be more difficult for other researchers to recreate independently.

## CONCLUSION

In providing formalized descriptions of underlying content models for thematic, semantic, and network text analysis, this chapter has served to illuminate distinctions among these three approaches to quantitative text analysis. Of greater practical value are the implications this formalism has for queries over the three data models. As a first implication, there is a precise mapping from the thematic content model to the relational database model. This allows us to use the full power of queries over the relational model in analyzing the quantitative results of a thematic text analysis.

Second, the semantic content model's tree structure requires a method for querying sets of trees. Although there is no well-developed theory for making queries over trees, I have suggested such queries may be constructed using partial trees.

Other implications follow from the fact that transitive relations in the network content model allow more complex queries than those that can be represented as partial trees. This complexity is passed on both to the user and to the programmer, who must write the underlying pattern-matching algorithms. The unrestricted character of the network content model allows the user to make a mind-boggling number of queries, as testified to, for example, by the numerous measures developed by Carley (this volume) and Kleinnijenhuis, de Ridder, and Rietberg (this volume). The challenge will be to determine which of the many possible measures are most useful in social science research.

Finally, the three content models have implications for the development of a single software system for performing thematic, semantic, or network text analysis. As indicated in the descriptions of the semantic and network content models, there is considerable expressive advantage in having the nodes of both the semantic and network models represent themes rather than individual phrases in text. In fact, this is how such representations are constructed in practice. To the extent to which themes in the semantic and network content models are phrase triggered, instances of these models can be reliably associated with the corresponding text. This type of text-model association significantly enhances the ease of auditing the coding of a particular body of text.

Once a semantic content model has been constructed for a particular block of text, a network content model could be constructed automatically. The first step would be to generate the set of nodes by mapping noun themes that appear as subjects, objects, and so on in the semantic content model into the nodes of a semantic network. This would render a noun theme that occurs in numerous clauses, as a single node in the corresponding network content model. Aggregating nodes in this way enables not only the identification of transitive relations in the corresponding network content model but also analyses based on queries over networks. In view of their interrelatedness (via the relating of themes in semantic and network text analysis and the aggregating of semantic relations in network text analysis), there is a sense in which this chapter might best be understood as an initial specification for a generic software tool suitable for all three types of quantitative text analysis.

# 16

# A THEORETICAL MAP FOR SELECTING AMONG TEXT ANALYSIS METHODS

Carl W. Roberts
Iowa State University

During the last decade a number of relational approaches have been developed for drawing statistical inferences about populations of texts. Text analyses prior to this time commonly used a thematic approach in which occurrences (or counts) of concepts comprised the variables under analysis. Relational alternatives to thematic text analysis can be grossly classified either as semantic text analyses, which map relations among concepts, or network text analyses, which map relations among statements. These three approaches to text analysis are not mutually exclusive. Instead they build upon each other, in the sense that the encoding of relations among concepts presupposes the identification of concept occurrences, and a network analysis makes use of information among statements of related concepts. This chapter starts with an examination of the data matrices that each type of text analysis affords and builds to a delineation of the universe of substantive questions that can be addressed via these three approaches to the analysis of texts and transcripts.

When social scientists embark on their first text analysis, they commonly begin by asking what each of these methods is "good for." What they want to know, of course, is what theoretically substantive questions can be addressed by the various text analysis methods currently in use. My purpose in this chapter is to address the "what is it good for" question—at least insofar as it relates to methods of quantitative text analysis.

In the introduction to this collection I drew a distinction between quantitative and qualitative text analysis, according to which only the former affords probabilistic inferences from samples to populations of text. As a first step in obtaining such probabilistic inferences, a sample of text must be obtained that is representative of the population of interest. In a second step, the sampled texts must be projected into a two-dimensional data matrix. No matter how sophisticated one's thematic, semantic, or network method of encoding texts, no matter how multidimensional the internal representation of one's data (e.g., as trees or networks; cf. Baker, this volume), the content of one's database must be "flattened" into two dimensions to make them suitable for statistical analysis. This (i.e., quantitative text analysis' data matrix requirement) greatly simplifies my task of delineating the domain of possible questions that quantitative text analyses are able to address. In particular, it allows the sought-after domain to be defined according to the various ways in which the columns (or variables) and rows (or units of analysis) of this data matrix can be constructed. As this domain gains definition, a theoretical map emerges on which text analysts can locate both their substantive question and the text analysis technique(s) to which it corresponds.

## VARIABLES

This book is organized according to what should now be a familiar tripartite view of quantitative text analysis methodology. Central to this view is the recognition that thematic, semantic, and network text analysis methodologies can be distinguished according to the types of variables generated in each. Variables derived from texts can be indicators of either the occurrence of a theme, the theme in a specific semantic role, or the theme's or theme relation's position within a network of semantically interrelated themes. Table 16.1 contains the type of data matrix generated in a thematic text analysis. Note that the data matrix has one row for each randomly sampled block of text and one column for each theme (or concept) that may occur

TABLE 16.1
Data Matrix for a Thematic Text Analysis

| ID Number | Theme 1 | Theme 2 | Theme 3 |
|-----------|---------|---------|---------|
| 1 | 2 | 0 | 0 |
| 2 | 0 | 0 | 1 |
| 3 | 1 | 3 | 1 |
| 4 | 0 | 2 | 1 |
| 5 | 0 | 0 | 0 |
| . | . | . | . |
| . | . | . | . |
| . | . | . | . |

in these text blocks. Cells in the data matrix indicate the number of occurrences of a particular theme within a specific block of text.

This is the type of data matrix analyzed in classic content analyses performed both before and after the advent of computer programs such as the General Inquirer (Stone, Dunphy, Smith, & Ogilvie, 1966). Encoding of textual data was occasionally embellished with secondary variables that measured the source's positive or negative sentiment regarding each theme (cf. Holsti, 1969; Pool, 1955). Yet it is essentially a matrix of word counts that forms the basis for a thematic analysis of texts.

Analyses of word counts yield inferences about the predominance of themes in texts. For example, Namenwirth and Weber's (1987) cultural indicators research reports shifts in the prevalence of various political and economic themes over time. Yet note that if, for example, certain types of political protest are found to occur in texts in which one also finds mentions of economic inflation, one is unable (on the basis of a data matrix of word counts) to determine if the protests are mentioned in the texts as being the cause or the effect of inflation. Information on semantic relations among themes such as "political protest" and "economic inflation" is not afforded by aggregated word-count data.

Relations among themes are encoded in a semantic text analysis, however. More generally, the data matrix generated in a semantic text analysis contains variables that identify themes as syntactic components within a semantic grammar. Table 16.2 illustrates a data matrix that might have been generated in a semantic text analysis. Note that the cells in the data matrix do not contain indicators of theme occurrences but contain discrete codes for the themes themselves. The column in which a specific theme's code appears indicates the theme's syntactic role within the researcher's semantic grammar. In generating Table 16.2 blocks of text were encoded as sequences of subject–action–object triplets. Inferences from such a data matrix might be made comparing the odds that within randomly sampled newspaper accounts of labor disputes, representatives of management ver-

TABLE 16.2
Data Matrix for a Semantic Text Analysis

| ID Number | Subject | Action | Object |
|-----------|---------|--------|--------|
| 1 | 11 | 35 | 64 |
| 2 | 9 | 22 | 89 |
| 3 | 14 | 35 | 72 |
| 4 | 11 | 36 | 72 |
| 5 | 17 | 30 | 55 |
| . | . | . | . |
| . | . | . | . |
| . | . | . | . |

sus of labor initiate collective bargaining or that within transcribed speech from a sample of minutes of prime-time television content, Blacks versus Whites refer to themselves as targets of aggression. More generally, and in contrast to thematic text analysis, semantic text analyses yield information on how themes are related according to an a priori specified semantic grammar.

Although writings on semantic text analysis methods date back to the 1950s (Gottschalk & Kaplan, 1958; Osgood, Saporta, & Nunnally, 1956), only in the last decade or two has there been a marked increase in their use. The breadth of these methods' applications can be found in Franzosi's (1989a) research on labor disputes, Gottschalk's (1979, 1982, 1995) on psychological states, Roberts' (1989, 1991) on ideology shifts, Schrodt's (1991, 1994) on contemporary political events, and Shapiro and Markoff's (Markoff, 1988; Markoff, Shapiro, & Weitman, 1974; Shapiro & Markoff, in press) work on public opinion in 18th century France. Yet if one wishes to analyze how semantically linked themes (or statements) are interrelated, these statements must first be combined into a network.

Network text analysis originated with the observation that once one has a series of encoded statements, one can proceed to combine these statements into a network. Moreover, once text blocks are rendered as networks of interrelated themes, variables can be generated to measure the positions of themes and theme relations within the networks. For example, let us imagine that we construct a network of themes in which all linkages indicate causal relations. Assigning the names theme-A and theme-B to any pair of themes in the network, one could develop a measure of "the causal salience of theme-A on theme-B" as the proportion of all sequences of causal linkages that are ones in which theme-A is the cause and theme-B is the effect. Note from the simple three-theme network in Figure 16.1 how calculation of "the causal-salience of theme-A on theme-B" draws on more than isolated semantically linked themes in blocks of text. It incorporates information on all themes and links within network representations of text blocks.

A data matrix such as that in Table 16.3 might be generated from a sample of networks that contained variables measuring the causal salience of each pair of the texts' themes. Network text analysts have developed many other measures of network characteristics. One example from this book is a theme's conductivity, which refers to the number of linkages that the theme provides between other pairs of themes (Carley, this volume). Another is of theme linkages that are logically implied but not explicitly stated in each block of text (Kleinnijenhuis, de Ridder, & Rietberg, this volume). As of this writing nearly all quantitative network text analysis research has been conducted either by Kathleen Carley or by a group of Dutch researchers in Amsterdam (Carley, 1986a; Carley & Palmquist, 1992; van Cuilenburg, Kleinnijenhuis, & de Ridder, 1986, 1988).

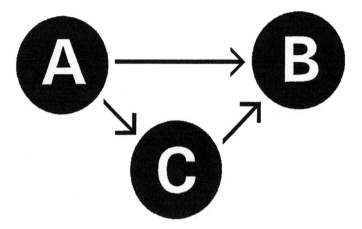

A. There are four sequences of causal linkages in this figure.

    1. A —> B
    2. A —> C
    3. C —> B
    4. A —> C —> B

B. Note that .50 is the proportion of all sequences of causal linkages in which A is the cause and B is the effect. That is, .50 is the "causal salience" of theme-A on theme-B.

FIG. 16.1. A network of causal relations among themes.

TABLE 16.3
Data Matrix for a Network Text Analysis

| | Causal Salience Measures | | | | | |
|---|---|---|---|---|---|---|
| ID Number | A on B | A on C | C on B | B on A | C on A | B on C |
| 1 | .50 | .25 | .25 | .00 | .00 | .00 |
| 2 | .25 | .00 | .50 | .00 | .25 | .00 |
| 3 | .00 | .00 | .25 | .25 | .50 | .00 |
| 4 | .00 | .00 | .00 | .50 | .25 | .25 |
| 5 | .00 | .25 | .00 | .50 | .00 | .25 |
| . | . | . | . | . | . | . |
| . | . | . | . | . | . | . |
| . | . | . | . | . | . | . |

## UNITS OF ANALYSIS

The discussion this far has been of three types of variables that can be used to characterize blocks of texts: the occurrence of a theme, the theme in a semantic role, and the network position of a theme or theme relation. The task now becomes one of specifying the types of units of analysis that are possible in a text analysis. Once done, a framework will have been established for delineating the realm of substantive inferences that can be drawn from the data matrices generated in quantitative text analyses.

In the earliest stages of every quantitative text analysis, the researcher is confronted with a "mountain of words" (a.k.a. a text population) about which statistical inferences are to be drawn. On the one hand, this text population may be an initially undifferentiated mass (e.g., a sample of minutes of speech on U.S. prime-time television could be drawn at random from the undifferentiated mountain of words that were uttered during a year's time). On the other hand, the text population may consist of clusters of sentences such as newspaper editorials, transcripts of interviews, diary entries, and so on. In either case, a representative sample can only be drawn once the text population has been divided into distinct text blocks, each of which is then assigned a unique number and sampled at random.[1]

The text population should not be mindlessly divided, however, even if it appears to the researcher as already a collection of discrete text blocks such as editorials, interviews, or diary entries. The statistical inferences that the researcher may legitimately draw from texts depend fundamentally on the units into which the text population is initially divided. Imagine a researcher, who wishes to analyze prime-time television data according to performers' mental models (or conceptual frameworks). In this case, the researcher would begin by dividing the text population into blocks associated with each performer. On the other hand, if the researcher wished to analyze the narratives (or storylines) depicted on prime-time television programs, the researcher would begin by dividing the text population into blocks associated with each program. However, performers may appear in more than one program, and programs will involve many performers. As a result, the researcher's inferences will differ, depending on this initial division of the text population.

In brief, the researcher who wishes to ask a substantive question of a population of texts must not only consider the thematic, semantic, and

---

[1] In this discussion I assume (without loss of generality) that the sampling unit and the unit of analysis are the same. With this assumption, one's units of analysis are identified as soon as one's text population has been divided into distinct text blocks. More important, the assumption allows me to separate the problem at hand (i.e., the problem of identifying one's units of analysis) from problems related to the clustering of units of analysis within sampling units. I return to the clustering problem in the following section.

TABLE 16.4
Types and Examples of Contextual Variables

---

Characteristics of source (gender, affiliation, biases, etc.)
Characteristics of message (local vs. domestic news, descriptive vs. evaluative orientation, etc.)
Characteristics of channel (radio vs. TV news, public vs. commercial network, written vs. spoken medium, etc.)
Characteristics of audience (sociocultural or historical setting within which text appeared)

---

network variables required to address the question but also the units of analysis yielded when this population is divided into text blocks. Thus far I have mentioned two types of units of analysis that might be yielded when a text population is divided, namely the conceptual framework of the text's source (e.g., the television performer's mental model) and the message that the text conveys (e.g., the program's storyline). Of course, there are others.

Consider Harold Lasswell's (1948) oft-cited depiction of communications research as the study of "Who says what, in which channel, to whom, and with what effect?" In his article-long answer to this question Lasswell argued that communications' effects can be largely understood as functions of their source, message, channel, and audience. Moreover, these four aspects of communication are the most common contextual variables used in analyses of texts and transcripts. Table 16.4 lists examples of the four corresponding types of contextual variables. Thus, other than source and message identifications, the researcher may also identify text blocks according to their channel (e.g., television, radio, electronic mail, etc.) or according to their intended audience (e.g., people within the various temporal and cultural contexts examined in historical-comparative research).

Comparisons among texts' sources, messages, channels, and audiences are only possible if each text block under analysis can be clearly identified according to its type of source, message, channel, and audience. The key in selecting a unit of analysis is not to assume that one's population of text is composed a priori of clearly distinguishable text blocks. On the contrary, it is the researcher's responsibility to divide this population into blocks that can be uniquely identified according to the contextual variables required for addressing the research question at hand.

## CAVEATS REGARDING THE CHOICE
## OF VARIABLES AND UNIT OF ANALYSIS

Before returning to the "What's it good for?" question, it is worthwhile considering what text-based data may not be good for. If text analysts lose perspective on the variables and units of analysis they have chosen, they may find themselves drawing illegitimate conclusions from their data. As it turns out, each text analysis method has its typical pitfalls.

Occasionally thematic text analysts will wrongly interpret co-occurrences of themes (i.e., correlations between word frequencies) as indicative of specific semantic relations among these themes. The associated warning is that if one's substantive question is about semantic relations, themes should not be counted but should be encoded according to a semantic grammar. Indeed, it was precisely to overcome thematic text analysis' limitation to inferences about theme occurrences that semantic text analysis methods were developed in the first place.

For semantic text analysts the typical pitfall stems from the fact that one's units of analysis are often clustered within one's sampling units. For example, in linguistic content analysis (Roberts, 1989, this volume, chapter 3; Eltinge, this volume) the unit of analysis is always the grammatical clause. Given that prior to sample selection each sampling unit must be assigned a unique number, one's sampling unit will rarely (i.e., except for the very smallest of text populations) be the clause. More commonly, one will sample text blocks (e.g., paragraphs, editorials, etc.) within which clauses are clustered. In such cases statistical analyses should not artificially inflate one's sample size by treating each unit of analysis as if it were a randomly sampled observation. Instead, inferential statistics must be adjusted to take the clustering into account.[2]

Every network is a cluster of nodes and arcs. Consequently, network text analysts must also be careful to take into account the within-network clustering of the themes and theme relations that respectively correspond to node and node-arc-node positions. Even more egregious errors may result if themes or theme relations are themselves treated as units of analysis.

Note that one could conceivably generate a rather large data matrix from a single network if one were to create a separate row in the matrix for each of the network's themes or theme relations and to place on each row the values of variables measuring each of these themes' or theme relations' various network positions. From a statistical perspective, the consequences of such a strategy are extremely problematic. Not only are the new units of analysis (namely, the themes or theme relations) not independent observations obtained via some random process, values on their associated variables are almost surely dependent observations with correlated errors (e.g., in a data matrix with one row per theme and with a column of conductivity scores for each theme [viz., the number of linkages that the theme provides between other theme pairs], dependence of scores across themes is assured

---

[2]One PC-based statistical package that adjusts standard errors for such complicated sampling designs is PC CARP (available from The Survey Section, 219 Snedecor Hall, Department of Statistics, Iowa State University, Ames, IA 50011).

because themes linked with highly conductive themes will, by virtue of this linkage, be more likely to be highly conductive themselves). If these error correlations are not taken into account in one's analyses, the possibilities of severely biased estimates and of underestimated standard errors cannot be discounted.[3] On the other hand, there is a simple remedy: Restrict one's statistical analyses to data matrices with "the network" as unit of analysis. Errors will be uncorrelated, if data on each row of one's data matrix is coded from a randomly sampled block of text.

## WHAT'S IT GOOD FOR?

Those who wish to draw statistical inferences about text populations will find themselves doing so based on a data matrix with text-related variables and, almost surely, contextual variables. Text-related variables in the matrix will measure occurrences of themes, theme relations within a semantic grammar, and/or network positions of themes and theme relations. Possible contextual variables will indicate the source, message, channel, and/or audience uniquely associated with each text block under analysis. Accordingly (and at the risk of becoming overly repetitive), the answer to the "what's it good for" question is that quantitative text analysis is good for drawing inferences about contextual and text-based variables, where contextual variables may include indicators of source, message, channel, and audience, and where text-based variables may include the frequency with which themes occur, the semantic relations among themes that do occur, and the network positions occupied by these themes and relations. Within these limits, the decision of which inferences to draw is, of course, where one's own imagination must take hold.

---

[3]These problems have not gone unnoticed by researchers in social network analysis (Strauss & Ikeda, 1990; Walker, Wasserman, & Wellman, 1994; Wasserman & Faust, 1994). If network text analyses are of clusters of conditionally independent pairs of themes (possibly ones related in multiple ways), considerable statistical sophistication will be needed to ensure unbiased estimators with appropriately large standard errors.

# REFERENCES

A maverick pollster promotes verbosity that others disdain. (1985, February 13). *Wall Street Journal* (eastern ed.), p. 1.

Abell, P. (1984). Comparative narratives: Some rules for the study of action. *Journal for the Theory of Social Behavior, 14*, 309–332.

Abell, P. (1987). *The syntax of social life: The theory and method of comparative narratives.* Oxford: Clarendon.

Abelson, R. P. (1968). Psychological implication. In R. P. Abelson, E. Aronson, W. J. McGuire, T. M. Newcomb, M. J. Rosenberg, & P. H. Tannenbaum (Eds.), *Theories of cognitive consistency: A sourcebook* (pp. 112–139). Chicago: Rand McNally.

Abelson, R. P., & Rosenberg, M. J. (1958). Symbolic psycho-logic: A model of attitudinal cognition. *Behavioral Science, 3*, 1–13.

Accornero, A. (1985). La 'terziarizzazione' del conflitto e i suoi effetti [The 'tertiarization' of conflict and its effects]. In G. P. Cella & M. Regini (Eds.), *Il conflitto industriale in Italia* [Industrial conflict in Italy] (pp. 275–341). Bologna: Il Mulino.

Adatto, K. (1990). The incredible shrinking sound bite (TV news and campaign image manipulation). *The New Republic, 202*, 20–24.

Agresti, A. (1990). *Categorical data analysis.* New York: Wiley.

Ahmed, A. G. (1989). Ecological degradation in the Sahel: The political dimension. In A. H. Ornas & M. A. Salih (Eds.), *Ecology and politics* (pp. 89–100). Uppsala: Scandinavian Institute of Africa Studies.

Aho, A. V., Sethi, R., & Ullman, J. D. (1986). *Compilers: Principles, techniques, and tools.* Reading, MA: Addison-Wesley.

Alker, H. R., Jr., Duffy, G., Hurwitz, R., & Mallery, J. C. (1991). Text modeling for international politics: A tourist's guide to RELATUS. In V. M. Hudson (Ed.), *Artificial intelligence and international politics* (pp. 97–126). Boulder, CO: Westview.

Allen, J. (1995). *Natural language understanding* (2nd ed.). Redwood, CA: Benjamin/Cummings.

Andrén, G. (1981). Reliability and content analysis. In K. E. Rosengren (Ed.), *Advances in content analysis* (pp. 43–67). Beverly Hills, CA: Sage.

Anonymous. (1989). A short guide to the General Inquirer. *Bulletin de Méthodologie Sociologique, 24*, 6–8.

Austin, J. L. (1975). *How to do things with words: The William James lectures delivered at Harvard University in 1955.* Cambridge, MA: Harvard University Press.

Axelrod, R. M. (Ed.). (1976). *The structure of decision: The cognitive maps of political elites.* Princeton, NJ: Princeton University Press.

Azar, E. A. (1982). *Conflict and peace data base, 1948–1978* [machine-readable data file]. College Park, MD: University of Maryland, Center for International Development and Conflict Management.

Azar, E. E., & Ben-Dak, J. (Eds.). (1975). *Theory and practice of events research.* New York: Gordon & Breach.

Baker, A. L., & Riley, D. D. (1993). *Data abstraction and object-oriented software development.* Published course notes, University-level Computer Science Program. Cary, NC: IBM Corporation.

Banks, D., & Carley, K. M. (1994). Metric inference for social networks. *Journal of Classification, 11*, 121–149.

Barcus, F. E. (1959). *Communications content: Analysis of the research, 1900–1958 (A content analysis of content analysis).* Ph.D. Dissertation, University of Michigan, Ann Arbor: University Microfilms.

Barker-Plummer, B. (1988). Look who's talking: Trends in attribution and sources in two elite newspapers. *Southwestern Mass Communication Journal, 4*, 55–62.

Berelson, B. (1954). Content analysis. In G. Lindzey (Ed.), *Handbook of social psychology* (Vol. I, pp. 488–522). Reading, MA: Addison-Wesley.

Berelson, B. (1971). *Content analysis in communication research* (Rev. ed.). New York: Hafner.

Berg, B. L. (1995). *Qualitative research methods for the social sciences.* Boston, MA: Allyn & Bacon.

Bergesen, A., & Jones, A. (1992). Decoding the standard modern dance. In R. Wuthnow (Ed.), *Vocabularies of public life: Empirical essays in symbolic structure* (pp. 169–181). London and New York: Routledge.

Berleant, D. (1995). *"Word experts" for word disambiguation.* Fayetteville: University of Arkansas, Department of Computer Systems Engineering.

Bierschenk, B. (1991). *The schema axiom as foundation of a theory for measurement and representation of consciousness.* Lund: Lund University, Cognitive Science Research, No. 31.

Blainey, G. (1988). *The causes of war* (3rd ed.). New York: The Free Press.

Bollème, G. (1965). Littérature populaire et littérature de colportage au 18e siècle [Popular literature and chapbooks of the 18th century]. In F. Furet (Ed.), *Livre et société dans la France du XVIII siècle* [Books and society in 18th century France] (Vol. 1, pp. 61–92). Paris and the Hague: Mouton.

Bond, D., Bennett, B., & Vogele, W. (1994). *Data development and interaction events analysis using KEDS/PANDA: An interim report.* Paper presented at the International Studies Association, Washington, DC.

Brook, B. S. (1969). Style and content analysis in music: The simplified "plaine and easie code." In G. Gerbner, O. R. Holsti, K. Krippendorff, W. Paisley, & P. J. Stone (Eds.), *The analysis of communication content* (pp. 287–296). New York: Wiley.

Bryan, M. (1988). *SGML: An author's guide to the Standard Generalized Markup Language.* Reading, MA: Addison-Wesley.

Burgess, P. M., & Lawton, R. W. (1972). *Indicators of international behavior: An assessment of events data research.* Beverly Hills, CA: Sage.

Bybee, R. W. (1985). The Sisyphean question in science education: What should the scientifically and technologically literate person know, value and do—As a citizen? In R. W. Bybee (Ed.), *Science technology society: 1985 yearbook for the National Science Teachers Association* (pp. 74–93). Washington, DC: National Science Teachers Association.

Carley, K. M. (1984). *Constructing consensus.* Unpublished doctoral dissertation, Harvard University, Cambridge, MA.

Carley, K. M. (1986a). An approach for relating social structure to cognitive structure. *Journal of Mathematical Sociology, 12,* 137–189.

Carley, K. M. (1986b). Knowledge acquisition as a social phenomenon. *Instructional Science, 14,* 381–438.

Carley, K. M. (1988). Formalizing the social expert's knowledge. *Sociological Methods and Research, 17,* 165–232.

Carley, K. M. (1993). Coding choices for textual analysis: A comparison of content analysis and map analysis. In P. Marsden (Ed.), *Sociological methodology, 1993* (pp. 75–126). Oxford: Blackwell.

Carley, K. M., & Kaufer, D. S. (1993). Semantic connectivity: An approach for analyzing semantic networks. *Communication Theory, 3,* 183–213.

Carley, K. M., & Palmquist, M. E. (1992). Extracting, representing, and analyzing mental models. *Social Forces, 70,* 601–636.

Carré, B. (1979). *Graphs and networks.* Oxford: Oxford University Press.

Cartwright, D. (1953). Analysis of qualitative material. In L. Festinger & D. Katz (Eds.), *Research methods in the behavioral sciences* (pp. 421–470). Niles, IL: Dryden.

Cerulo, K. (1992). Putting it together: Measuring the impact of aural and visual symbols. In R. Wuthnow (Ed.), *Vocabularies of public life: Empirical essays in symbolic structure* (pp. 111–129). London and New York: Routledge.

Chiang-Soong, B., & Yager, R. E. (1993). The inclusion of STS material in the most frequently used secondary science textbooks in the U.S. *Journal of Research in Science Teaching, 30,* 339–349.

Chomsky, N. (1957). *Syntactic structures.* The Hague: Mouton.

Cicourel, A. (1970). The acquisition of social structure: Toward a developmental sociology of language and meaning. In J. Douglous (Ed.), *Understanding everyday life* (pp. 136–168). Chicago: Aldine-Atherton.

Cicourel, A. (1974). *Cognitive sociology.* New York: The Free Press.

Clay, J. W., & Holcomb, B. K. (1986). *Politics and the Ethiopian famine of 1984–1985.* Peterborough, NH: Cultural Survival Transcript Printing.

Cliffe, L., & Davidson, B. (Eds.). (1988). *The long struggle of Eritrea for independence and constructive peace.* Nottingham, England: Bertrand Russell House.

Clocksin, W. F., & Mellish, C. S. (1984). *Programming in Prolog* (2nd ed.). Berlin: Springer-Verlag.

Colby, B., Kennedy, S., & Milanesi, L. (1991). Content analysis, cultural grammars, and computers. *Qualitative Sociology, 14,* 373–384.

Coleman, D. L. (1991). *Formalized structured analysis specifications.* Unpublished doctoral dissertation, Iowa State University, Ames.

Conference on goals for science and technology education grades K–12. (1983). *A revised and intensified science and technology curriculum grades K–12 urgently needed for the future.* A report to the National Science Board commission on precollege education in mathematics, science and technology. Washington, DC: National Science Foundation.

Connelly, F. M., Whalstrom, M. W., Finegold, M., & Elbaz, F. (1977). *Enquiry teaching in science, a handbook for secondary school teachers.* Toronto: The Ontario Institute for the Study of Education.

Cooley, C. (1902). *Human nature and social order.* New York: Scribner's.

Coombs, C. (1953). Theory and methods of social measurement. In L. Festinger & D. Katz (Eds.), *Research methods in the behavioral sciences* (pp. 471–535). New York: Dryden.

Corsaro, W. A., & Heise, D. R. (1990). Event structure models from ethnographic data. In *Sociological methodology, 1990* (pp. 1–57). Oxford: Basil Blackwell.

Cropper, S., Eden, C., & Ackermann, F. (1990). Keeping sense of accounts using computer-based cognitive maps. *Social Science Computer Review, 8,* 345–366.

Crowell, V. L., Jr. (1937). The scientific method: Attitudes and skills essential to the scientific method, and their treatment in general science and elementary biology textbooks. *School Science and Mathematics, 37,* 525–531.

Cuilenburg, J. J. van, Kleinnijenhuis, J., & Ridder, J. A. de. (1986). A theory of evaluative discourse: Towards a graph theory of journalistic texts. *European Journal of Communication, 1,* 65–96.

Cuilenburg, J. J. van, Kleinnijenhuis, J., & Ridder, J. A. de. (1988). Artificial intelligence and content analysis: Problems of and strategies for computer text analysis. *Quality and Quantity, 22,* 65–97.

D'Haenen, H., Morez, V. E., Weert, D. de, Cornet, C., Mulders, I. van, & Kaufman, L. (1985). Primary versus secondary depression: A psychometric approach, preliminary results. *Acta Psychiatrica Belgica, 85,* 381–389.

Dale, T. A. (1991). *Changing perceptions of robots in science fiction.* Unpublished honors thesis, Department of Social and Decision Sciences, Carnegie Mellon University, Pittsburgh.

Danielson, W. (1988). *User manual, General Content Analyzer, version 1.1.* Austin, TX: Wayne Danielson.

Date, C. J. (1995). *An introduction to database systems* (6th ed.). Reading, MA: Addison-Wesley.

Davis, K. (1938). Mental hygiene and the class structure. *Psychiatry, 1,* 55–65.

Delisle, N., & Garlan, D. (1990). A formal specification of an oscilloscope. *IEEE Software, 7,* 29–36.

Denzin, N. K., & Lincoln, Y. S. (Eds.). (1994). *Handbook of qualitative research.* Thousand Oaks, CA: Sage.

DeWeese, L. C. (1976). Computer content analysis of printed media: A limited feasibility study. *Public Opinion Quarterly, 40,* 92–114.

Digman, J. (1994). Historical antecedents of the five-factor model. In P. Costa & T. Widiger (Eds.), *Personality disorders and the five-factor model of personality* (pp. 13–17). Washington, DC: American Psychological Association.

Dijk, T. van. (1972). *Some aspects of text grammars.* Paris: Mouton.

Dik, S. C. (1981). *Functional grammar.* Dordrecht, the Netherlands: Foris.

Dixon, R. M. W. (1991). *A new approach to English grammar on semantic principles.* Oxford: Clarendon.

Dornbusch, S. M., & Hickman, L. C. (1959). Other-directedness in consumer-goods advertising: A test of Riesman's theory. *Social Forces, 38,* 99–102.

Dowty, D. R. (1979). *Word meaning and Montague grammar: The semantics of verbs and times in generative semantics and in Montague's PTQ.* Dordrecht, the Netherlands: Reidel.

Dunphy, D. C. (1966). Studies in psychotic language. In P. J. Stone, D. C. Dunphy, M. S. Smith, & D. M. Ogilvie (Eds.), *The General Inquirer: A computer approach to content analysis* (pp. 287–340). Cambridge, MA: MIT Press.

Durham, W. (1979). *Scarcity and survival in Central America: Ecological origins of the Soccer War.* Stanford, CA: Stanford University Press.

Duschl, R. A. (1986). Textbooks and the teaching of fluid inquiry. *School Science and Mathematics, 86,* 27–32.

Eick, S. G. (1994). Graphically displaying text. *Journal of Computational and Graphical Statistics, 3,* 127–142.

Ekman, P., Friesen, W. V., & Taussig, T. G. (1969). VID-R and SCAN: Tools and methods for the automatic analysis of visual records. In G. Gerbner, O. R. Holsti, K. Krippendorff, W. Paisley, & P. J. Stone (Eds.), *The analysis of communication content* (pp. 297–312). New York: Wiley.

Eltinge, E. M. (1988). Linguistic content analysis of the Holt, Rinehart and Winston series of high school biology textbooks: A longitudinal study focusing on the use of inquiry (Doctoral dissertation, Iowa State University, Ames, 1988). *Dissertation Abstracts International, 49,* 2606A.

Eltinge, E. M., & Roberts, C. W. (1993). Linguistic content analysis: A method to measure science as inquiry in textbooks. *Journal of Research in Science Teaching, 30,* 65–83.

Fauconnier, G. (1985). *Mental spaces: Aspects of meaning construction in natural language.* Cambridge, MA: Bradford.

Feldman, M. S. (1994). *Strategies for interpreting qualitative data.* Thousand Oaks, CA: Sage.

Fielding, N. G., & Lee, R. M. (Eds.). (1991). *Using computers in qualitative research.* Newbury Park, CA: Sage.

Fischer, D. H. (1977). *Growing old in America.* New York: Oxford.

Fiske, A. (1991). *Structures of social life: The four elementary forms of human relations (Communal sharing, authority ranking, equality matching, market pricing).* New York: The Free Press.

Flexner, S. B., & Hauck, L. C. (Eds.). (1987). *The Random House Dictionary of the English Language* (2nd ed.). New York: Random House.

Franzosi, R. (1987). The press as a source of socio-historical data: Issues in the methodology of data collection from newspapers. *Historical Methods, 20,* 5–16.

Franzosi, R. (1989a). From words to numbers: A generalized and linguistics-based coding procedure for collecting event-data from newspapers. In C. Clogg (Ed.), *Sociological methodology, 1989* (pp. 263–298). Oxford: Basil Blackwell.

Franzosi, R. (1989b). One hundred years of strike statistics: Methodological and theoretical issues in quantitative strike research. *Industrial and Labor Relations Review, 42,* 348–362.

Franzosi, R. (1990a). Computer-assisted coding of textual data: An application to semantic grammars. *Sociological Methods and Research, 19,* 225–257.

Franzosi, R. (1990b). Strategies for the prevention, detection and correction of measurement error in data collected from textual sources. *Sociological Methods and Research, 18,* 442–471.

Franzosi, R. (1994). From words to numbers: A set theory framework for the collection, organization, and analysis of narrative data. In P. Marsden (Ed.), *Sociological methodology, 1994* (pp. 105–136). Oxford: Basil Blackwell.

Franzosi, R. (1995). *The puzzle of strikes: Class and state strategies in postwar Italy.* Cambridge: Cambridge University Press.

Freeman, R. B. (1986). Unionism comes to the public sector. *Journal of Economic Literature, 24,* 41–86.

Frege, G. (1959). *The foundations of Arithmetic: A logico-mathematical enquiry into the concept of number.* Oxford: Blackwell. (Original work published 1884)

Frost, R. (1986). *Introduction to knowledge base systems.* New York: Macmillan.

Fuchs, V. R. (1968). *The service economy.* New York: National Bureau of Economic Research and Columbia University Press.

Galtung, J. (1967). *Theory and methods of social research.* New York: Columbia University.

George, A. (1959). Quantitative and qualitative approaches to content analysis. In I. de Sola Pool (Ed.), *Trends in content analysis* (pp. 7–32). Urbana, IL: University of Illinois Press.

Gerbner, G. (1988). *Violence and terror in the mass media.* Paris: Unesco.

Gerbner, G., Holsti, O. R., Krippendorff, K., Paisley, W. J., & Stone, P. J. (Eds.). (1969). *The analysis of communication content: Developments in scientific theories and computer techniques.* New York: Wiley.

Gerhart, S. (1990). Applications of formal methods: Developing virtuoso software. *IEEE Software, 7,* 6–10.

Gerner, D. J., Schrodt, P. A., Francisco, R., & Weddle, J. L. (1994). The analysis of political events using machine coded data. *International Studies Quarterly, 38,* 91–119.

Ghanem, S. (1990). *The change in the reporting style of newspapers.* Unpublished seminar paper, Department of Journalism, University of Texas, Austin.

Giorgis, D. W. (1989). *Red tears: War, famine and revolution in Ethiopia.* Trenton: The Red Sea Press.

Glaser, B. G., & Strauss, A. L. (1967). *The discovery of grounded theory, strategies for qualitative research.* Chicago: Aldine.

Gleick, P. H. (1992). Water and conflict. *The occasional paper series of the project on environmental change and acute conflict* (No. 1). Peace and Conflict Studies Program, University of Toronto.

Gleser, G. C., Gottschalk, L. A., & Springer, K. J. (1961). An anxiety scale applicable to verbal samples. *Archives of General Psychiatry, 4,* 109–118.

Gleser, G. C., Winget, C. N., & Seligman, R. (1979). Content scaling of affect in adolescent speech samples. *Journal of Youth and Adolescence, 8,* 282–297.

Goldhamer, D. H. (1969). Toward a more general Inquirer: Convergence of structure and context of meaning. In G. Gerbner, O. R. Holsti, K. Krippendorff, W. J. Paisley, & P. J. Stone (Eds.), *The analysis of communication content: Developments in scientific theories and computer techniques* (pp. 343–354). New York: Wiley.

Goldstein, J. S. (1992). A conflict-cooperation scale for WEIS events data. *Journal of Conflict Resolution, 36,* 369–385.

Goldstein, J. S., & Freeman, J. R. (1990). *Three-way street: Strategic reciprocity in world politics.* Chicago: University of Chicago Press.

Goldstone, J. A. (1992). Imminent political conflicts arising from China's environmental crises. *The occasional paper series of the project on environmental change and acute conflict* (No. 2). Peace and Conflict Studies Program, University of Toronto.

Good, R. (1993). Editorial: Science textbook analysis. *Journal of Research in Science Teaching, 37,* 619.

Gottlieb, A. A., Gleser, G. C., & Gottschalk, L. A. (1967). Verbal and physiological responses to hypnotic suggestion of attitudes. *Psychosomatic Medicine, 29,* 172–183.

Gottschalk, L. A. (1955). Psychologic conflict and electroencephalographic patterns. Some notes on the problem of correlating changes in paroxysmal electoencephalographic patterns with psychologic conflicts. *Archives of Neurology and Psychiatry, 73,* 656–662.

Gottschalk, L. A. (1968). Some applications of the psychoanalytic concept of object relatedness: Preliminary studies on a human relations scale applicable to verbal samples. *Comprehensive Psychiatry, 9,* 608–620.

Gottschalk, L. A. (1974). A hope scale applicable to verbal samples. *Archives of General Psychiatry, 30,* 779–785.

Gottschalk, L. A. (1976). Children's speech as a source of data toward the measurement of psychological states. *Journal of Youth and Adolescence, 5,* 11–36.

Gottschalk, L. A. (Ed.). (1979). *The content analysis of verbal behavior: Further studies.* New York: Spectrum.

Gottschalk, L. A. (1982). Manual of uses and applications of the Gottschalk–Gleser verbal behavior scales. *Research Communications in Psychology, Psychiatry and Behavior, 7,* 273–327.

Gottschalk, L. A. (1984). Measurement of mood, affect, and anxiety in cancer patients. *Cancer, 53,* 2236–2242.

Gottschalk, L. A. (1985). The pharmacokinetics of some psychoactive drugs and relationships with clinical response. *Methods and Findings in Experimental and Clinical Pharmacology, 7,* 275–282.

Gottschalk, L. A. (1987). Content category analysis—the measurement of the magnitude of psychological dimensions in psychotherapy. In R. L. Russell (Ed.), *Language in psychotherapy: Strategies of discovery* (pp. 13–70). New York: Plenum.

Gottschalk, L. A. (1994). The development, validation, and applications of a measurement of cognitive impairment from the content analysis of verbal behavior. *Journal of Clinical Psychology, 50,* 349–361.

Gottschalk, L. A. (1995). *Content analysis of verbal behavior: New findings and computerized clinical applications.* Hillsdale, NJ: Lawrence Erlbaum Associates.

Gottschalk, L. A., & Bechtel, R. (1982). The measurement of anxiety through the computer analysis of verbal samples. *Comprehensive Psychiatry, 23,* 364–369.

Gottschalk, L. A., & Bechtel, R. (1989). Artificial intelligence and the computerization of the content analysis of natural language. *Artificial Intelligence in Medicine, 1,* 131–137.

Gottschalk, L. A., & Bechtel, R. (1993). *Psychologic and neuropsychiatric assessment applying the Gottschalk–Gleser content analysis method to verbal sample analysis using the Gottschalk–Bechtel computer scoring system.* Palo Alto, CA: Mind Garden.

Gottschalk, L. A., Biener, R., Noble, E. P., Birch, H., Wilbert, D. E., & Heiser, J. F. (1975). Thioridazine plasma levels and clinical response. *Comprehensive Psychiatry, 16*, 323–337.

Gottschalk, L. A., Buchsbaum, M. S., Gillin, C., Wu, J., Reynolds, C., & Herrera, D. B. (1991). Positron emission tomographic studies of the relationship of cerebral glucose metabolism and the magnitude of anxiety and hostility experienced during dreaming and waking. *Journal of Neuropsychiatry and Clinical Neuroscience, 3*, 131–142.

Gottschalk, L. A., Cleghorn, J. M., Gleser, G. C., & Iacono, J. M. (1965). Studies of relationships of emotions to plasma lipids. *Psychosomatic Medicine, 27*, 102–111.

Gottschalk, L. A., Eckardt, M. J., Pautler, C. P., Wolf, R. J., & Terman, S. A. (1983). Cognitive impairment scales derived from verbal samples. *Comprehensive Psychiatry, 25*, 6–19.

Gottschalk, L. A., Falloon, I. R. H., Marder, S. R., Lebell, M. B., Gift, T. E., & Wynne, L. C. (1988). The prediction of relapse of schizophrenic patients using emotional data obtained from their relative. *Psychiatry Research, 25*, 261–276.

Gottschalk, L. A., & Frank, E. C. (1967). Estimating the magnitude of anxiety from speech. *Behavioral Science, 12*, 289–295.

Gottschalk, L. A., Fronczek, J., & Abel, L. (1993). Emotions, defenses, coping mechanisms, and symptoms. *Psychoanalytic Psychology, 10*, 237–260.

Gottschalk, L. A., & Gleser, G. C. (1964). Distinguishing characteristics of the verbal communications of schizophrenic patients. In Association for Research In Nervous and Mental Diseases (Ed.), *Disorders of communication* (pp. 400–413). Baltimore: Williams & Wilkins.

Gottschalk, L. A., & Gleser, G. C. (1969). *The measurement of psychological states through the content analysis of verbal behavior.* Los Angeles: University of California Press.

Gottschalk, L. A., Gleser, G. C., & Springer, K. J. (1963). Three hostility scales applicable to verbal samples. *Archives of General Psychiatry, 5*, 254–279.

Gottschalk, L. A., Gleser, G. C., D'Zmura, T., & Hanenson, I. B. (1964). Some psychophysiological relationships in hypertensive women: The effect of hydrochlorothiazide on the relation of affect to blood pressure. *Psychosomatic Medicine, 26*, 610–617.

Gottschalk, L. A., Gleser, G. C., Daniels, R. S., & Block, S. (1958). The speech patterns of schizophrenic patients. A method of assessing relative degree of personal disorganization and social alienation. *Journal of Nervous and Mental Disease, 127*, 153–166.

Gottschalk, L. A., Gleser, G. C., Springer, K. J., Kaplan, S. M., Shanon, J., & Ross, W. D. (1960). Effect of perphenazine on verbal behavior patterns. *Archives of General Psychiatry, 2*, 632–639.

Gottschalk, L. A., Gleser, G. C., Wylie, H. W., & Kaplan, S. M. (1965). Effects of imipramine on anxiety and hostility levels derived from verbal communications. *Psychopharmacologia, 7*, 303–310.

Gottschalk, L. A., Haer, J. L., & Bates, D. E. (1972). Effect of sensory overload on psychological state. *Archives of General Psychiatry, 27*, 451–457.

Gottschalk, L. A., Hausmann, C., & Brown, J. S. (1975). A computerized scoring system for use with content analysis scales. *Comprehensive Psychiatry, 16*, 77–90.

Gottschalk, L. A., & Hoigaard-Martin, J. (1986). A depression scale applicable to verbal samples. *Psychiatry Research, 17*, 153–167.

Gottschalk, L. A., & Kaplan, S. M. (1958). A quantitative method of estimating variations in intensity of a psychologic conflict or state. *Archives of Neurology and Psychiatry, 78*, 656–664.

Gottschalk, L. A., Kunkel, R. L., Wohl, T., Saenger, E., & Winget, C. N. (1969). Total and half body irradiation: Effect on cognitive and emotional processes. *Archives of General Psychiatry, 21*, 574–580.

Gottschalk, L. A., & Lolas, F. (1987). *Estudios sobre analisis del comportamiento verbal* [Studies on the analysis of verbal behavior]. Santiago, Chile: Editorial Universitaria.

Gottschalk, L. A., & Lolas, F. (1989). Cross-cultural characteristics of the Gottschalk–Gleser content analysis method measuring the magnitude of psychological dimension. *Transcultural Psychiatric Research Review, 26*, 83–111.

Gottschalk, L. A., & Lolas, F. (1992). The measurement of quality of life through the content analysis of verbal behavior. *Psychotherapy and Psychosomatics, 25*, 1–9.

Gottschalk, L. A., Lolas, F., & Viney, L. L. (Eds.). (1986). *The content analysis of verbal behavior: Significance in clinical medicine and psychiatry.* New York: Springer-Verlag.

Gottschalk, L. A., Mayerson, P., & Gottlieb, A. (1967). The prediction and evaluation of outcome in an emergency brief psychotherapy clinic. *Journal of Nervous and Mental Disease, 29*, 172–183.

Gottschalk, L. A., & Rey, F. (1990). The emotional effects of physical or mental injury on Hispanic people living in the U.S.A. as adjudged from the content of their speech. *Journal of Clinical Psychology, 46*, 915–922.

Gottschalk, L. A., Springer, K. J., & Gleser, G. C. (1961). Experiments with a method of assessing the variations in intensity of certain psychological states occurring during two psychotherapeutic interviews. In L. A. Gottschalk (Ed.), *Comparative psycholinguistic analysis of two psychotherapeutic interviews* (pp. 115–138). New York: International Universities Press.

Gottschalk, L. A., Stone, W. N., Gleser, G. C., & Iacono, J. M. (1966). Anxiety levels in dreams: Relation to changes in plasma free fatty acids. *Science, 153*, 654–657.

Gottschalk, L. A., Stone, W. N., Gleser, G. C., & Iacono, J. M. (1969). Anxiety and plasma free fatty acids. *Life Sciences, 8*, 61–68.

Gottschalk, L. A., Winget, C. N., & Gleser, G. C. (1969). *Manual of instructions for using the Gottschalk–Gleser content analysis scales: Anxiety, hostility, social alienation–personal disorganization.* Los Angeles: University of California Press.

Gottschalk, L. A., Winget, C. N., Gleser, G. C., & Lolas, F. (1984). *Analisis de la conducta verbal* [Analysis of verbal conduct]. Santiago, Chile: Editorial Universitaria.

Grabiner, J. V., & Miller, P. D. (1974). Effects of the Scopes trial: Was it a victory for evolutionists? *Science, 185*, 832–837.

Griemas, A. J. (1984). *Structural semantics: An attempt at a method.* Lincoln, NE: University of Nebraska Press. (Original work published 1966)

Griffin, L. J. (1993). Narrative, event–structure analysis, and causal interpretation in historical sociology. *American Journal of Sociology, 98*, 1094–1133.

Grobman, A. B. (1969). *The changing classroom: The role of the Biological Sciences Curriculum Study.* Garden City, NY: Doubleday.

Gurr, T. R. (1974). The neo-Alexandrians: A review essay on data handbooks in political science. *American Political Science Review, 68*, 243–252.

Guttag, J. V., & Horning, J. (1993). *LARCH: Languages and tools for formal specification.* New York: Springer.

Habermas, J. (1979). *Communication and the evolution of society.* Boston: Beacon.

Halliday, M. A. K. (1970). Language structure and language function. In J. Lyons (Ed.), *New horizons in linguistics* (pp. 140–165). New York: Penguin.

Halliday, M. A. K. (1978). *Language as social semiotic.* London: Arnold.

Halliday, M. A. K. (1994). *An introduction to functional grammar* (2nd ed.). London: Arnold.

Harbeson, J. W. (1988). *The Ethiopian transformation: The quest for the post-imperial state.* Boulder: Westview Press.

Harmon, P., & King, D. (1985). *Expert systems: Artificial intelligence in business.* New York: Wiley.

Harms, N. C., & Yager, R. E. (1981). *What research says to the science teacher* (Vol. 3). Washington, DC: National Science Teachers Association.

Hawthorne, M. (1994). The computer in literary analysis: Using tact with students. *Computers and the Humanities, 28*, 19–27.

Hayes-Roth, F., Waterman, D. A., & Lenat, D. (Eds.). (1983). *Building expert systems.* Reading, MA: Addison-Wesley.

Hazarika, S. (1993). Bangladesh and Assam: Land pressures, migration and ethnic conflict. *The occasional paper series of the project on environmental change and acute conflict* (No. 3). Peace and Conflict Studies Program, University of Toronto.

Heider, F. (1946). Attitudes and cognitive organizations. *Journal of Psychology, 21*, 107–112.

Heise, D. R. (1988). Computer analysis of cultural structures. *Social Science Computer Review, 6*, 183–196.

Heise, D. R. (1991). Event structure analysis: A qualitative model of quantitative research. In N. G. Fielding & R. M. Lee (Eds.), *Using computers in qualitative research* (pp. 136–163). Beverly Hills, CA: Sage.

Heise, D. R., & Lewis, E. M. (1988). *Introduction to ETHNO, version 2.* Raleigh, NC: National Collegiate Software Clearinghouse.

Helgeson, S. L., Blosser, P. E., & Howe, R. W. (1977). *The status of pre-college science, mathematics and social science education: 1955-75.* (The Center for Science and Mathematics Education, The Ohio State University, Columbus, OH). Washington, DC: U.S. Government Printing Office.

Herron, M. D. (1971). The nature of scientific enquiry. *School Review, 79*, 171–212.

Hesse-Biber, S., Depuis, P., & Kinder, T. S. (1991). HyperRESEARCH: A computer program for the analysis of qualitative data with an emphasis on hypothesis testing and multimedia analysis. *Qualitative Sociology, 14*, 289–306.

Hickman, F. M., & Kahle, J. B. (Eds.). (1982). *New directions in biology teaching.* Reston, VA: National Association of Biology Teachers.

Hockey, S., & Martin, J. (1987). The Oxford Concordance Program version 2. *Literary and Linguistic Computing, 2*, 125–131.

Hoey, M. (1994). Signalling in discourse: A functional analysis of a common discourse pattern in written and spoken English. In M. Coulthard (Ed.), *Advances in written text analysis* (pp. 26–45). London: Routledge & Kegan Paul.

Hofstein, A., & Yager, R. E. (1982). Societal issues as organizers for science education in the '80s. *School Science and Mathematics, 82*, 539–547.

Holsti, O. R. (1966). External conflict and internal consensus: The Sino-Soviet case. In P. J. Stone, D. C. Dunphy, M. S. Smith, & D. M. Ogilvie (Eds.), *The General Inquirer: A computer approach to content analysis.* Cambridge, MA: MIT Press.

Holsti, O. R. (1969). *Content analysis for the social sciences and humanities.* Reading, MA: Addison-Wesley.

Homer-Dixon, T. F. (1991). On the threshold: Environmental changes as causes of acute conflict. *International Security, 16*, 77–79.

Homer-Dixon, T. F. (1994). Environmental scarcities and violent conflict: Evidence from cases. *International Security, 19*, 5–40.

Hopcroft, J. E., & Ullman, J. D. (1969). *Formal languages and their relation to automata.* Reading, MA: Addison-Wesley.

Hubert, L. J. (1987). *Assignment methods in combinatorial data analysis.* New York: M. Dekker.

Hurd, P. D., Bybee, R. W., Kahle, J. B., & Yager, R. E. (1980). Biology education in secondary schools of the United States. *The American Biology Teacher, 42*, 388–404, 409–410.

Iker, H. P., & Harway, N. I. (1969). A computer system towards the recognition and analysis of content. In G. Gerbner, O. R. Holsti, K. Krippendorff, W. Paisley, & P. J. Stone (Eds.), *The analysis of communication content* (pp. 381–406). New York: Wiley.

Janis, I. L. (1949). The problem of validation in content analysis. In H. D. Lasswell, N. Leites, & Associates (Eds.), *Language of politics: Studies in quantitative semantics* (Chapter 4). New York: George W. Stewart.

Johnson, D. (1989). *Examination of change-related words over time.* Unpublished seminar paper, Department of Journalism, University of Texas, Austin.

Johnson, P., Sears, D., & McConahay, J. B. (1971). Black invisibility: The press and the Los Angeles riot. *American Journal of Sociology, 76*, 698–721.

Johnson-Laird, P. N. (1970). The perception and memory of sentences. In J. Lyons (Ed.), *New horizons in linguistics* (pp. 261–270). New York: Penguin.

Johnson-Laird, P. N. (1983). *Mental models: Toward a cognitive science of language, inference, and consciousness.* Cambridge, MA: Harvard University Press.

Jones, C. B. (1990). *Systematic software development using VDM* (2nd ed.). International Series in Computer Science. Englewood Cliffs, NJ: Prentice-Hall.

Kabanoff, B., Waldersee, R., & Cohen, M. (in press). Espoused organizational values and their relation to organizational change themes: A content analysis study. *Academy of Management Journal*.

Kahn, D. (1967). *The codebreakers: The story of secret writing*. New York: Macmillan.

Kaplan, A. (1943). Content analysis and the theory of signs. *Philosophy of Science, 10*, 230–247.

Kaplan, R. D. (1988). *Surrender or starve*. Boulder: Westview Press.

Kaufer, D. S., & Carley, K. M. (1993a). *Communication at a distance: The effects of print on socio-cultural organization and change*. Hillsdale, NJ: Lawrence Erlbaum Associates.

Kaufer, D. S., & Carley, K. M. (1993b). Condensation symbols: Their variety and rhetorical function in political discourse. *Philosophy and Rhetoric, 26*, 201–226.

Kelle, U. (Ed.). (1995). *Computer-aided qualitative data analysis: Theory, methods, and practice*. Beverly Hills, CA: Sage.

Kelly, E. F., & Stone, P. J. (1975). *Computer recognition of English word senses*. Amsterdam: North Holland Press.

Kepecs, J. (1979). The teaching of psychotherapy by use of brief typescripts. In L. A. Gottschalk (Ed.), *The content analysis of verbal behavior: Further studies* (pp. 871–886). New York: Spectrum.

Kimberly, A. H., & Kimberly, K. H. (1991). International migration and foreign policy: A survey of the literature. *The Washington Quarterly, 14*, 32–41.

Klahr, D., Langly, P., & Neches, R. (Eds.). (1987). *Production system models of learning and development*. Cambridge, MA: MIT Press.

Klamer, A. (1984). *The new classical macroeconomics: Conversations with the new classical economists and their opponents*. Brighton: Wheatsheaf.

Klein, H. (1991). INTEXT/PC: A program package for the analysis of texts in the humanities and social sciences. *Literary and Linguistic Computing, 6*, 108–111.

Kleinnijenhuis, J. (1990). *Op zoek naar nieuws: Onderzoek naar journalistieke informatieverwerking en politiek* [In search of news]. Amsterdam: Free University Press.

Kleinnijenhuis, J., & Rietberg, E. M. (1991a). *Codeerinstructie politiek-economische teksten* [Coding instruction for political and economic texts]. Unpublished manuscript, Department of Political Science, Free University, Amsterdam.

Kleinnijenhuis, J., & Rietberg, E. M. (1991b). *Experiment codeurbetrouwbaarheid* [Experiment on coder reliability]. Unpublished manuscript, Department of Political Science, Free University, Amsterdam.

Koch, U., & Schofer, G. (Eds.). (1986). *Sprachinhaltsanalyse in der psychosomatischen und psychiatrischen Forschung: Grundlagen und Anwendungsstudien mit den Affekstkalen von Gottschalk und Gleser* [Content analysis of speech in psychosomatic and psychiatric research]. Weinheim und Munchen: Psychologie Verlags Union.

Krippendorff, K. (1969). Models of messages: Three prototypes. In G. Gerbner, O. R. Holsti, K. Krippendorff, W. J. Paisley, & P. J. Stone (Eds.), *The analysis of communication content* (Chapter 4). New York: Wiley.

Krippendorff, K. (1980). *Content analysis: An introduction to its methodology*. Beverly Hills, CA: Sage.

Krueger, R. A. (1994). *Focus groups: A practical guide for applied research* (2nd ed.). Thousand Oaks, CA: Sage.

Kuckartz, U. (1994). Using MAX in surveys: Experiences and new features. In F. Faulbaum (Ed.), *SoftStat '93. Advances in statistical software 4* (pp. 377–384). Stuttgart: Gustav Fisher Verlag.

Lakoff, G., & Johnson, M. (1980). *Metaphors we live by*. Chicago: University of Chicago Press.

Lampkin, R. H. (1951). Scientific inquiry for science teachers. *Science Education, 35*, 17–39.

Lasswell, H. D. (1942). The politically significant content of the press: Coding procedures. *Journalism Quarterly, 19*, 12–23.

Lasswell, H. D. (1946). Describing the contents of communications. In B. L. Smith, H. D. Lasswell, & R. D. Casey (Eds.), *Propaganda, communication, and public opinion* (pp. 74–94). Princeton: Princeton University Press.

Lasswell, H. D. (1948). The structure and function of communication in society. In L. Bryson (Ed.), *The communication of ideas* (pp. 37–51). New York: Harper & Row.

Lasswell, H. D., & Kaplan, A. (1950). *Power and society: A framework for political inquiry.* New Haven: Yale University Press.

Lasswell, H. D., Leites, N., & Associates. (1949). *Language of politics: Studies in quantitative semantics.* New York: George W. Stewart.

Lasswell, H. D., Lerner, D., & Pool, I. de Sola. (1952). *The comparative study of symbols.* Stanford, CA: Stanford University Press.

Lebell, M. B., Marder, S. R., Mintz, J., & Mintz, J. (1990). Predicting schizophrenic relapse by a speech sample of family emotional climate. In C. N. Stefanos, A. D. Rabavilas, & C. R. Soldatos (Eds.), *Psychiatry: A world perspective. Pharmacotherapies; psychotherapies; other therapies* (Vol. 3, pp. 802–807). Amsterdam: Elsevier.

Lebovitz, A. H., & Holland, J. C. (1983). Use of the Gottschalk–Gleser verbal content analysis scales with medically ill patients. *Psychosomatic Medicine, 45,* 305–320.

Lerner, D. (1950). The American soldier and the public. In R. K. Merton & P. F. Lazarsfeld (Eds.), *Continuities in social research* (pp. 212–251). Glencoe, IL: The Free Press.

Levy, J. S. (1989). The diversionary theory of war: A critique. In M. Midlarsky (Ed.), *Handbook of war studies* (pp. 259–288). Boston: Unwin Hyman.

Lindkvist, K. (1981). Approaches to content analysis. In K. Rosengren (Ed.), *Advances in content analysis* (pp. 23–41). Beverly Hills, CA: Sage.

Lindsay, P. H., & Norman, D. H. (1972). *Human information processing: An introduction to psychology.* New York: Academic Press.

Lolas, F., Kordy, H., & von Rad, M. (1979). Affective content of speech as a predictor of psychotherapy outcome. In L. A. Gottschalk (Ed.), *The content analysis of verbal behavior. Further studies* (pp. 225–230). New York: Spectrum.

Lolas, F., Mergenthaler, E., & von Rad, M. (1982). Content analysis of verbal behavior in psychotherapy research: A comparison between two methods. *British Journal of Medical Psychology, 55,* 327–333.

Lolas, F., & Rad, M. von. (1977). Angustia y agresivadad en pacientes psicosomaticos y psiconeuroticos. Analisis de contenido de la expresion verbal [Anxiety and aggression in psychosomatic and psychoneurotic patients]. *Acta Psiquiatria Psicologia Americana Latina, 23,* 184–193.

Lowenthal, L. (1956). Biographies in popular magazines. In W. Petersen (Ed.), *American social patterns* (pp. 63–118). New York: Doubleday.

Lowery, L. F., & Leonard, W. H. (1978). A comparison of questioning styles among four widely used high school biology textbooks. *Journal of Research in Science Teaching, 15,* 1–10.

Lowi, M. R. (1992). West Bank water resources and the resolution of conflict in the Middle East. *The occasional paper series of the project on environmental change and acute conflict* (No. 1). Peace and Conflict Studies Program, University of Toronto.

Luborsky, L., Docherty, J., Todd, T., Knapp, P., Mirsky, A., & Gottschalk, L. A. (1975). A content analysis of psychological states prior to petit mal EEG paroxysms. *Journal of Nervous and Mental Disease, 160,* 282–298.

Maher, B. A., McKean, K. O., & McLaughlin, B. (1966). Studies in psychotic language. In P. J. Stone, D. C. Dunphy, M. S. Smith, & D. M. Ogilvie (Eds.), *The General Inquirer: A computer approach to content analysis* (pp. 469–503). Cambridge, MA: MIT Press.

Mahl, G. (1959). Exploring emotional states by content analysis. In I. de Sola Pool (Ed.), *Trends in content analysis* (pp. 89–130). Champaign, IL: University of Illinois Press.

Markoff, J. (1988). Allies and opponents: Nobility and the third estate in the spring of 1789. *American Sociological Review, 53,* 477–496.

Markoff, J., Shapiro, G., & Weitman, S. (1974). Toward the integration of content analysis and general methodology. In D. R. Heise (Ed.), *Sociological methodology, 1975* (pp. 1–58). San Francisco: Jossey-Bass.

Marshall, C., & Rossman, G. B. (1994). *Designing qualitative research* (2nd ed.). Thousand Oaks, CA: Sage.

Martindale, C. (1990). *The clockwork muse: The predictability of artistic change.* New York: Basic Books.

McClelland, C. A. (1968). Access to Berlin: The quantity and variety of events, 1948–1963. In J. D. Singer (Ed.), *Quantitative international politics* (pp. 159–186). New York: The Free Press.

McClelland, C. A. (1976). *World event/interaction survey codebook.* (ICPSR 5211). Ann Arbor: Inter-University Consortium for Political and Social Research.

McClelland, D. C. (1958). Methods of measuring human motivation. In J. W. Atkinson (Ed.), *Motives in fantasy, action, and society* (Chapter 1). New York: Van Nostrand.

McClelland, D. C. (1961). *The achieving society.* New York: Van Nostrand.

McClelland, D. C., Atkinson, J. W., Clark, R. A., & Lowell, E. L. (1953). *The achievement motive.* New York: Appleton-Century-Crofts.

McClelland, D. C., Atkinson, J. W., Clark, R. A., & Lowell, E. L. (1958). A scoring manual for the achievement motive. In J. W. Atkinson (Ed.), *Motives in fantasy, action, and society* (Chapter 12). New York: Van Nostrand.

McConnell, M. (1982). Teaching about science, technology and society at the secondary school level in the United States: An educational dilemma for the 1980s. *Studies in Science Education, 9,* 1–32.

McGranahan, D., & Wayne, I. (1948). German and American traits reflected in popular drama. *Human Relations, I,* 429–455.

McTavish, D. G., & Pirro, E. B. (1990). Contextual content analysis. *Quality and Quantity, 24,* 245–265.

Mechling, J. E. (1975). Advice to historians on advice to mothers. *Journal of Social History, 9,* 44–63.

Merriam, J., & Makower, J. (1988). *Trend watching: How the media create trends and how to be the first to uncover them.* New York: AMACOM.

Merritt, R. L. (1966). *Symbols of American community: 1735–1775.* New Haven: Yale University Press.

Merritt, R. L., Muncaster, R. G., & Zinnes, D. A. (Eds.). (1993). *International event-data developments: DDIR phase II.* Ann Arbor: University of Michigan Press.

Miles, M. B., & Huberman, A. M. (1994). *Qualitative data analysis: An expanded sourcebook* (2nd ed.). Thousand Oaks, CA: Sage.

Miller, G. (1990). WordNet: An on-line lexical database. *International Journal of Lexicography, 3,* 235–312.

Mills, C. W. (1942). The professional ideology of social pathologists. *American Journal of Sociology, 49,* 165–180.

Mitchell, J. C. (1983). Case and situation analysis. *The Sociological Review, ns 31,* 187–211.

Moon, T. J., Mann, P. B., & Otto, J. H. (1956). *Modern biology.* New York: Holt, Rinehart & Winston.

Morovic, J., Skocic, D., Skocic, P., & Buranji, I. (1990). The content analysis method in studying communication with group psychotherapy of schizophrenics. *Socijalna Psihijatrija, 18,* 33–39.

Mosteller, F., & Wallace, D. L. (1964). *Inference and disputed authorship: The federalist.* Reading, MA: Addison-Wesley.

Muhr, T. (1991). ATLAS/ti: A prototype for the support of text interpretation. *Qualitative Sociology, 14,* 349–371.

Munton, D. (1978). *Measuring international behavior: Public sources, events and validity.* Dalhousie University: Centre for Foreign Policy Studies.

Murray, H. A. (1938). *Explorations in personality.* New York: Oxford University Press.

Naisbitt, J. (1982). *Megatrends.* New York: Warner Books.

Namenwirth, J. Z. (1973). The wheels of time and the interdependence of value change. *Journal of Interdisciplinary History, 3*, 649–683.

Namenwirth, J. Z., & Brewer, T. L. (1966). Elite editorial comment on the European and Atlantic communities in four countries. In P. J. Stone, D. C. Dunphy, M. S. Smith, & D. M. Ogilvie (Eds.), *The General Inquirer: A computer approach to content analysis* (pp. 401–430). Cambridge, MA: MIT Press.

Namenwirth, J. Z., & Weber, R. P. (1987). *Dynamics of culture.* Winchester, MA: Allen & Unwin.

Neuman, R. (1989). Parallel content analysis: Old paradigms and new proposals. *Public Communication and Behavior, 2*, 205–289.

North, R. C., Holsti, O. R., Zaninovich, M. G., & Zinnes, D. A. (1963). *Content analysis: A handbook with applications for the study of international crisis.* Evanston, IL: Northwestern University Press.

O'Donnell, J. (1989). *Public administration values as portrayed in* The New York Times *and* The Los Angeles Times, *1886–1986.* Unpublished seminar paper, Department of Journalism, University of Texas, Austin.

Ogilvie, D. M., Stone, P. J., & Kelly, E. F. (1982). Computer aided content analysis. In R. B. Smith & P. K. Manning (Eds.), *A handbook of social science methods* (pp. 219–246). Cambridge, MA: Ballinger.

Ogilvie, D. M., Stone, P. J., & Schneidman, E. S. (1966). Some characteristics of genuine versus simulated suicide notes. In P. J. Stone, D. C. Dunphy, M. S. Smith, & D. M. Ogilvie (Eds.), *The General Inquirer: A computer approach to content analysis* (pp. 527–535). Cambridge, MA: MIT Press.

Olsen, M. (1989). TextPack V: Text analysis utilities for the personal computer. *Computers and the Humanities, 23*, 155–160.

Olzak, S. (1989a). Analysis of events in the study of collective action. *Annual Review of Sociology, 15*, 119–141.

Olzak, S. (1989b). Labor unrest, immigration and ethnic conflict in urban America, 1880–1914. *American Journal of Sociology, 94*, 1303–1333.

Osgood, C. E. (1959). The representational model and relevant research methods. In I. de Sola Pool (Ed.), *Trends in content analysis* (Chapter 2). Champaign, IL: University of Illinois Press.

Osgood, C. E., Saporta, S., & Nunally, J. C. (1956). Evaluative assertion analysis. *Litera, 3*, 47–102.

Osgood, C. E., Suci, G. J., & Tannenbaum, P. H. (1957). *The measurement of meaning.* Urbana, IL: University of Illinois Press.

Otto, J. H., & Towle, A. (1965). *Modern biology.* New York: Holt, Rinehart & Winston.

Otto, J. H., & Towle, A. (1977). *Modern biology.* New York: Holt, Rinehart & Winston.

Otto, J. H., & Towle, A. (1985). *Modern biology.* New York: Holt, Rinehart & Winston.

Paisley, W. J. (1969). Introduction: The recording and notation of data. In G. Gerbner, O. R. Holsti, K. Krippendorff, W. J. Paisley, & P. J. Stone (Eds.), *The analysis of communication content: Developments in scientific theories and computer techniques* (pp. 283–286). New York: Wiley.

Palmquist, M. E. (1990). *The lexicon of the classroom: Language and learning in writing classrooms.* (Doctoral dissertation, Carnegie Mellon University, 1990). *Dissertation Abstracts International, 51*, 1940A.

Palmquist, M. E. (1993). Network-supported interaction in two writing classrooms. *Computers and Composition, 10*, 25–57.

Parr, T., Dietz, H., & Cohen, W. (1990). *Purdue compiler construction tool set* (Tech. Rep. TR-EE 90-14). West Lafayette: Purdue University School of Electrical Engineering.

Parsons, T., & Shils, E. (1951). *Towards a general theory of action.* Cambridge, MA: Harvard University Press.

Peters, V., & Wester, F. (1990). *Qualitative analysis in practice. Including user's guide Kwalitan version 2.* Nijmegen, the Netherlands: Department of Research Methodology, University of Nijmegen.

Peterson, C., Schulman, P., Castellon, C., & Seligman, M. (1992). The explanatory style scoring manual. In C. Smith (Ed.), *Motivation and personality: Handbook of thematic content analysis* (pp. 401–418). Cambridge, England: Cambridge University Press.

Pipan, T. (1989). *Sciopero contro l'utente* [Strike against the consumer]. Torino: Bollati Boringhieri.

Pontalti, C., Arnetoli, C., Dastoli, C., Grespi, L., Martini, A., & Valle, S. (1981). Emotional meanings of couple transactions: Analysis with Gottschalk's schizophrenia scale. *Archivio di Psicologia, Neurologia e Psichiatria, 42*, 357–367.

Pool, I. de Sola. (1951). *Symbols of internationalism.* Stanford, CA: Stanford University Press.

Pool, I. de Sola. (1952). *Symbols of democracy.* Stanford, CA: Stanford University Press.

Pool, I. de Sola. (1955). *The prestige press: A comparative study of political symbols.* Cambridge, MA: MIT Press.

Pool, I. de Sola. (Ed.). (1959). *Trends in content analysis.* Champaign, IL: University of Illinois Press.

Porter, G., & Ganapin, D. (1988). *Resources, population, and the Philippines' future: A case study* (WRI Paper No. 4). Washington, DC: World Resources Institute.

Porter, M. F. (1980). An algorithm for suffix stripping. *Program, 14*, 130–137.

Propp, V. (1968). *Morphology of the folktale* (2nd ed.). Austin, TX: University of Texas Press. (Original work published 1928)

QCAD Systems, Inc. (1987). *QPARSER+ translator writing system reference manual.* San Jose: QCAD Systems.

Ramallo, L. (1966). The integration of subject and object in the context of action: A study of reports written by successful and unsuccessful volunteers for field work in Africa. In P. J. Stone, D. C. Dunphy, M. S. Smith, & D. M. Ogilvie (Eds.), *The General Inquirer: A computer approach to content analysis* (pp. 536–547). Cambridge, MA: MIT Press.

Raud, R., & Fallig, M. (1993). Automating the coding process with neural networks. *Quirk's Marketing Research Review, 7*, 14–47.

Ridder, J. A. de. (1994a). *Computer-aided evaluative text analysis: CETA 2.1* (user's manual). Groningen: ProGamma.

Ridder, J. A. de. (1994b). *Van tekst naar informatie: Ontwikkeling en toetsing van een inhoudsanalyse-instrument* [From text to information]. Amsterdam: University of Amsterdam.

Riessman, C. K. (1993). *Narrative analysis.* Newbury Park, CA: Sage.

Roberts, C. W. (1989). Other than counting words: A linguistic approach to content analysis. *Social Forces, 68*, 147–177.

Roberts, C. W. (1991). Linguistic content analysis. In H. J. Helle (Ed.), *Verstehen and pragmatism: Essays on interpretative sociology* (pp. 283–309). Frankfurt: Peter Lang.

Rumelhart, D. E. (1975). Notes on a schema for stories. In D. G. Bobrow & A. Collins (Eds.), *Representation and understanding: Studies in cognitive science* (pp. 211–236). New York: Academic Press.

Russell, S. L. (1990). *The measurement of narcissism through the content analysis of verbal behavior.* Unpublished doctoral dissertation, University of California, Irvine.

Rychner, M. D., & Newell, A. (1979). An instructable production system: Basic design issues. In F. Hayes-Roth & D. A. Waterman (Eds.), *Pattern-directed inference systems* (pp. 135–153). New York: Academic Press.

Samuelson, P. A. (1967). *Economics: An introductory analysis.* New York: McGraw-Hill.

Sanderson, P. M., James, J. M., & Seidler, K. S. (1989). SHAPA: An interactive software environment for protocol analysis. *Ergonomics, 32*, 1271–1302.

Schank, R. C., & Abelson, R. P. (1977). *Scripts, plans, goals, and understanding: An inquiry into human knowledge structures.* New York: Wiley.

Schlesinger, L. (1993). How to hire by wire. *Fast Company, 1*, 86–91.

Schofer, G. (Ed.). (1980). *Gottschalk–Gleser Sprachinhaltsanalyse Theorie und Technik: Studien zur Messung angslicher und aggressiver Affekte* [Gottschalk–Gleser verbal content analysis theory and technique]. Weinheim und Basel: Beltz Verlag.

Schrodt, P. A. (1991). Pattern recognition of international event sequences: A machine learning approach. In V. M. Hudson (Ed.), *Artificial intelligence and international politics* (pp. 169–193). Boulder, CO: Westview.

Schrodt, P. A. (1993). Machine coding of event data. In R. L. Merritt, R. G. Muncaster, & D. A. Zinnes (Eds.), *Theory and management of international event data: DDIR phase II* (pp. 117–140). Ann Arbor: University of Michigan Press.

Schrodt, P. A. (1994). Event data in foreign policy analysis. In P. J. Haney, L. Neack, & J. A. K. Hey (Eds.), *Foreign policy analysis: Continuity and change* (pp. 145–166). New York: Prentice-Hall.

Schrodt, P. A., Davis, S. G., & Weddle, J. L. (1994). KEDS: A program for the machine coding of event data. *Social Science Computer Review, 12*, 561–588.

Schrodt, P. A., & Gerner, D. J. (1994). Validity assessment of a machine-coded event data set for the Middle East, 1982–1992. *American Journal of Political Science, 38*, 825–854.

Schwab, J. J. (1962). The teaching of science as enquiry. In J. J. Schwab & P. F. Brandwein (Eds.), *The Teaching of Science* (pp. 1–103). Cambridge, MA: Harvard University Press.

Schwab, J. J. (1963). *Biology teachers' handbook.* New York: Wiley.

Searle, J. R., & Vanderveken, D. (1985). *Foundations of illocutionary logic.* Cambridge, England: Cambridge University Press.

Semait, B. W. (1989). Ecological stress and political conflict in Africa: The case of Ethiopia. In A. H. Ornas & M. A. Salih (Eds.), *Ecology and politics* (pp. 37–50). Uppsala: Scandinavian Institute of Africa Studies.

Senge, P. (1990). *The fifth discipline.* New York: Doubleday.

Shalev, M. (1978). Lies, damned lies and strike statistics: The measurement of trends in industrial conflicts. In C. Crouch & A. Pizzorno (Eds.), *The resurgence of class conflict in Western Europe since 1968* (Vol. 1, pp. 1–20). New York: Holmes & Meier.

Shapiro, D. H., & Bates, D. E. (1990). The measurement of control and self-control: Background, rationale, and description of a control content analysis scale. *Psychologia—An International Journal of Psychology in the Orient, 43*, 147–162.

Shapiro, G., & Markoff, J. (in press). *Revolutionary demands: A content analysis of the cahiers de doléances of 1789.* Stanford, CA: Stanford University Press.

Shils, E. (1948). *The present state of American sociology.* Glencoe, IL: The Free Press.

Shneidman, E. S. (1969). Logical content analysis: An explication of styles of 'concludifying'. In G. Gerbner, O. R. Holsti, K. Krippendorff, W. J. Paisley, & P. J. Stone (Eds.), *The analysis of communication content: Developments in scientific theories and computer techniques* (pp. 261–280). New York: Wiley.

Silverman, D. (1993). *Interpreting qualitative data: Methods for analyzing talk, text, and interaction.* Beverly Hills, CA: Sage.

Simpson, P. K. (1990). *Artificial neural systems: Foundations, paradigms, applications, and implementations.* Elmsford, NY: Pergamon.

Sly, D. S. (1991). *Computer-aided content analysis: An application to transcripts of prime-time television.* M.S. Creative Component, Department of Statistics, Iowa State University.

Smil, V. (1992). Environmental change as a source of conflict and economic loss in China. *The occasional paper series of the project on environmental change and acute conflict* (No. 2). Peace and Conflict Studies Program, University of Toronto.

Smith, C. P. (1992). *Motivation and personality: Handbook of thematic content analysis.* Cambridge, England: Cambridge University Press.

Smith, J. M. (1992). *SGML and related standards: Document description and processing languages.* New York: Ellis Horwood.

Smith, M. S., Stone, P. J., & Glenn, E. N. (1966). A content analysis of twenty presidential nomination acceptance speeches. In P. J. Stone, D. C. Dunphy, M. S. Smith, & D. M. Ogilvie (Eds.), *The General Inquirer: A computer approach to content analysis* (pp. 359–400). Cambridge, MA: MIT Press.

Sowa, J. F. (1984). *Conceptual structures.* Reading, MA: Addison-Wesley.

Spencer, L. M., & Spencer, S. M. (1993). *Competence at work: Models for superior performance.* New York: Wiley.

Spivey, J. M. (1988). *Understanding Z: A specification language and its formal semantics.* Cambridge, England: Cambridge University Press.

Stake, R. E., & Easley, J. (1978). *Case studies in science education* (Vols. 1 & 2). Washington, DC: U.S. Government Printing Office.

Starkweather, J. A. (1969). Measurement methods for vocal interaction. In G. Gerbner, O. R. Holsti, K. Krippendorff, W. Paisley, & P. J. Stone (Eds.), *The analysis of communication content* (pp. 313–318). New York: Wiley.

Stevens, S. S. (1951). Mathematics, measurements and psychophysics. In S. Stevens (Ed.), *Handbook of experimental psychology* (pp. 1–49). New York: Wiley.

Stone, P. J. (1969). Improved quality of content-analysis categories: Computerized disambiguation rules for high frequency English words. In G. Gerbner, O. R. Holsti, K. Krippendorff, W. Paisley, & P. J. Stone (Eds.), *The analysis of communication content* (pp. 199–222). New York: Wiley.

Stone, P. J. (1986). Content analysis. In T. Sebeok (Ed.), *Encyclopedic dictionary of semiotics* (Vol. 1, pp. 147–151). New York: Mouton.

Stone, P. J., & Bernstein, A. (1965). Content analysis applications at Simulmatics. *American Behavioral Scientist, 8,* 16–18.

Stone, P. J., Dunphy, D. C., & Bernstein, A. (1966). The analysis of product image. In P. J. Stone, D. C. Dunphy, M. S. Smith, & D. M. Ogilvie (Eds.), *The General Inquirer: A computer approach to content analysis* (pp. 536–547). Cambridge, MA: MIT Press.

Stone, P. J., Dunphy, D. C., Smith, M. S., & Ogilvie, D. M. (1966). *The General Inquirer: A computer approach to content analysis.* Cambridge, MA: MIT Press.

Stone, P. J., & Weber, R. P. (1992). Content analysis. In E. F. Borgatta & M. L. Borgatta (Eds.), *Encyclopedia of Sociology* (Vol. 1, pp. 290–295). New York: Macmillan.

Strauss, D., & Ikeda, M. (1990). Pseudolikelihood estimation for social networks. *Journal of the American Statistical Association, 85,* 204–212.

Strike disrupts airports in France. (1993, October 21). *The New York Times,* Midwest Ed., p. C4.

Stryker, S. (1980). *Symbolic interactionism.* Menlo Park, CA: Benjamin Cummings.

Stuart, J. A. (1982). An identification of life science concepts in selected secondary school science textbooks. *School Science and Mathematics, 82,* 189–200.

Suedfeld, P., Tetlock, P., & Streufert, S. (1992). Conceptual/integrative complexity. In C. Smith (Ed.), *Motivation and personality: Handbook of thematic content analysis* (pp. 393–400). Cambridge, England: Cambridge University Press.

Suhrke, A. (1993). Pressure points: Environmental degradation, migration and conflict. *The occasional paper series of the project on environmental change and acute conflict* (No. 3). Peace and Conflict Studies Program, University of Toronto.

Tafoya, E., Sunal, D. W., & Knecht, P. (1980). Assessing inquiry potential: A tool for curriculum decision makers. *School Science and Mathematics, 89,* 43–48.

Tamir, P. (1983). Inquiry and the science teacher. *Science Education, 67,* 657–672.

Tamir, P. (1985). Content analysis focusing on inquiry. *Journal of Curriculum Studies, 17,* 87–94.

Tamir, P., & Lunetta, V. N. (1978). An analysis of laboratory inquiries in the BSCS yellow version. *The American Biology Teacher, 40,* 353–357.

Tamir, P., & Lunetta, V. N. (1981). Inquiry-related tasks in high school science laboratory handbooks. *Science Education, 65,* 477–484.

Tamir, P., Nussinovitz, R., & Friedler, Y. (1982). The design and use of a practical tests assessment inventory. *Journal of Biological Education, 16,* 42–50.

Tesch, R. (1989). Computer software and qualitative analysis: A reassessment. In G. Blank, J. L. McCartney, & E. Brent (Eds.), *New technology in sociology* (pp. 141–154). New Brunswick, NJ: Transaction.

Tesch, R. (1990). *Qualitative research: Analysis types and software tools*. New York: Falmer Press.

Thaller, M. (unpublished). *DESCRIPTOR: Programs for the analysis of descriptions of medieval pictorial sources.*

Tilly, C. (1981). *As sociology meets history*. New York: Academic Press.

Tilly, C. (1986). *The contentious French*. Cambridge, MA: Harvard University Press.

Toennies, F. (1988). *Gemeinschaft und Gesellschaft* [Community and society]. New Brunswick, NJ: Transaction.

Treu, T. (Ed.) (1987). *Public service labour relations: Recent trends and future prospects*. Geneva: International Labour Organization.

Tschuschke, V. G., & MacKenzie, K. R. (1989). Empirical analysis of group development: A methodological report. *Small Group Behavior, 20*, 419–427.

Uliana, R. (1979). Measurement of black children's affective states and the effect of interviewer's race on affective states as measured through language behavior. In L. A. Gottschalk (Ed.), *The content analysis of verbal behavior: Further studies* (pp. 173–218). New York: Spectrum.

Vaughn, C. D., & Leff, J. P. (1976). The measurement of expressed emotion in the families of psychiatric patients. *British Journal of Social and Clinical Psychology, 15*, 157–165.

Vico, G. (1961). Discovery of the true Homer. In T. G. Bergin & M. H. Fish (Trans.), *The new science of Giambattista Vico* (Book 3, pp. 245–282). New York: Anchor.

Viney, L. L., & Manton, M. (1975). Sampling verbal behavior in Australia: The Gottschalk–Gleser content analysis scales. *Australian Journal of Psychology, 25*, 45–55.

Viney, L. L., & Wang, W. (1987). *Psychosocial maturity of children in Australia and the People's Republic of China*. Unpublished manuscript, University of Wollongong, New South Wales, Australia.

Vogt, W. P. (1993). *Dictionary of statistics and methodology*. Newbury Park, CA: Sage.

Volk, W. von, & Tschuschke, V. G. (1982). Studies of affect changes during group psychotherapy using content analysis (Gottschalk–Gleser). *Zeitschrift fuer Klinische Psychologie und Psychotherapie, 30*, 52–67.

Vygotsky, L. S. (1962). *Thought and language*. Cambridge, MA: Harvard University Press.

Wahls, T., Baker, A. L., & Leavens, G. T. (1994). *The direct execution of SPECS-C++: A model-based specification language for C++ classes* (Tech. Rep. TR94-02). Department of Computer Science, Iowa State University, Ames.

Walker, M. E., Wasserman, S., & Wellman, B. (1994). Statistical models for social support networks. In S. Wasserman & J. Galaskiewicz (Eds.), *Advances in social network analysis: Research in the social and behavioral sciences* (pp. 53–78). Thousand Oaks, CA: Sage.

Walsh, G. (1988). Trade unions and the media. *International Labour Review, 127*, 205–220.

Wasserman, S., & Faust, K. (1994). *Social network analysis: Methods and applications*. New York: Cambridge University Press.

Webb, E. J., Campbell, D. T., Schwartz, R. D., & Sechrest, L. (1966). *Unobtrusive measures: Nonreactive research in the social sciences*. Chicago: Rand McNally.

Webb, E. J., & Roberts, K. H. (1969). Unconventional uses of content analysis in social science. In G. Gerbner, O. R. Holsti, K. Krippendorff, W. J. Paisley, & P. J. Stone (Eds.), *The analysis of communication content: Developments in scientific theories and computer techniques* (pp. 319–332). New York: Wiley.

Weber, M. (1973). Kritische Studien auf dem Gebiet der Kulturwissenschaftlichen Logik [Critical studies in the logic of the cultural sciences]. In J. Winckelmann (Ed.), *Gesammelte Aufsätze zur Wissenschaftslehre* [Collected Essays on the Scientific Method] (pp. 215–290). Tübingen: Mohr. (Original work published 1906)

Weber, R. P. (1990). *Basic content analysis* (2nd ed.). Newbury Park, CA: Sage.

Weitman, S. (1973). National flags: A sociological overview. *Semiotica, 8*, 328–367.

Weitzman, E. A., & Miles, M. B. (1995). *Computer programs for qualitative data analysis: A software sourcebook*. Thousand Oaks, CA: Sage.

Welch, W. W., Klopfer, L. E., Aikenhead, G. S., & Robinson, J. T. (1981). The role of inquiry in science education: Analysis and recommendations. *Science Education, 65*, 35–50.

White, A. (1989). *Female and male references on front page samples of* The Los Angeles Times *and* The New York Times, *1900–1987*. Unpublished seminar paper, Department of Journalism, University of Texas, Austin.

White, H. C. (1992). *Identity and control: A structural theory of social action.* Princeton, NJ: Princeton University Press.

Wicklund, R. A., & Brehm, J. W. (1976). *Perspectives on cognitive dissonance.* Hillsdale, NJ: Lawrence Erlbaum Associates.

Willats, B. D. (1990). *The growth of national government: A content analysis.* Unpublished seminar paper, Department of Journalism, University of Texas, Austin.

Winget, C. N., Seligman, R., Rauh, J. L., & Gleser, G. C. (1979). Social alienation–personal disorganization assessment in disturbed and normal adolescents. *Journal of Nervous and Mental Disease, 167*, 282–287.

Winter, E. (1994). Clause relations as information structure: Two basic text structures in English. In M. Coulthard (Ed.), *Advances in written text analysis* (pp. 46–68). London: Routledge & Kegan Paul.

Winterbotham, F. W. (1974). *The ultra secret.* New York: Harper & Row.

Wittgenstein, L. (1973). *Tractatus logico-philosophicus.* Frankfurt am Main: Suhrkamp. (Original work published 1921)

Wolcott, H. F. (1994). *Transforming qualitative data: Description, analysis, and interpretation* (2nd ed.). Thousand Oaks, CA: Sage.

Zinnes, D. A. (1976). *Contemporary research in international relations.* New York: The Free Press.

# AUTHOR INDEX

## A

Abel, L., 124, 291
Abell, P., 58, 80, 81, 285
Abelson, R. P., 42, 79, 192, 194, 199, 285, 298
Accornero, A., 134, 285
Ackermann, F., 219, 287
Adatto, K., 39, 285
Agresti, A., 168, 285
Ahmed, A. G., 150, 285
Aho, A. V., 246, 247, 285
Aikenhead, G. S., 160, 302
Alker, H. R., Jr., 221, 285
Allen, J., 248, 267, 285
Andrén, G., 72, 285
Arnetoli, C., 298
Atkinson, J. W., 226, 296
Austin, J. L., 66, 286
Axelrod, R. M., 79, 192, 286
Azar, E. A., 153, 196, 286

## B

Baker, A. L., 7, 8, 60, 215, 251, 253, 276, 286, 301
Banks, D., 188, 286
Barcus, F. E., 41, 286
Barker-Plummer, B., 110, 286
Bates, D. E., 124, 291, 299
Bechtel, R., 7, 8, 53, 118, 119, 187, 210, 214, 231, 239, 290
Bell, M. M., 2
Bennett, B., 154, 286
Berelson, B., 11-13, 16, 20, 21, 23, 24, 27-29, 36, 286
Berg, B. L., 2, 286
Bergesen, A., 16, 286
Berleant, D., 47, 286
Bernstein, A., 42, 300
Biener, R., 119, 124, 291
Bierschenk, B., 221, 286
Birch, H., 291

Blainey, G., 151, 156, 286
Block, S., 118, 129, 291
Blosser, P. E., 159, 293
Bollème, G., 25, 286
Bond, D., 154, 286
Brehm, J. W., 206, 302
Brewer, T. L., 230, 297
Brook, B. S., 41, 286
Brown, J. S., 118, 291
Bryan, M., 244, 286
Buchsbaum, M. S., 291
Buranji, I., 123, 296
Burgess, P. M., 153, 286
Bybee, R. W., 160, 170, 286, 293

## C

Campbell, D. T., 19, 20, 301
Carley, K. M., 4-6, 8, 79-82, 87, 90, 91, 98, 99, 171, 173-175, 187, 188, 196, 218, 250, 273, 278, 286, 287, 294
Carré, B., 200, 287
Cartwright, D., 11-14, 16, 27, 287
Castellon, C., 48, 298
Cerulo, K., 16, 287
Chiang-Soong, B., 162, 287
Chomsky, N., 263, 287
Cicourel, A., 79, 287
Clark, R. A., 226, 296
Clay, J. W., 149, 150, 287
Cleghorn, J. M., 118, 124, 291
Cleveland, C., 54
Clifton, D., 45, 54
Clocksin, W. F., 250, 287
Cohen, M., 53, 294
Cohen, W., 247, 297
Colby, B., 221, 287
Coleman, D. L., 42, 252, 253, 287
Connelly, F. M., 161, 287
Cooley, C., 79, 287
Coombs, C., 17, 287
Cornet, C., 288
Corsaro, W. A., 15, 29, 287

Cropper, S., 219, 287
Crowell, V. L., Jr., 160, 288
Cuilenburg, J. J. van, 198, 200, 218, 278, 288

D

D'Haenen, H., 123, 288
D'Zmura, T., 118, 291
Dale, T. A., 4, 6, 99, 171, 172, 288
Daniels, R. S., 118, 129, 291
Danielson, W., 4, 8, 36, 40, 58, 103, 106, 211, 267, 288
Dastoli, C., 298
Date, C. J., 244, 257, 288
Davis, K., 10, 288
Davis, S. G., 153, 158, 299
Delisle, N., 253, 288
Denzin, N. K., 3, 288
Depuis, P., 219, 293
DeWeese, L. C., 46, 288
Dietz, H., 247, 297
Digman, J., 48, 288
Dijk, T. van, 57, 136, 288
Dixon, R. M. W., 147, 148, 192, 193, 288
Docherty, J., 295
Dornbusch, S. M., 15, 288
Dowty, D. R., 66, 288
Duffy, G., 221, 285
Dunphy, D. C., 12, 18, 21, 36, 41,42, 49, 106, 229, 277, 288, 293, 295, 297-300
Durham, W., 148, 288
Duschl, R. A., 160, 169, 288

E

Easley, J., 159, 300
Eckardt, M. J., 122, 291
Eden, C., 219, 287
Eick, S. G., 221, 288
Ekman, P., 41, 288
Elbaz, F., 161, 287
Eltinge, E. M., 4, 5, 8, 71, 76, 159, 166, 168, 282, 288

F

Fallig, M., 42, 298
Falloon, I. R. H., 291
Fauconnier, G., 81, 288
Faust, K., 283, 301
Feldman, M. S., 3, 289

Fielding, N. G., 3, 289, 293
Finegold, M., 161, 287
Fischer, D. H., 19, 20, 289
Fiske, A., 47, 53, 289
Francisco, R., 153, 154, 158, 289
Frank, E. C., 118, 291
Franzosi, R., 4, 5, 8, 26, 27, 31, 56-58, 72, 81, 131, 132, 135-138, 216, 217, 232, 233, 278, 289
Freeman, J. R., 156, 290
Freeman, R. B., 135, 289
Frege, G., 60, 289
Friedler, Y., 161, 300
Friesen, W. V., 41, 288
Fronczek, J., 124, 291
Frost, R., 244, 289
Fuchs, V. R., 135, 289

G

Galtung, J., 17, 22, 24, 289
Ganapin, D., 148, 298
Garlan, D., 253, 288
George, A., 28, 289
Gerbner, G., 14, 23, 39, 41, 286, 288-290, 293, 294, 297, 299-301
Gerhart, S., 253, 289
Gerner, D. J., 153, 154, 158, 289, 299
Ghanem, S., 108, 109, 289
Gift, T. E., 62, 291
Gillin, C., 291
Giorgis, D. W., 149, 289
Glaser, B. G., 214, 215, 289
Gleick, P. H., 148, 289
Glenn, E. N., 28, 299
Gleser, G. C., 5, 59, 118, 119, 121, 122-125, 129, 213, 289-292, 294, 295, 298, 301, 302
Goldhamer, D. H., 230, 290
Goldstein, J. A., 154, 156, 290
Goldstone, J. S., 148, 290
Good, R., 160, 290
Gottlieb, A. A., 118, 124, 290, 292
Gottschalk, L. A., 4, 5, 8, 40, 59, 117-119, 121-125, 129, 188, 213, 214, 231, 265, 278, 289-292, 294, 295, 298, 301
Grabiner, J. V., 162, 292
Grespi, L., 298
Griemas, A. -J., 57, 292
Griffin, L. J., 67
Grobman, A. B., 161, 292
Gurr, T. R., 136, 292

Guttag, J. V., 252, 253, 292

H

Habermas, J., 63, 292
Haer, J. L., 124, 291
Halliday, M. A. K., 57, 60, 66, 136, 292
Hanenson, I. B., 118, 291
Harbeson, J. W., 149, 292
Harmon, P., 248, 292
Harms, N. C., 159, 292
Harway, N. I., 41, 293
Hausmann, C., 118, 291
Hawthorne, M., 220, 292
Hazarika, S., 148, 292
Heider, F., 192, 197, 293
Heise, D. R., 15, 29, 58, 67, 80, 81, 287,
    293, 296
Heiser, J. F., 291
Helgeson, S. L., 159, 162, 293
Herrera, D. B., 291
Herron, M. D., 160, 161, 169, 293
Hesse-Biber, S., 219, 293
Hickman, L. C., 15, 162, 170, 288, 293
Hockey, S., 212, 293
Hoey, M., 57, 293
Hofstein, A., 162, 170, 293
Hoigaard-Martin, J., 122, 124, 291
Holcomb, B. K., 149, 150, 287
Holland, J. C., 118, 295
Holsti, O. R., 10-12, 14, 20-23, 41, 192,
    229, 277, 286, 288-290, 293, 294, 297,
    299-301
Homer-Dixon, T. F., 147, 148, 293
Hopcroft, J. E., 250, 293
Horning, J., 252, 253, 292
Howe, R. W., 159, 293
Huberman, A. M., 3, 296
Hubert, L. J., 185, 293
Hurd, P. D., 160, 162, 169, 293
Hurwitz, R., 221, 285
Huxtable, P., 158

I-J

Iacono, J. M., 118, 291, 292
Ikeda, M., 283, 300
Iker, H. P., 41, 293
James, J. M., 221, 298
Janis, I. L., 11-13, 17, 21, 293
Johnson, D., 112, 293
Johnson, M., 57, 294

Johnson, P., 39, 293
Johnson-Laird, P. N., 66, 81, 293
Jones, A., 16, 286
Jones, C. B., 252, 253, 294

K

Kabanoff, B., 53, 294
Kahle, J. B., 160, 162, 170, 293
Kahn, D., 239, 294
Kaplan, A., 21, 23, 41, 294, 295
Kaplan, R. D., 149, 294
Kaplan, S. M., 118, 278, 291
Kaufer, D. S., 80, 87, 99, 287, 294
Kaufman, L., 288
Kelle, U., 3, 294
Kelly, E. F., 47, 49, 165, 294, 297
Kennedy, S., 173, 221, 287
Kepecs, J., 124, 294
Kimberly, A. H., 150, 294
Kimberly, K. H., 150, 294
Kinder, T. S., 219, 293
King, D., 248, 292
Klamer, A., 202, 294
Klein, H., 212, 294
Kleinnijenhuis, J., 6, 8, 79-81, 188, 191,
    196, 198, 200, 201, 218, 227, 248, 267,
    273, 278, 288, 294
Klopfer, L. E. ,160, 302
Knapp, P., 295
Knecht, P., 161, 300
Koch, U., 122, 123, 294
Kochan, T., 294
Kordy, H., 124, 295
Krippendorff, K., 12-14, 23, 25-27, 41,
    201, 286, 288-290, 293, 294, 297, 299-
    301
Krueger, R. A., 3, 294
Kuckartz, U., 220, 294
Kunkel, R. L., 118, 124, 291

L

Lakoff, G., 57, 294
Lampkin, R. H., 161, 294
Lasswell, H. D., 4, 23, 35, 40, 41, 47, 103-
    106, 114, 115, 226, 281, 293-295
Lawton, R. W., 153, 286
Leach, E., 15
Leavens, G. T., 253, 301
Lebell, M. B., 124, 291, 295
Lebovitz, A. H., 118, 295

Lee, R. M., 3, 289, 293
Leff, J. P., 39, 301
Leites, N., 293, 295
Leonard, W. H., 162, 295
Lerner, D., 10, 103-106, 114, 295
Levi-Strauss, C., 15
Levine, C. H., 297
Levy, J. S., 151, 295
Lewis, E. M., 15, 293
Lincoln, Y. S., 3, 288
Lindkvist, K., 40, 295
Lindsay, P. H., 174, 183, 295
Lolas, F., 118, 119, 123, 124, 291, 292, 295
Lowell, E. L., 226, 296
Lowenthal, L., 25, 31, 295
Lowery, L. F., 162, 295
Lowi, M. R., 148, 295
Luborsky, L., 124, 295
Lunetta, V. N., 161, 300

M

MacKenzie, K. R., 123, 301
Maher, B. A., 229, 295
Mahl, G., 228, 295
Makower, J., 46, 296
Mallery, J. C., 221, 285
Mann, P. B., 162, 296
Manton, M., 123, 301
Marder, S. R., 124, 291, 295
Markoff, J., 1, 2, 8, 9, 17, 23, 31, 56, 132, 136, 225, 232, 233, 278, 295, 296, 299
Marshall, C., 3, 296
Martin, J., 122, 124, 212, 220, 293
Martindale, C., 43, 296
Martini, A., 298
Mayerson, P., 118, 123, 292
McClelland, C. A., 153, 154, 296
McClelland, D. C., 24, 26, 44, 226, 296
McConahay, J. B., 39, 293
McConnell, M., 170, 296
McGranahan, D., 26, 296
McTavish, D. G., 212, 296
Mechling, J. E., 24, 296
Mellish, C. S., 250, 287
Mergenthaler, E., 124, 295
Merriam, J., 46, 296
Merritt, R. L., 25, 152, 296, 299
Milanesi, L., 221, 287
Miles, M. B., 3, 209, 215, 216, 219-221, 296, 301
Miller, G., 47, 52, 221, 296

Miller, P. D., 162, 292
Mills, C. W., 10, 11, 296
Mintz, J., 124, 295
Mirsky, A., 295
Mitchell, J. C., 3, 296
Moon, T. J., 162, 296
Morez, V. E., 288
Morovic, J., 123, 296
Mosteller, F., 24, 296
Muhr, T., 215, 296
Mulders, I. van, 288
Munton, D., 153, 296
Murray, H. A., 45, 226, 296

N

Naisbitt, J., 46, 296
Namenwirth, J. Z., 43, 58, 230, 267, 277, 297
Neuman, R., 46, 297
Newell, A., 250, 298
Noble, E. P., 291
Norman, D. H., 174, 183, 295
North, R. C., 22, 123, 297
Nunally, J. C., 192, 197, 297
Nussinovitz, R., 161, 300

O

O'Donnell, J., 110, 297
Ogilvie, D. M., 12, 18, 21, 36, 40, 41, 49, 106, 277, 288, 293, 295, 297-300
Olsen, M., 213, 297
Olzak, S., 26, 27, 233, 297
Osgood, C. E., 12-14, 20, 22, 23, 25-27, 30, 41, 47, 192, 197, 217, 228, 278, 297
Otto, J. H., 162, 296, 297

P

Paisley, W. J., 14, 16, 23, 41, 286, 288-290, 293, 294, 297, 299-301
Palmquist, M. E. 4, 6, 8, 79-81, 99, 171, 173, 174, 181, 182, 218, 278, 287, 297
Parr, T., 247, 297
Parsons, T., 4, 41, 47, 115, 297
Pautler, C. P., 122, 291
Perry, J. L., 297
Peters, V., 216, 297
Peterson, C., 48, 298
Pipan, T., 134, 298
Pirro, E. B., 212, 296

Pontalti, C., 123, 298
Pool, I. de Sola, 23, 40-42, 52, 103, 104-106, 114, 228, 277, 289, 295, 297, 298
Porter, G., 148, 298
Porter, M. F., 247, 298
Propp, V., 57, 298

R

Rad, M. von, 123, 124, 295
Ramallo, L., 39, 298
Raud, R., 42, 298
Rauh, J. L., 124, 302
Rey, F., 123, 292
Reynolds, C., 291
Richards, L., 2
Ridder, J. A. de, 6, 8, 79-81, 188, 191, 196, 198, 200, 218, 227, 248, 267, 273, 278, 288, 298
Riessman, C. K., 3, 298
Rietberg, E. M., 6, 8, 79-81, 188, 191, 196, 248, 267, 273, 278, 294
Riley, D. D., 253, 286
Roberts, C. W., 8, 54, 55, 69, 71, 77, 81, 136, 163-166, 168, 188, 189, 210, 217, 233, 263, 264, 275, 278, 282, 288, 298
Roberts, K. H., 19, 301
Robinson, J. T., 160, 302
Rosenberg, M. J., 192, 285
Ross, W. D., 291
Rossman, G. B., 3, 296
Rumelhart, D. E., 57, 298
Russell, S. L., 46, 124, 298
Rychner, M. D., 250, 298

S

Saenger, E., 118, 291
Samuelson, P. A., 202, 298
Sanderson, P. M., 221, 298
Saporta, S., 192, 197, 217, 278, 297
Schank, R. C., 79, 298
Schlesinger, L., 45, 298
Schofer, G., 122, 123, 294, 298
Schrodt, P. A., 4, 5, 8, 58, 59, 147, 152-154, 158, 214, 265, 278, 289, 299
Schulman, P., 48, 298
Schwab, J. J., 161, 299
Schwartz, R. D., 19, 20, 301
Searle, J. R., 66, 299
Sears, D., 39, 293
Sechrest, L., 19, 20, 301

Seidler, K. S., 221, 298
Seligman, M., 48, 298
Seligman, R., 123, 124, 290, 302
Semait, B. W., 149, 299
Senge, P., 50, 299
Sethi, R., 246, 247, 285
Shalev, M., 132, 299
Shanon, J., 291
Shapiro, D. H., 124, 299
Shapiro, G., 1, 2, 4, 6-9, 17, 20, 23, 31, 56, 59, 69, 76, 132, 164, 210, 225, 232, 233, 278, 296, 299
Shils, E., 18, 41, 297, 299
Shneidman, E. S., 17, 299
Silverman, D., 3, 299
Simpson, P. K., 248, 299
Skocic, D., 123, 296
Skocic, P., 123, 296
Sly, D. S., 215, 299
Smil, V., 148, 299
Smith, C. P., 38, 298-300
Smith, J. M., 244, 299
Smith, M. S., 12, 18, 21, 28, 36, 41, 49, 106, 277, 288, 293, 295, 297-300
Sowa, J. F., 79, 300
Spencer, L. M., 45, 48, 300
Spencer, S. M., 36, 45, 48, 49, 54, 300
Spivey, J. M., 253, 300
Springer, K. J., 118, 129, 289, 291, 292
Stake, R. E., 159, 300
Starkweather, J. A., 41, 300
Stevens, S. S., 17, 300
Stone, P. J., 3, 4, 12-14, 16-18, 20-23, 27, 28, 31, 35, 36, 40-42, 47, 49, 106, 165, 227, 228, 230, 231, 277, 286, 288-290, 293-295, 297-301
Stone, W. N., 118, 124, 292
Strauss, A. L., 214, 215, 289
Strauss, D., 283, 300
Streufert, S., 48, 300
Stryker, S., 79, 300
Stuart, J. A., 162, 300
Suci, G. J., 41, 297
Suedfeld, P., 48, 300
Suhrke, A., 148, 150, 300
Sunal, D. W., 161, 300

T

Tafoya, E., 161, 300
Tamir, P., 160, 161, 166-168, 300
Tannenbaum, P. H., 41, 285, 297

Taussig, T. G., 41, 288
Terman, S. A., 122, 291
Tesch, R., 209, 216, 219-221, 300, 301
Tetlock, P., 48, 300
Thaller, M., 15, 301
Tilly, C., 26, 27, 31, 233, 301
Todd, T., 295
Toennies, F., 114, 115, 301
Towle, A., 162, 297
Tschuschke, V. G., 123, 301

U

Uliana, R., 123, 301
Ullman, J. D., 246, 247, 250, 285, 293

V

Valle, S., 298
Vanderveken, D., 66, 299
Vaughn, C. D., 39, 301
Vico, G., 26, 301
Viney, L. L., 118, 123, 292, 301
Vogele, W., 154, 286
Vogt, W. P., 2, 301
Volk, W. von, 123, 301
Vygotsky, L. S., 79, 301

W

Wahls, T., 253, 301
Waldersee, R., 53, 294
Walker, M. E., 283, 301
Wallace, D. L., 24, 296
Walsh, G., 134, 143, 301
Wang, W., 123, 301
Wasserman, S., 283, 301
Wayne, I., 26, 103, 211, 296
Webb, E. J., 19, 20, 301
Weber, M., 67, 301

Weber, R. P., 12, 31, 40, 43, 48, 53, 105,
230, 267, 277, 297, 300, 301
Weddle, J. L., 153, 154, 158, 289, 299
Weert, D., de, 288
Weitman, S., 15, 56, 132, 232, 233, 278,
296, 301
Weitzman, E. A., 3, 209, 215, 216, 219-
221, 301
Welch, W. W., 160, 302
Wellman, B., 283, 301
Wester, F., 216, 297
Whalstrom, M. W., 161, 287
White, A., 108, 109, 302
White, H. C., 79, 302
Wicklund, R. A., 206, 302
Wilbert, D. E., 291
Willats, B. D., 110, 302
Winget, C. N., 118, 123, 124, 290-292, 302
Winter, E., 60, 66, 302
Winterbotham, F. W., 239, 302
Wittgenstein, L., 192, 302
Wohl, T., 118, 291
Wolcott, H. F., 3, 302
Wolf, R. J., 122, 291
Wu, J., 291
Wylie, H. W., 118, 291
Wynne, L. C., 291

Y

Yager, R. E., 159, 160, 162, 170, 287, 292,
293
Yuan, H., 54

Z

Zaninovich, M. G., 22, 297
Zinnes, D. A., 22, 151, 152, 296, 297, 299,
302

# SUBJECT INDEX

## A

A priori categorization, 43
Academic writing, 171, 181
Actionable research, 44
Actions "short of strike," 134, 142-144
Active listening, 44
Affirmative action, 45
Agriculture, 36, 103, 108
Ambiguity, 12, 55, 59-61, 63, 64, 67, 68, 72, 76, 77, 95, 105, 117, 118, 121, 164, 165, 180, 194, 197, 200, 212, 217, 262, 263
Ambivalent Hostility Scale, 117
American National Election Studies, 42
Annenberg, 23, 41-43
Anxiety Scale, 117, 119, 121, 126
Aristotelian logic, *see* Formal logic
Artificial Intelligence (AI), 43, 52, 76, 117, 118, 125, 225, 227, 231, 235, 248, 250
Aspect grammar, 66
Audience, 13, 20, 22-27, 37, 62, 63, 66-68, 165, 181, 191, 192, 217, 228, 281, 283
literacy of, 24, 25
Automatic text abstracting, 52

## B

Base, 198
defined, 198
of a nuclear sentence, 200
of an a-cyclic path, 198
Behavioral Event Interview, 45
Biological Science Curriculum Study (BSCS), 161, 162, 169
Biomedical research, 124
Black invisibility, 39
Boolean, 69, 152, 227, 236, 237, 253, 254, 256, 257
defined, 253
Bounded rationality, 47
Bundle of paths, 199, 200, 205

Business cycle, 135
Buzzwords, 87-89, 94
defined 88

## C

*Cahiers de doléances*, 28, 56, 58, 233
Car-rental agents, 44
Categorization schemes, 41, 42, 44, 48-51, 53, 166
CAVE (Content Analysis of Verbal Explanations), 48
Causal-salience, 278, 279
Chain, 197, 204-206
variance within, 200
Chain argument, 6, 204-206
Char (defined), 253
Classroom, 159, 161, 169, 171, 181, 182, 184
Clause type, 164, 165
evaluation, 66, 68-69, 71, 164, 165
importance of context in determining, 164
justification, 66, 68-69, 71, 164, 165
perception, 66, 68, 71, 164, 165
recognition, 66, 68, 71, 164, 165
selection of, 164
Clause (defined), 70
Coder, *see also* Rater, 7, 15, 16, 21, 28, 31, 43, 47, 53, 58-60, 66, 67, 69, 70, 71, 72, 76, 77, 105, 106, 147, 154, 158, 164-166, 174, 175, 180, 188, 189, 192, 196, 201, 225, 226, 227, 230-233, 236-238, 259, 264, 268, 269
agreement, 71, 183
as a black box, 232
as research instrument, 232, 233, 238
as surrogate scientist, 226, 227, 232
human, 15, 16, 31, 47, 53, 147, 158, 180, 189, 227, 230-233
intuition of, 76

Coding, 10, 11, 14, 17, 20, 23, 26-28, 38, 42, 46-48, 66, 67, 70, 71, 81, 90-92, 99, 100, 104-106, 117, 137, 147,153, 154, 158, 163, 165, 166, 171, 174, 175, 180, 181, 188, 189, 192, 195, 196, 201, 206, 211, 212, 214, 216, 217, 225-229, 231-233, 235, 237, 258, 259, 274
    computer-aided, 147, 153, 154, 158
    concrete vs. abstract, 237
    consistency, 147, 154
    hierarchical organization in, 234, 235, 237
    manual, 38, 46
    rules for, 70, 71, 154, 165, 229
    with human coders, 31
Cognitive Impairment Scale, 117, 122
Cognitive maps, 4, 79, 81, 84, 99, 171, 173, 181, 189, 192, 201, 218, 280, 281
Coherence, *see* Semantic coherence
Common ground, 68
Communication Process as object of investigation, 23
Communications Development Company (CDC), 43, 44, 46, 47, 50, 53
Communism, 36, 103, 107, 194
Competency
    job- or work-related, 35, 44, 45, 48-50
    relating, 49
    striving, 49
    thinking, 49
Compilers, 246, 247
Computational Lingistics (CL), 247, 248
Computer programs, *see* Software
Computer-aided text analysis, 3, 40, 171, 172, 180, 187
    capabilities, 50
Concepts, 174-176, 181, 183-188
    defined, 81
    positional properties of, 99
    relations among, 81
Concept list, *see* Dictionary
Conceptual networks, 79-85, 87, 93, 96-98, 100
    defined, 81
Conceptual theory, 48
Concordance, 41, 212, 215, 220
    from the Bible, 41
Conductivity, 6, 84, 86-89, 91-93, 95-98, 278, 282
    extended (defined), 86
    local (defined), 86
Conflation, 247

Conflict, 5, 26, 60, 131-138, 140, 144, 145, 147-158, 196, 248
Consensus, 6, 30, 80, 81, 86-92, 94-96, 98, 99, 171, 177, 186, 218, 230
Content analysis, 1, 2, 9-31, 37, 38, 40, 41, 47, 48, 53, 59, 64, 69, 70, 72, 103-106, 115, 117-119, 121-125, 131, 132, 136-138, 159, 163, 164, 167, 170, 191, 192, 200, 201, 206, 212, 213, 215, 217, 225-231, 233, 240, 241, 258, 277, 282
    as inference, 12, 13, 16, 17, 20, 22, 23, 27, 31
    as measurement, 14, 16-18, 28
    as science, 11, 13, 14, 21, 22, 29, 30
    computerized, 119, 225, 227, 229, 231
    criteria of, 11
    minimal definition of, 1, 9, 13
    objectivity in, 11-14, 30
    of nonverbal materials, 14-16
    replicability of, 12, 13, 30
    systematic procedures in, 11-14, 23, 26, 27, 29, 30
    validity of, 12, 13, 18, 19, 22, 27,30, 31
Content model, 7, 251-254, 258-274
Contentious events, 26
Context, 6, 12, 17, 18, 21, 37-39, 46, 47, 50, 51, 55, 57, 60, 64, 66, 68-70, 76, 105,121, 135, 154, 164, 165, 170, 212, 213, 215, 227, 239, 259, 263, 267
    of situation, 57, 67-69, 76
Contextual information, 45, 215
Counter-sorter, 40, 105
Cross-cultural research, 119
Cross-sentence capabilities, 52

D

Data model, 251-253, 255-257, 261-265, 273
Data reduction, 180, 181, 187, 188
Database, 7, 131, 137, 138, 143, 172, 244, 245, 247, 251-253, 255-257, 261, 273, 276
    data retrieval, 51
Deception, 67, 228
Defensive demands, 135, 142
Density, 6, 84-89, 91-93, 95-98, 100
    extended (defined), 86
    local (defined), 85
Depersonalization, 109
Depression Scale, 117, 122

Depth-interviewing, 43
Dictionary, *see also* Vocabulary, 5, 19, 36, 37, 43, 49, 52, 106, 109, 119, 154, 158, 166, 171, 210, 211, 213, 225, 228, 230, 231, 259
  bilingual, 52
  concept list, 171-173, 182
  Harvard IV-4, 49
  spell-checker, 52
Direct link, 83, 206
  defined 83
Disambiguation, 21, 51, 213
Discourse analysis, 14, 15
Discourse style, 67
Display of text, 51
Divergence, 200, 205, 206
Document management systems, 245

E

Ellipsis, 70, 259, 265
Emblems, 87, 89, 94
  defined, 89
Environmental change, 147, 148, 157
Ethiopia, 5, 8, 147-158
Evaluative assertion analysis, 30, 217
Event characteristics, 5, 136, 144
Event counts, 136, 144
Event data, 26, 147, 148, 152-156, 214
Evokability, 84-86, 91-93, 98
  extended (defined), 86
  local (defined), 85
Evolution
  of concepts, 87, 99
  of knowledge, 89, 99
  of networks, 80
Expense, 42, 43, 58, 147, 153, 154, 158, 230, 231, 237, 242, 244
Expressed emotion, 39
Extended network, 83, 84, 86, 92, 96
  defined, 83
Extra-textual information, 240, 244
Extraction, 7, 79, 80, 171, 174, 218, 239, 240, 245-250

F

Factoids, 87-89, 93, 94, 98
  defined, 88
*Facts on File*, 153
Famine, 5, 147, 149-151, 155, 157
Flow of symbols, 104, 106, 114, 115

Focal concept, 83, 85-87, 91-95
  defined, 83
Focus groups, 43
Formal language theory, 7, 245-248, 250
Formal logic, 61, 63, 255
French Revolution, 23, 25, 56, 233
Frequency
  of a bundle, 199, 201
  of a nuclear sentence, 198
  of a path, 198
Functional forms, 57, 61, 63-69, 71, 72, 74, 77
  criteria for selection among, 66
  sequence of, 57
Functional grammar, 57, 192, 193
Functional linguistics, 60, 66

G

Gallup, 35, 36, 39, 45-50
*Gemeinschaft*, 114
General Motors Research Laboratories, 46
Genetics, 5, 159, 163, 169, 170
*Gesellschaft*, 114, 115
Government, 5, 56, 58, 59, 103, 108, 110, 112, 114, 115, 131-133, 135, 138, 140, 141, 149-152, 201, 202, 204-207, 234-236
  local, 110, 140, 141, 235
  national, 110
Grammar, *see* Semantic grammar, Functional grammar
Grand theory, 4, 41, 47-50, 115
Graphs, 83, 107, 108, 167, 170, 188, 263, 267, 273
Grounded research, 47
Grounded theory, 48, 214, 215, 219

H

Handwritten materials
  conversion of, 243
High school, 5, 159, 161, 162, 169, 170
Highlighting, 57-59, 68, 144, 267
  of relevant text, 58
  of text structure, 58
Holt series, 159, 162, 169
Hoover Institute, 104

Hope Scale, 117, 122
Hostility Inward Scale, 117
Hostility Outward Scale, 117, 119
Human element, 109
Hyperbole, 67

I

Ideal, 194, 195, 197, 201, 202, 204, 205
Ideal types, 87
Identity, 44
IF-THEN, 193, 197
Illocution, 66
Imageability, 84-86, 91-93, 96, 100
    extended (defined), 86
    local (defined), 85
Implicit knowledge, 174
Indirect link (defined), 83
Industrial sector, 5, 133, 135, 138, 140,
    143, 144
Inexpensive, see Expense
Inference, 2, 3, 8, 12, 13, 16-18, 20-27,
    29, 31, 35-39, 48, 50, 52, 53, 55, 56,
    59, 60, 76, 77, 82, 84, 120, 163, 188,
    191, 192, 197, 198, 200, 209, 217,
    219, 240, 248, 249, 269, 272, 275-277,
    280, 282, 283
    rules for, 191, 192, 197, 198, 200, 240
Information Retrieval (IR), 246, 247
Information superhighway, 53
Instrumental text analysis, 7, 59, 209,
    225, 227-231
Insurgence, 149, 150
Integer (defined), 253
Intensity, 6, 14, 38, 85-89, 91-93, 95-98,
    136, 213
    extended (defined), 86
    local (defined), 86
Intention, 23, 37, 65-69, 134, 164, 170,
    181, 217
    types of, 66, 164, 170, 217
Interactions, 94, 98, 114, 144, 147,148,
    152, 154, 156, 157, 172, 181, 182, 185-
    187, 194
IQ, 45
Irony, 67
Italy, 5, 8, 26, 56, 123, 131-133, 138, 140,
    141, 143-145
    judges, 143
    ministries, 140, 141, 143
    politicized system of labor relations,
    140, 143

K

Key-word-in-context (KWIC), 212, 213,
    215

L

Labor disputes, 4, 5, 56-58, 131-135, 138,
    140, 144, 277, 278
    as multiple-actor, multiple-
    action phenomena, 132, 144
    counter-cyclical, 133, 135, 141, 144
    disruption, 133, 134, 137, 140, 143, 144
    pro-cyclical, 135
    public involvement in, 133, 134, 140,
    143, 144
Lagged variables, 155-157
Language, see also Formal language
    theory, Natural language, Query
    language, Specification language
    agglutinated, 52
    as a network, 80
    canonical structure of, 136
    model of, 100
    position in the structure of, 96
    representation of, 98
    used to induce consensus, 90
Latent content, 1, 6, 20, 21, 191, 192,
    197, 199, 200, 204-206, 229
    as indirect relationships, 206
Leaf structure, 163, 169, 170
Linguistic approach
    advantages of, 137
Linguistic Content Analysis (LCA),
    64, 69-72, 74, 76, 159, 163-168, 170,
    217, 282
Linguistics, 7, 14, 15, 24, 55, 58, 61, 64,
    66, 69, 70, 72, 76, 79, 106, 117,121, 124,
    131, 132, 136, 137, 159, 163, 164, 167,
    170, 201, 217, 225, 247, 267, 282
    approach to text analysis, 131, 132,
    136, 137
Link, 197-200, 202, 204-206
    ij-links, 198
Literary texts, 172
Local network, 83, 92-97
    defined, 83
Logical operator, 215, 256, 257
    defined, 256
Long-term storage, 244
Lossy integration, 80, 87, 98
Lotus-Notes forum, 46

## M

Machine translation, 7, 72, 243
Machine-readable format, 47, 53, 158, 241
Magnetic tape, 244
Mainframe, 35, 41-43, 52, 53, 180, 211, 212
Manifest content, 11, 13, 20-23, 191, 192, 200, 204-206
   as direct relationships, 206
Maps, 4, 68, 83, 96, 171, 173-176, 180-185, 187-189, 192, 218, 225
   intersection of, 96, 176, 183, 185
Matrix, 7, 56, 72, 76, 85, 166, 209-213, 215-219, 248, 276-279, 282, 283
McBer, 44-50
Meaning object, 6, 191, 192, 194, 195
Measurement, 2, 14, 16-20, 24, 27-29, 117, 120, 121, 124, 166, 228, 231
   of explanatory style, 48
   of inquiry, 166
   of integrative complexity, 48
   of psychological dimensions, 117
Media analysis, 46
Megatrends, 46
Mental model, *see* Cognitive map
Mental states, *see also* Psychological states 60, 66, 120, 128
*Modern Biology,* 159, 162

## N

Narrative grammar, 57
Narrative of inquiry, 166
Narratives, 26, 29, 57, 80, 81, 131, 132, 136, 137, 144, 166, 167, 280
National Opinion Research Center, 42
Natural language, 60, 62, 118, 227, 232, 236, 247, 248, 251, 265, 267
   analysis techniques for, 248
Need-achievement, 49
Network, 1, 3-8, 77, 79-100, 173, 191, 192, 196, 197, 199, 200, 202, 206, 210, 214, 217, 218, 221, 248, 249, 251, 252, 258, 267-276, 278, 279-283
   representation as, 191, 192, 202, 267, 268, 278
   theory of, 192
Network text analysis, 1, 3-8, 77, 79, 191, 196, 200, 206, 210, 217, 252, 267, 268, 270, 273-276, 278, 279, 282, 283

Neural networks, 7, 42, 51, 52, 248, 249
Newspapers, 4-6, 14, 25, 26, 30, 35, 36, 46, 56, 57, 104-108, 110, 112, 114, 115, 131, 132, 136-138, 144, 200-202, 204-207, 230, 232, 277, 280
   *Corriere della Sera,* 138
   *De Volkskrant,* 200-202
   *Frankfurter Allgemeine Zeitung,* 230
   front-page news, 114
   *L'Unità,* 138
   *La Stampa,* 138
   *Le Monde,* 230
   *London Times,* 230
   *Los Angeles Times,* 36, 103, 106, 108, 109, 115
   *Messaggero,* 138
   *New York Times,* 36, 103, 105, 106, 108, 109, 115, 153, 230
   *NRC Handelsblad,* 200-202
   *Times of London,* 153
   *Wall Street Journal,* 43
   *Washington Post,* 197
Nexis, 46, 152, 158
Nontextual information, 51
Nuclear sentence, 6, 191-198, 200, 201, 202, 204, 205, 217, 218

## O

Objectivity, 120
Offensive demands, 135, 142-144
Open-ended questions/answers, 35, 42, 45, 56, 215, 258, 259
Operationalization, 31, 41, 48, 100, 166, 168, 226, 227, 232
Optical Character Recognition (OCR), 7, 53, 241-243, 245
   accuracy, 242
Optical media, 244
Order-quote, 193, 197
Ordinary concepts, 87-90, 92-94
   defined, 88
Organizational culture, 50, 53

## P

Paraphrase, 72, 193
Parsing, 59, 153, 191, 192, 217, 218, 247, 248, 263, 264, 267
Partiality of actors, 197
Passive voice, 64, 71, 193

Path, 197-200
  defined, 198
  indirect, 197
Path algebra, 200
Pattern detection, 52
Pattern matching, 7, 248, 266, 273
Pattern recognition, 51, 214
Performative utterances, 66
Personality theories, 48
Personnel selection, 45, 48
Phenomenon of interest, 4, 55-59
  same as unit of analysis, 56
Place-holders, 87, 89, 94, 98
  defined, 89
Political actors, 138, 140, 143, 144, 153,
  154, 201
Population of texts, 1-3, 29, 55-57, 59,
  60, 68, 76, 77, 163, 275, 280, 282
  division into units of analysis, 280,
  281
  homogeneity of, 57
  theoretical relevance of, 68
Pragmatics, 21, 67
Predicate types, *see also* Relationship
  types, 194-196, 199
    ACT, 195, 197, 199
    AFF, 195, 197, 199
    CAU, 195, 199
    EVA, 195, 197, 199
    REA, 195, 199
Preprocessing, 7, 197, 210, 239, 240, 245,
  250
Presidency, U.S., 110, 112, 152, 194, 195,
  197
Prespecified categories, 41
Production systems, 7, 248-250
Professionals, 103, 110, 111
Pronoun reference, 52, 153
Propositional calculus, 197
Prototypes, 87-89, 94, 98
  defined, 88
Psycho-logic, 192
Psychological states and traits, 5, 40,
  117, 119, 121, 231
Psychosocial research, 123
Public opinion, 30, 45, 46, 56, 134, 217,
  278
Public relations, 134, 135, 143, 144
Punched cards, 40, 42, 105
Pyramid style of journalistic
  writing, 154

Q

Qualitative content/text analysis, 2, 3,
  11, 27-29, 42, 210, 211, 215, 219, 275
Quality, 194, 197, 201, 204, 205
  of a bundle, 201
  of a bundle of paths, 199
  of a chain, 205
  of a direct relationship, 205
  of a link, 198, 204, 205
  of a nuclear sentence, 194, 200
  of a path, 198, 199
  of a predicate, 194
  of chain arguments, 205
Quantification words, 109, 110
Quantifier (defined), 256
Quantitative text analysis, 1-3, 7, 8, 16,
  29, 55, 70, 72, 209, 215, 251, 273-276,
  280, 283
Query language, 251, 252, 255, 257
  SQL, 257
Question-and-answer systems, 52
Quotation, 10, 14, 40, 66, 110, 193, 197,
  198, 215, 255

R

RADIR project, 104
Rater, *see also* Coder, 120, 121, 171, 174,
  179, 180, 183, 187
Reality, 193-195, 201
Rebellion, 149, 150, 152, 154, 157, 158
Recording unit, 196
Refugees, 5, 147, 149-158
Regressive imagery, 43
Relational content analysis, 191, 206
Relational table, 252, 261, 262
Relationship (defined), 81
Relationship types, *see also* Predicate
  types, 81, 172, 173, 183, 196, 218
Reliability, 10, 22, 23, 38, 70, 104, 117,
  118, 120-123, 125, 132, 147, 149, 153,
  162, 168, 171, 174, 180, 183, 188, 189,
  196, 201, 211, 228, 230, 232, 239, 273
  in non-English languages, 122
  of computers, 38, 106
  rescoring, 38
  signal-detection analysis, 174, 183
Religious rituals, 112, 113, 115
Representation of intended
  meaning, 66-68, 163-165

Representational text analysis, 164, 209, 225, 227-231, 233, 237, 238
Reuters, 5, 60, 147, 152-154
Reuters leads, 152
Robot, 4, 171-177, 179-181, 183, 187, 188

S

Say-quote, 193, 197
Scaling versus coding, 231, 232, 237
Scanners, 53, 241, 243
Scanning, 215, 241, 242, 245
Scapegoat hypothesis, 151, 156
Science as facts, 159-161, 163
Science as inquiry, 5, 159-163, 166, 169, 170
Science education, 160-162, 170
Science fiction, 4, 171, 172, 179, 180, 238
Science textbook, 159
Semantic coherence, 105
Semantic grammar, 4, 55-61, 63, 64, 66-70, 72, 76, 77, 81, 131-133, 136, 137, 144, 165, 216, 217, 233, 264-266, 277, 278, 282, 283
    generic, *see also* Clause type, 4, 55, 58-61, 63, 66, 68-70, 72, 76, 77
    phenomenal, 55, 58, 68
Semantic invariance, 62, 65
Semantic text analysis, 3-6, 55, 57-60, 72, 77, 210, 213, 216, 263, 264, 266, 267, 275, 277, 278, 282
Semantic triplet, 136
Sequence,
    defined, 254
    string as, 255
Service sector, 5, 131-135, 137, 138, 140-144
Set (defined), 254
Shared knowledge, *see* Consensus
Signal-detection analysis, 174, 183
Simple primitive type, 253
Simulmatics, 42
Social Alienation-Personal Disorganization Scale, 117, 119, 121-123
Social change, 87, 103, 106, 108, 114, 115
    perception of, 103, 112
Sociohistorical records, 90, 91
Software, 209-221
    ATLAS, 214
    CETA, 6, 196, 199, 217, 268
    CODEF, 91

CODEMAP, 91
CUBE, 85
FlexText, 215
for OCR, 241-243
for qualitative text analysis, 219
GENCA, 106, 210
Gottschalk-Gleser System, 5, 59, 119, 121-125, 213
instrumental orientation, 210, 213
InText, 211
KEDS, 5, 59, 153, 158, 214
Kwalitan, 215
Lex, 246, 247
MCCA, 212
MECA, 83, 91, 174, 183, 218
Micro OCP, 212
NUD*IST, 2, 219
PC CARP, 282
PC-ACE, 137, 216
PLCA, 69, 73, 75, 163, 165, 217
representational orientation, 210, 214, 216, 217
SKI, 6, 174, 175, 189, 268
Text Base Alpha, 216
TextPack, 43, 211, 213
The General Inquirer, 5, 21, 42, 43, 209, 211, 213, 225, 227, 228, 230, 231, 277
WordNet, 47, 52, 221, 247
Sound bytes, 39
Specification language, 253
Speech acts, 57, 60-63, 65-67, 72
    functions of, 57
    with multiple meanings, 59, 60, 63, 68, 71
Sputnik, 161, 173
Standard Generalized Markup Language (SGML), 244
State as employer, 133, 143
Statements, 173-176, 181, 183-188
    defined, 82
    implicit, 174
Statistics
    analysis of variance, 179
    cluster analysis, 51, 53, 221
    correlation, 18, 19, 22, 151, 155-157, 179, 282, 283
    factor analysis, 22, 41, 42, 48, 51
    logistic regression, 168, 169
    multiple regression, 22, 155
    quadratic assignment procedure, 185
    t-test, 6, 204, 205

Stemming algorithm, 228, 247
Stereotypes, 87, 89, 94-96, 98, 99
    defined, 89
Story grammar, 57, 221
Strike statistics, 131-133, 135
Structured primitive type, 253-255
Subject-Action-Object, 132, 136
Subject-Verb-Object (S-V-O), 56, 57, 59,
    153, 154
Subjectivity, 14, 67, 120, 170, 231
Suicide notes, 39
Surface grammar, 55, 59, 60, 66, 71, 72,
    77, 217, 264, 265
Symbolic environment, 103-107, 112,
    114, 115
Symbols, 14-18, 21, 22, 28, 30, 87, 89, 90,
    94, 95, 104-109, 114, 115, 126-128, 226,
    242, 248, 253
    defined, 89
Synsets, 47
Syntactic components, 56, 58, 59, 277
Syntax grammar, 55, 59, 60, 77, 136


                            T-U

Tabulation machines, 40
Taxonomy, 80, 87, 89, 92, 98, 99
Television, 26, 39, 59, 114, 278, 280, 281
    MTV, 37, 38
Text decomposition, 51, 52
Text grammar, 57
Text structure, 57-60, 66, 77
Text-routing procedures, 52
The American Soldier, 10
Thematic Apperception Test, 45
Thematic text analysis, 3-5, 35, 37-40,
    46, 47, 52, 53, 68, 77, 210, 214, 252,
    258-262, 266, 267, 273, 275, 276, 278,
    282
    applied objectives of, 53
    computer-based, 47
    situating of, 44, 53
Theme profiles, 45
Themes, 35
    achievement, 44
    affiliation, 44
    as attributes, 36
    as subjects, 36
    evolution into images, 36
    in British speeches, 43
    in party platforms, 43
    in poetry, 43

    intensity, 38
    musical, 36, 37
    power, 44
Theoretical map, 275, 276
Theories of the middle range, 48
Theory of meaning, 100
Time-consuming, 153, 240
Transcripts, 1, 35, 37, 44, 47, 165, 182,
    183, 209, 212, 241, 275, 280, 281
Transitive Evaluative Transfer, 199, 200
Transitivity, 199, 200, 204, 272-274
Translation, 7, 37, 39, 72, 76, 226,  232,
    233, 236, 243, 245, 246, 248
Tree representation, 263-266, 273
Trend report, 46
Triangulation, 20
Tuple, 56, 57, 59, 252, 253, 255-262, 264,
    265, 268-271
    defined, 255
Two-place predicate, 64, 192, 193
Understatement, 67
Unified theory of social relations,  48
Unit of analysis, 7, 56, 57, 59, 163, 167,
    196, 219, 276, 280-283


                            V-Z

Validity, 18, 19, 22, 35, 39, 40, 50, 63, 77,
    104, 107, 108, 117-123, 125, 154, 163,
    165, 167, 168, 180, 188, 230-232
    construct validity, 117, 118, 121-123
    in non-English languages, 122
Verb pattern/phrase, 153, 154, 214
Verb-Object (V-O), 56
Verbal behavior, 117-119, 121
Verbatim text, 251
Verbs of attribution, 110
Violence on television, 39
Vocabulary, see also Dictionary, 5, 15, 19,
    21, 24, 29, 50, 68, 83, 85, 90, 99, 104,
    166, 213, 228, 237, 243
    defined, 83
Wheels of time, 43
Word experts, 47
Word frequency/count, 5, 41, 44, 51,
    213, 219, 277
Word sense/meaning, 47, 51
Word-processors, 51
Work-to-the-rule, 143
Writing instruction, 181
ZUMA, 43, 211, 213